Ridge.

"WE ARE IN FOR IT!"

The Shenandoah Valley from Winchester to Mount Jackson, Virginia, Sketched by Jed Hotchkiss.

Courtesy of The Handley Library, Winchester, Virginia

"WE ARE IN FOR IT!"

The First Battle of Kernstown
March 23, 1862

By

Gary L. Ecelbarger

White Mane Publishing Company, Inc.

This White Mane Publishing Company, Inc. publication
was printed by
Beidel Printing House, Inc.
63 West Burd Street
Shippensburg, PA 17257-0152 USA

In respect for the scholarship contained herein, the acid-free paper used in this book meets the guidelines for permanence and durability of the Committee on Production Guidelines for Book Longevity of the Council on Library Resources.

For a complete list of available publications
please write
White Mane Publishing Company, Inc.
P.O. Box 152
Shippensburg, PA 17257-0152 USA

Library of Congress Cataloging-in-Publication Data

Ecelbarger, Gary L., 1962–
    We are in for it! : the first Battle of Kernstown, March 23, 1862
/ by Gary L. Ecelbarger.
        p.   cm.
    Includes bibliographical references and index.
    ISBN 1-57249-053-5 (alk. paper)
    1. Kernstown, Battle of, 1862.   I. Title.
E473.72.E25   1997
973.7'31--dc21   97–22162
                                                            CIP

PRINTED IN THE UNITED STATES OF AMERICA

To all the soldiers, Blue and Gray, who fought at Kernstown on
March 23, 1862:
May your story never be forgotten

Table of Contents

List of Photographs and Illustrations

List of Maps

The base map for this book was created by digitizing a copy of Jed Hotchkiss' "Sketch of the Battle of Kernstown." Subsequent chapter maps were then made using sections of the base map.

LEGEND

LAND FEATURES

Natural Features

Terrain Topography

Woodlands

Streams

Man-made Features

VALLEY PIKE Roads and lanes

------- Wooden fences

_____ Stone fences

□ Structures

MILITARY FEATURES

☐ Confederate Forces

■ Union Forces

Carroll Commander

67th Ohio Unit designation

Artillery

× Skirmisher

Unit in column formation

Regiment in front

Company in front

Cavalry

Troop movements

MAP FEATURES

North Arrow

600   0   600   1200   1800   2400
Scale: in feet

Scales on each map are in feet, but have been modified in length.

Legend by Marcus D. Lemasters

The Battlefield of
KERNSTOWN, VA.:
Sunday, March 23, 1862

WINCHESTER

Map by Marcus D. Lemasters

Preface

Years after the guns of the Civil War were silenced, a former private in the Stonewall Brigade remembered Kernstown as "one of the hardest little battles of the war." A Federal counterpart offered even greater tribute to this engagement: "Most of the boys were in more or less of the great battles fought subsequently," wrote a former Indiana private in 1889, "but I'll warrant that none of them was ever under a hotter fire than when in front of the stone wall at Kernstown." A Union officer in the same regiment offered this startling analysis of Kernstown: "The infantry fire, to the extent of the line, was as heavy as it was at Antietam, Gettysburg, or the Wilderness."[1]

As far as the veterans were concerned, those post-war statements were not laced with hyperbole. Kernstown was a momentous event for both the green recruit who "saw the elephant" there and for the more experienced volunteer soldier who used this battle as the benchmark to gauge previous and subsequent engagements of the Civil War. Brothers fought side by side and, in at least two families, against each other. Two opposing colonels risked their lives to salvage their military reputations; another commander's career was jeopardized for his on-the-field decisions that resulted in the most famous court-martial trial in Confederate history. One division commander suffered the only defeat of his career at Kernstown while the demagoguery of the division commander who opposed him launched one of the most remarkable campaigns in military history. After the war victors and victims conducted pilgrimages to the hallowed ground where their comrades fell. Survivors living in two different states reunited every March 23 for at least thirty years to commemorate the anniversary of what one regimental commander at Kernstown unabashedly labelled: "The greatest battle of the late war."[2]

Although the veterans grasped the impact of Kernstown, incredibly, to date, a very minimal understanding of the battle exists.

The Stone Wall at Kernstown, Visited by Tourists in 1885
Courtesy of M.O.L.L.U.S. of Massachusetts,
United States Army Military History Institute,
Carlisle Barracks, Pennsylvania,
Hereafter cited as U.S.A.M.H.I.

No book-length treatment of it has ever been attempted. The only narratives dealing with Kernstown occasionally appeared as obscure chapters in biographies written about General Thomas J. "Stonewall" Jackson and in the handful of histories about his famous 1862 Shenandoah Valley Campaign. Not surprisingly, detailed tactical approaches of Kernstown have been shunned in these histories as Jackson's partisans carefully avoided dwelling on his only defeat of the campaign. To compensate, most of what has been written about Kernstown focuses on the aftermath of the battle, a period in which Jackson's tactical defeat is transformed into a strategic victory. The authors of nearly every extant biography of Stonewall or anthology of his campaign manage to depict Kernstown in a totally "Southern" light. The only Northern sources referenced are official reports of the battle and an occasional published regimental history. Consequently, those who decided to recount the fight at Kernstown managed to do so without any serious recognition of the winning force—one of the few times in military annals that feat has been accomplished. The result is a regrettable void that has prevailed in the Civil War literature for over 130 years.

In 1991 I visited the Kernstown battlefield for the first time. Retracing the steps of Civil War soldiers on the fields where they fought and fell is an enlightening experience. This is why National

Military Parks are visited throughout the United States. But Kernstown is unique. It is "unmarked" land, much of which has been virtually unchanged since the Civil War. Two interpretive markers depict the events of March 23, 1862 and one United Daughters of the Confederacy stone marker sits on the southern outskirts of Kernstown near a post-battle church off Route 11—the old Valley Turnpike. That is it. Most of the battlefield sits on private property, making a comprehensive understanding of Kernstown a difficult process.

Kernstown's obscurity piqued my interest to the mystery of what happened there on March 23, 1862. Using easily accessible military reports, a few published soldiers' accounts, and a troop movement map published in a popular history of Stonewall Jackson's Valley Campaign, I drove around the perimeter of the battlefield and viewed it from all publicly accessible locations I could find. I stood at the interpretive marker at Opequon Church and faced Pritchard's Hill. I then pulled out my map, studied it, and pondered. Why did Stonewall send infantry to Sandy Ridge if no Federals defended the height? Why did Colonel Fulkerson advance to Sandy Ridge on a circuitous route that brought his flank within 500 yards of Federal artillery when the road he left could have taken him directly onto the hill in a safer manner? What was the regimental line of battle from both sides? Where was General Jackson during the battle? How many Northern troops fought at Kernstown: 7,000? 9,000? 11,000?

All published interpretations of the Battle of Kernstown forced me to ask rather than answer those questions; therefore, I endeavored to uncover primary accounts from both sides. I quickly realized a phenomenon that was illustrated with the aforementioned words of the veterans. Union and Confederate soldiers felt the significance of Kernstown both immediately and years later. They wrote prolifically about the events of January 1 to April 1, 1862. This was a period when these opposing forces squared off against each other on numerous occasions, climaxing on March 23 on the hills south of Winchester. City and county newspapers published hometown soldiers' colorful accounts of the action; hundreds of letters reached loved ones at home. Normally brief diary entries suddenly tripled in length at the time of the Kernstown battle. Winchester's citizens had something to say about it too. After all, this was the first of thirteen times that their town was officially occupied by opposing forces. Union and Confederate war departments also held official hearings concerning the conduct of the battle. Every natural and man-made terrain feature of the Kernstown battlefield (including the mile posts that existed on the Valley Turnpike) was carefully sketched six months afterwards by Jedediah Hotchkiss, the war's best cartographer. All of these rich primary accounts survive in libraries, historical societies, and state and military archives.

Three years of research allowed me to accumulate over 300 first-hand Northern and Southern accounts specific to the actions surrounding and including the Battle of Kernstown. Based on these findings, I echo the unified sentiments of all of the 1862 Shenandoah Valley Campaign historians who previously demonstrated that the men that comprised Jackson's division were fascinating warriors; however, the Federal sources I uncovered revealed men who were equally engrossing. Putting it all together, I answered most of my questions and came to the conclusion that much of what took place at the Battle of Kernstown had been misinterpreted. Still, a missing piece to the complete understanding of this battle could only be found by tramping the same terrain where 10,000 Americans waged war in a manner not seen east of the Allegheny Mountains since the first battle of Manassas was fought eight months earlier.

Today the Kernstown battlefield stretches across the property lines of four landowners. They generously permitted me to study their property countless times to map regimental movements and battle lines. The 1862 battlefield has been encroached by the necessities of the late twentieth century; a bypass route cuts into the eastern portion of Sandy Ridge, and the eastern side of the Valley Turnpike is lost to development. Notwithstanding these blemishes, I was relieved to discover that the same buildings these armies passed and their leaders occupied, the same terrain features they eloquently described in their contemporary writings, and the base of the same stone wall over which the main segment of this battle was fought remain intact. The puzzle now appears complete.

The following is a comprehensive and objective treatment of the first battle of Kernstown. The history encompasses January 1–April 5, 1862, in ten chapters. Chapter One uses the backdrop of the Bath-Romney campaign to introduce some key Union personalities associated with Kernstown. It describes the winter expedition from the Northern perspective to offer a brief but original look at that campaign. Chapter Two introduces key Confederates while they were encamped at Winchester. Chapter Three pits the two forces against each other where they remain for the rest of the narrative. Whereas the first three chapters encompass twelve weeks of winter activity that preceded the battle, Chapters Four through Eight detail the twelve hours of battle. Nineteen interpretive troop movement maps guide the reader through these five chapters. Chapter Nine covers the two weeks that followed the battle to highlight the strategic aftermath of the Battle of Kernstown. Chapter Ten features the Joint Committee of the Conduct of the War's investigation and the Richard Brooke Garnett court-martial trial. Both events set the stage to analyze the reasons for successes and failures at Kernstown. An epilogue is included to interweave the post-battle careers of several of the personalities associated with Kernstown.

"We Are In For It!" is a story for the Civil War neophyte because it introduces him to the Union and Confederate soldiers by frequently quoting the volunteers' colorful descriptions of drills, marches, battle, life and death. The narrative should also appeal to the more experienced Civil War aficionado because it uses (almost exclusively) primary sources to uncover a fascinating story that has been hidden for over 130 years. Finally, and most importantly, *"We Are In For It!"* is the only historiography of the first battle of Kernstown that describes and analyzes the battle at the regimental and company level from both sides and emphasizes the impact of this engagement on participants and subsequent campaigns. The serious student of the Civil War will find the book fills a void that has prevented a comprehensive understanding of the 1862 Shenandoah Valley Campaign. My objective is to provide insight to the events leading up to and including March 23, 1862, so that one will finish the book with an appreciation of Kernstown that equals that of the veterans who fought there, and a respect for this battle which dignifies the hundreds of Americans who made the ultimate sacrifice at Kernstown in fighting for their beliefs.

Acknowledgments

A comprehensive battle or campaign history is a project that can never be completed without the help of experts in related fields and the generosity of those with interest in the work. Although this book carries the name of only one author, it is important to recognize those who provided him with the information necessary to complete such an undertaking.

Foremost on the list is Winchester resident Marcus Lemasters, the cartographer for this book. Accurate troop movement maps are essential elements to a battle narrative, and Lemasters has truly enhanced this project with his expertise in computer topography. He digitized a terrain map prepared by Jed Hotchkiss (General Thomas J. Jackson's mapmaker) to enable specific areas of the Kernstown battlefield to be highlighted based on the narrative descriptions. Lemasters's maps are unique in that they depict troop movements and actions at the company level and indicate every 1862 fence and wood line that existed on the battlefield.

Other Winchester and Frederick County residents deserve special mention for their assistance. Ben Ritter is a valuable source of knowledge on Winchester during the war and he contributed several photographs for this project. He also directed me to Nathaniel Banks's intelligence file and several primary sources of information. One of the most underrated depositories of Civil War manuscripts is Handley Library in Winchester. Thanks to Rebecca Ebert and the archive staff there for their assistance in obtaining soldier and citizen diaries dealing with the Kernstown campaign. James Tubessing guided me on my first trip to Sandy Ridge. His knowledge, gleaned from relic hunting (with permission) there in the 1960s, unlocked the door to where the heaviest and the lightest fighting took place at the stone wall. I am also indebted to R. Lee Taylor, Eugene Dearing, Eugene Lupton, and Marshall Beverly (representing F & M Bank) for allowing me to inspect the terrain of their respective properties, much of which is unchanged from its 1862 appearance. Jerry Reid of Stephens City was also helpful in providing an updated Confederate casualty list for this battle.

I also wish to acknowledge the many friends who provided me with sources from their respective areas of interest. This includes Dan Jenkins (Jackson's Winter Campaign), Bill Miller (Jedediah Hotchkiss and Camp Curtin), David Richards (84th Pennsylvania), Lt. Colonel John P. McAnaw, USA (retired) (Military Tactics and Topography), David Taylor (29th Ohio), and Julian Mohr (1st Ohio Light Artillery). Marilyn Clark-Snyder was particularly generous in providing me with many of her ancestor's letters. Special thanks are extended to E. B. Vandiver III, Tom Kissinger, and Regina Trodden for critiquing a draft of the narrative. Karen Fojt donated much of her time to line edit the manuscript for me. Her efforts are appreciated. Scott Patchan and Rod Gainer deserve special mention. Both accompanied me on numerous excursions to distant archival depositories to accomplish our respective research projects. They also reviewed portions of the manuscript and provided suggestions for improving this interpretive history.

The personnel of the Library of Congress, National Archives, and state and county historical societies have offered first-rate guidance to this project. More than fifty librarians and archivists aided my research (see "Manuscripts" in the bibliography for their respective archives); they all deserve special recognition. The advice and information provided by military historians has also been vital. Robert K. Krick (Fredericksburg and Spotsylvania National Military Park), Dr. Richard Sommers (U.S. Army Military History Institute), Michael Musik (National Archives), and Guy Swanson (Museum of the Confederacy) were particularly generous in donating their time and efforts to enhance this history.

This book could not have been produced without the assistance of those closest to me. A special thank you to Elvin J. Ecelbarger for balancing the skill of a technical writer with the patience, understanding, and reassurance that only a father can provide. His countless hours spent reviewing, editing, and critiquing my manuscript will never be forgotten. My sister Karla also earns my appreciation for her read of the narrative. Finally, I thank my wife, Carolyn, for her many sacrifices made over the past four years to enable me to research and write this book. Her name appears last on this list, but she is, and always will be, first in my heart.

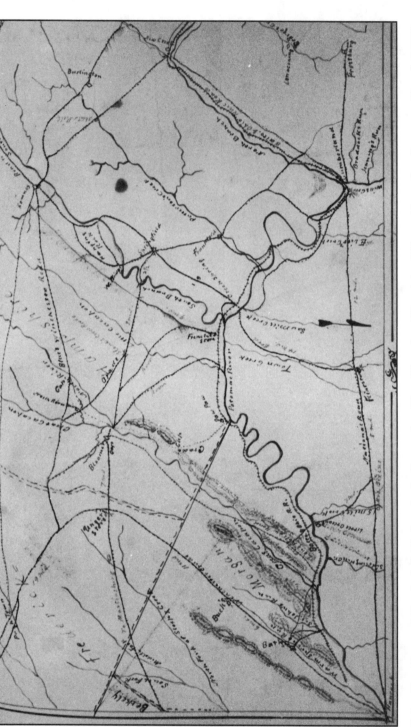

Brigadier General Frederick W. Lander's Campaign Map Showing Theater of Operations for January–March 1862. Winchester Is Located Beyond the Upper Left Corner, Cumberland in Lower Right, Hancock and Bath in Lower Left, and Bloomery Gap and Paw Paw in Center. Upper Section of Map Is South; Lower Section of Map Is North.

Frederick Lander Papers, Carton #3, #6544, Library of Congress, Manuscript Division

Chapter One

"A LITTLE DASH IS A GOOD ELEMENT"

No military force could have been more ill-prepared to fight.

On the last day of 1861, the 84th Pennsylvania Volunteer Infantry Regiment departed Camp Curtin in Harrisburg, Pennsylvania, and boarded a twenty-one-car train. Twenty-six hours later, the soldiers disembarked from their boxcars at Hagerstown, Maryland, and marched westward along the National Pike. They arrived at Hancock on the night of January 2, 1862, greeted by blustery winds and sub-freezing temperatures. Now only the Potomac River separated them from Virginia and Dixie.

The 84th Pennsylvania, a new regiment in a war that was nine months old, fell one company short of claiming full strength. Nine companies (766 volunteers) had rendezvoused at Harrisburg at the end of November. Most of the recruits hailed from the mountainous regions of central Pennsylvania; therefore, the state capital was the largest city they had ever seen. As with most of the other new regiments at Camp Curtin, the 84th consisted of individual companies which had been organized in small towns by the men who served as their original captains. On December 23, the nine companies consolidated into the 84th Pennsylvania under the overall command of Colonel William G. Murray. Unlike most regiments ordered to the front, the volunteers in the 84th Pennsylvania headed for enemy territory without one of the necessities to wage war—they had no rifles![1]

Unlike many recruits pulled from the cities, the mountain men in the 84th knew how to handle guns. Indeed, many company designations attested to that proficiency: the "Muncy Rifles," the "Clearfield Rifles," and the "Mechanic's Rifles" to name a few. However, for over a month they had been forced to train with sticks

1

instead of guns. No weapons in training camp rendered target practice obsolete. These deficiencies made these untested troops even greener.[2]

The 84th Pennsylvania finally received their arms on the morning of January 3 when their guns arrived on canal boats which docked near one of the Chesapeake and Ohio (C & O) Canal warehouses at Hancock. Rather than obtaining the popular and reliable .58-caliber Springfield rifle or the English .577-caliber Enfield rifle, the men of the 84th received the Prussian-manufactured Belgian musket. This cumbersome, grossly inferior .69-caliber import was cursed with a crooked barrel. Men forced to use them called them "pumpkin slingers" and "European stovepipes." One Civil War general pointed out the danger as well as the impracticality of the weapon when he stated that the Belgians "burst at the first firing, and were more dangerous at their butts than at their muzzles."[3] The Pennsylvanians were concerned that the weapons would be nearly useless in the condition they arrived in. The barrels were packed with thick tallow, and the cartridges contained moist powder which forced the need to pack several rounds of ammunition into the muzzle before the powder would ignite. The unit's historian highlighted the danger of this combination by reminiscing, "When they were carried over into Virginia, and the warmth of the fire reached the explosive grain, you can think now, as you realized then, that even the Belgian was not built to throw more than one ball at the same fire without repairs to one or the other—the gun or the man."[4]

The men barely had time to even attempt to clean their shoddy weapons at Hancock. Two frantic members of a Federal force stationed six miles away in Virginia territory brought Colonel Murray an order to join them at the front. They were expecting an attack from Confederate forces who had skirmished with an Illinois detachment on the Winchester Grade Road ten miles south of the Potomac River. Eight companies of Murray's regiment ferried across the Potomac immediately and headed south into Virginia. By midnight they reached Bath, a small village named for the elegant bath houses created to exploit the area's abundant natural springs. Here, shortly after midnight, the 84th Pennsylvania joined an advance force consisting of a 240-man detachment of the 39th Illinois Infantry, a Chicago regiment also without battle experience. This unit did have better rifles; they had been fitted with Springfields in late 1861 after spending the first two months of their existence without firearms.[5]

Snow blanketed the mountainous region on the night of January 3. The soldiers found quarters in the homes of Bath residents while the officers of the two regiments held a council. Over 180 enemy campfires illuminated the countryside to the south. Since Colonel Murray outranked the newly appointed colonel of the 39th Illinois, Thomas O. Osborn, he took charge of the whole force.[6] Both regiments were loosely assigned to Brigadier General Benjamin Franklin Kelley's Railroad District which was encamped at Romney and was responsible for protecting the vital Baltimore and Ohio (B & O) Railroad from Confederate attempts at sabotage. Kelley, who had requested to be relieved owing to ill health from an injury received at Philippi, answered to Brigadier General William S. Rosecrans, commander of the Department of Western Virginia. General Kelley had sent the 39th Illinois from Hancock to Bath two weeks earlier and had ordered Colonel Osborn to get the newly arrived 84th Pennsylvania to strengthen his position. He also promised to send another regiment to reinforce them.[7] Aside from the rest of Kelley's division at Romney, over fifty miles west of Bath, the closest Federal troops belonged to the Army of the Potomac; Major General Nathaniel Prentiss Banks commanded a division stationed at Frederick, Maryland, over fifty miles to the east.[8] (See Map 1)

The Union force faced a potential disaster. Together, Colonels Murray and Osborn counted fewer than 1,500 men in their total force at Bath, Hancock, and the vicinity around the two towns. As promised, the 13th Indiana would arrive from Romney to reinforce them sometime the following morning. Another new Pennsylvania regiment en route from Camp Curtin would also arrive late on the fourth of January. Fully consolidated, the Federal force would total four infantry regiments, one cavalry company, and a section (two cannons) of the 4th U.S. Artillery, under Lieutenant F. D. Muhlenburg. These troops would confront a Confederate force of nearly 9,000 men under the command of Major General Thomas J. Jackson. The opposition included a militia detachment, the 7th Virginia Cavalry, six artillery batteries with twenty-seven cannons, and four infantry brigades of fifteen regiments. Most of the Confederates had been battle tested. Jackson's force had left Winchester on New Year's Day, moving northward toward the railroad.[9] The light from his division's campfires bode ill tidings for the woefully overmatched Murray and Osborn.

The Federal officer's council concluded early in the morning of January 4, and the men awoke at approximately 4:00 A.M. as word quietly passed around to "fall in." Four companies of the 39th Illinois and eight companies of the 84th Pennsylvania climbed Warm Spring Ridge, an elevation that dominated the western edge of Bath. It ran northeast to southwest from the Potomac River at Hancock. Lieutenant Muhlenburg's two cannons were also pulled to the top of the towering ridge. The handful of remaining companies ascended periphery ridges. All waited for Jackson to approach.[10]

Shortly after 8:00 A.M., General Jackson's Confederate force marched towards Bath. While the veterans of Colonel William Gilham's brigade led the advance directly northward on the Winchester Grade Road, a body of Southern militia marched on a parallel road west of Warm Spring Ridge, ostensibly to cut off the retreat route of the Federal infantry and artillery stationed on the top. The militia encountered stiff resistance from Federal skirmishers on the hill who—concealed by standing and fallen trees and rocky out-croppings—lay a concentrated fire into the unsuspecting Southerners and easily repulsed them. Unfortunately for Jackson, the surprised militia panicked at the opening fire which threw the entire flanking force into disarray and ended the immediate threat to the Union right.[11] Colonel Murray swiftly concentrated his firepower toward the east where the remaining Southern infantry advanced over the snow-covered path leading into town. He had arranged his artillery to produce a plunging fire on the cold and aggravated veterans of Jackson's division. After learning of the mini-disaster that had befallen the militia, Confederate Brigadier General William Wing Loring, a subordinate officer to General Jackson, ordered his whole command to halt. Murray's poorly armed complement on Warm Spring Ridge, estimated at only 820 effectives, had successfully held over ten times their number in check for over four hours.[12]

General Jackson's calculated plan for the campaign assumed he would capture Bath by January 3. Slow marching and hesitant subordinates had already placed him one day behind schedule and, by midday of January 4, Jackson realized that he had to commit more troops to the assault to prevent being kept from his destination an additional night. He ordered General Loring to attack the ridge and dislodge the Union force. Two Tennessee regiments scaled the height to envelop the Federals. At 3:00 P.M. Colonel Murray pulled his skirmishers in when he saw large numbers of Southerners flanking on both sides and advancing toward him. Realizing that his own firepower would be inadequate because of the 84th Pennsylvania's tallow-caked guns, Murray ordered the entire command to withdraw to the Maryland side of the Potomac River.[13]

The Federal retreat and subsequent Confederate pursuit steered both forces toward Sir John's Run, a northerly flowing tributary that fed the Potomac River about two miles northwest of Bath. A detachment of the 39th Illinois had been on picket since early morning at the B & O Railroad depot located at the confluence of these waterways. Late in the morning, the 13th Indiana, commanded by Lieutenant Colonel Robert Foster, arrived at the depot by rail from Cumberland. The Hoosier regiment disembarked and marched toward Bath with its regimental band filling the air with martial music. The

Illinois detachment was jubilant because the additional manpower and ammunition would increase the effective Federal force in the area by over thirty percent.

Soon the Federals from Warm Spring Ridge approached the Sir John's Run railroad depot. Colonel Murray rode to the rail station where he met Lieutenant Colonel Foster of the 13th Indiana and Major Sylvester W. Munn of the 39th Illinois. After a brief council they decided to stand and fight. The three commanders about-faced their regiments and readied themselves to meet the oncoming Southerners. Major Munn asked Foster for ammunition. To his surprise the Hoosier commander stated that he had only two rounds per man—he had been told they would receive more when they reached Bath. Colonel Murray heard this in stunned disbelief. Realizing he lacked any appreciable firepower, he immediately changed his plans from fighting to retreating across the Potomac. Lieutenant Colonel Foster ordered his regiment to the rail cars and they headed back to Cumberland. They took their ammunition with them—all but two companies of the 13th Indiana carried smoothbores; their musket balls were worthless to the Pennsylvania and Illinois soldiers.[14]

With the Confederates closing in, the Federals abandoned much of their baggage at the rail depot and scampered to the river. The artillery and several members of the 39th Illinois forded the icy Potomac; ill members rode on the backs of healthy ones. Colonel Murray sent his horse across with his servant before realizing that there was not time enough for his regiment to cross—the baggage wagons and artillery were jamming the ford. He ordered his command to follow the rail line eastward to the next ford at Alpine Station, directly across the river from Hancock.[15] With little sleep and no food for twenty-four hours, Murray and his regiment double-quicked the five and one-half miles along the winding course of the Potomac until they approached the station. They were joined by several members of the 39th Illinois who had been too hard-pressed to cross at Sir John's Run. Without warning, the command was overtaken by a detachment of the 7th Virginia Cavalry. An Illinois picket consisting of two detached companies fired on the Southern cavaliers from a nearby hill, unhorsing four riders and ending the immediate threat. Some bluecoats rode across the river on a ferry to the safety of the Maryland side, while the rest took to the icy chest-high water and waded across. By nightfall, Murray's full command rested in Hancock, Maryland—except for one member who fell victim to the Potomac's frigid current and was swept away. The drowned soldier was the only Federal casualty of the day.[16]

That evening, with the Confederates now occupying Bath and the two railroad depots a few miles north of town, General Jackson ordered his artillery to fire across the river. The rounds falling on Hancock caused little serious damage as the brick houses that lined the main road protected the soldiers resting behind them. Lieutenant Muhlenburg returned fire from the elevations at Hancock.[17] While this artillery exchange lit the sky above him, Colonel Murray waited for reinforcements to arrive.

The Federals at Hancock improved their strength at midnight when the 110th Pennsylvania Volunteer Infantry finally moved in. This regiment boarded trains near Camp Curtin on January 2 and arrived at the Hagerstown depot early the following morning, January 3. They marched a few miles west of town and camped for the night. The next morning, the officers entered hotels to grab breakfast while the men headed for the saloons. Four companies of the 110th hailed from Philadelphia while the rest were recruited from country and mountain locales. According to the regimental historian, both city boys and country boys drank until "half the regiment was tanked up full." The heterogeneity of the regiment had created severe animosity within the ranks—the country and mountain companies resented the fact that all of the regimental officers were Philadelphians even though city recruits were in the minority. As the troops left the saloons, several drunken country boys attempted to rectify the situation by taking the flag from the Philadelphian elected to carry the colors. The predictable occurred—one or two fights quickly grew into a melee. Officers stopped the fight within a few minutes, placed the drunken men in their ranks under guard, and marched them out of the city along the freshly macadamized National Pike. The limestone macadam was six inches deep with pieces as large as goose eggs—potential weapons for angry drunken soldiers who had yet to be issued arms. A member of the regiment mused, "when whiskey is in, wit is out." The inebriated soldiers verbally abused their guards shortly after leaving Hagerstown which fostered an even uglier and deadlier brawl. This time the intra-regimental battle lasted over twenty minutes as the men went at each other with clubs and stones. As chunks of limestone filled the air, the officers intervened by striking men with their swords and pistols. Word of the insurrection travelled fast and the 1st Maryland Cavalry arrived from Williamsport to quell the riot. When the dust cleared, three men lay dead and over forty suffered serious, some mortal wounds. The 110th's late-night arrival at Hancock concluded a forced march of twenty-six miles that day. The weary men took shelter in churches and other buildings to rest and to reflect on the catastrophic consequences that result when discipline disintegrates.[18]

Several hours after the 110th Pennsylvania appeared, the Hancock force welcomed a new commander. Colonel Murray relinquished overall command to Brigadier General Frederick West Lander. General Lander had celebrated his fortieth birthday three weeks earlier. Born in Salem, Massachusetts, in 1821, Lander had enjoyed a respected and illustrious career by the start of 1862. His education and training as an engineer landed him his first major responsibility as chief civil engineer for the Northern Pacific Railway Survey, Northern Route, of 1853. Four years later Lander progressed to superintendent and chief engineer of Fort Kearney, South Pass, and the Honey Lake Wagon Road. These duties allowed him to improve on the Oregon Trail as a migration path and to act as a special agent for the Indians along the trail. Of greater military significance, Lander's activities on five treacherous expeditions made him an expert in sustaining and transporting men and supplies over rough terrain.

An imposing figure at six feet two inches in height, Frederick Lander was one of those rare people who seem to make a lasting impression after even the briefest of acquaintances. Nathaniel P. Willis, a renowned poet, described him from a chance meeting prior to 1862 at Willard's Hotel in Washington:

> I selected him as the *American-esque* man of whom to make a sketch as the finest specimen of the class. He passed me in the corridor of the hotel, crossed the sidewalk to his horse, mounted and rode away; and he did it all as exactly as an English horseguardsman would *not* have done it.

> There was not an angle in his whole movement. With no signs of the martinet, no military stiffness or restraint, he was wonderfully alert and agile, wiry and fearless, as well as careless and graceful. He had the proper "pathfinder" look like a hunter trained on the prairie. And his horse seemed pleased to be a part of him. It was a centaur of wavy lines—steed and rider animated by but one thought—and, as he galloped away up the avenue and disappeared around the Treasury colonnade, I speculated

**Brigadier General
Frederick West Lander**
*From a Matthew Brady Photograph,
Author's Private Collection*

on the superiority which it certainly exhibited to the angu-
larities of a dragoon.[19]

Frederick Lander had fallen in love with and married renowned
British actress Jean Margaret Davenport in 1860. She had moved
to the United States eleven years earlier and her career flourished
as it had in Europe. In the months prior to the outbreak of the Civil
War, Lander had completed a confidential mission to Governor Sam
Houston of Texas on behalf of the United States. His role was apparently to mediate an attempt to prevent the Lone Star State's
secession. His efforts failed and, after hostilities erupted, he entered the service as an aide-de-camp of Major General George Brinton
McClellan. Lander was active in the western Virginia campaign of
1861 and eventually was appointed brigadier general of volunteers
to rank from May 17, 1861. General Lander arrived too late to take
part in the Federals' disaster at Ball's Bluff. Nevertheless, the day
after the battle, October 22, he was severely wounded in the leg
while leading a holding force of sharpshooters at Edwards' Ferry.
The trimly bearded and mustached general recuperated in Washington where he was informed at year's end that he was to relieve
General Kelley as division commander at Cumberland and Romney, specifically to reopen the B & O Railroad in that segment of
Virginia. Lander had entered Hagerstown en route for Cumberland
on January 4 when he was informed of the military action transpiring across the river in Virginia. He wired a message from Hagerstown
at 7:15 P.M.: "I shall not leave Hancock, Maryland." Lander arrived
at Hancock shortly before daylight and set up his headquarters in a
store that also was equipped with a telegraph office.[20]

General Lander exuded confidence from experience. He was not
the type to ever be intimidated—even now, when he was vastly outnumbered by Southern infantry and woefully outgunned by the Confederate artillery. He started receiving telegraphs quickly from General Banks in Frederick. Banks's division was the closest supporting
body of troops with five regiments spread out between Hagerstown
and Williamsport. Based on information from his scouts, Banks had
telegraphed Lander at Williamsport that he thought the Confederate
attacking force was small, although he had not received reports of
exact numbers. Realizing that Lander would immediately inherit only
two regiments, one squadron of cavalry, and two artillery pieces, Banks
informed the new commander that his own 1st Maryland Infantry
was ready to move to Hancock. Banks's gesture was unique—as a
division commander in the new Federal Army of the Potomac, he was
offering to transfer his regiment to an entirely different army, for
Lander was subordinate to General William Rosecrans, commander

of the Department of Western Virginia. Since General Rosecrans could not be reached at his headquarters at Wheeling—and his whereabouts were unknown—Lander relied on Army of the Potomac commander General McClellan for orders and reinforcements.[21]

General Lander, with no sleep the previous night, assessed his force on the arctic Sunday morning, January 5 (the temperature at Cumberland hovered at eight degrees at 7:00 A.M.). His infantry consisted of three regiments numbering 2,041 soldiers. He had been promised a brigade of support from Banks's division, but these men were still at least a day's march away. Banks's intelligence also corrected his initial estimates of a small Confederate force across the river. The numbers were in; Banks now believed that Lander opposed 6,000 Southerners and six guns.[22] By now, Lander knew that these numbers also were severe underestimations. The Federals could see Jackson's division across the river and could count at least ten Confederate cannons crowning a dominant elevation representing the northern hill of Horse Ridge—just 1,000 yards away.

While the Confederates positioned their guns across the river, the 110th Pennsylvania marched to the edge of town to pick up their Belgian muskets at a docked canal boat. These guns, as the 84th Pennsylvania already knew, were unserviceable until the tallow could be worked out of the barrels. After the Keystoners built fires in the streets and melted the fat out, they discovered that "the hole in the pivot [was] too small to admit the powder in [their] American cartridges, the grains being too large." One member admitted that the men appeared "a little scared" at the prospect of going into battle with the poor weapons; not surprisingly, a few men left the ranks never to be seen again.[23]

At 9:30 A.M., as the Pennsylvanians cleaned their Belgians, two Southerners approached the riverbank on the Virginia side waving a flag of truce. Lander, recognizing the enemy's formal move to communicate, sent an aide over on a small flatboat to pick up the messenger. The Federal detachment brought one of the men across the river where he was blindfolded and escorted to Lander's headquarters in the telegraph room. A crowd of Federals quickly gathered around the escorted Southerner. Word passed through the lines identifying him as Lieutenant Colonel Turner Ashby of the 7th Virginia Cavalry. Those who had read or heard of him wanted a closer look at the respected cavalier. Ashby entered the telegraph office, but General Lander wisely moved him to an adjacent room based on the premise that he might be able to read telegraphy.[24] Ashby hand-delivered a message from his superior who, at this point, still did not know who was commanding the Union forces. General Lander opened the note which read:

> *Head Quarters, Valley District*
> *Opposite Hancock*
> *January 5, 1862*

To the Officer Com'dg
the United States Forces
in and near Hancock, Md.

Sir,

    It is my purpose to cross the river and take possession of the town of Hancock.

    If in opposing the execution of this purpose, you make use of the town of Hancock, or the citizens of the town aid you in your opposition, I will cannonade the town.

    If neither of these things is done, I will refrain as practicable from firing upon it.

    An immediate reply to this communication is required.

> *T. J. Jackson*
> *Maj. Genl. P.A.C.S.*
> *Comdg Valley District*[25]

Colonel Ashby attempted to bluff General Lander into believing that Jackson's strength was 15,000. If Lander refused to surrender his force, two hours would be allotted for noncombatants to evacuate before the town was bombarded. Hearing this, General Lander flew into a rage. He scolded the messenger with animated anger: "Colonel Ashby, give my regards to General Jackson and tell him to bombard and be damned! If he opens his batteries on this town he will injure more of his friends than he will of the enemy, for this is a damned sesech place anyhow!"

The Union commander cooled down after a few minutes, then politely told Ashby that his superior deserved the courtesy of an official response. Lander scribbled a nearly illegible note informing General Jackson that he would indeed dispute Jackson's attempt to take the town, and that the Confederate commander must take full responsibility for the consequences if he felt justified in shelling the homes of innocent civilians. General Lander never revealed his identity to Ashby and closed his note with the title Jackson bestowed upon him: "The Officer Commanding the United States Forces." Lander gave the note to Ashby, then shook his hand, saying "General Jackson and yourself, Colonel Ashby, are gentlemen and brave men, without question, but you have started out in a God Damned bad cause!"[26] With that closing, the blindfold was placed over Ashby's eyes and he was escorted from the room. Colonel Murray then exchanged polite greetings with the Southern officer, and his last words to Ashby warned him of the Federal plans: "We'll meet you in Dixie."[27]

Lander watched Ashby return to the Virginia shore, then he telegraphed General Banks to inform him of Jackson's ultimatum. Lander reasoned that he could not give up the town without a fight. Several impediments prevented his tiny force from leaving—1,000 rifles frozen in canal boats at the edge of town, no transportation to move the army over the icy and snow-covered terrain, and no supplies to sustain his men on the march. He also reminded Banks that most of his men were armed with Belgians, a weapon he considered to be "a curse to the army." Lander planned to engage Jackson long enough for Banks to trap him by moving in force from Martinsburg. "I will make as hard a struggle as I can," Lander wrote, ending his message by emphasizing, "I will keep the enemy engaged as long as the men will stand to give you a chance south of him."[28]

Hancock's citizens, consisting primarily of women and children, quickly packed necessities and evacuated the area. Some male residents shouldered antiquated muskets and proffered their services. General Lander positioned his meager force to gain every advantage he could. Squadrons of bluecoats were assigned to guard the fords to prevent a direct Confederate assault. Others were ordered to take cover behind the brick houses that lined Hancock's main street. With water buckets handy, they would be ready to douse fires caused by artillery fire.[29] The elevated ground behind Main Street was dominated by two brick churches—an Episcopal church and a Catholic church 100 yards east of it. Lieutenant Muhlenburg placed his six-pounder and ten-pounder Parrott behind the churches on the high ground used for cemeteries. Lander used the 110th Pennsylvania as a ruse; he directed them to enter a thick woods on high ground, and then moved them from the treeline to open ground to make the Confederates think that reinforcements were arriving. A company detached from the regiment dug loopholes into a warehouse wall facing the river ford. Two men in the 110th Pennsylvania convinced their captain that it would be wise to conduct prayer services—it was Sunday after all—prior to the cannonading.[30]

At 2:00 P.M., the battle opened with artillery greetings from Confederate guns across the river. Muhlenburg answered with fire from the high ground behind the churches, disrupting the peaceful environment fostered by the cemeteries that dominated the area. The artillerist behind the red church was not accurate and the Southerners did not even flinch when he fired. The gun behind the brown church told a different story. It wreaked havoc on the Confederates and forced them to employ a code to warn each other of potential danger. If a Southerner cried out "Brown Church," all would scurry to duck the incoming round. Shouts of "Red Church" indicated no worries and caused no movement. "Brown Church" and "Red Church" became subsequent watch words for Confederate artillerists.[31]

The Confederate artillery fire, though striking no one, terrified the Pennsylvania and Illinois soldiers. As cannonballs and shell fragments struck the ground and buildings around them, the foot soldiers watched in admiration and awe as General Lander rode along Main Street shouting words of encouragement: "Soldiers, do your duty; there is work for you today; If I am killed somebody else will take my place." A Pennsylvanian, much impressed by Lander's leadership, later told his hometown friends: "There was something about the appearance of the man that indicated that he was equal to the station, and there was not a soldier looked upon his countenance, but that felt confidence at his ability."[32]

The artillery duel sputtered late Sunday afternoon, but was renewed early on January 6. The Federal shots were so accurate that Jackson and his staff were forced from their viewing positions behind the Southern batteries. The lone bridge in the area (across the Big Cacapon River) was burned, and the B & O Railroad tracks were destroyed by the Confederates prior to their departure from the area. The next day the Confederates, having ransacked a house of a Union sympathizer at Bath and burning some buildings at Alpine Station during their three-day occupation, headed south. Their destination was Unger's Store, a crossroads that could direct them either southward back to Winchester or westward to Romney. Across the river at Hancock, the new Federal recruits showed equal disrespect for private property by wantonly destroying the provisions of people they were supposed to be protecting. Later in the day a small detachment of Federals entered Alpine Station and found destroyed railroad tracks, property in ashes, and fresh graves of Confederate soldiers who succumbed to the elements of a severe winter campaign. They also found notes left by Southerners admonishing the bluecoats to leave the Dixie borders and go home.[33]

General Lander's erratic temper festered on the blustery Tuesday following his successful defense of Hancock. He remained furious at the lack of support from Banks. He had fully expected Banks to acquire a sizable force from Baltimore, cross the Potomac at Williamsport, and attack Jackson from Martinsburg. At 1:00 P.M. Lander telegraphed the division commander in Frederick and asked him to relay his request for permission to move his whole force across the Potomac and attack the tail of Jackson's moving division. "It must be a forced march under scant subsistence," Lander reasoned, "but I hope to harass him long enough to do some good and will try not to lose the command." He further explained that the telegraph station at the Big Cacapon bridge was destroyed by the Confederates, forcing him to rely on a horse relay to communicate with General Kelley. This system of delivery was now impossible because of the heavy ice and snow that encrusted the mountains.

A black servant from one of the Confederate brigades escaped the force and was brought to Lander. Lander interrogated the slave and acquired (mis)information on enemy troop strength. Lander telegraphed Banks that he believed Jackson's total force numbered over 13,000 effectives with twenty-four cannons and an immense baggage train. Romney was without a commander now that General Kelley was recuperating in Cumberland. That vital western Virginia town had been Lander's original destination. The confrontation at Hancock had delayed him, and he now demanded direct orders to use his undersized Hancock force to cross the river that night and "fall on the rear of the enemy." He coldly ended his proposal to Banks by admitting that he "shall probably drown or freeze some men" by attempting this endeavor.[34]

General Banks read Lander's telegram with shock and anger at the proposal and criticisms; he then sent it directly to General McClellan in Washington. McClellan quickly responded with a telegram to prevent the renegade from destroying his force:

To Nathaniel P. Banks

Washington, January 7, 1862

Say to General Lander that I might comment very severely on the tone of his dispatches but abstain. Give him positive orders to repair at once to Romney and carry out the instructions I have sent already to fall back on the Railway.

It would be folly to cross the river at Hancock under present circumstances, except with a small corps of observation, but not to follow up the enemy.

(General Lander is too suggestive and critical.)

G. B. McClellan
Maj. Genl. Comdg[35]

General McClellan's rebuke nullified Lander's aggressive plans. Now, after completing only his third day as a division commander, Lander left his force at Hancock and moved toward Romney via the National Pike running through the Maryland panhandle. He had become familiar with a portion of the division he had inherited and must have been pleased at the successful accomplishments of his new recruits. The Pennsylvania and Illinois regiments, despite shoddy equipment and adverse conditions, had performed well enough to thwart an enemy that dramatically overwhelmed them in number. These three regiments would stay at Hancock temporarily and be commanded by Brigadier General Alpheus S. Williams who was advancing with a brigade from Banks's division to reinforce the Maryland town. The men would rejoin Lander near Cumberland while the general moved the Romney force northward to closely cover the railroad. (See Map 1)

Now Lander would get to see the rest of the force he was to incorporate into his division. They were Western regiments—primarily Ohio, Indiana, and western Virginia soldiers—and they had been a success story for the Union in 1861. He knew many of the men as a result of his participation in McClellan's victorious western Virginia campaign of the previous summer. As Lander headed for Romney late on January 7, a portion of his new force was already completing a mission that accentuated the daring aggressiveness that befit their new commander.

General Benjamin F. Kelley, although detached from his Romney force while recuperating in Cumberland, had been concerned that Jackson would overwhelm General Lander at Hancock; therefore, he decided to create a diversion to draw the aggressive Southerner away from his threatening position near Bath. Kelley reasoned that if Jackson believed a strong force was approaching Winchester from the west, the Confederates would abort their campaign and return to their winter camps at Winchester.[36] On the snowy evening of January 6, 1862, Kelley ordered a raid on a Confederate militia detachment at a mountain pass along the Northwestern Turnpike known as Hanging Rock Pass or Blue's Gap—named after the Confederate militia colonel whose home occupied the area. General Kelley chose Colonel Samuel H. Dunning of the 5th Ohio to spearhead the attack. Dunning received his superior's Cumberland telegram late in the evening of January 6 and quickly organized a force to march the sixteen miles from Romney to the pass. It consisted of thirty-six infantry companies (six companies each from six different regiments) supported by eight cannons and detachments from three cavalry regiments.

The Federal force at Romney buzzed with excitement upon hearing the orders. This was welcome news for the volunteer soldier, for the winter's inactivity had left the soldiers disappointed about army life. A despondent private in the 1st West Virginia complained about the stagnancy to his sister on January 2, "I am well as usual, considering the corn meal we're fed on, and very little of even that. I think they must be trying to starve us as it seems impossible to kill us off in battle. . . . Christmas and New Years passed off very quietly here, hardly any difference from other days." This soldier and many of his regimental mates would have a different story to tell the following week.[37]

The 1st West Virginia Infantry, like many veteran Union regiments, converted from three-month to three-year enlistments after the terms of the former expired. The regiment now was a mix of seasoned veterans and recruits eager to fight. Kelley had been the original colonel of the 1st West Virginia's three-month men prior to his promotion to the regiment's division commander. Colonel Joseph Thoburn, the new commander of the three-year Union Virginians, was also a veteran of the original organization. He received his appointment on August 30, 1861, and was at the helm to lead the regiment on the Hanging Rock expedition.[38]

Thoburn was born in Antrim County, Ireland, and had moved to Canada with his parents in 1825 before he celebrated his first birthday. The Thoburns settled in Belmont County, Ohio, one year later, where Joseph attended and eventually taught school. He studied the science and art of medicine in Columbus which enabled him to enter a partnership for a lunatic asylum. Dr. Thoburn subsequently moved to Brownsville, Pennsylvania, then settled in Wheeling, Virginia, where he continued his practice, married, and raised a young family. His wife and three young children remained in Wheeling when the thirty-six-year-old colonel left to fight for his country in 1861. Thoburn entered the service as the surgeon of Kelley's three-month men. In this role he participated in the Rich Mountain Campaign and attended the wounded Colonel Kelley when he became a casualty at Philippi.[39] Thoburn's elevation from surgeon to colonel was of little surprise to his men; they admired the Irish leader's qualities. Colonel Dunning's planned expedition would be Thoburn's first test to demonstrate his abilities.

Although Dunning expected to start from Romney by 9:00 P.M. to surprise the Blue's Gap force before daybreak, organizational delays held up the expedition for nearly four hours. Approximately 2,000 infantrymen answered Dunning's call—an unusually small number because of illness and large numbers of men on picket duty. The volunteers taking part in the excursion gathered at camp and responded with spirited shouts and cheers to inspirational speeches made by their regimental officers. Between 12:30 and 1:00 A.M. on January 7, the column set off in the bitter cold. The 4th and 5th Ohio with Lieutenant Colonel Philip Daum's battery of artillery led the advance, followed by the 8th Ohio, 1st West Virginia, 14th Indiana, and the 7th Ohio. The 1st West Virginia Cavalry companies squeezed between the infantry regiments during the march. Despite the blustery weather, the confident foot soldiers were in good spirits at the prospect of fighting; they made the hills ring with patriotic songs as they passed the outposts that protected Romney two hours into the march. The surprised pickets asked where they were headed. When they answered that they were going to "whip the rebels," the outpost force wished them luck and admitted that they wished they could go along too.

The Federal detail marched down the frozen Northwestern Turnpike. They passed through cleared country land on their march eastward toward the North River Mountains that formed Blue's Gap. An Ohio soldier marvelled at the frame houses, spacious barns, and cultivated fields that dominated both sides of the road; he believed these farms portrayed a "higher order of civilization" compared to the more dilapidated homes seen in other areas of western Virginia. The column resembled a huge serpent winding through the winter night. The serpent, however, did not move smoothly. Frequent halts were ordered to let the men rest. The soldiers took advantage of every opportunity and threw themselves down on the snow-covered hillsides where many stole catnaps only to be abruptly awakened to "fall in" and resume the march.[40]

Colonel Dunning's detail made remarkable time in the frigid morning weather, covering fifteen miles in slightly over six hours. About one mile from the gap, Dunning ordered his artillerists to plant their cannons on a cleared hill. As the early morning light dawned on the North River valley landscape, the colonel could easily see the Confederate force attempting to burn the lone bridge that crossed the river. Dunning called on his own regiment, the 5th Ohio, to double-quick to the bridge and save it. His men responded with shouts; their spirits were ready. Their tired bodies were wanting, however, and although they moved slowly their presence, coupled with sporadic rifle fire, surprised the militia detachment which retreated back across the bridge where the rest of the Confederate force was notified of the pending attack. In the meantime, the Ringgold and Washington Cavalry (the latter named after the western Pennsylvania town they were recruited from) captured several of the militia pickets before they could react to the developing assault. The Federals crossed the bridge and, under Colonel Dunning's orders, halted at the gap. The opposing Confederate militia force consisted of four infantry regiments, one artillery section under Captain Wilfred Cutshaw, and a cavalry company under the command of Captain George Sheetz. Their primary fortifications against this mostly veteran Yankee force were the rifle pits trenched on the eastern edge of the mountain pass. These pits were now threatened; the 4th Ohio scaled the southern hill that lined the gap while the 5th Ohio climbed the opposite side. Colonel Dunning led his own regiment on the northern side after getting directions from a black servant at Colonel Charles Blue's residence. The bluecoats advanced toward the rifle pits with loud yells and cheers, and the Confederates fled from their positions without sustaining a fight.

The Union regiments remaining near the bridge heard the crack of rifle fire emanating from both sides of the gap.[41] Once the action on the hillsides died down, they charged through the gap, led by Colonel Samuel Sprigg Carroll and his 8th Ohio Infantry. Colonel Thoburn rode forward several hundred yards in front of his 1st West Virginia. He quickly returned to his men and announced, "Boys, if you want to see them, you will have to run. Come on. Follow me!" Thoburn wheeled his horse toward the mountains and led his men through the gap, followed by the 7th Ohio, while the 14th Indiana brought up the rear. They met no resistance. The Southerners were fleeing into the hills in front of them. By the time the cavalry moved up from the bridge, it was too late. The 800 militia already had a two-mile head start and easily escaped into the steep and densely wooded hills where the horsemen were not able to chase them.[42] Unfortunately for the Confederates, they had to travel light to make their escape. Two cannons were left at the gap: a six-pounder smooth-bore and a ten-pounder rifle. A caisson, plenty of ammunition, 300 muskets, wagons, and ten artillery horses also remained for the bluecoats to take. Seven militia pickets were taken prisoner and seven were killed. Immediately after the brief fight ended, a Hoosier soldier sat on a stump and helped himself to a hot breakfast left by an adversary. Looking to his side, he caught sight of two of the dead lying just a few yards from his makeshift dining table. One was shot through the head ("hole big enough to put your fist through"), while the other's head was split in two by a sabre stroke.[43]

Colonel Dunning ordered his men to torch the Blue house and the adjacent mill, reasoning that the buildings had been and could still be used as enemy quarters in the near future. From the moment those orders were given, his control over the men evaporated. The Buckeyes fired the mill, then shot at the miller as he fled from the burning building. After the soldiers began their return march to Romney at about noon, other houses were plundered and burned, and several livestock were stolen or killed.[44] This was the third time in two days that citizens became victims of war. At Bath and Alpine Station, the Confederates had plundered and destroyed some of the homes they were quartered in; the Federals did likewise at Hancock. The raid at Hanging Rock seemed particularly cruel, but it was the only one of the three incidents where total war was waged on opposing soil rather than on allied ground.

Dunning's orders were to return to Romney once the gap was cleared. By 5:00 P.M. on January 7, his tired soldiers reentered Camp Keys with turkeys and hens hanging off their gun barrels, and carrying haversacks filled with newly acquired supplies. They had been very successful on this brutal winter day. In sixteen hours, these 2,500 men (including cavalry and artillery) marched thirty-two miles and defeated a foe, capturing small arms and cannons in the process. However, what General Kelley did not know at the time was that Colonel Dunning could have taken his force to a poorly protected Winchester, a mere twenty-five miles east of Blue's Gap, because Jackson's division had remained at Unger's Store between Bath and Winchester. By doing so, the Union forces could have caged the Confederates with formidable "bars" at Williamsport to the east, Romney to the west, Hancock to the north, and Winchester to the south.

The destruction of the Blue's Gap stronghold drew mixed but predictable reactions, depending on whose side commented on the action. Jackson's militia force, approaching Romney from Unger's Store, passed by the devastated Blue's farm a few days after the Federals left it. Seeing the slaughtered livestock strewn along the turnpike and the burnt civilian property, a member of the Rockingham militia seethed. "We may go back to the darkest and uncivilized age of the world," he announced, "and we will not find in all wars among the savage tribes, such dark and atrocious deeds committed, as those which has just been done by the Lincolnites of the present day." Lander received an immediate dispatch from Kelley after the expedition force returned to Romney. Quickly describing the early morning attack, Kelley proudly announced the success of his plan. Lander was very impressed with the performance of the men he was about to inherit from Kelley, but he was also angry at McClellan's orders to move the Romney force back to the railroad as soon as he arrived there. Noting that McClellan commanded a huge army that was going nowhere that winter, Lander scribbled at the bottom of Kelley's dispatch, "See the difference between Kelley and the Army of the Potomac? A little dash is a good element."[45]

The Romney force received its new commander, without fanfare, on the evening of January 8 when General Lander entered town via Cumberland. He had little time to size up the veteran force he had been given for he had been ordered to move his men closer to the B & O Railroad to better protect that vital rail link. By Thursday, January 9, the sutlers and quartermasters sent most of their military supplies to Cumberland. Trains were constantly leaving and entering Green Spring, the station on the B & O line nearest Romney. Stocks of stores and supplies were being shipped out while horses, troops, and ammunition stayed in to protect Romney from what was believed to be General Jackson's imminent attack. His Confederate force was estimated by some to number about 16,000 when, in actuality, it was less than half that size. Scouting parties scoured the countryside for twenty miles while other troops threw up entrenchments and mounted guns. Despite the widespread apprehension and bustle of activity, Lieutenant L. C. Robinson of the 5th Ohio was given two days' furlough to complete some non-military business. The Company F officer travelled northward to Cumberland that busy Thursday and married his hometown sweetheart from Cincinnati. The ceremony was performed with the distraction of rattling swords and glittering bayonets all around them.[46]

Although Lander did not want to give up Romney without a fight, he followed General McClellan's orders: "Fall back in time. Be careful not to be caught." Beginning late on Friday, January 10, the Romney force evacuated their camps and relocated through a driving sleet to the north, wading several ice-cold creeks during their retreat. The dreary weather and withdrawal orders ignited Lander's short fuse this night. He exploded when the chaplain of the 14th Indiana asked him about arrangements to evacuate the sick men in his regiment. "God damn you, the 14th Regt., the whole army, everybody and everything," Lander roared, adding for good measure, "and if I have forgotten anything, God damn it too." Later in the withdrawal, he ordered the Ringgold Cavalry (a Pennsylvania cavalry company) to ford a creek, even though heavy precipitation had swollen the tributary beyond its banks. No fewer than four four-horse teams were swept away in an attempt to pontoon the stream. A cavalry lieutenant saved himself from drowning by grabbing an overhanging tree limb, then watched his horse become permanently engulfed by the swift creek waters. As Lander watched the catastrophic scene unfold in front of him, he uttered, "The next time I undertake to move an army, and God almighty sends such a rain, I will go around and cross hell on the ice."[47]

The soldiers planted their tent stakes at their new campsite near Patterson's Creek, a Virginia tributary of the Potomac River two miles downstream from where the B & O Railroad crosses the C & O Canal and Potomac River at North Branch Bridge. The camp, sitting approximately seven miles southeast of Cumberland, quickly turned into a quagmire. An Indiana soldier, expecting to find an immaculate campsite, needed only three words to describe the major features of his new home: "Mud! Mud! Mud!"[48] An Ohio newspaper correspondent was more colorful in his denunciation of the camp:

Take any Ohio pig-sty in the wet weather, enlarge its dimensions to a hundred acres or more, make it everywhere as slimy and mortary as the worst pig-sty of any dimensions, cover it with a thin layer of snow and trample this into the mud with thousands of feet til the dirty discolored whiteness only serves to show how nasty it is—soften the whole mass of mud and snow by a gentle thaw—put railroad track by the side of the area, and make its dirty freight cars and coal burning locomotives the only symbol of cleanly comfort anywhere visible—put a two story brick house in the middle of the mud, with muddy sentries pacing the muddy porch before the door—surround it with the dirt colored tents of many regiments, orderly pitched in the mire, with streets of the spongy soil made semi-liquid—put trenches along the rows of tents and make them gradually fill with the slipping mud from the banks—build wood fires in the mud, and set in kettles and pans on the burning logs to "cook" the abundant rations, tie up the poor begrimed horses in the swampy places to the rear of the tents, range the wagons to their rear, in still more unapproachable mire, cover the whole ground with the flower of Ohio's and Indiana's soldiers in discolored great coats and inexpressible inexpressibles and boots, scatter them everywhere, drearily stalking about in the mud, collecting on the little islands of comparatively solid ground, stretched out on the damp straw or damper ground that makes the floor of their tents, hovering like the witches in MacBeth around the dirty fires, everywhere listless, hands in their pockets, a dull stare in their eyes, nothing to do and unable to do anything; close in the old scene with the grand old Virginia mountains to the South, glistening in the spotless covering of purest snow, and crowned with the verdures of the pines, looking across the filthy camps and the clear Potomac toward the gentle knoll and the rich marshes that stretch between on the Maryland shore; and then please to understand that you have before you the winter encampment of the Western Division of the army of the Potomac.[49]

The notorious Camp Kelley stretched along the Virginia side of the Potomac and served as winter quarters for Lander's division for nearly a month. Between January 11 and January 31 Jackson's Confederates occupied and, subsequently, evacuated Romney, returning to more comfortable quarters at Winchester by the first week of February.[50]

Lander had been in division command since January 5; however, he did not learn until January 10 that he belonged to the Army of the Potomac and not the originally intended Department of Western Virginia. Although the Federals were inactive the rest of January, Lander's division took true form at the Patterson's Creek camp. By the end of January, the division exceeded 10,000 men structured in three brigades of sixteen infantry regiments, five batteries of artillery, four cavalry companies, and a company of sharpshooters from Lander's home state of Massachusetts. The force was a mix of new organizations, and veterans from Kelley's Railroad District and Brigadier General Robert H. Milroy's Cheat Mountain District (formerly belonging to Brigadier General Joseph J. Reynolds) from the Department of Western Virginia.[51]

Before January closed, the men of Lander's division saw the paymaster for the first time in several months. The acquisition of over forty dollars per man did much to relieve the grumblings of winter life; however, the back pay did little to change the soldiers' impressions of this part of Virginia. One infantryman stated, "I have heard much of Virginia; I have now seen some of it; but to my surprise, I find this a most barren, hilly, and rough looking place. It is almost desolate. I have seen but one female since we touched the soil of Virginia; all seem to have fled, but where I know not. The houses (all I have seen) are small and scarce."[52]

With the exception of the Ball's Bluff fiasco in October of 1861, the Union armies in the east had been inactive since the Battle of Manassas was fought the previous summer. As January turned to February, the public's attention remained focused on the Army of the Potomac quartered around Washington. Its commander, General George McClellan, had survived a severe bout of typhoid fever about the time Lander was taking over his new command. Now McClellan was healthy again and actively planning a campaign to capture Richmond via the landing at Urbanna and a rapid march by way of West Point. In the meantime, his 100,000-plus army continued daily drills in and around the capital city. Most of his men were inexperienced recruits, and few of his veterans had yet to taste victory in a Civil War engagement.

Lander's Western division contrasted sharply from the rest of the Army of the Potomac. His veterans were the very reason McClellan now commanded the largest army in the Western Hemisphere. The Westerners had won sweet victories for him at Philippi and Rich Mountain, miniscule engagements that still effectively boosted the responsibilities of their former commander as well as confidence in themselves. Despite the grumblings of poor camp conditions and debilitating illnesses contracted from closed-in winter quarters, the confidence of the veterans became infectious and swept through the ranks of the green regiments. The commanding presence of General Lander also inspired the new troops. "The army is fully organized under the leadership of the gallant Lander," wrote a sanguine Pennsylvanian on January 20, "and you may soon hear some more of his brilliant exploits. His name is a tower of strength and a dread to the Secesh."[53]

Lander was a familiar figure to veterans who had seen him as an aide-de-camp to McClellan several months earlier. He was tall and slender with black hair that draped in slight curls upon his neck. The finely proportioned general was considered a born commander by many. But he looked different this time. Lander walked with an abrupt gait from his Edwards' Ferry injury, and he appeared paler than he did during McClellan's western Virginia campaign.[54] It was obvious that Frederick Lander was not well. On February 2, he became very ill—sick enough to cause his division's planned maneuvers for the day to be cancelled. One of Lander's aides explained away the ailment as "one of the congestive chills to which he is subject," but rumors spread through the camp fingering an alternative source of his illness. The rumors parroted similar hearsay spread to explain Lander's erratic behavior during the Romney evacuation. Lieutenant Colonel Thomas Clark of the 29th Ohio wrote his wife on February 6, "There is a current report that the sudden sickness of General Lander the other day was delirium tremors. I neither affirm or deny it."[55] Clark's rumor proved to be false, but alcohol flowed freely throughout Lander's district due to his enforcement of a controversial policy—whiskey rations.

Lander placed a premium in dispersing half-gill whiskey allotments, laced with quinine, to his troops throughout January and February of 1862. Unfortunately, some of the general's subordinates found ways to exceed their two-ounce allotments. A contingent of women living in Cumberland became outraged at the unhidden use of alcoholic beverages. They sent a petition to Lander, requesting him to put a stop to the liquor traffic in the area. "The front doors are closed to the soldiers," they complained, "while the back doors are open to the officers." Colonel Otto Burstenbinder of the 67th Ohio was apparently one of the officers the ladies were complaining about. He also was an object of disdain for fellow Buckeye, Lieutenant Colonel Clark of the 29th Ohio, a teetotaler, who witnessed the "tipsy" colonel treating a few captains in camp to a swig from his bottle. Burstenbinder offered the whiskey to Clark, who refused it by declaring, "Never use it, sir, and I have but devilish little respect for officers who drink." Noting that the inebriated Burstenbinder disappeared in a few minutes, Clark predicted that the colonel would be ousted soon by his disgusted regiment. Colonel Otto Burstenbinder was arrested on March 16 and finally dismissed from the service of the United States in July.[56]

Lander's whiskey and quinine rations did little to alleviate illness in his troops. He could see that Camp Kelley was not healthy for his command. Fortunately, he received orders to depart the inhospitable terrain; no soldier disagreed with packing up and moving this time. Lander transported his division eastward by railroad cars to new campgrounds during the second week of February. His men now enjoyed the cold, but less muddy confines of Camp Chase near Paw Paw, Virginia, twenty-five miles downriver from Cumberland and forty miles northwest of Winchester. The soldiers rested a short hike away from the 3,118-foot tunnel that had been cut into the rocky Maryland shore so that canal boats could avoid a six-mile bend in the Potomac that began two miles south of Paw Paw. On the Virginia side of the river, a 100-foot railroad tunnel traversed the camp. Once the Westerners' Sibley tents arrived, they deemed their new campsite "comfortable." Lander's new base of operations better enabled him to protect the railroad while it was being repaired. Regiments from the division were still entering Camp Chase as late as February 13. On this day, several regiments left to embark on a new mission.[57]

At the same time Major General Ulysses S. Grant was attacking Fort Donelson in the western theater of operations, General Lander set out to complete a forced reconnaissance to break up a "rebel's nest" at Bloomery Gap, one of the rare passes in the Cacapon Mountains existing approximately halfway between Paw Paw and Winchester. The gap, only fifteen miles southeast from the new Union camp, had been a source of Confederate bushwacking, and Lander wanted the threat removed. Portions of six infantry regiments (the 5th, 8th and 67th Ohio, 13th Indiana, 14th Indiana, and 7th West Virginia), several hundred members of his cavalry, and a battery of artillery lined the road leading south from Paw Paw. Lander set out late in the afternoon of Thursday, February 13.[58] At approximately 5:00 P.M., he dashed up to his attacking force and raised his cap as he rode along the lines on his charger. Lander spoke briefly with his aides, moved to the right of his formed lines, and set the column in motion.[59]

Taking part in his second raid in as many months was Samuel Sprigg Carroll, colonel of the 8th Ohio. Carroll graduated from West Point in 1856 and started his military career as a lieutenant in the 10th U. S. Infantry prior to the opening of the war. He lobbied for, and received, a colonel's commission with the 8th Ohio and joined that command in Romney in December of 1861. The red-haired and bearded Maryland native (his nickname was "Brick Top") had been described by a fellow officer in the Ohio regiment as "a dashing officer, anxious to distinguish himself, and above all to qualify his regiment for its duties." Carroll's regiment had not been in the original plan for the Hanging Rock expedition in January, but he had convinced Colonel Dunning to include it. Both he and his regiment served there, and subsequently, with "high notice and distinction."

General Lander chose Carroll and his regiment to spearhead the planned assault at Bloomery Gap.[60]

The most immediate obstacles confronting Lander's force were natural ones, particularly the rain-swollen Big Cacapon River and the formidable Cacapon Mountains. The expedition reached the bank of the river in six hours where the men built fires and rested. When his engineer corps told him that they had no means for bridging the river, Lander cursed in a voice that "out-roared the roaring flood." A member of the 14th Indiana, within earshot of Lander's oaths, later described his general as "one of the most wicked men I ever saw. Profanity seemed to him a recreation and no time or place was sacred from his oaths." Fortunes improved when a member of the 8th Ohio, who had been an engineer for a circus prior to the war, helped the engineers bridge the river by pushing wagons into the waterway and laying planks on top of their beds. It delayed the expedition by four hours.[61]

By the time morning's light penetrated the Cacapon Mountains, the Union force had successfully traversed a narrow path and advanced to within two miles of the gap. The 67th Ohio and 13th Indiana had taken a divergent road to cut off the militia retreat, but they never got involved in the action. The 1st West Virginia Cavalry, commanded by Colonel Henry Anisansel, a French-Swiss immigrant who lived in Canonburg, Pennsylvania, prior to the war, overtook the infantry and proceeded to lead the expedition. Just before entering the gap, Lander ordered Anisansel to move his advance force forward, make a reconnaissance, and capture the enemy's baggage. Lander told the cavalier that he would send infantry support. At that point Lander rode to the rear to bring up the 14th Indiana and 7th West Virginia.

**Colonel Samuel Sprigg Carroll,
8th Ohio Infantry**
U.S.A.M.H.I.

Anisansel and his small force met surprising resistance at the pass, and they buckled under the pressure of advanced regiments of the approximately 700 Confederate militia stationed there. While the cavalry was being held in check, General Lander rode up, swearing furiously at the horsemen for not charging forward. Anisansel tried to explain that he was waiting for infantry support, but Lander would hear none of it. Yelling, "Follow me! I'll lead you!" Lander galloped to the head of the West Virginia cavaliers, who had now been joined by the Pennsylvania and Ohio horse soldiers, and led them forward. They charged through the gap where an unsuspecting contingent of militia companies had formed.[62] The Union force displayed confusion, but the rebel militia was completely surprised, and several members were killed and captured. Lander apprehended Colonel Robert F. Baldwin of the 31st Virginia Militia, then the general watched an Ohio horseman argue with another Southern militia officer. Lander rode up to the cavalry private and commanded him to disarm the Rebel, but the Ohioan complained that he had refused to surrender his sword to a Yankee. Lander was furious; he dismounted, walked up to the officer, and seized him by his shoulder. In a rage, Lander shook the Southerner and ordered him to surrender. The startled Confederate immediately unbuckled his sword and handed it over to Lander. The general then turned to his Ohio private and said, "If you find another man like this, don't multiply words with him." He then remounted his steed and rode ahead.[63] The militia force was devastated; thirteen lay dead with an additional sixty-five—including seventeen officers—taken prisoner.[64]

But Lander was not through. He ordered Anisansel to move forward a second time and capture the Southern baggage wagons attempting to escape a few miles ahead. Anisansel rode forward but met stiff resistance from a body of militia that rallied behind a stone fence. They poured an effective volley into the cavalry, killing two and knocking out Anisansel's horse. The steed abruptly fell into the mud and herniated the luckless colonel. The baggage wagons escaped capture which enraged Lander still further. The general then ordered Colonel Carroll to clear the country all the way to Unger's Store, the limit of Lander's command in the Western Department. Carroll, with his two regiments, did as he was told without encountering any resistance. The entire force returned to Paw Paw Friday night. Carroll's troops also made it back with little delay, surpassing their performance at Hanging Rock by marching forty-five miles in less than twenty-eight hours. Upon his return to headquarters, Lander was pleased to learn of an additional coup accomplished, again, by Colonel Dunning. He had led a small force from Romney on a forty-mile raid where he broke up a "guerrilla haunt" at Moorefield, capturing 225 head of cattle at a cost of only two wounded men.[65]

Lander was pleased that the B & O Railroad was now almost completely opened for the first time in nearly six months, and the enemy did not exist anywhere within the entire scope of his command. He wired the news of his success to General McClellan, going out of his way to commend Colonel Carroll for acting as "a most efficient and gallant officer." He also complained about his own health, broken down by the toils of the day, and requested that he be relieved from duty. Lander then set his next plan in motion; he levelled charges against Colonel Anisansel, court-martialing him for cowardice and misconduct in the presence of the enemy.[66]

The affair at Bloomery Gap, wagged by the soldiers as "Lander's Midnight Bloomery Dash," exposed both the best and the worst in General Lander. Those that witnessed him that day knew he was buoyed by something other than the good news about Forts Henry and Donelson. It appeared to them that the general was drunk that day, and many resented the way he was sacrificing Anisansel for actions that were beyond his control. "He [Anisansel] halted his command in order to feel the enemy as a careful man should," complained one of the Ringgold's, continuing to defend the cavalry officer, "While he was doing this, General Lander came up at full charge, drunk, cursing, and damning, and put Colonel Anisansel under arrest for cowardice." An infantry officer, not part of the expedition, offered his opinion of Lander: "I do not question General Lander's bravery but don't want him to get up a drunken courage that has no fear, reason or anything else that should mark an officer of his rank."[67] A loyal member of Anisansel's regiment also was impressed with Lander's dash and daring at Bloomery Gap, but also alluded strongly to his commander's drinking. "No one doubts General Lander's bravery," he wrote, "and he has a kind of savage enthusiasm, well calculated to lead men in battle; but of his fitness, at times, to have command of an army, and especially on the morning of said fight, many who saw him have serious doubts." The same soldier reasoned that his commander's problem could not be kept a secret much longer and predicted to his hometown newspaper, "the public, no doubt, will arrive at the same conclusions if he holds his present position any length of time."[68]

General McClellan was unaware of his former aide's health problems, but he knew he needed Lander for a planned campaign to capture Winchester. McClellan realized that by transferring the Western division from Cumberland to Paw Paw, Lander would be close enough to link up with General Banks, who was prepared to cross the Potomac at Harpers Ferry and sweep southward to Winchester. Lander's telegram requesting to be relieved alarmed McClellan; within two hours he responded with a telegram of his own telling the ailing general, "Don't talk about resigning." McClellan appeased his friend by suggesting that he rest at Cumberland to recuperate before the planned movements. Secretary of War Edwin M. Stanton sent a congratulatory telegram three days later to tell Lander that President Abraham Lincoln was impressed by the performance of his command. Stanton also took a back-handed swipe at McClellan's inactive army when he lauded Lander, "You have shown how much may be done in the worst weather and worst roads, by a spirited officer, at the head of a small force of brave men, unwilling to waste life in camp when the enemies of their country are within reach."[69]

Six days after returning from Bloomery, Lander was apparently feeling confident and optimistic. He sent a message to Stanton, boasting of the accomplishments of his subordinate officers and men. Lander continued by claiming that his division's successes were possible only because of his experience in mountain transportation. He complained about the army's organization, frankly stating that Americans were behind the French in that aspect of war, but were well ahead of Europe in the art of transportation. Lander begged Stanton for orders to move his men again—realizing, perhaps, that this time his health depended on it. Close to admitting the seriousness of his illness, Lander ended his telegram to Stanton by warning him, "I am never so sick as when I cannot move."[70]

While awaiting orders for a new campaign, Lander's soldiers rested in their Paw Paw camps. Many recuperated from illnesses contracted in the cold and damp climate of the mountains. The only news of note was Grant's victories in the West; still, this appeared to satisfy the soldiers for the present. Creative measures were employed to fill the time and prevent the boredom induced by stagnancy. The 7th Ohio decided to use the respite to demonstrate its bias against the Southern government. They celebrated the anniversary of Confederate President Jefferson Davis's inauguration by noisily burning him in effigy on their campgrounds.[71]

On February 22, General Lander took advantage of the atmosphere of pageantry associated with Washington's Birthday to review his division of Westerners. For most of the men, the occasion allowed them to see their commanding general for the first time. The temperature had warmed into the forties for a third straight day, lifting the spirits of the men and their commanding general. Lander witnessed a thirteen-volley salute in his honor, followed by each regiment breaking into columns by company and passing him in review. Then the men formed solid squares, allowing the general to ride up to each regiment and inspire them with a speech. As Lander left one unit to address the next one in line, thunderous cheers filled the intervals. The complement was appropriate—a daring general firing up his dashing troops. Although some were taken by the martial atmosphere, the cynical members of the ranks remained unswayed. "Thus it goes," wrote a member of the 29th Ohio that night, "nothing to do for weeks only to show ourselves once in a while to our officers, and scour our guns, at the tune of $13 per month." Despite the unenthusiastic approach adopted by some of Lander's foot soldiers, all were confident about the prospects of taking Winchester away from General Jackson and his Southern army. Lander certainly exhibited no qualms about the prospect of meeting General Jackson in battle. Responding to a false rumor that the Confederates were moving northward from Winchester again, Lander confidently announced to McClellan that he would surprise Jackson from behind and "beat him to death."[72]

Regimental officers spent the next several days in Lander's headquarters; Colonel Henry Anisansel was tried by a military court of law there and acquitted of all the charges Lander levelled against him. Although Lander was displeased at the court's final ruling, more important matters diverted his attention. He was informed that a movement upon Winchester was inevitable. McClellan telegraphed his subordinate, warning him to keep his men "perfectly in hand, and be ready for a spring." The Army of the Potomac commander deemed the possession of Winchester and Strasburg imperative to effectively cover the railroad in the rear. McClellan believed simultaneous movements in the Northern Valley and in the Tidewater region would compel Confederate General Joseph E. Johnston to evacuate his defenses near Centreville to counter the two-pronged thrusts. After promising Lander that his men would share in the pending operation against Jackson at Winchester, McClellan confided to him that he had plans for a more important expedition for Lander and his Westerners when their immediate goal was attained and the Confederates were removed from the Shenandoah Valley.[73]

General Banks crossed his division from Harpers Ferry into Virginia on February 27. McClellan was there to watch the crossing, then he wired Lander and fittingly ordered the Massachusetts native to advance to Bunker Hill, a small town south of Martinsburg. Banks and McClellan advanced to Charlestown the next day. They occupied the town and waited for Lander to move his division toward Martinsburg, fifteen miles northwest of Charlestown. Unsubstantiated reports reached McClellan indicating that thousands of Confederates were reinforcing Winchester from Manassas. Inexplicably, Lander had not occupied Martinsburg by March 1. McClellan feared that Lander took the wrong road so "Little Mac" attempted to recall him.[74]

There was no need to do so. On March 1, most of Lander's division had marched from their Paw Paw camps toward Martinsburg beginning at 4:00 P.M. They scaled one mountain range, crossed the Big Cacapon River on pontoons, and bivouacked in a pine forest on the ascent of the Shenandoah Mountains late that night. Mysteriously, the next day, the men were ordered back to Camp Chase at Paw Paw. A heavy snow storm hit the area which angered the men as much as the countermanded orders. When they returned to their camps, the men received shocking news that explained the reason for their confused movements.[75]

Lander was ailing tremendously on the morning of March 1, staying in his bed at Paw Paw headquarters while his heavily supplied force attempted to advance to Martinsburg. By late afternoon, Lander's condition worsened; when he failed to rally as he had always done before, his doctors sedated the general with morphine. Simon F. Barstow, Lander's assistant adjutant general, recalled the troops on March 2 and notified McClellan of Lander's condition, optimistically stating that the general may rise from his bed later that Sunday. By 4:15 P.M., reality hit Barstow that his superior had now been in a medical stupor for nearly twenty-four hours and he informed McClellan that "Lander cannot last an hour." The general's mortal condition was described as congestion of the brain, induced by Lander's four-month-old Edwards' Ferry wound. Lander's hard-working and hard-drinking lifestyle may have exacerbated his poor health. Questionable medical care may have also aided his demise. All these debilitating factors turned a once vibrant and fearless leader into a pale and comatose victim with no chance for recovery, and no chance for survival. General Frederick West Lander died at 5:00 P.M. on March 2, 1862. "This campaign killed him," complained an emotional Simon F. Barstow when he announced Lander's death to McClellan, "for he held on in spite of failing health and strength, to the last."[76]

Rather than participate in a grand assault against Winchester on March 3, the Westerners of Lander's division stood under arms for three hours through another rainy winter day. All flags at Paw Paw flew at half staff for General Lander's funeral ceremonies. The 7th Ohio held the post of honor; they never marched better. Their band led the procession as the Buckeyes escorted the draped coffin over a road lined on both sides by nearly 12,000 troops standing at "present arms" position. The turbulent weather befit the tumultuous leader whose remains were followed by his troops—many who loved him, some who despised him, all who respected him—to the railroad depot. As the steam-driven cars churned toward Pittsburgh to take Lander home to Salem, Massachusetts, one of his Indiana soldiers echoed the opinion of many who served under the fallen warrior:

> Thus ended the career of one of the most daring and strong headed men the world ever knew.[77]

Chapter Two

"The Crisis Is Upon Us"

Winchester was whitened by snowfall on Sunday, March 2, 1862. Its citizens had suffered through a miserable winter, and the unyielding precipitation this day did little to alleviate their colds, sore throats, or dispositions. Lingering illnesses prevented some from enjoying the highlight of the day, morning church services.[1]

The Presbyterian Church on Kent Street rang with resounding voices, a spirited response to the sermon given by the Reverend James Robert Graham. The thirty-seven-year-old Graham arrived from his native New Jersey in 1851 and had been a Winchester resident ever since. This day Graham's audience included one parishioner who drew as much attention as the reverend himself. Major General Thomas J. Jackson and his staff presided among the worshippers.[2]

Thomas Jonathan Jackson was one month past his thirty-eighth birthday. The third child and second son of Julia Beckwith Neale and lawyer Jonathan Jackson, Thomas was born in the small town of Clarksburg, (West) Virginia, and was named after his maternal grandfather. Although he had received a meager boyhood education, Jackson's uncle helped him secure an appointment at the forty-year-old United States Military Academy at West Point. He graduated in 1846 with a class that turned out twenty future Civil War generals.

After graduating the academy, young Jackson was assigned to the 1st Artillery and served in the Mexican War, earning laurels for his performance near Mexico City. Jackson left Mexico with two brevets, but he resigned from the military to accept a professorship at the Virginia Military Institute (V.M.I.) in Lexington, Virginia. Jackson married twice there. His first wife, Elinor Junkin, was the daughter of Washington College President and Presbyterian minister, the Reverend Dr. George Junkin. She died delivering a stillborn child in 1854. Jackson remarried in 1857, this time to Anna Morrison, a daughter of another Presbyterian minister and college president. Thomas and Anna Jackson resided in Lexington until 1861.[3]

In April of 1861, Jackson, like many of his West Point classmates and V.M.I. colleagues, sided with the Confederacy and was commissioned a colonel of Virginia forces. His first assignment landed him at Harpers Ferry where he spent much of the spring of 1861 organizing recruits into a military force, including four companies from Winchester and the surrounding environs of Frederick County who were brigaded under his command. Jackson was promoted to brigadier general in June. His troops defended Winchester from an advancing Federal force under Major General Robert Patterson until the Southerners were called to the aid of Brigadier General Pierre G. T. Beauregard who was about to battle the Northern army near the town of Manassas, Virginia.[4]

The conversion from man to legend arose on the sun-baked terrain of Henry Hill on July 21, 1861. Here, General Jackson held his brigade in line, concentrated thirteen cannons near his position, and turned a sure Confederate defeat at Manassas into a resounding victory. "There stands Jackson like a stone wall," marvelled a fellow general who attempted to reorganize his withdrawing troops on Henry Hill, "rally behind the Virginians." The name stuck to both the general and his five-regiment brigade. Jackson's performance did not go unnoticed by his superiors. In October he was promoted to a higher rank while the Southern press published his exploits to fascinate their readers. In less than six months, "Stonewall" Jackson's meteoric rise from V.M.I. major to major general became the talk of the South.[5]

The Confederate War Department marked Stonewall's promotion by rewarding him an independent command of the newly formed Valley District in General Joseph E. Johnston's Department of Northern Virginia. Jackson's command included the Shenandoah Valley and regions of northwestern Virginia outside the mountains that formed the Valley. Jackson returned to Winchester on November 4, 1861; the Stonewall Brigade joined him there over the next two weeks. With Winchester as his new base of operations, General Jackson sent for his wife by playfully writing her, "Will little ex-Anna Morrison come and keep house for me and stay until the spring of the campaign of 1862?" Mrs. Jackson joined her husband in Winchester during the closing weeks of 1861.[6]

Stonewall's appearance was best captured by the lens of Nathaniel Routzahn, a Winchester photographer whose 1862 portrait of the general has been considered a perfect likeness of him. Standing at approximately five feet ten inches, Jackson appeared trim and relaxed. A broad forehead, thin lips, and full beard could not divert one's attention from Jackson's most distinguishing feature—his eyes. Those eyes were described as "always direct and penetrating"—characteristics captured in the Routzahn portrait; however, the limits of photography at the time hid the deep blue-gray hue that left a lasting impression on peers and subordinates alike.[7]

In early 1862, no one outside of General Jackson's family knew the man as well as the Reverend Graham. In addition to being regular attenders at the preacher's church, Jackson and his wife resided in the Graham's North Braddock Street home during their stay in Winchester. The Jacksons and Grahams struck a warm friendship which allowed the observant Graham to witness a side of the man that contrasted sharply with the legend that developed over the next fifteen months. The preacher considered Stonewall "a simple gentleman"; there was little about him that would attract special observation. His manners were neither polished nor constrained; his bearing was neither dignified nor embarrassed. Graham considered him neither graceful nor ungainly in his movements and denied witnessing

any of the peculiarities that others noted in the general. Personally, Graham described Stonewall as methodical in manner, cheerful in conversation, free in expression, and firm in principle. Not surprisingly, the reverend attributed religion to be responsible for Jackson's strength of character. Graham claimed that Stonewall's "simple, earnest, Scriptural faith in God" dominated his whole being and took absolute possession of him. Graham firmly believed that Jackson was a man of God "first and last and always."[8]

Major General Thomas J. Jackson, Photographed by Nathaniel Routzahn in 1862
Courtesy of Ben Ritter

Although Jackson had met with success early in his Civil War career, his fortunes turned sour during his first months as an independent division commander.

Two winter campaigns met with mixed, if not dubious, results. First came the December 1861 expedition to destroy Dam Number 5, a waterway block of the Potomac River that regulated the water levels of the C & O Canal near Williamsport, Maryland. His success achieved there was merely temporary; the Federals had the canal working again in a few days. Then came the miserable Bath-Romney expedition, a January campaign marred by brutal weather and bickering subordinates. Jackson had only some paltry Federal supplies captured at Bath to justify the winter maneuver. The losses and missed opportunities turned the campaign into a debacle, leaving a lingering foul taste in the mouths of all involved.

Jackson's first loss was the missed golden opportunity to capture all the Federals at Bath and, subsequently, at Hancock on January 3–6, 1862. Embarrassed by the realization that his men failed to cut off the retreat and capture a small Federal force on Warm Spring Ridge, Jackson sought out who he believed was responsible for the failure and came across the name of Colonel William Gilham, the brigade commander whose regiments led the Confederate division into Bath and allowed several hours to transpire before the height was assaulted. Jackson attempted to court-martial Gilham for allowing Colonel Murray's Federal detachment to escape across the Potomac River at Sir John's Run on January 4.

Gilham, a fellow faculty member with Jackson at V.M.I. before the war, had resigned from the service and returned to his teaching position in January. Because he no longer led one of Jackson's brigades, Jackson's charges against him never were aggressively pursued by the Confederate War Department. This did not prevent the colonel from firing back at his superior's accusations. Gilham blamed Jackson for the failed opportunity at Bath, pointing out the fact that of the three roads that led to Unger's Store from Winchester, the division commander had chosen "the very worse one" resulting in a very slow approach to the resort town. He also charged Jackson with the responsibility for failing to capture the 84th Pennsylvania, 39th Illinois, and the artillery pieces with them on Warm Spring Ridge. Gilham cited Jackson's decision to use militia to surround the Federals instead of his own Stonewall Brigade as the source of the failure. "Had he sent volunteers instead of militia to enter the town on the left, and cut off the retreat towards [Cacapon] or Sir John's Run Depot, we should have been in town early in the day," Gilham reasoned, "and must have [captured] the enemy before he reached the river opposite Hancock."[9] It appeared that both the uninspired attack by Gilham, as well as the poor judgment in deployment by Jackson, resulted in Colonel Murray's escape from

Bath and General Lander's subsequent successful defense of Hancock.

Gilham's brigade had initially been part of Brigadier General William Wing Loring's command. Loring and his men had spent the latter months of 1861 in the western Virginia theater until ordered to reinforce Jackson's command. They arrived at Winchester on December 26, 1861. The one-armed Loring, second in command to Jackson at the time, was allowed to retain command of his own troops—three infantry brigades consisting of ten regiments from Virginia, Tennessee, Georgia and Arkansas and two batteries of eight cannons. Loring's presence tripled the size of Jackson's original brigade and when they marched off toward Bath on January 1, 1862, the unusually warm sunny weather appeared to be a pretense for a successful cooperative effort for the two commands that formed the over-8,000-strong Valley District army.[10]

Unfortunately, the campaign turned cold and ugly, largely from the intolerable winter weather that ravaged the mountainous country northwest of Winchester. Nearly one-fifth of the force was ill during January and February. Many died from disease while only a handful of men succumbed from battle wounds. Lieutenant Colonel George Lay, the inspector-general employed by Jackson's superior, General Joseph E. Johnston, noted that conditions could have been much worse for many of the soldiers had already contracted measles during the previous spring. Lay also believed that the number of sick was not unusual for the winter months, but he did concede that a disproportionate number of ill men originated from General Loring's brigades.[11]

Loring temporarily lost over 1,150 men to illness during the campaign, a major factor in the torn relationship that divided the Valley District force. The disunity that developed between Loring's men and the Stonewall Brigade, and between Jackson and Loring, intensified the harshness associated with the Bath-Romney expedition. Loring's men despised the Stonewall Brigade, accusing Jackson's regiments of receiving special treatment during the winter campaign that resulted in great discomfort for Loring's troops. The situation came to a head on January 23 when Jackson ordered his Stonewall Brigade, under the command of Brigadier General Richard Brooke Garnett, to return to winter quarters at Winchester while instructing General Loring to remain in Romney with his three brigades. A member of the Stonewall Brigade pitied Loring's men, for while he enjoyed the comfortable confines of Winchester, the former Army of the Northwest had to endure "the most miserable hole in creation" by remaining in Romney. Loring's men took out their frustrations by verbally abusing Garnett's men, hurling epithets at them and calling them "F.F.V's" (First Families of Virginia), "Jackson's Pets," "militia" and "cowards."[12]

The worst moments of the arduous campaign occurred in late January when General Loring, under pressure from his angry subordinates, went behind Jackson's back and successfully lobbied the Confederate cabinet in Richmond to recall his troops from Romney. Secretary of War Judah P. Benjamin telegraphed Jackson on January 30, ordering him to bring Loring and his brigades back to Winchester. Stonewall was angry at the interference with his command and swiftly replied to the secretary's orders in writing, informing him that his order had been complied with and that Jackson was tendering his resignation from the service of the Confederate army.[13]

Jackson's resignation sent shock waves through his former brigade. "We are all deeply grieved at the prospect of loosing our brave old Genl." wrote a member of the 4th Virginia. "We all know in loosing him we loose the firmest stone in our wall." The soldiers' worries were swiftly swept away, for it took only one week for friends, citizens, and politicians to convince Stonewall to withdraw his resignation. Jackson then worked to formally punish the officers who impeded his campaign. During the first week of February, General Johnston received Jackson's list of five specifications charging General Loring with neglect of duty during the campaign. Charges against Colonel Gilham soon followed, even though he no longer served as an officer in the Valley District. Both court-martials were dismissed when Confederate President Jefferson Davis decided that carrying the charges through would do no good for the service.[14]

Although the litigious general did not enjoy the completion of the court-martials, the Confederate War Department placated him by removing Loring from the Valley District. General Loring was promoted to major general by President Davis and was reassigned away from the Shenandoah Valley. Colonel Gilham returned to V.M.I. prior to his regiments' arrival at Romney in January. Unfortunately for Jackson, much of Loring's command was also taken away from Stonewall's jurisdiction, significantly reducing the strength of his division. The Tennessee, Georgia, and Arkansas regiments of Loring's command were doled out to Tennessee and eastern Virginia. The remaining five Virginia regiments and lone battalion were ordered to Manassas to reinforce General Johnston's command there, but Jackson decided to hold these units with him at Winchester when he learned of Federal forces massing north of him.[15] The militia regiments, failing time and time again at Bath, Hanging Rock, Moorefield, and Bloomery Gap, had diminished in number to the point where they no longer could be relied upon. By March 3, Jackson's Valley District force became an all-Virginia division comprised of three brigades containing ten regiments, one five-company battalion, one regiment of cavalry, and five artillery batteries numbering twenty-six guns.[16]

Jackson's new brigade commanders of Loring's former regiments satisfied him more than the previous officers who had led the men during the Bath-Romney campaign; however, the two men Jackson chose were outspoken critics of Stonewall's decision to leave them in Romney in January. Colonel Jesse Burks replaced Colonel Gilham as commander of a brigade consisting of his own former regiment, the 42nd Virginia, and the 21st Virginia, 48th Virginia, and Irish Battalion. Colonel William B. Taliaferro, one of Loring's brigade commanders and another vocal dissenter of Jackson's leadership, had also removed himself from Jackson's command. Taliaferro had served in the Virginia legislature prior to the war and decided to use his political clout to obtain a general's commission from President Davis. Taliaferro left Romney for Richmond late in January and had not yet returned. Jackson replaced him with Colonel Samuel V. Fulkerson of the 37th Virginia. Fulkerson was a surprising choice for promotion considering that he had also been a critic of Jackson's winter campaign and had even written a letter to two congressmen in Richmond to solicit a reassignment for Loring's regiments, then in Romney. Colonel Fulkerson's diminutive brigade consisted of one artillery battery and two infantry regiments, the 23rd and 37th Virginia.[17]

Despite the removal of his subordinate nemeses, Stonewall Jackson was far from satisfied with his existing subordinate command structure. Colonels Burks and Fulkerson were new to brigade command. The only other general-grade officer in the Valley District commanded Jackson's former brigade. The Stonewall Brigade (the 2nd, 4th, 5th, 27th, and 33rd Virginia infantry regiments) retained the sobriquet that they and their former commander earned on the hills along Bull Run. Brigadier General Richard Brooke Garnett commanded them since early December of 1861, and the men of his new brigade had taken a great liking to him. Unfortunately for Garnett, General Jackson did not share his men's ardor for the brigadier. Prior to levelling court-martial charges against General Loring and Colonel Gilham, Jackson sent a letter to the War Department complaining about Garnett's handling of the brigade during the early days of 1862. Although General Garnett remained in command in March of 1862, he also remained, unwittingly, under the suspicious eye of his superior officer.[18]

General Richard "Dick" Garnett was enjoying his prestigious rank for only the fourth month in an army career that spanned twenty years. The Essex County, Virginia, native was one of twin sons

born to William and Anna Garnett of Essex County (the twin brother
died in 1855). Garnett's uncle, a brigadier in the U.S. Army, influenced then-President Andrew Jackson to secure a position at West
Point for his nephew. The young Garnett entered the academy in
1836, failed one year, and suffered conduct rankings that ultimately
affected his final class standing. Dick Garnett graduated with the
rank of second lieutenant, twenty-ninth out of a class of fifty-two in
1841.[19] He served in the 6th U.S. Infantry after graduation, then
was detached as an aide to his uncle in New Orleans during the
Mexican War. Eventually Lieutenant Garnett transferred to the
Western territories and served there in the early 1850s. The year
1855 became a landmark one for Garnett; he received a promotion
and fathered a son. The boy, William "Billy" Garnett, was half Tidewater Virginian and half Miniconjou Sioux (the child's mother was
an American Indian named Looking Woman). In May of 1857, Captain Garnett participated in Lieutenant Colonel Joseph E. Johnston's
expedition to survey the southern Kansas boundary, a tenuous region of "Bloody Kansas." It was a difficult experience for the captain
who expressed his bitterness to the secretary of war soon afterwards, venting about later West Point graduates and classmen who
graduated lower than he did but were receiving promotions above
his current captain's rank. Garnett complained about being deeply
humiliated over the process that promoted over twenty juniors above
his head to fill ranks in newly formed army regiments. His argu-
ment, though convincing, resulted in no further promotions for
Garnett in the Old Army.[20]

Captain Garnett had been stationed in northern California with
his Company K, 6th Infantry, when Fort Sumter was fired upon in
April of 1861. He quickly resigned from the U.S. Army to fight for
Virginia and the Confederacy. On September 2, Garnett accepted
the rank of lieutenant colonel and was assigned to Cobb's Georgia
Legion. He worked two months in this capacity until receiving his
promotion to brigadier general on November 14, 1861. Ironically,
Garnett's leap-frog from lieutenant colonel to brigadier general suggests that he benefited from the same convoluted system of promotion that he railed against four years earlier. Not surprisingly, Colonel Thomas R. R. Cobb was upset at Garnett's promotion: "I think
Davis meant this as a lick for me." Notwithstanding his objections
to Garnett's sudden ascent, Cobb had previously considered his
former lieutenant colonel to be a "a perfect gentleman" and "an
excellent officer."[21]

Garnett arrived in Winchester on December 7, two weeks
past his forty-fourth birthday, and assumed command of the
Stonewall Brigade. Although stepping into the imprints of very

large shoes left by Stonewall Jackson, the rank and file of the
Stonewall Brigade took an immediate liking to their new light-haired,
blue-eyed brigadier general.[22] The brigade veterans, however, were
more experienced in battle than their new commander. Although
the Bath-Romney Expedition provided General Garnett with the
experience of moving large bodies of men, the Stonewall Brigade
had been held in reserve during the few violent actions of the campaign. As February turned to March, many of General Richard
Brooke Garnett's academy mates had "seen the elephant" by participating in the Mexican War and early Civil War battles; however,
Garnett had been out of West Point for over twenty years and had
yet to take part in a battle-sized engagement.

During the waning days of the 1862 winter, General Jackson's
greatest impediment no longer was Loring, Gilham, the weather, or
the inexperience of his brigade commanders. The month of March
was named for the Greek god of war, but when it arrived Stonewall
no longer had a force large enough to achieve lasting success through
fighting. The ten-plus infantry regiments shared only the Virginia
name. Half of the units were from Loring's old command and they
still harbored grudges against General Jackson and the Stonewall
Brigade. The court-martial charges and subsequent departure of
General Loring exacerbated the hard feelings they displayed against
their division mates and their commander. General Jackson's primary concern in early March lay not with the disunity of his command, but rather the size of it. Original Confederate one-year terms
of service were due to expire in April. To induce re-enlistments within
the ranks, the Confederate Congress enacted the Bounty and Furlough Act in December of 1861 to grant furloughs and monetary
rewards for those soldiers who would re-enlist for the duration of
the war. Additionally, regimental and company officers were also
temporarily excused from the field to persuade hometown citizens
to turn into soldiers and join the ranks of those who had chosen to
continue to fight for their new country and its rights. Although the
long-range effect was expected to swell the muster rolls, General
Jackson learned that the immediate pitfall was the depletion of his
ranks as officers and men disappeared by the scores on temporary
leave. The size of Jackson's command shrunk precipitously; although
he had over 8,500 men on January 1, 1862, early March found him
with little more than 4,500 infantry, cavalry, and artillery soldiers
to defend Winchester against an approaching Union army.

That Federal force greatly outnumbered Stonewall's Valley District army. General Nathaniel Banks, with his own division and two
brigades of Brigadier General John Sedgwick's division, had crossed
the Potomac River at Harpers Ferry and had advanced to Charlestown

and Bunker Hill; General Lander's former division was fast approaching Martinsburg, and Sedgwick's remaining brigade at Harpers Ferry
was set to join the rest of the division in Virginia. Although General
Jackson and his staff enjoyed an exhilarating church sermon on
March 2, the presence of 30,000 bluecoats resting in camps within
one day's march disrupted any feelings of peace and tranquility
they may otherwise have been harboring.[23]

On Tuesday, March 4, 1862, Winchester citizen Kate Sperry
sat down to enter her daily reflections in her journal. "Today one
year ago Abe Lincoln was inaugurated President of the United States,"
she remembered, adding "what changes since then."[24]

Most of the changes experienced by Miss Sperry's town transpired during the 125 years prior to the Civil War. The city of Winchester had represented the American frontier since the first white
settlers inhabited the area in the 1730s. A young surveyor named
George Washington made Winchester his base of operations when
he pushed into the mountainous regions of western Virginia and
ultimately initiated the French and Indian War. Daniel Morgan, one
of the city's most famous citizens, organized troops from the area
and the rugged band transformed into one of the best fighting units
of the Revolution. Hessian soldiers that had been imprisoned in the
Winchester area built many of the solid stone homes. The same
limestone used for architecture also fertilized abundant crop and
grain fields throughout Frederick County, of which Winchester was
the county seat.

Winchester developed and thrived as the major marketing center of the lower (northern) Shenandoah Valley during the 1800s.
Situated in the broadest corridor of the Valley, Winchester was separated from the Piedmont region of Virginia by the majestically beautiful Blue Ridge Mountains, approximately twenty-five miles east of
the town, running in a northeasterly direction. The North Mountains, an extension of the Allegheny chain, enclose Winchester ten
miles west of town. The fifty-five-mile saw-toothed Massanutten
Mountain divides the Valley beginning fifteen miles south of Winchester near Strasburg. A traveler advancing south from Strasburg
could explore the Page (or Luray) Valley to the east, or the wider
Shenandoah Valley to the west. The directional nomenclature of
the Valley appears to be reversed because the Shenandoah River
flows northward. A traveler moving south would be heading "up"
the Valley while one moving north would be heading "down" the
Valley.

Winchester's road network was largely responsible for its pre-
eminence as the marketing and purchasing center for the entire
Lower Valley. No fewer than nine roads, running in all directions,

spoked from the Winchester hub. The Berryville Pike transported people and supplies eastward and through the mountains at Snicker's Gap. The Northwest Turnpike linked Winchester and Romney. The Pughtown Road carried travelers toward Bath and the Potomac River below Hancock, Maryland. The Millwood Pike extended eastward, crossing the Blue Ridge at Ashby's Gap and continuing into Alexandria as the Little River Turnpike. Front Royal linked with Winchester by an old grade road and a newer plank road. Martinsburg could be reached by moving north on a pike that eventually extended toward Shepherdstown. Running parallel to the Martinsburg Pike was the Winchester and Potomac Railroad, Winchester's only rail link. The railroad ran from a depot in the northern section of town to Harpers Ferry thirty miles north at the neck of the Valley where it connected with the B & O Railroad.[25]

The most important road was the Valley Turnpike or Valley Pike, a ninety-mile north-south route that traversed the entire Valley and had termini at Winchester in the north and Staunton in the south. The Valley Pike was a modern road. Built in the 1830s, the road was macadamized with crushed limestone over a cement bed and lined in several areas with shoulder high stone walls. It contrasted sharply with the inferior dirt roads in the Valley and was regarded as the only dependable path to take during rainy weather. The Valley Pike was so reliable that water transport via the Shenandoah River all but became obsolete by 1860.[26]

The Valley Turnpike, 1885. Photo Taken Near Middletown, Virginia.
U.S.A.M.H.I.

Winchester's populace had endured frontier conflicts with Indians in the 1700s and, in 1862, was faced with residing in a town that was cherished by both sides in a civil war. The 1860 Federal census reveals a Winchester population of 4,392 living as members of 701 different families. Blacks comprised nearly one-quarter of the citizenry; nearly half of the 1,355 African Americans and their descendants were free, and most of the 708 slaves in Winchester worked as household servants. Although the majority of Winchester and Frederick County voting residents had cast their ballots for John Breckinridge during the November 6, 1860 national election that put Abraham Lincoln in the U.S. president's chair, the town unequivocally favored remaining in the Union when they selected anti-secession delegates to represent the area in a special state election the following February. The election results temporarily kept Virginia in the Union. When President Lincoln issued the call for 75,000 troops three days after Fort Sumter was fired upon, the Virginia convention passed an ordinance of secession, effectively taking the state out of the Union.[27]

After Virginia officially seceded from the Union, Winchester's citizenry rabidly supported their army that would attempt to win the fight for a new nation. Symbols of disunion competed with each other throughout the town; even the old Union Hotel had two of its sign letters deliberately removed to extinguish any notion that the town supported Northern efforts to keep the country unified. A small pro-Union faction remained in Winchester when war arrived. At least fifty citizens supported the preservation of the United States, a definitive minority existing in a town growing more fervently Confederate as each day passed. General Jackson distrusted the Unionists and grew increasingly cautious of their activities with a Federal army so close to him. On at least one occasion Stonewall ordered select soldiers to arrest a Unionist who he believed was passing information to the Federals.[28]

One of the Winchester Unionists was Julia Chase, who kept a near-daily diary of activities that came under her notice. During the first week of March, Miss Chase paid close attention to the flurry of activity and panic which pervaded the town. Several citizens were either sending family members and supplies south of town, or were packing up and leaving altogether. "The Virginians have always said never surrender, that they never ran," she observed, quipping, "Pretty good number are running now fast enough."[29]

Miss Chase soon learned that no other options were available. By March 6, Winchester's populace was well aware that sizable Federal forces extended to Charlestown, twenty miles northeast, and Bunker Hill, twelve miles north of Winchester. Major John A.

Harman, chief quartermaster of the Valley District, received word from General Jackson that the estimated strength of the enemy at these two points numbered 17,000 effectives and they could attack at any moment. Harman realized the out-numbered Confederates had no chance against the Federals. He wrote to his brother that day:

> At last the crisis is upon us. . . . We are in no condition to meet such a force. I am very much afraid that we will stay here too long. We cannot hold the place. I have sent off all the stores and nothing remains, but four heavy guns of importance. What is to become of us remains for Providence to decide. I am afraid to go into the fight with our present disorganized force. I am cool and awaiting events. Will came in yesterday evening. He is afraid it is too late to do anything.[30]

Harman's fears were realized the next day. On March 7, the Federal force at Bunker Hill made the first threat toward Winchester by advancing southward along the Martinsburg Pike. The bluecoats came within view of a company of Confederate infantry stationed at Stephenson's Depot, four miles north of Winchester. Cavalry pickets were driven in toward town, forcing Turner Ashby to take control of the situation. Ashby ordered one of his captains of the 7th Virginia Cavalry to keep the enemy in check while he formed rearward skirmish lines in timber and behind stone fences and brick houses. Ashby's deployment was successful; the Federals did not expect stiff resistance, and Jackson had enough time to mass his infantry behind Ashby in a provocative show of force. The Federal reconnaissance force, realizing they were outnumbered, withdrew and retired to Bunker Hill. No battle would come off this day.[31]

Lieutenant Alexander Swift "Sandie" Pendleton worked as an aide-de-camp for the Valley District. He was the twenty-one-year-old son of William Nelson Pendleton, the initial commander of the Rockbridge Artillery. The young officer had been attending graduate classes at the University of Virginia at the outbreak of the war and immediately joined General Jackson's staff. Pendleton was considered a brilliant intellect and "most popular" with fellow officers and men. But Sandie was also critical of his fellow officers. He charged Colonel James Walkinshaw Allen of the 2nd Virginia with cowardice for his performance at the Battle of Manassas. Sandie was disappointed that the skirmish on March 7 had not developed into a bigger fight, for he believed that it would have offered Colonel Allen the opportunity to redeem himself in battle. Sandie had personal reasons for rooting for Allen's success—the colonel married Pendleton's first cousin several years earlier.[32]

Colonel Allen's commanding presence was well suited for his rank. Standing six feet three inches in height, Allen was described as popular, graceful, and handsome. The thirty-three year old carried an undeserving blemish on his military record that he wished to erase. As a child, Allen lost his right eye after he was struck by a fragment from a percussion cap. The handicap did not hinder him from receiving his education at V.M.I. where he graduated with distinction. A Union man, Allen taught at the institute prior to the war, married Julia Pendleton, and purchased a farm in Jefferson County where he lived until the war broke out in 1861.

Allen was elected colonel of the 2nd Virginia Infantry of the Stonewall Brigade. His one-sided blindness was destined to impair him; unfortunately, it did so at the worst possible time. At the Battle of Manassas, when his regiment was drawn up in line of battle, a Yankee shell tore through a pine limb above him, sending the dismembered branch into Allen's face where it struck him directly in his good eye. Temporarily but totally blinded, Allen was unable to organize his command and he and his regiment suffered for it. Allen was subsequently criticized for poor leadership and accused of cowardice.[33] Few opportunities to redeem himself had arisen since the Manassas fight.

March 7 passed without atonement for Colonel Allen when the Federal reconnaissance-in-force returned toward Bunker Hill. On March 8, Major Harman packed all division supplies in preparation for what he considered an inevitable retreat from Winchester. Harman also noted that the size of Jackson's division had dwindled to approximately 3,000 men. He cited sickness, furloughs and militia deserters as the root causes for the diminution of size and strength.[34] Militia desertions underscored, however, the true threat to security within the Valley District. Twenty-seven members of Jackson's volunteer force left the ranks and wound up in Federal hands, beginning with the Bath-Romney campaign and continuing into March. At least thirty other men were captured during that period. The loss of these soldiers did not significantly strain Jackson's already thinned ranks, but several of the deserters and captives openly divulged information to General Banks that became far more valuable to him than any acquired through his Union spies.

Throughout the campaign, Banks's assistants logged information from refugees, deserters, contraband, and Confederate captives. Two of the most recent interrogees were T. J. McVeigh, the chaplain of the 2nd Virginia, who was captured near the Blue Ridge Mountains west of Berryville when he attempted to get his servant, and Arthur S. Markell, a twenty-year-old lieutenant of Company A of the 5th Virginia. Markell deserted both his regiment and his boyhood home of Winchester on March 4, the day after McVeigh was captured. Both men provided valuable intelligence to Banks, acknowledging that parts of General Loring's command were sent westward and Major General Gustavus W. Smith's division had not yet reinforced Jackson as had been expected by the men in the ranks. McVeigh stated that only ten regiments protected Winchester, while Markell's testimony revealed that supplies had already been sent away in anticipation of a Federal advance. Banks remained poised to attack Winchester (McClellan desired this to assure security for the B & O Railroad), but he was still leery of the possibility that reinforcements from Manassas could strengthen the city's defenses. The Manassas army, under General Joseph Johnston, withdrew southwest on March 9. Banks waited for conclusive evidence to convince him that no reinforcements from Johnston had come to Jackson's aid.[35]

That valuable information arrived in the form of eighteen-year-old Jacob Poisel of the 2nd Virginia who delivered himself to the Federal pickets of General Williams's command on March 9 at Bunker Hill. Poisel was a diminutive, slightly-built private; at five feet two inches tall he appeared more suited for the cavalry than the infantry. The boy lived in Hedgesville, a town five miles northwest of Martinsburg. He claimed that he had been forced to enlist in the Hedgesville Blues, a company that eventually became incorporated as part of Colonel Allen's 2nd Virginia Infantry. Waiting for the opportunity to escape, Private Poisel woke up that frigid Sunday morning (the temperature dipped to sixteen degrees at the Sheets Mill weather station near Romney) with his mind made up. He had encamped with the rest of the regiment north of Winchester on the Pughtown Road. He left his camp at 7:00 A.M. and walked—undetected by Confederate pickets—northward on the Martinsburg Pike where he crossed the enemy lines and deserted to the Federal side at Bunker Hill. General Williams briefly interrogated Poisel and decided his information was so valuable that he sent the young deserter to speak directly with General Banks.

Banks noted the importance of the unexpected coup by keeping two separate files on the intelligence received from this unlikely source. Poisel confirmed much of the information provided by previous deserters and captives, but freely expanded that intelligence to reveal a Southern force that was no match for what Banks had to offer. The private informed Banks that two of Loring's regiments were gone, no reinforcements had come in, and supplies had already been packed and moved south. Poisel continued by naming the regiments and commanders of the Stonewall Brigade. He also stated that company strength averaged about thirty men and that his company was armed with "percussion smoothbores." He divulged that trenches had been dug across the Martinsburg Pike, but his brigade shifted camps to the Pughtown Road on Saturday evening (March 8) where no earthworks had yet been prepared. The remainder of Loring's old command was encamped on the other side of town. The valuable turncoat was sent to Sandy Hook where he took the oath of allegiance to the Union on March 10 and was subsequently discharged.[36]

By Monday morning, March 10, 1862, Stonewall Jackson realized that the Federals were becoming more aggressive in their attempt to capture Winchester. Banks had become less hesitant and now controlled four roads leading into Winchester from the north and east. The Federals were reinforced north of Winchester when Lander's former division arrived at Martinsburg nine days late due to the death of their commander. A portion of Banks's force took possession of Berryville, approximately ten miles east of Winchester, which signalled the inevitability of a two-pronged attack toward Winchester. The 30,000 available Federals outnumbered the Valley District by over eight fold. General Jackson sent away his four big guns representing the final government stores leaving Winchester. Although the army and citizens prepared for a Federal occupation of Winchester, General Jackson's demeanor baffled Quartermaster John Harman. Visiting him that morning, Harman noted that Stonewall was still indicating that he did not want to give up the town without a fight.[37]

Union troops inched cautiously toward Winchester on Tuesday morning, March 11, 1862. The men in the ranks of Jackson's Valley District army packed up their equipment, satisfying the orders of the upper command. The men cooked all their rations and spent the next few hours resting until summoned by the long roll to form lines at approximately 2:00 P.M. They could hear Federal cannons booming from the direction of Berryville.

Turner Ashby's 7th Virginia Cavalry fronted the Southern line of breastworks hastily prepared two miles north of Winchester in an open field near the Martinsburg Road. General Garnett's Stonewall Brigade occupied the works on the high ground behind the cavalry as well as a skirt of woods near the railroad. By 3:30 P.M. the Virginians could see the Federal pickets approaching within four miles of them. Watching the enemy's bayonets glisten in the setting sun, members of Jackson's division felt confident that the long-awaited fight would finally materialize.[38]

Those impressions changed when campfire smoke started rising through the woods near Mrs. Carter's house a few hundred yards south of Stephenson's Depot. Major Frank Jones, temporarily in command of the 2nd Virginia, believed the enemy force from Martinsburg would wait the night out until Banks's column arrived within striking distance from Berryville. Although the Yankee scouts were within rifle shot, Jones was prepared to wait until morning to fight it out.[39]

General Jackson had other ideas. A New York native soldiering in Jackson's infantry watched a brief council held in front of his company's position, "with the leading officers Jackson, Fulkerson, Burks, Cambell [sic], Allen and others. I watched it with an eagle's eye. I thought gloom and despair was visible in their faces as our men were drawed up in line. . . ." Stonewall apparently did not choose to fight. Instead, he ordered his troops to fall back and prepared to march them southward through the town. Jackson also instructed Quartermaster Harman to send the army supply wagons south of Winchester. The impression to all the citizens now appeared to be evacuation.

Stonewall took many precautions. He was well aware of the strong Union element in the area and decided it would harm his army if Banks received more valuable information if he took over the town. Members of his division witnessed Unionists heading toward Federal lines. (A member of the 42nd Virginia had seen "several fat old codgers and two horse buggies" defecting toward Bunker Hill just a few days before.) Captain John Quincy Adams Nadenbousch, the acting provost marshal of Winchester, acted upon Jackson's orders and arrested the most partisan Union men of Winchester. Approximately twenty citizens were taken prisoner, including the elderly and ill Charles Chase, the father of diarist Julia Chase. She remarked bitterly at the indignation she felt to see her ailing father carried from his parlor sofa and she finished her diary entry for the day with the simple lamentation, "Sad, sad day to us."[40]

For the secessionists in Winchester, the majority of the inhabitants, an uneasy feeling of uncertainty and trepidation permeated the town. The women spent the early afternoon hiding family papers, silver and other valuables, expecting the Yankees to invade Winchester and their homes. Some watched the bustle of activity from their porches as Southern horsemen dashed in front of them toward the expected battlefield north of town. Rumors rippled through the streets telling of thousands of Federals within a few miles of their residences. All expected the "terrible conflict" to be waged at any time.[41]

By nightfall the excitement turned to fear as some of the army was seen withdrawing through the town to the south. The rumor mill now spoke of Jackson evacuating Winchester without a fight.

Some refused to believe it, thinking that Jackson was merely collecting his force below the town to prepare an assault; others feared the worst—the army was leaving them and heading toward Staunton. Mrs. Cornelia McDonald, the wife of former 7th Cavalry Colonel Angus McDonald, spent the rest of the night in "violent fits of weeping at the thought of being left, and what might happen to that army before we should see it again."[42]

Much of Jackson's division withdrew through the town experiencing as much disappointment as that felt by the citizens they were supposed to protect. Major Frank Jones marched the 2nd Virginia four miles south of town "with heavy hearts" where they bivouacked on the turnpike. Jones was particularly saddened; the locust tree under which he rested was within sight of "Careysbrooke", his deserted home.[43] A member of the 4th Virginia waxed melancholy at the prospect of leaving Winchester, a town that they had considered home for nearly a year. Realizing the ties that bound many of his regiment, brigade, and division to Winchester should keep them there, the soldier lamented, "But it was to no avail. They had but to bid their sweethearts good bye, take one last kiss and leave them to their fates. This was sad indeed. Many expressed themselves that they would sooner fight than leave those endearments behind."[44]

Stonewall Jackson never intended to evacuate Winchester without a fight. As the regiments moved toward Newtown, Jackson called a night council of his brigade and regimental officers. They met at Jackson's winter headquarters, the North Braddock Street home of Colonel Lewis T. Moore, formerly of the 4th Virginia. The subordinate officers gathered to hear what their division commander had to say. The audaciousness of Jackson's plan took them by surprise. Stonewall told his subordinates that he sent the men south of Winchester merely to get supper and a couple hours of rest. He proposed to take the men from their camps near Kernstown, move them north of town during the night, and launch a rare night attack on an unsuspecting portion of the Federal army encamped near Stephenson's Depot.

General Jackson was, however, unaware of the locations of his wagons and troops. He proposed the plan believing that his supplies sat at the turnpike hamlet of Kernstown, a village only three miles south of Winchester. Stonewall did not know that the wagons rolled to Newtown, an additional four miles south of Kernstown. Miscommunication between Jackson and his quartermaster jeopardized the timing and feasibility of his plan. His infantry was spread out between Newtown and Bartonsville. Committing to Jackson's proposal involved a forced night march of nearly ten miles for some

Dr. Hunter H. McGuire, C.S.A.
*Courtesy of Winchester-Frederick
County Historical Society*

of the men in order to face off against the Federals north of Winchester before daylight.

An unidentified officer at the meeting informed Jackson of the disposition of his division. The subordinates, thinking better than to attempt Stonewall's proposed feat with dispersed and woefully outnumbered soldiers, voted down the commanding general's plan, preferring to continue evacuating the area. Jackson urged them a second time to reconsider—Winchester should not be relinquished. They rebuffed their leader a second time, killing his plan once and for all.[45]

Without unified support to engage the Federals in battle, Stonewall terminated his council to carry out a new and totally antithetical plan. His officers dispersed to rejoin their respective commands. At approximately midnight, Stonewall called upon Sandie Pendleton and instructed him to order the regiments to move south at daylight. Only Turner Ashby and the 7th Virginia Cavalry remained north of Winchester to contest the now inevitable Union takeover of Winchester. The Southern general moved to the tail of his column and rested near a fence corner close to Bartonsville.[46] The next morning he would lead his men southward, just as his subordinates wished.

At daylight on Wednesday, March 12, Dr. Hunter McGuire, Jackson's trusted friend and surgeon, joined Stonewall as the army began to lurch southward. The general and the physician looked upon their defenseless town from a height near Newtown, realizing Winchester would become a Federal possession within hours. The bitterness of rebuke and failure burned within Stonewall, releasing the energy of anger and resolve in a commander who had suffered through two miserable months of war. McGuire was awed at the savage transformation that seized Jackson on that hill. With a face displaying the rage generated from the previous night's rejection, Stonewall turned to the doctor and fiercely announced, "That is the last council of war I will ever hold!"[47]

Stonewall Jackson proved to be a man of his word.

Chapter Three

"LIKE A BULL WITH A GAD-FLY"

On Wednesday morning, March 12, 1862, Colonel Turner Ashby and a squadron of his 7th Virginia Cavalry patrolled the Martinsburg Pike north of Winchester. Keeping the Federals at bay as long as feasibly possible, he finally ordered his command to withdraw to the south. He had survived a close call the previous evening when a Union cannonball severed the hind leg of his black horse, taking the animal out from under him. This particular morning the undaunted Ashby rode his white charger, "Tom Telegraph," a horse of prestigious stock, as he slowly led his men to rejoin Jackson's division already en route toward Staunton, the terminus of the Valley Pike ninety miles south of Winchester. As General Banks's bluecoats enveloped Winchester's northern borders, the seemingly unconcerned Ashby followed his men down the road, coolly stopped to take a biscuit offered to him by one of the town's ladies, and then casually trotted to Newtown. By sunrise, the town of Winchester lay completely in the mercy of the forces of the United States Army.[1]

Those Federals quickly responded to the open invitation. Celebrating a spring-like morning that dawned under a cloudless sky, two brigades of Banks's division crept forward toward the vacated earthworks that traversed the roads north of Winchester. General Alpheus S. Williams, heading one of the brigades, watched with excitement as ten regiments of blue-clad infantry, ten cannons, and four companies of cavalry cautiously moved forward toward Winchester in a long single row. Looking from a distance, Williams described the soldiers as resembling "a swarm of ants" as they clamored up the parapets. The Federals took the earthworks without opposition and headed toward Winchester. By 7:00 A.M. the vanguard of the Union forces entered the town.[2]

The mayor of Winchester, John B. T. Reed, and select members of the city council greeted Generals Alpheus S. Williams and Charles S. Hamilton at the outskirts of town. There they formally surrendered Winchester and asked for protection of private property. One council member proceeded to argue with a Federal colonel about previous destruction of private property by Union armies in Virginia. A Federal private sided with his officer and called the councilman a liar, while another soldier told his colonel that a pair of handcuffs should effectively quiet the citizen. The Union colonel let the matter drop and the troops marched into town greeted, this time, by closed doors and shutters.[3]

The remaining citizens of Winchester had dreaded the inevitable and now it had arrived. "Must it be told—the glory has departed from Shiloah [sic]," lamented Kate Sperry, "never was anything more appropriate—to think after all our trouble in fortifying the town for the enemy to come and take quiet possession is too much." The Federals entered via Market Street and Main (Loudoun) Street. They marched in quietly, begrudgingly impressing the staunchest Southerners with their immaculate blue uniforms and fine brass bands that serenaded each regiment with renditions of "Hail Columbia" and "The Battle Hymn of the Republic." John Peyton Clark sarcastically described the melodies: "Music it may have been to them but to us it grated a harsh discord which easily could be felt." One citizen seethed when she heard a band segue from "Yankee Doodle" to "Dixie." "They steal everything from us," she complained in her diary.[4]

The temperature soared over thirty degrees in seven hours. By mid-afternoon a month-high reading of sixty-nine degrees was registered at Sheets Mill (near Romney) and sixty-seven degrees was recorded at Georgetown. Several Winchester residents greeted the Union army as warmly as had the weather. Many Unionists waved handkerchiefs in celebration; others placed the Star Spangled Banner outside their doors—the first time that flag was shown in town in nearly a year. The 12th Indiana raised the Stars and Stripes over the courthouse to signify that the Union now ruled the area. Unionist Julia Chase wrote "Glorious news" in her diary entry celebrating the Federal takeover of Winchester. Chase further admitted regret that the troops failed to arrive two days earlier to save her father from capture.[5]

Major General Nathaniel P. Banks, whose brigades were the first to enter the town, telegraphed Washington to notify General McClellan's chief of staff that Winchester had been occupied and that the railway and telegraph would be operating soon between the town and Harpers Ferry. Banks sent the message from

Charlestown and arrived in Winchester late that Wednesday night. He slept at the George W. Seevers house on the corner of Stewart and Boscawen streets on the west side of town. Banks used a physician's office one block east of the Seevers house as his head-quarters office. General Banks's headquarters now carried more prestige than did his winter division headquarters at Frederick, Maryland. Abraham Lincoln's President's General War Order Number Two officially placed Banks in charge of the army's new Fifth Corps. Brigadier General Williams replaced Banks as division commander and took charge of the three infantry brigades that Banks had led throughout the winter season. General Sedgwick and his division, sitting idle at Berryville, were reassigned to the army's Second Corps and subsequently departed the Valley.[6]

Sedgwick's departure left Banks with a small corps consisting of only two divisions. Williams headed the first division while the second division of the Fifth Corps consisted of the late Frederick W. Lander's Ohio, Indiana, Pennsylvania, and western Virginia troops. After Lander's untimely death on March 2, the Westerners were placed under the interim command of Colonel Nathan Kimball, the leader of the division's First Brigade. By the time they reached Martinsburg, the division had transferred to the command of Lander's replacement—Brigadier General James Shields.

General Shields was nearly fifty-six years old and had been characterized as short-tempered and independent for most of his adult life. He would eventually be the only man in United States history elected to represent three different states in the Senate; however, in 1862, Shields's past was equally as colorful. Born in County Tyrone, Ireland, he had been shipwrecked off Scotland at the age of sixteen while attempting to emigrate to the United States and stayed there four years. Eventually he made his way to America, settled in Illinois where Shields taught French, studied law, fought Indians in the Black Hawk War and led a brigade of New York and South Carolina regiments in the Mexican War. He was injured through the lung so severely at Cerro Gordo that his surgeon was able to debride the wound by passing a silk handkerchief entirely through Shields's body. The feisty Irishman survived his injury and returned to Illinois where years earlier he had challenged a lawyer to a duel for writing slanderous newspaper articles about him. The affair was settled peacefully and that Illinois lawyer, a lanky fellow named Abraham Lincoln, was able to advance his career to the White House. On August 19, 1861, Lincoln appointed Shields a brigadier general of volunteers, but the newly commissioned general finished the year without any troops to lead.[7]

While Shields sat out the winter, he offered advice to General George McClellan concerning plans of operations for the Army of the Potomac's commander. On January 10, Shields wrote McClellan from Washington to offer "a few hints" in relation to the general mode of prosecuting the war. Shields concluded that Richmond in the East and Memphis in the West were the Union army's two objectives. Shields believed the capture of Yorktown should be the first important operation on the campaign against Richmond.[8] In essence, Shields provided McClellan with support for the initial blueprint of McClellan's Urbanna campaign. Shields had been placed at the top of the list to receive a division command. General Lander's death provided that opportunity.

Shields stood in stark contrast to the late General Lander both in appearance and manner. Whereas Lander was an imposing and somewhat reckless general, Shields was a smaller-statured and more disciplined officer. Standing five feet eight inches with a trim build and dark features, he was a personable, handsome, and well-known figure to the men in his new division. They took an instant liking to their new commander and described him as "an Irishman by birth, an American by choice, and a patriot because he could not be otherwise." "He was, undoubtedly, a man possessed of many fine qualities—warm-hearted, brave, and zealous," remarked an artillery officer who served under Shields, pinpointing the general's greatest fault when he added, "but vainglorious to the last degree."[9]

Shields had been offered command of the Irish Brigade toward the end of 1861, but declined it owing to poor health at the time. A few weeks later Shields addressed his fellow Irishmen from the Herndon House in Washington in an effort to smooth over any hard feelings against him. The speech illustrated the qualities he felt imperative for an army to be victorious in the field:

Brigadier General James Shields
U.S.A.M.H.I.

. . . But I am sure if I had the command of the Irish Brigade I would either break you in or break you down, for I am a most rigid disciplinarian. It is only in discipline, rigidly enforced, that we can have

any confidence in our strength. An armed mob does not con-
stitute an army. It is only in discipline and the perfect obedience to orders, and not in numbers, that we may calculate on
success. No great victories have been gained with large armies;
therefore, I enjoin upon you strict obedience to the laws and
I will promise if discipline and obedience are enforced, the
next time we will have Bull Run reversed.

There are three things which I am resolved never to
do: I will never break my oath of allegiance to this country. I
will never betray my trust. I will never fly back upon my
adopted country in an hour of peril like this.[10]

The troops General Shields inherited certainly were not used
to strict discipline, but they had tasted success against General
Jackson's Confederate division the previous winter. The Westerners arrived at Winchester, 11,000 strong, behind Banks's men and
camped near Stephenson's Depot, three miles north of town on the
Martinsburg Road. The men christened their new home "Camp
Shields." The general who the camp was named after took his headquarters at Mary Tucker Magill's house on Loudoun Street in northern Winchester. Although disappointed at missing the opportunity
to be the first troops in Winchester, Shields's men approved of their
campsite. The Shenandoah Valley was a refreshing change for the
Westerners who had spent the previous months in more desolate
areas of western Virginia. "It is by far the best country I have seen
in the East and equal to any I have seen in the West," wrote an
Illinois private to his parents, adding, "I would consent to live here
if uncle sam will give me a farm at the close of this war." An Indiana
soldier echoed these sentiments; he considered the Valley "incom-
parably lovely, the uniform unevenness of the rural scenery adding
to the beauty of the high state of cultivation that Yankee machinery
has brought to the Valley of Virginia."[11]

Another treasure the Valley offered the Federal soldier was the
sight of Virginia women—a pleasure the soldiers sorely missed when
encamped around Romney, Patterson's Creek, and Paw Paw. The
ladies were predictably unfriendly to the Union soldiers, but this
did not seem to diminish their appeal. "To me they look tempting
and bewitching," is how one Western soldier described Shenandoah
Valley women. The Federal apparently disregarded the impact of
war in the area when he added, "In fact, I'd like to marry in this
Valley."[12]

Although encamped north of town, Shields's men visited Winchester daily. The city drew mixed reactions from the blue-clad soldiers. A member of the 13th Indiana described the historic town as
"a large place but very filthy and dirty." Another Hoosier called it "a

great secesh hole." In no uncertain terms, an Ohio native expressed his opinion about Winchester when he wrote to his friends in Wood County: "Winchester is about 100 years behind the age—a dirty slovenly, ill-paved, rickety, unpainted, foul-smelling town." By and large, though, the Federals approved of Winchester. A Pennsylvania native considered Winchester "a very finely built town, the houses being most of brick and stone." An Ohio soldier described it as "about the only decent looking town I have seen in Virginia." A member of the 14th Indiana decided that the town resembled many in his home state and informed his parents, "Winchester is a very nice town. It is too pretty a place to belong to secession and I think we have permanently taken it from them."[13]

The Westerners of Lander's former division campaigned independently throughout the winter. Consolidation with General Banks's former division did not sit well with many of these men; many considered themselves better soldier material than the New Englanders of Williams's three brigades. A Pennsylvania soldier spoke his mind to his home-town friends in Clearfield County about the disparity between the two divisions of the Fifth Corps:

> Now you should see these soldiers of General Banks. They parade the streets in white gloves, white shirts and boots blacked to looking-glass perfection; upon my word it makes us laugh. By *us* I mean we of Gen. Shield's Division—the mud-trampers, baggage-carriers and field-sleepers. Gen. Banks has lain at Frederick for months, in winter quarters— nicely housed—tents in house-order—and any quantity of provisions. On the other hand our Division has been moving about all the time—half of the time without tents, sleeping on the wet ground with one blanket around us; nothing to eat except hard johnnies; miles away from our baggage; no change of clothes for two or three weeks. Is it any wonder that we laugh at these polished, powdered jacks?[14]

By coincidence, the U.S. War Department set a plan in motion that granted Shields's men the independence they desired. General McClellan's Urbanna campaign had been scrubbed. Instead the grand assault on Richmond would be accomplished by transporting the Army of the Potomac from Washington to Fort Monroe and Newport News on the Yorktown Peninsula. The revised plan entered its final planning stages. The first troops would embark on steamers at Alexandria on March 17. President Lincoln insisted on a covering force to guard the nation's capital while the army moved southward. McClellan believed that Jackson's division no longer posed a serious threat in the Valley and decided to pull Banks from the region. The commanding general's plan placed Banks at Manassas to cover the approaches to Washington. McClellan would provide Banks with a large cavalry force to secure the vast country in front of Manassas. Believing that Confederate Generals Jackson and Joseph E. Johnston retired en masse to Gordonsville, McClellan decided that only a small force in the Valley was required to guard the area while the Manassas Gap Railroad and B & O Railroad were being repaired. McClellan considered an operating railroad in the area imperative to open communications between Washington and Strasburg in the Shenandoah Valley. On March 16 Banks received McClellan's order to leave all of General Shields's division in the region until the railroad was running again.[15]

Members of Williams's division were all too happy to receive their transfer orders, although it would still be a few days before they could leave Winchester. They had to wait until a bridge over the Shenandoah River east of Berryville was reconstructed; Jackson destroyed the previous span before he evacuated the area. The day before Banks's received McClellan's plan, a few companies of Federal cavalry, four pieces of artillery, and five companies of infantry from the 13th Massachusetts left town on an armed reconnaissance. They immediately bumped into Ashby's 7th Virginia Cavalry a few miles south of town and attempted to capture the horsemen, but returned empty handed. Lieutenant Colonel Wilder Dwight, 2nd Massachusetts, claimed that a wagon train had an equal chance of catching Ashby's men as Union cavalry had. Dwight lauded the skills and training of the Southern horsemen. "Where our men have to dismount and take down the bars," he wrote, "they fly over fences and across country like birds." The ladies of Winchester likely took the horsemanship skills of Ashby's cavaliers for granted until they witnessed the amateur riding style of the Northern dragoons. One of the women mocked, "I wish you could see the ridiculous manner in which they ride; they go about on their horses as if they were drunk." Kate Sperry also ridiculed the Federal cavalry. "They are splendidly equipped and very gay," she admitted, "but such bobbing up and down in the saddles is ridiculous to behold—not one of them can ride fit to be seen." In contrast, Miss Sperry praised the abilities of Colonel Turner Ashby. "I never saw such a reckless, daring fellow in my life," she raved.[16]

The mere mention of Turner Ashby's name conjured up the image of the quintessential cavalier. The Fauquier County native descended from a prestigious family of soldiers, including a grandfather who made a reputation for himself as a captain during the Revolutionary War. With dark eyes to match his dark complexion, Turner Ashby sported a full beard and mustache, reminding many of an Arab. At five feet ten inches tall, he was blessed with deceptive strength hidden within his wiry frame. The thirty-three-year-old's horsemanship was superb and without peer. One of Stonewall Jackson's staff considered him "the most picturesque horseman ever seen in the Shenandoah Valley." Ashby reminded one of Stonewall's foot soldiers of "one of the cavaliers that we read about in romances. The spirit of chivalry, poetry and knighthood seemed to envelope him, and start one to dreaming dreams of the olden times." His soft-spoken demeanor so contradicted his striking appearance that many admirers remember clearly what Ashby looked like; however, few recalled anything he ever said.[17]

Ashby's omnipresence awed, mystified, and frustrated his opponents throughout the winter of 1861–1862. One Federal officer paid tribute to his bravery by stating, "I think our men had a kind of admiration for him as he sat upon his horse and let them pepper away at him as if he enjoyed it." "This Ashby was the terror and the wizard of the Shenandoah," wrote another officer of the 8th Ohio, "he was represented as being always mounted on a white horse, of being everywhere present and of wearing a charmed life; consequently everything astride of a white horse in front, in rear, along the mountains, near at hand or in the distance, was at once conjured up in the minds of the soldier to be Ashby. His apparition had presented itself frequently during the day, evening, and morning, and still hovered about fitfully in the advance." A Massachusetts soldier succinctly explained why, during March of 1862, the Federal soldiers exhibited the utmost respect for Turner Ashby: "He is light, active, skillful, and we are tormented by him like a bull with a gad-fly."[18]

Ashby's greatest fault lay with his dubious performance as a disciplinarian. He ascended to the colonelcy of the 7th Virginia Cavalry on February 12. Five weeks later, he found himself responsible for seventeen cavalry companies and one artillery company, 600 men in all. On March 17, he informed Confederate Secretary of War Judah P. Benjamin that he expected five more companies to swell his ranks within a few days. Ashby admitted that his men were poorly armed, citing that at least one of his men

**Colonel Turner Ashby,
7th Virginia Cavalry**
Courtesy of Ben Ritter

skirmished recently by riding bareback and carrying a club.[19] Circumstances in the Valley usually prevented him from remaining idle long enough to engage his regiment in organized drilling. After the war a lieutenant in his command stated "I do not recollect that during my service under Gen. Ashby we ever had time to drill. . . . It was one continued 'Go! go!'—and Ashby always went." Despite the colonel's limitations, his effectiveness as a leader was gauged by his men's loyalty and their subsequent accomplishments; here Ashby had few peers. Perhaps Lieutenant Colonel (then Captain) R. Preston Chew, the head of Ashby's horse artillery, summarized best the experience to serve under the gallant cavalier. Less than two years after the close of the war, Chew eloquently countered Ashby's critics:

> It was then popular to say Gen. Ashby exercised no control over his men beyond personal influence, that there was no discipline in his command. It was boasted that his successes were gained, not by skillful manaeuvre, but by the reckless dash and courage of himself and his men; but I will do him the justice to say that he could always command more men for duty from the same muster rolls than any cavalry commander under whom I have since served. While he was not possessed of brilliant intellect, his complete self-possession under all circumstances, and that absence for fear and regard for personal security, enabled him at all times to exercise a cool and clear judgement. I have served at different times during the war with almost all the prominent cavalry leaders of Virginia, and I have never seen one who possessed the ability to inspire troops under fire with the courage and enthusiasm that Ashby's presence always excited. His modesty, combined with his gentleness, rendered him agreeable to all who came in contact with him. He was always bold in his operations with cavalry, and believed in charging the enemy whenever opportunity afforded. He adopted in the beginning of the war the tactics of cavalry by which later in the war other cavalry commanders could only secure success—namely, always meeting the enemy by bold and determined charges, and when defeated, to press them with utmost vigor.[20]

Colonel Ashby's skills proved invaluable to his superior, General Thomas J. Jackson. While Stonewall leisurely led his division southward toward Mount Jackson, he ordered Ashby and his command, including most of the 7th Virginia Cavalry and eighteen-year-old Captain R. Preston Chew's three-gun battery of horse artillery, to remain close to Winchester to keep the Valley District commander apprised about Federal operations in and around the town. Ashby readily complied, relying on a network of partisan citizens-turned-spies in the region as well as sending some of his own men directly into Federal-controlled Winchester—disguised as farmers selling eggs. Whenever small detachments of Banks's corps advanced southward to capture him, Ashby embarrassed them with his skill and audacity which prevented the Federals from determining Jackson's whereabouts. Some were even misled to believe that Jackson had a larger force than merely one regiment of cavalry near Winchester.[21]

On Monday afternoon, March 17, Ashby's men thwarted another Federal southward-advancing reconnaissance from Winchester. When this force, led by Colonel John Mason of the 4th Ohio, returned without information, General Williams thought it prudent to send a larger force toward Strasburg to assure that no sizable Confederate force was in the area before Banks took his division out of the Valley. Williams found himself temporarily in charge of Valley operations while his superior, General Banks, spent a few days in Washington. Williams's headquarters in Winchester was at the Ann Powell house on Amherst Street. It was here where Williams received Colonel Mason's reconnaissance report.

David Hunter Strother served on Banks's staff as a topographical engineer. He entered the Powell home that cold afternoon and found several officers there, including General Shields, "in high feather" drinking punch. Shields was feeling very confident and was formulating a plan to circumvent the pesky Ashby. Shields's division report completed earlier that day indicated an available force of nearly 11,000 infantry, cavalry, and artillery. Williams informed Colonel Mason that he would lead the larger reconnaissance the following morning, and would be supported by Shields's full division, to which his regiment belonged. Later that day, Strother called upon Shields to hear the plan he had been concocting. Shields explained that Mason would take a brigade on the Front Royal Road which ran circuitously from Winchester linking with the Valley Pike on its left at Middletown over ten miles away. Mason's goal was to flank Ashby on the left while the main body advanced southward along the Valley Pike, keeping Ashby "amused" while Mason struck his rear at Middletown. Strother, pleased with Shields's spirit, asked and received permission to join the main body; however, he also believed a bull had a better chance of catching a fox than Shields did of catching Ashby. Strother reasoned that Shields was merely baiting Jackson into a fight.[22]

Strother's bull-versus-fox analogy proved pathetically prophetic. Colonel Mason led two companies of his own 4th Ohio, the 8th Ohio, Captain Joseph Clark's regular artillery battery, and one squadron of Michigan cavalry on the Front Royal Road for their circuitous approach to Middletown. His men were up and marching by 3:00 A.M. The distance between Winchester and Middletown totalled thirteen miles for a traveler on the Valley Pike, but Mason's flanking route increased the distance to the town to over twenty-two miles. Mason's instructions were to get behind Ashby and seize the bridge that crossed Cedar Creek south of Middletown to cut off the retreat of any Confederates between there and Winchester. At 2:00 P.M. Mason's force reached its destination only to find that Ashby had out-foxed him. The Confederate cavalier had left a picket force at the location which Mason drove through Middletown with ease. Once Mason's men reached the Cedar Creek bridge, they could only watch in frustration as Ashby's entire force sat safely on the other side. Mason could not cross to catch him—Ashby had covered the bridge with tar and set it on fire, ironically completing the Federal leader's objective for him. Ashby intensified the discomfort of the tired Federals by planting Chew's three guns on a height south of the creek and lobbing shells directly at them from 900 yards away. Mason ordered his battery forward, supported by three companies of the 8th Ohio, while the remaining infantry lined the banks of the creek and returned fire through the smoky air. Two Federal cavalrymen were wounded in the exchange. Mason sent his adjutant northward on the Valley Pike to find General Shields who was moving southward in force in an attempt to annihilate Ashby.[23]

David Hunter Strother and Colonel Thornton Brodhead (commanding the 1st Michigan Cavalry on the expedition) took their time leaving Winchester that day knowing they would easily catch up to Shields's main body snaking along the turnpike. They mounted their horses early in the afternoon and rode southward on the macadamized road, passing the small hamlets of Kernstown and Newtown. At this time they trotted up to the tail of the division, passed the entire column, and caught up to Shields and his staff at the vanguard of the mass just north of Middletown. Shields admitted to Strother that his troops got a late start, but the general reasoned that he was deliberately moving slowly to allow Colonel Mason enough time to get well ahead of them to cut off the Confederate retreat. Within a few miles of Middletown, the staff climbed a bluff to scan the countryside. This is where Mason's adjutant found Shields and delivered the colonel's disappointing information. Strother vented his disgust at the news. "Our plan," he later wrote, "was as feasible as that of a child who tries to catch a bird by throwing salt on his tail."

Shields's division advanced to the creek, guided by the distant smoke rising from the burning bridge. They reached it as the sun set behind the Allegheny Mountains. The general examined the ground and decided to cross the creek both above and below the burning bridge; he deemed the waterway fordable at these two points. With night coming on, a cavalry officer convinced Shields that the crossing should wait because the light from the burning bridge needlessly exposed the soldiers to Confederate artillery fire. Strother despaired at what he considered to be a lack of enthusiasm in the men, but Shields acquiesced to the cavalier's request. Fires were forbidden that evening; nevertheless, some enterprising Federals boiled coffee over the burning embers of the fallen bridge. During the night boards were placed over the partially submerged bridge timbers to span the shallow waterway for the next morning's planned crossing.[24]

In the meantime, Colonel Ashby retired his force four miles from the creek to the town of Strasburg where the men took quarters in houses to shelter themselves from the cold. At midnight Ashby abruptly woke his men from their slumbers when he learned that the Federals had bridged Cedar Creek; he withdrew his force a few hundred yards south of Strasburg where they rested at the roadside until the light of day drew upon them. Ashby led them nearly two more miles southward on the Valley Pike where the dominant ridge line of Fisher's Hill overlooked the area. Ashby well knew that he opposed a sizable Union force and was doing so with one regiment of cavalry, four companies of infantry detached from the Valley District army, and three cannons—less than 700 men in all—but he was determined to make a stand. He ordered Captain Chew to place his artillery in a good commanding position on the height and waited for the Federals to react.[25]

By 8:00 A.M. Shields's division plodded forward, crossed their makeshift bridge, and filed into Strasburg. The general was vocally annoyed at the delayed creek crossing, particularly when he believed it could have been forded without a bridge. At the southern side of town, Shields and his staff rode to the summit of Quarry Hill where they could see Ashby astride his white horse near the top of Fisher's Hill over a mile away. Ashby ordered his gunners to fire rounds at the Federals, but the shells fell well short of their mark. Shields ordered all his brigade commanders forward—Colonel Nathan Kimball commanding his First Brigade, Colonel Jeremiah C. Sullivan leading his Second Brigade, and Colonel Erastus B. Tyler heading his Third Brigade—and added Colonel Mason to the council. According to Mason (the only one who recorded the event), Shields "stated that he was under the impression that Jackson's whole force was in front of us, and he should make his dispositions for battle immediately."

With that, Shields ordered all of his available artillery forward and placed a battery on the height. Lieutenant Colonel Philip Daum, the division's chief of artillery, spent two hours maneuvering the guns in an attempt to place them on flanking hills undetected. Confederate cavalry and artillerymen watched the entire event unfold; eight rifled cannons were positioned at an elevation equal to the Confederates one mile to the northeast. The Union infantry brigades supported the rear. Mason's force from the previous day was sent on a flanking path along the turnpike which skirted the Southerners to their right. Before morning had closed, twenty Union cannons were firing away at Ashby while Mason's detachment, led by the 1st Michigan Cavalry, fast approached Ashby's flank. "It looked like we were going to be picked up in short order," wrote a member of Company I, 2nd Virginia, who believed they held on to the height too long. At what seemed to be the last possible second, Ashby ordered his guns to limber and withdraw a mile to the rear.

Lieutenant Colonel Daum stood on the flanking hill with eight rifled cannons belonging to Captain Joseph Clark's 4th U.S. Artillery, Battery E. Watching the head of the Michigan column emerging from the distant glen, Daum mistook them for Ashby's men and ordered Captain Clark to fire his guns at them. Clark protested, knowing they were Union horsemen, but eventually conceded to the stubborn Daum's instructions. Within seconds friendly fire took out four Federal horses—including one poor animal that was torn in two behind the saddle (the rider was uninjured by the shell, which passed through his coattails). Daum's faux pas did not cost any human lives. The Michigan cavalry was quick to forgive the cannoneers after receiving indirect praise from the gunners by learning that they were mistaken as Ashby's men because of their swift advance. According to one horseman, his company "congratulated [the artillerists] on their promptitude and good marksmanship, and let the matter drop."[26] Shields organized his force and moved forward once again.

Ashby's newest position rested on an elevation one mile south of Fisher's Hill. Watching the Union batteries rolling toward them, the Southerners opened upon them with the two rifled pieces of Chew's battery only to have the fire returned in triplicate. The 8th Ohio spearheaded the Federal assault. Colonel Carroll commanded the left (southern) wing and Lieutenant Colonel Franklin Sawyer proceeded with the right-hand companies. Confederate shot and shell plowed into the ground directly in front of the officers on horseback. The Southern aim was so precise that Carroll was forced to dismount; he claimed the shots would have cut him in two otherwise. As the regiment began to scale the height, Ashby disappeared like a flash and took up a new position southward. The procedure repeated itself, again with the same results. The day-long repetitious sparring desensitized members of the 8th Ohio to the artillery rounds thrown by Chew's guns. By late afternoon the foot soldiers were seen turning their rifles around and swatting at the incoming shot as though they were playing ball. By 5:00 P.M. Ashby held his force a few miles north of Woodstock while Shields's men remained two miles north of them. With darkness approaching, Shields decided that the reconnaissance had been advanced as far as could be expected; therefore, after leaving a strong picket in their most advanced position, he withdrew his division seven miles northward on the Valley Pike to Strasburg. There they camped for the night.[27]

Turner Ashby took his force of 700 southward three miles beyond Woodstock and camped for the night at Narrow Passage. Throughout the day, Ashby slowed the momentum of a 10,000-man enemy division, limited their advance to approximately nine miles, and kept Shields more than fifteen miles from General Jackson's infantry camp. Additionally, a detachment of the 7th Virginia Cavalry burned three railroad bridges to further impair the Manassas Gap line. Ashby's brilliant performance relied on his experience, natural skills, and knowledge of the terrain he covered. His achievement impressed the Federals. David Hunter Strother, who worked at Shields's side throughout the day, admired Shields's "pluck and enterprise," but he dished out greater accolades to his opponent. Strother closed his diary passage for the day's events by admitting "Ashby has played his part handsomely in disputing our advance, displaying a great deal of personal boldness and military tact in checking so large a column as ours with his small force." A Union horse soldier commended the 7th Virginia Cavalry for possessing the essential ingredients for success: ". . . fine horses, a perfect knowledge of the country, and a colonel who is professedly one of the bravest in the South."[28]

Stonewall Jackson and his Valley District division rested at Camp Buchanon at Red Banks, a turnpike hamlet ten miles south of Woodstock and approximately three miles north of Mount Jackson. They gradually fell back to this location on March 16 and remained there through March 19. The camp occupied a wooded area near the Ripley house. The foot soldiers were surrounded by the gently rolling countryside sporadically dotted with sturdy farmhouses. The North Fork of the Shenandoah River skirted the right of the camp, separating the men from the Massanutten Mountain. One member of the 4th Virginia took this all in and deemed his location "a tolerably nice place for a camp." Despite the pleasant and presently unthreatened surroundings, Major Frank Jones, 2nd Virginia, still despaired over leaving his wife and children in Winchester. Successfully passing a letter to his wife through enemy lines, Jones reminded her that it was one week ago that he was forced to leave, adding "how long it seems, how sad. Oh how sad is this separation." Major Elisha "Bull" Paxton of the 27th Virginia benefited from having his wife safely tucked away at their Lexington home well south of the Confederate line. Without the emotional hardship of leaving a family in the hands of an opponent, Paxton pragmatically wrote his wife, "Whilst it is a sad thought to give up one's home to the enemy, with many of us it is destined to be a necessity which will contribute more than all other causes to the ultimate achievement of our independence. It is utterly impossible to defend every section."[29]

Stonewall Jackson headquartered himself and his staff in the hamlet of Hawkinstown at the home of Israel Allen, a prosperous elderly farmer. Wednesday night, March 19, while Stonewall's staff rested in their posh surroundings (including feather beds), the general labored in his private office on the second floor. He wrote a letter to Turner Ashby that evening, addressing it to "My dear Colonel." Apparently, Jackson had received no information from the cavalier during the day for he listed bridges between Strasburg and Mount Jackson that he wished Ashby to destroy, not knowing that Ashby had already burned most of them. Jackson knew a Federal force started the day at Strasburg; however, he was unaware of who led those troops. Jackson informed his cavalry commander that he expected militia forces to arrive the following day and wished to know where the enemy was and how far he predicted they would advance. Jackson closed the letter, handed it to a courier, and sent him northward to find Ashby.

Jackson's courier returned that night to provide Stonewall with knowledge of Ashby's accomplishments, but also misinformed him that the enemy had closed to approximately ten miles from Camp Buchanon. Ashby was unaware at the time that Shields had withdrawn the Federals back to Strasburg. Shields left a strong picket in the most advanced position of the day and Ashby retired southward prior to the Federals' departure. These two deployments instigated the false impression that Shields was still in pursuit which forced Stonewall to plan to move his men and supplies southward again.[30]

Although Stonewall was hampered by a depleted division, his superior, Joseph E. Johnston, pressured him to close the gap between the Confederate Valley District force and Banks's Fifth Corps in the Valley. Johnston, who had pulled back his army from Manassas to the Rappahannock River, was disappointed to learn on March 19 that Jackson had marched his division forty miles south of Winchester. Johnston spelled out to his subordinate in a return dispatch what his mission was in the Valley:

Would not your presence with your troops near Winchester prevent the enemy from diminishing his force there? I think it certain that it would. It is important to keep that army in the valley—& that it should not reinforce McClellan. So try to prevent it by keeping as near as prudence will permit.[31]

Johnston in turn was receiving pressure from Richmond. McClellan's Peninsula campaign was no secret; the Confederate War Department received continuous information from Washington shortly after the first troop ships sailed from Alexandria on March 17. Johnston was urged by General Robert E. Lee, advisor to President Jefferson Davis, to detach Major General James Longstreet from his army to hard-pressed tidewater North Carolina. Realizing the survival of the Confederacy depended on keeping Union troops dispersed, Lee also believed that McClellan's campaign could be delayed if President Lincoln felt threatened. "Can you by a rapid forward movement threaten Washington and thus recall the enemy?" Lee queried Johnston.[32] Johnston's best hope to satisfy the Confederate War Department would be Jackson's Valley District force. They may not be able to advance far enough to approach Washington, but Jackson's presence in the northern Valley may be enough of a threat to disrupt McClellan's plans.

Thursday, March 20, dawned in the Valley under a chilling northeast wind foretelling an approaching storm. Colonel Jesse Burks, leading Jackson's Third Brigade, and Colonel John Echols, the head of the 27th Virginia Infantry, both turned thirty-nine years old that day, but there was no time to celebrate their birthdays. Jackson ordered his supply wagons to move toward Rude's Hill, an elevation four miles south of Mount Jackson on the turnpike. Fostered by fears that Shields's division had closed to within five miles of the Valley District army, confusion rippled through the packed-up camp. The few remaining available wagons overflowed with knapsacks and bedding; disposable supplies were piled so they could be destroyed once the regiments marched off. Shortly after 2:00 P.M. the infantry set off and marched southward through Mount Jackson in a bone chilling rain. Frank Jones described the short hike as "cold and cheerless." He and the rest of the men camped in an open field without tents as nighttime blanketed the Valley. Here the men received orders to prepare to march again the next day. The continued retreats frayed the soldiers' nerves. "If our men would just step forward now in this emergency and make a demonstration towards the enemy, . . . the effect would be great," noted a frustrated member of the 4th Virginia, who continued by complaining, "But we leave a section and the enemy comes in and fares as well as we. This will not do. Some sacrifice of life, property and time must be undergone before we shall win our independence."[33]

Stonewall Jackson had little left in his arsenal to placate General Lee, General Johnston, and the aggressive-minded soldiers in his division. The general's veteran volunteer force numbered fewer than 4,000 effectives due to casualties and leaves of absence. Jackson toiled endlessly to gather and arm a militia force to reinforce his ranks long enough to allow the reenlisted veterans of his division to return from their furloughs. Although the militia had failed him in northwestern Virginia, Stonewall appeared willing to give them another try. He labored to secure money and equipment to incorporate militia forces from twelve Valley counties into his division. Prior to evacuating his headquarters at the Allen house, Stonewall received two members of the Augusta County militia who reported that they were prepared for muster at a camp fifteen miles southwest of Staunton. Jackson asked many questions of the two militia men and became intrigued with one of them, a New York native who made a name for himself as an engineer for the Confederates in their western Virginia campaign of 1861. Jackson later divulged plans to detail that man, named Jedediah Hotchkiss, from the militia and use him as an engineer on his staff.

Those plans would have to wait. Jackson joined his command that evening at Rude's Hill. Jackson took his headquarters at the home of Reverend Anders Rudolph Rude, an upper class residence sitting prominently at the foot of the hill with the same name. As the temperatures fell to convert the evening rain into sleet and snow, Stonewall sat in Rude's parlor and shared the warmth from the fireplace with several members of the Liberty Hall Volunteers, a company of Washington College students who became incorporated into the 4th Virginia Infantry. Jackson had the company detached to serve as his headquarters guard and the boys enjoyed the advantages, including a warm shelter during a wet and freezing night, that came with the duty. The college company chatted freely with Stonewall who appeared unusually cheerful and at ease for a commander beset with military impediments. One company officer fondly remembered the evening that Jackson "made himself one of the boys" as one of the only times Stonewall Jackson mingled with his men.[34]

Two inches of snow covered the Rude's Hill camp on Friday morning, March 21, and snow continued to fall until 10:30 A.M. The unusual inauguration of the spring season for 1862 did little to mellow the spirits of Jackson's Valley District soldiers. For the first time in nearly ten days, they broke camp and marched northward rather than southward. It was a short hike; the men returned to the wooded environment of Camp Buchanon to the west of the turnpike while Jackson's staff returned to Israel Allen's house at Hawkinstown.

Rumors rippled through the ranks that the Federals were leaving Winchester to quell riots in Baltimore.

Sandie Pendleton arrived at Allen's house in the morning, ate a large breakfast, then wrote his mother a letter. "We are carrying an independent war here," Sandie explained. "We hear nothing from the outer world and rely solely upon our own strong arms and providence." Pendleton also put a complete spin on the reason for the initiation of a forward movement. Pendleton believed that the Federals were not leaving Winchester, but rather were in force at Strasburg, 10,000 strong. With the militia turning out strongly, Pendleton surmised that General Jackson planned to drive the Federals across the Potomac. "They have come as far up the Valley as they can without a fight," he postured, "and if a fight does come off they will undoubtedly be sorry for it, as we have the choice of position and will hazard everything upon success."[35]

General Jackson rode with an assistant to the Augusta County militia camp at noon and inspected the new recruits there. Later that afternoon he rode to the Allen house through an uncomfortable rain. Jackson sat at his desk in the private second-floor room and wrote a letter to his superior, General Joseph Johnston. Despite the rumors of the evacuation of Winchester, Jackson agreed with his young aide, Sandie Pendleton, that the Federals were still in Strasburg, at least 10,000 strong, and that they intended to pursue him to Staunton. Still lacking muskets for his militia, Stonewall planned on using those troops for detached labor duties. In the meantime he would take his division ten miles northward to Woodstock.[36] In the face of what he believed to be a force outnumbering him nearly three to one, Stonewall appeared ready to meet them in battle rather than retreat from them.

The news that Jackson relayed to his superior came to him from Turner Ashby who received the information from a spy in Strasburg; however, the intelligence proved to be erroneous. No Federal force existed in the Strasburg area on March 21. The day previous, during a driving rainstorm, General Shields deemed his reconnaissance completed and returned his men on a brutal twenty-two-mile march that carried the bluecoats through Winchester and back to their camps north of town. They covered the distance with an impressive three-miles-per-hour pace, leaving Strasburg at 11:00 A.M. and arriving at their old camp by dark at 7:00 P.M. The three-day sojourn was the first full division activity under Shields's command. Although no major accomplishments were achieved, the movement allowed each regiment to gauge the performance of sister units within the command. Most were complimentary of other regiments; however, the poorly disciplined 110th Pennsylvania received failing grades as far as one opinionated soldier was concerned. Lieutenant Colonel Thomas Clark of the 29th Ohio noted with disgust that several members of the 110th Pennsylvania found the time to steal hens from an old widow's chicken coop during the march. "I wish the 110th Regt. could be swapped off for a team of unserviceable mules and then condemned and shot," penned the livid officer to his wife. The chicken poaching was an isolated incident, however, as Shields appeared to generally have tight control of discipline in the ranks. Although General Jackson had no idea where Shields's division was located on March 21, the Federal Westerners somehow knew exactly where Stonewall and his men encamped. "Jackson and his force have fallen back upon Mount Jackson," accurately wrote an Ohio soldier that day. "It is more than likely that we will mount Jackson before long and if he don't kick too high we will ride him out of that part of the country sure."[37]

Although he was unable to capture Ashby's command or penetrate his defense, Shields believed the reconnaissance was successful, for it assured him that Jackson was at least forty miles from Winchester and Ashby's small force should pose no serious threat to Lower Valley operations. Pickets thrown to the south of Winchester were believed to be sufficient to ready the division for a further advance. Banks had returned to Winchester from Washington and apparently agreed with his subordinate's conclusion. The Fifth Corps engineers successfully rebuilt the Castleman's Ferry Bridge with an eighty-foot oak span that crossed the Shenandoah River east of Berryville. With the bridge reconstructed, Banks could easily send Williams's division through Snicker's Gap in the Blue Ridge and direct them to Centreville. The first brigade of Williams's division struck their tents on March 21 and departed Winchester to the east. The two other brigades made final preparations to move out the next day. With Shields and his division tucked away in their camps three miles north of town on the Martinsburg Road, nearly everyone living in Winchester believed he would depart the Valley northward to Harpers Ferry and Williams would move eastward. It appeared to many that the Federals were evacuating town.[38]

Colonel Jonah Tavener, an elderly militia officer living in Loudoun County, entered the Shenandoah Valley through Snicker's Gap during the late afternoon of Friday, March 21. Too old to serve the Confederacy directly, Tavener spotted the first of Williams's three brigades winding eastward on the Berryville Pike toward the newly repaired bridge over the Shenandoah and believed he had valuable information to aid the Southern cause. He passed undetected to the south of the blue-clad infantry, then flanked to the south of Winchester to deliver his information. Tavener found Ashby's outposts not far from town and requested to be taken to their commander immediately. Ashby knew Tavener personally and greeted his newest spy with pleasure after hearing the news he had to deliver. Ashby sent a courier to deliver the intelligence to Jackson.

Colonel Ashby's information forced Stonewall Jackson to alter his plans. Jackson originally intended to march his division ten miles the next day from Mount Jackson to Woodstock. Now knowing no opposition existed between Winchester and Mount Jackson, Stonewall redesigned his plan to march as far as possible the following day to "employ" the Federals before they left the Valley. General Johnston's prodding had taken effect, but Jackson's mission was to detain Federal troops in the Valley without getting too near to them so that he would be forced to fight a superior force. The Confederate War Department received intelligence on Saturday morning, March 22, that seventeen Federal regiments had left Winchester, confirming the old militia colonel's report. With Union troops already seen leaving the Valley, Jackson's objective appeared to be jeopardized.[39]

That cloudy Saturday morning, Ashby gathered his cavalry command of 290 horseman and Captain Chew's gunners. From his Woodstock camp, Ashby led them northward once again. The artillerists marched confidently and eagerly expected to enter Winchester unopposed. Late that morning a boy from Winchester found Ashby south of Newtown and told him that Winchester had been evacuated that day. When Ashby rode closer to town, another sympathetic citizen found him and confirmed the earlier report. Ashby detached a courier to relay the intelligence to General Jackson whose division was also marching northward from Red Banks, nearly thirty-five miles behind Ashby.

Expecting little resistance from a skeleton force remaining in the vicinity, Ashby's cavalry and horse artillery strode through Kernstown at approximately 2:00 P.M. on Saturday afternoon. After two days of rain, sleet, and snow, this day warmed above fifty degrees without detectable precipitation. All roads, except the Valley Pike, were still muddy quagmires; therefore, Federal cavalry focused on the limestone turnpike for picketing. Major Angelo Paldi commanded a squadron from the second battalion of the 1st Michigan Cavalry and stationed it on the pike two miles south of Winchester. Pickets from the squadron rode to Kernstown to water their horses at Hoge Run. Their respite was interrupted when they watched the leading elements of Ashby's 7th Virginia Cavalry advancing through the village in front of them. Ashby pushed the Federal cavalry pickets across Abraham's (also known as Abrams) Creek and back toward Abraham Hollingsworth's three-story stone gristmill in an area appropriately known as Milltown.

Major Paldi and Company F's Captain Henry K. White head-quartered themselves in one of the houses at Milltown. They watched as rider after rider from their squadron gallop past the house to warn the camp north of Milltown. Before Paldi and White could react, fifteen horsemen from Ashby's advanced force rode up and surrounded the house. The ill-equipped cavalry officers improvised to stall their seemingly inevitable surrender. Major Paldi raised the window sash while Captain White snapped an empty revolver at the Southern cavaliers. Before Ashby's men could take advantage of their unarmed prey, several members from the 1st Michigan Cavalry thundered up the Valley Pike toward Milltown and drove the outnumbered Confederates away to save their officers.[40]

Major Paldi galloped back to Winchester where he found Colonel Thornton F. Brodhead. His partial cavalry regiment of four companies, along with four companies of the 46th Pennsylvania Infantry, (the only leftover infantry unit remaining from Williams's division), guarded the immense stores of supplies for Banks's corps and were the only force in the southern Winchester area. Shields's division remained encamped three miles north of Winchester on the Martinsburg Road. Brodhead respected Ashby's cavaliers and left nothing to chance. He sent his chief subordinate, Lieutenant Colonel John T. Copeland, with the remaining three Michigan companies and the Pennsylvanians to reinforce Paldi's pickets. Brodhead then sent a courier to General Banks at the Seevers house where one of the three companies camped as the headquarters guard. Another courier delivered a request to General Shields to bring up support to drive the Confederates away. To the aide's surprise, Shields discredited the intelligence and remained north of town.

An hour passed, providing Colonel Ashby time to position his horsemen and his three-gun battery. Captain Chew's battery ascended a low ridge northwest of the intersection of the Cedar Creek Grade Road and the Valley Pike. The intersection's most familiar feature was Hillman's Tollgate, but the toll collector had been absent ever since the Federals took over the area ten days earlier. Chew's gunners fired their first rounds approximately 3:30 P.M. Meanwhile, Lieutenant Colonel Copeland arrived with the remaining Michigan cavalry companies to hold Ashby in check until support arrived. Realizing that an aggressive force of approximately 300 Southerners contested him, Colonel Brodhead sent another urgent message to General Shields for immediate support.[41]

This time Shields complied and Winchester's residents witnessed their second spectacle of the day. Williams's remaining brigades left town that morning with bands playing and soldiers marching eastward in parade fashion. Now a more hurried troop movement passed from north to south. Shields and his staff, escorted by one company of the 1st West Virginia Cavalry, rode horses in the van. They were followed by Huntington's artillery battery and the 8th Ohio and 67th Ohio infantry regiments from Colonel Nathan Kimball's First Brigade. Kimball's other regiments and the remaining two brigades of Shields's division lagged in the rear. Some residents climbed upon the roofs in an attempt to see what the cannonading was all about south of town.[42]

As Shields advanced through Winchester, Turner Ashby ordered a squadron to charge down the pike to break up the Michigan picket force and enter Winchester. The Southern horsemen galloped across the Abraham's Creek bridge with exultant yells and headed toward the cluster of mills. To their surprise, two hidden companies of cavalry rose from behind the stone fence that lined the road north of the creek and delivered a hurried volley at the charging horsemen. The Union cavalry disclosed their poor marksmanship; they aimed their carbines too high and injured no one. However, it effectively drove Ashby's men back to the southern side of the creek by 4:00 P.M. Within minutes of the repulse, Shields and his reinforcements entered Milltown from the north.[43]

The Valley Turnpike, Looking North from Hillman's Tollgate. Turn-of-Century View of Abrams Creek (low ground) and Milltown Beyond.
Courtesy of Ben Ritter

Shields was surly from events occurring earlier in the day. He had complained to General Banks about seeking reprisals for what he considered to be the miscreants of Winchester who "fly before us and leave their wives and children in our power, and while doing this wreak their vengeance on the poor Union men who happen to be found amongst them." Shields did not believe the first request for aid and was still skeptical after deciding to move in response to the second call for troops. He heard the Confederate cannons while moving through Winchester and took personal charge to out-muscle them. Shields rode forward with Captain James F. Huntington's 1st Ohio Light Artillery, six rifled pieces of Battery H, and positioned them on an eminence near the mill, well within the sight of Chew's gunners opposing them. While aligning the cannons on the left of the battery, an incoming shell found its mark on the head of one of the artillery horses and exploded on impact. The bomb blast killed the horse and its driver, Private Jacob Yeager, while shell fragments flew in all directions. A second artillery horse was hit while another shell fragment struck Shields above the left elbow, breaking the humerus bone and injuring the general's shoulder and left side.[44]

Shields dropped to the ground in pain. Dr. H. M. McAbee, the surgeon of the 4th Ohio Infantry, arrived quickly to aid the general. Shields requested to be helped back on his horse, but fainted as soon as he was placed in an upright position. An open carriage was ordered and became another target for Chew's gunners who forced the empty vehicle off the turnpike. Once again, Shields fainted when held upright so Dr. McAbee sent for an ambulance to take him back to town. In the meantime, staff aides carried Shields to one of the houses near the mill to escape the raining shot and shell. A boy living in the residence asked why the general was carried inside. When told about the shell fragment that injured Shields's arm, the lad reportedly responded, "I wish it had struck him through his damned head." The ambulance wagon eventually arrived and carried the wounded commander back to Winchester.[45]

Command of the Second Division, Fifth Corps, Army of the Potomac immediately transferred to General Shields's second in command, Colonel Nathan Kimball. He was already on the field with the leading elements of his First Brigade. Kimball seemed a solid replacement for division chief, owing to the steady ascent of responsibility he earned in military endeavors. Kimball's early life is a mystery; it is unknown if he was born in 1822 or 1823. What is known is that he had grown up in Washington County, Indiana, dropped out of college after two years and attempted to make a living as a teacher and a farmer before opting to study medicine in 1843. Taught by his brother-in-law, the new physician suspended his practice in

1846 when duty called him to serve in the Mexican War. He raised and captained a Hoosier company called the Posey Guards which was incorporated into the 2nd Indiana Infantry. The regiment broke in disorder at the Battle of Buena Vista, but Kimball rallied his company and continued fighting.

After that war, Captain Kimball returned to civilian life as a doctor in Martin County, Indiana, and practiced medicine for over a decade until Fort Sumter was fired upon. Once again Captain Kimball raised and captained a Martin County company which became part of the 14th Indiana Volunteer Infantry. Nathan Kimball's Mexican War experience won him a colonel's commission in May of 1861. He and his regiment were part of the victorious western Virginia campaign of 1861. Kimball performed well in command of his regiment and was awarded the First Brigade of Lander's division early in 1862, though maintaining the rank of colonel. He temporarily led the division at Paw Paw after General Lander died. With the injury to General Shields, the brigade colonel took command of the Westerners once again.[46]

Nathan Kimball could never be accused of ostentatious displays, for he was not a flamboyant commander. He led by solid, steady example and his troops responded positively to his style. Kimball occasionally mingled with his troops. In January, a Hoosier in the 14th Indiana sang "Maggie by My Side" while quartered at miserable Camp Kelley. The soldier heard a friend behind him ask if he did not wish her by his side; the singer lamented that he did. Then he heard someone else say, "Pretty good. I wish you had her here too." Realizing the voice did not match any of his tentmates, the soldier turned and met the familiar features of Colonel Kimball. Kimball's good-hearted surprises were minor, but did much to boost the morale of his soldiers. They had grown to depend on him to carry them through any hardship, realizing that during his absence whenever adverse circumstances brought them down, it would be different "if Colonel Kimball was here." Most importantly, Nathan Kimball's men held the utmost respect for him. "He is a matchless soldier, and he loves his men, and they all know it, and so they love him," declared James Oakey of the 14th Indiana, insisting that Kimball's men "would follow him anywhere at anytime, and against any odds."[47]

Nathan Kimball's immediate responsibility on the late Saturday afternoon of March 22, 1862 was to clear the Confederates from his front. Kimball had no trouble accomplishing his first task, thanks to artillery power. Huntington's battery, supported by several pieces from Captain Lucius N. Robinson's Battery L, 1st Ohio Light Artillery, returned fire on Ashby's force within minutes of

Shields's wounding. The 67th and 8th Ohio swept along the left and right of the Valley Pike, supported by cavalry companies. With oncoming darkness, Ashby withdrew his severely outmanned force and took them to Newtown, six miles south of Milltown, where the Confederates quartered themselves in churches and houses to escape the cold.[48]

One member of Ashby's cavalry found shelter closer to the skirmish arena. Private John N. Kitchen attached himself to Ashby's 7th Virginia Cavalry only five days previous to the skirmish (he had transferred from Jeb Stuart's command). Kitchen was a blue-eyed, full-framed Clarke County native who suffered from a nebulous disability for which he had obtained a certificate, but had yet to be formally discharged. Kitchen did not participate in the

Colonel Nathan Kimball, Commanding Second Division, Fifth Corps, Army of the Potomac

U.S.A.M.H.I.

skirmish; he shirked the action and took refuge in a Kernstown citizen's home to the east of the Valley Pike. After the skirmish, when Ashby pulled his command back through Kernstown to Newtown, Kitchen rode east instead of south and found shelter at the widow Hamilton's house on the Front Royal Plank Road. This road, unlike the muddy Old Front Royal Road running in a parallel track to the west, was bedded with clay and sand with traversing wooden planks across it. Kitchen's quarters rested only two and one half miles south of Winchester, well within designated Union picket areas.[49]

Lieutenant Colonel Joseph Copeland of the 1st Michigan Cavalry commanded the Federal cavalry that evening. He ordered the available cavalry to picket the westerly and southerly routes leading from Winchester. The Federal horsemen galloped past the 8th Ohio, splashing muddy water all over the tired and miserable soldiers. Captain John Keys's Ringgold squadron was ordered to scout the Front Royal Road. Keys's command consisted of two dozen men moving blindly through the darkened countryside. Two members of the squadron, acting on their suspicions, dismounted near Hamilton's residence and scaled the fence. To their surprise, they heard a man's voice which alerted one of the Federals to drop back and inform their captain. Keys received the information and rode ahead of the rest of his squadron to join the two scouts at the lane leading to Hamilton's farmhouse. There they waited as a man left the house and strode down the lane on horseback. Keys surprised him, ordered him to dismount, and removed his weapons. Keys questioned his prisoner, the wayward John Kitchen, and deemed his knowledge valuable enough to take him directly to Banks's quarters in Winchester. Kitchen's carelessness and bad fortune resulted in a coup for the Union cavalry.[50]

Ashby reached Newtown with John Kitchen as his only loss for the day, but he realized that insufficient rest and forage for over one week had dwindled the total strength of his eight companies to fewer than 300 men. Ashby believed the hard campaigning had been necessary and was successful. Although unable to enter Winchester that day, he had acquired confirming information that only four regiments remained in Winchester with orders to proceed to Harpers Ferry the next day. He saw the equivalent of three opposing regiments (including cavalry) Saturday afternoon and was unaware that General Shields's full division remained at Winchester with no orders or intentions of leaving on Sunday. The misinformed cavalry chief believed he could take over Winchester with the support of one infantry regiment. Ashby detailed a courier southward that evening to find General Jackson and hand him the summary of the afternoon's events and the request for reinforcements.[51]

Ashby's courier found General Jackson ten miles south of Newtown at Strasburg, quartered near Hupp's Hill. His division completed a day-long march that varied between fourteen and twenty-six miles, depending on where the men camped the previous evening. Fulkerson's men marched the shortest distance from Woodstock to Fisher's Hill; Garnett's brigade marched twenty-four miles from Camp Buchanon to Cedar Creek; and Burks's brigade advanced nearly twenty-six miles from a camp near Rude's Hill to Fisher's Hill. Ashby's message was the second one that Stonewall received from him that day. Both accounts revealed the Federals had evacuated Winchester and a token force of four regiments was all that remained to oppose him. These notes, coupled with information from a spy who confirmed Ashby's intelligence, convinced Jackson that he could attack the small Federal force that lingered around the town.[52]

Jackson's division had withered, however, to the size of a brigade. Stonewall carried fewer than 3,500 infantrymen to the Strasburg area Saturday evening. Militia forces had not been mustered and armed in time and were left behind. The volunteer veterans with Jackson were footsore and weary. Before he turned in at his Cedar Creek camp for the night, Major Frank Jones pulled out his diary and ended his March 22 entry by noting, "Men very much fatigued and a large number of stragglers strayed from the regiment." Jackson knew his force had become scant and his men were not in the best condition, but how could a mere four enemy regiments hold back over 3,000 men supported with six artillery batteries? Not knowing that an opposing force that doubled his lay near Winchester, Jackson passed orders for his troops to march at daybreak.[53]

The next morning Stonewall Jackson rose before dawn to prepare the day's events. He detached four companies of Stonewall Brigade infantry to join Ashby, providing the cavalry colonel with half the support he requested. Those men departed their Cedar Creek camps before 5:00 A.M. The rest of the army was up and in line on the Valley Pike by 6:30 A.M. The sun had come up half an hour earlier, but an extensive cloud barrier cast an ominous darkness over the valley corridor. The sounds of clanging accoutrements and hoarsely barked orders, as well as the sight of thousands of miniature clouds of heated breath filled the chilly morning air. Twenty minutes later Jackson wrote a hasty dispatch to General Johnston, telling his superior: "With the blessing of an ever-kind Providence I hope to be in the vicinity of Winchester this evening." Stonewall then set his column of Virginia troops in motion to liberate one of their towns in the Old Dominion from Federal occupation.[54]

The date was March 23, 1862. On the same date in 1775, Patrick Henry stood up in St. John's Church in Richmond and passionately declared to the Virginia Convention, "I know not what course the others may take; but as for me, *give me liberty or give me death!*" By the time the 1862 day ended, Virginia would mark another event in its almanac for March 23—a day that played out the theme of Patrick Henry's speech exactly four score and seven years later.

Chapter Four

"JACKSON IS AFRAID OF ME"

March 23, 1862, was the first Sabbath of spring and despite the fact that their city was occupied by Federal troops, the citizens of Winchester tried to go about their normal Sunday morning activities. Mrs. Mary Charlton Greenhow Lee, a widow who lived on Market Street, attended the nearby Kent Street Presbyterian Church which had been General Jackson's house of worship throughout the preceding winter. It was the first time she had left her home in twelve days ("since our army left us"). Mrs. Lee thought church would be a panacea for her troubles. The Reverend Graham, she noted, gave a particularly strong sermon marked with a good Southern prayer. The ever-observant Mrs. Lee, who admittedly felt nothing but contempt for Northerners, noted that no Federal troops attended the service that morning. "They are not a church going people," she surmised in her diary.[1]

Other Winchester citizens shared Mrs. Lee's concerns this day. Several companies of Stonewall Jackson's division were recruited from Frederick County which left many of the soldiers' families restless. Nearly all were aware of the Saturday skirmish south of town, but few knew that only Ashby's cavalry was involved. They were praying for the day that their sons could release them from Federal occupation; many expected the day to be soon.

Shields's troops occupied themselves with camp preparations after spending the night sleeping on the nearly frozen soil without tent shelter. The 7th Indiana Infantry of Colonel Erastus B. Tyler's Third Brigade bivouacked near the edge of town on Saturday night. The men were subsequently ordered back to their camp north of Winchester on Sunday morning. Many of the soldiers used the respite to converse and, in some cases, tease each other. Private A. I. Canary showed off a picture he received from a girlfriend back in Indiana to his comrades, claiming the attractive lady was "the girl he left behind him." One of the recipients of Canary's braggadocio, Private G. K. Covert, asked to see the picture. Canary more than willingly complied and, to his shock, Covert announced he was keeping the picture, claiming he had as much right to it as Canary did. A long scuffle ensued, but when it was over Covert retained the possession of Canary's picture and slipped it into his left breast pocket.[2] The tin type was destined to save the man's life.

The other four regiments of Tyler's brigade had returned to Camp Shields near Stephenson's Depot the previous night and awoke on Sunday expecting an uneventful day. Evidence of soul searching became apparent during the normal morning flurry of regimental dispatches. Sixty-year-old Captain John F. Moore of the 29th Ohio tendered his resignation to Colonel Lewis P. Buckley. The hard marching over the past two months, particularly the twenty-two miler conducted three days earlier, was too much for the elderly captain who felt unable to perform the daily duties of a foot soldier.[3] Only two years younger than Captain Moore, Colonel Buckley accepted the resignation. It would still require three weeks for the resignation to be officially granted.

Most of Colonel Nathan Kimball's First Brigade slept on their arms throughout Saturday night and welcomed the opportunity to encamp on Sunday morning, particularly since their tents had not arrived the night before. Colonel William G. Murray of the 84th Pennsylvania looked for good campgrounds on the eastern side of the Valley Pike, south of Winchester. His men welcomed the chance to rest. After completing the long march the previous Thursday, Murray had issued orders for daily two-hour drills, the first time such a regimen had been imposed on the men.[4]

William Gray Murray was born in Longford, Ireland, in the summer of 1825 and his parents had moved to America when he was nine months old. His father settled the Murray family in various towns in the Mohawk Valley of New York, where he prospered in the mercantile trade until the financial crisis of 1835–1836 destroyed his fortune, forcing the family to move to Harrisburg, Pennsylvania. William Murray was raised for the mercantile life there, but opted for the military when the Mexican War broke out. He volunteered as a private in the Cameron Guards and rose through the ranks to finish the war as a second lieutenant of the 11th United States Infantry. Murray returned to private life as a businessman

Colonel William Gray Murray, 84th Pennsylvania Infantry
Courtesy of Blair County Historical Society, Altoona, Pennsylvania

in Hollidaysburg, Pennsylvania, where he served as the town's post-master while supporting a wife and three children.

At the outbreak of the Civil War, Murray had declined a captain's commission in the regular service, opting instead to remain with his wife who was suffering through the final stages of tuberculosis. She died in August of 1861; soon afterwards Governor Andrew Gregg Curtin authorized Murray to recruit a regiment of infantry as part of Pennsylvania's answer to President Lincoln's call for 300,000 troops. Murray complied and was commissioned a colonel of the 84th Pennsylvania Volunteers, a regiment consisting predominantly of central state mountaineers who were raised with the rifle but were not prepared to handle the Belgians they were issued.[5]

By March 23, Murray's regiment was reduced to approximately one quarter of its original muster strength. The rest were either ill or had been sent on special duty to guard other occupied Lower Valley towns. In addition to his depleted ranks, Colonel Murray had been plagued with other concerns. Approving a thirty-day leave of absence that morning for ailing Captain Robert M. Flack reminded Murray of his most pressing problem: he had been the victim of an attempted mutiny by his subordinate officers, including the captain he was excusing from duty.[6] The wording of the letter Colonel Murray received Friday, March 21, clearly summarized the intentions of others in the regiment:

> Though it is painful yet duty, owed alike to our country and the men of the Regiment, compels us, Officers of the Line, to address you on the subject of your resignation. It is the opinion of the undersigned that though endowed with many traits which distinguish in civil life, you have yet failed to discover that peculiar genius which qualifies for martial command. To have in charge the lives, interests, and proud hopes of a regiment of patriotic and noble hearted men is a responsibility of so great moment that no one but he who is competent should assume or retain it. The conduct of the regiment since its organization has been, it is respectfully submitted, not only unsatisfactory but criminal. Lives are not to be imperilled wantonly because of inefficiency ascribable to the incompetency of command. . . .
>
> Believing that your pride as a high lived gentleman will induce you to regard the wishes of your officers and men, it is respectfully asked that you resign your position as Colonel of the 84th Regiment of Pennsylvania Volunteers.

The letter was endorsed by seventeen of the line officers of the regiment and a similar letter, written on March 10, was sent to

Governor Curtin in Harrisburg.[7] Murray refused to step down and, two days later, he still stood stubbornly in command; however, with his leadership now in question at the State House of Pennsylvania, the colonel would have to prove himself in battle. In the meantime, grueling drills became Murray's answer to his subordinates' accusations of poor conduct and discipline.

While the Second Division prepared breakfast, General Banks and General Shields analyzed the situation in the Seevers house on the corner of Boscawen and Stewart streets, where Shields had been taken after his injury. The house had served as Banks's sleeping quarters since he arrived at Winchester on March 12. General Shields was furious about his injury; it was still possible that his shattered arm would require amputation. He would not have been concerned if the wounding had occurred in a significant battle, but he was disgusted to be mutilated in a mere skirmish.[8]

Banks and Shields spent much of the morning discussing the implications of the previous evening's skirmish. Neither believed that Ashby's attack was significant; after all, the aggressive cavalryman had been nipping at Banks's heels ever since he occupied the Lower Valley. Why should this be any different? Cavalryman John Kitchen, the prisoner from Ashby's force who was captured by the Ringgolds, had been brought to Banks late the previous evening. Banks interrogated Kitchen who told the general that Ashby was under the impression that Federal troops had left Winchester, and that Jackson's forces were on the road from Strasburg under the same impression.[9] Despite this frank and revealing testimony, Banks discounted its veracity. A new day brought a fresh approach to the situation and, as far as Banks was concerned, this man's assertions contradicted all the evidence he had in his possession. With the Confederates pulled back from Manassas and no sign of supporting troops for Jackson's Valley District, there existed no real indication that General Jackson was anywhere near the Lower Valley; therefore, Banks prepared to leave Winchester by the afternoon.

General Shields was also convinced that no serious fighting would come about for quite a while. With the exception of some Fifth Corps staff that Banks would leave behind for assistance, Shields now commanded the only Federal force in the Lower Valley since Williams's last brigade departed the previous afternoon. The general brimmed with confidence in his new role. He sent for Colonel Jeremiah C. Sullivan, the former head of the 13th Indiana who was promoted to command the Second Brigade of Shields's division. Sullivan, whose brigade had spent the night picketing the roads south of Winchester, arrived promptly and told Shields his pickets had seen nothing of Ashby that night. Shields was not surprised.

He told Sullivan he believed the enemy was indeed gone and that there was no indication that they would be fighting Jackson in the near future. Shields went on to claim that he knew the Confederate general well, and he boasted that "Jackson is afraid of me."

Shields had not endeared himself to his brigade commander this particular morning. Colonel Sullivan felt that Shields exhibited "a propensity for underrating his troops." Sullivan also had proof that his troops were poorly supplied, particularly concentrating on the lack of shoes in his force (In eight days he would formally complain to his superiors that his 2,500-man brigade was "absolutely barefoot"). He had planned to rest his men in camps this Sunday since they had been up all night picketing. Shields disapproved, telling Sullivan that certain skirmish movements had been made that his brigade was unaware of. General Shields ordered Sullivan to select good campground south of Winchester and to drill his troops in the art of skirmishing "to get them ready for a fight that would come off at some future time." Sullivan's objections fell on disinterested ears, so he left headquarters to tell his tired troops the unpleasant news.[10]

Colonel Samuel Sprigg Carroll's 8th Ohio Infantry needed no skirmish training. The 8th Ohio, a regiment in Nathan Kimball's First Brigade, had developed into a crack skirmishing force, an earned reputation of which Carroll's men were very proud. The 8th Ohio was one of only two infantry units engaged the previous evening. Carroll's men had performed well by driving Ashby's horse soldiers away from Winchester. The colonel, also believing that the previous evening's skirmish showed no foreboding signal of an imminent battle, felt that this Sunday was the opportune time for him to see his wife and children. They were in Martinsburg and had been trying to join him on the march. Carroll received permission, probably through General Shields, to head northward to retrieve his family.[11]

Colonel Jeremiah C. Sullivan, Commanding Second Brigade, Second Division, Fifth Corps, Army of the Potomac

U.S.A.M.H.I.

Two companies from Colonel Carroll's 8th Ohio relieved the pickets from Colonel Sullivan's Second Brigade, the force left to picket
the roads leading to and from Winchester overnight.[12] Company C
moved to the southern outpost near the tiny hamlet of Kernstown,
a village named for an eighteenth-century Frederick County pioneer. Kernstown lay three miles south of Winchester on the Valley
Pike. Although its population and number of dwellings were dwarfed
by the large marketing center north of it, Kernstown had managed
to secure a relative degree of independence. The Valley Pike ran
through the hamlet and three other roads spoked from Kernstown
to meet with the Front Royal Road on the east, the Middle Road to
the west, and curved into the Valley Pike at Bartonsville to the southwest. This small road network allowed some businesses in Kernstown
to survive, including a butcher and wheelwright shop, smithy, coo-
perage, general store, and the Beemer Tavern which rested south of
Hoge Run, where the turnpike veered gently eastward. Hoge Run, a
tributary of Opequon Creek and named after one of the area's first
settlers, ran in a southeast direction across the Valley Pike at
Kernstown, emptying into the creek two miles southeast of the village. Additionally, Opequon Church, a sturdy stone Presbyterian
house of worship, stood near the village west of the turnpike on the
site of the original structure built in 1736. The church and the
creek are said to be named for Opeckenough, the chief of a Tidewater tribe whose braves drove the Iroquois out of the Valley in the
1600s (Legend has it that the successful chief's son was Shawnee;
he was destined to organize his own tribe).

After the Indians left at the end of the seventeenth century, a
mixture of Pennsylvania Germans, Quakers, and Scotch-Irish settlers occupied Kernstown and the hilly landscape that surrounds
it. The war took several inhabitants from Kernstown; however, the
small shops continued to stay in business during the early months
of 1862. Kernstown apparently fell into disrepair by the time the
Federals occupied Winchester. An Ohio soldier, passing through
the hamlet, was struck by the untidy condition of the village and
described Kernstown as "a shabby town that looked wretched enough
in comparison with the beautiful country that surrounded it." Another Ohioan tempered his remarks about Kernstown to his family;
he explained that it resembled many towns on the Valley Pike, ". . .
as long as the moral Law, only one street along the Pike; the regular
old fashion Post towns, 2 or 3 Stage offices or Hotels."[13]

One of the wealthier Irish residents of Kernstown was Joseph
P. Mahaney. His two-story red brick house stood approximately
twenty yards west of the pike at the southern outskirts of Kernstown.
The Valley Pike turned from south to southwest in front of Mahaney's

dwelling. Mahaney was a sixty-three-year-old farmer and widower whose real estate had been valued at approximately 10,000 dollars in 1860. Mahaney did not witness the flourish of activity that developed along the turnpike in front of his home on Saturday evening. Known for his Union sympathies, the Kernstown resident had been taken prisoner by General Jackson when Stonewall evacuated Winchester on the night of March 11. Mahaney and twenty other Union men were subsequently incarcerated in Staunton.[14]

On Sunday morning, March 23, 1862, the Mahaney property in southern Kernstown was reoccupied, not by its owner, but by Captain R. Preston Chew's horse artillery. Turner Ashby had returned to the Winchester area and this time he had reinforcements. Four companies of infantry from the Stonewall Brigade—Companies D, H, and I from the 2nd Virginia and Company H of the 27th Virginia, all under the command of Captain John Quincy Adams Nadenbousch—had joined Ashby one hour earlier. Captain Nadenbousch, a former mill proprietor from nearby Martinsburg, had led Company D of the 2nd Virginia until given charge of a four-company battalion earlier in the week. They supported Colonel Ashby as he harassed the Federals during their Strasburg reconnaissance of March 18–March 20; now many of the same men were ordered to move from Strasburg at the break of dawn to reinforce Ashby again. This they did, meeting Ashby at Bartonsville with his command by 8:00 A.M. The men were working on empty stomachs but were eager for action.[15]

Ashby had moved his command of cavalry, infantry, and horse artillery from Bartonsville, a hamlet that rested on the turnpike between Kernstown and Newtown, and advanced them another two miles northward along the Valley Pike. The cavalry commander halted his horse artillery one-quarter mile south of Hoge Run and Captain Chew ordered one of his artillery pieces, the British Blakely gun, to unlimber on the slightly elevated lawn in rear of the Mahaney house.[16] In the meantime, several

Captain John Quincy Adams Nadenbousch, 2nd Virginia Infantry, Company D
Courtesy of Ben Ritter

horsemen from the 7th Virginia Cavalry galloped through Kernstown toward the unsuspecting Federal pickets.

John Stough and David Lewis, two members of Company C, 8th Ohio, wandered beyond their outpost in search of something to eat. Supposing no danger existed, the two friends "found" a pie while picketing near Kernstown and sat down to share it. Both pickets noted a squad of cavalry forty yards ahead of them, east of the Valley Pike. Believing they were Union horsemen, the Buckeyes continued to eat their breakfast without concern. Behind them a company of Federal cavalry came galloping up the Valley Pike. Stough and Lewis witnessed the squad of cavaliers in front of them fire at the Federal horsemen, then fall back. At that point the two infantrymen realized how close they had come to being attacked by Ashby's men. They wisely withdrew one-half mile northward and rejoined their company.[17]

Within minutes of the return of the 8th Ohio's wayward pickets, Captain Chew's artillerists loaded the Blakely gun on the lawn of the Mahaney house. Chew quickly examined the cannon and ordered it to be fired at the Federal pickets less than one mile north of this position. The quiet morning was suddenly interrupted at 9:00 A.M. by the peculiar rifle-like sound of Ashby's "English pet."[18]

The recipient of Chew's first shot was Colonel Jeremiah C. Sullivan. Sullivan had been riding on the heights south of Winchester, scouting good campgrounds for his command in accordance with General Shields's orders, when Chew's artillery salvo greeted him. Sullivan quickly sent his adjutant back to Colonel Nathan Kimball, who was still in charge of the forces on the field. Kimball arrived within minutes of the opening shot and prepared to meet the force in his front.[19]

Kimball reacted quickly and decisively. He had massed his own First Brigade, Daum's artillery, and a squadron of cavalry south of town the previous night. This movement obeyed General Shields's instructions to move at daylight to drive out or capture the force in his front.[20] Although Shields, with a little influence from Banks, believed the area was cleared on Sunday morning, no one bothered to tell Nathan Kimball. He was preparing to move the division forward when Chew's Blakely gun opened fire. Kimball now had a ready force to react to the aggressive Southern cavalier.

Kimball recalled Colonel Carroll from his attempt at a family reunion and ordered him to advance his regiment along both sides of the turnpike to drive the force out from their front. Confederate cavalry pickets had advanced to the heights west of the Valley Pike approximately three-quarters of a mile north of the Mahaney house. Lieutenant Colonel Franklin Sawyer of the 8th Ohio had command of the western skirmish line, initially consisting of Companies B, E and H, but picking up two more (C and D) along the route. These companies advanced with loud cheers and drove Ashby's most advanced squadron off the heights and forced them southward toward Chew's artillery position below Kernstown.[21]

Kimball scaled the hill and ordered artillery to support him on the summit. This height was known as Pritchard's Hill. One of the area's pioneer settlers, William Hoge, made the hill his home in 1735. He eventually donated the land near Hoge Run at the southern base of the hill for Opequon Church in 1745. In 1756 the ground was granted to Rees Pritchard. Pritchard's grandson built a red brick house on the southern portion of the height in 1854, just to the east of Hoge's cabin.[22] The crest of the hill consisted of three cleared knolls, each peak about seventy yards from the others, forming a triangle. The two knolls that formed the base of the triangle lay to the south of the peak. It was an ideal location for artillery positions for it allowed adequate distance for the cannons to recoil. Fortunately for Nathan Kimball and the Federal division, Ashby had neglected to place Chew on the height that morning, choosing a more modest elevation south of Pritchard's Hill instead. A more dominating Southern occupation of the height would have inflicted several casualties on any Union force that attempted to clear it.

Colonel Kimball quickly discovered the treasure in his possession. Pritchard's Hill provided a commanding view of the area from Winchester to Bartonsville. A higher elevation, called Sand or Sandy Ridge by the locals, lay one mile to the west of Pritchard's Hill. Kimball chose not to occupy this height, realizing the force in his front lay more to the east of his position. A dirt road, appropriately called the Middle Road, bisected the valley created by the two heights. It was muddy and impassible for heavy wagons this morning, and all the low plain to the east of it was marshy from the drenching rains which had soaked the fields during the previous week. Forces would not feasibly use the road, particularly when the macadamized Valley Pike paralleled it one mile to the east.[23] These factors may have convinced Colonel Kimball not to place a force on Sandy Ridge. His neglect of that height would haunt him before the afternoon was over.

Lieutenant Colonel Daum's artillery arrived on the height shortly after Kimball made it his headquarters. Initially, Daum chose only rifled pieces to occupy the hill. His former unit, Battery A, 1st West Virginia Artillery, was the first on the hill and was now under the command of Captain John Jenks. Daum ordered Jenks to place his partial battery of four ten-pounder Parrotts on the western base knoll and to immediately return Chew's fire. Captain Joseph Clark's

Battery E, 4th U.S. Artillery, soon brought an additional six ten-pounder Parrotts. These guns were placed to the left of Jenks's battery on the eastern base knoll and soon fired away at Chew's outmanned three-gun battery. Two more rifled cannons from Battery B, 1st West Virginia, added additional firepower to the Union artillery position.[24]

Federal infantry supported the cannons. The closest available regiment, the 67th Ohio of Kimball's brigade, climbed Pritchard's Hill and took position near Jenks's pieces. The 5th Ohio of Sullivan's brigade had been heading for their camp after picketing the whole night. Marching on the Cedar Creek Grade Road, it was immediately sent to Pritchard's Hill to support Federal cannons. They protected the Parrotts of Battery B, 1st West Virginia.[25]

Despite the repulse of his left flank early on, Ashby continued to advance east of the turnpike. The two other guns of Chew's battery, a twelve-pounder howitzer and a Tredegar iron six-pounder, were wheeled north of Kernstown. Ashby also ordered Captain Nadenbousch and his four Stonewall Brigade companies forward to support the guns which rolled beyond a stone wall that ran eastward and perpendicular to the Valley Pike, directly across the road from the dirt lane that led to the Pritchard house. The wall touched the southern edge of an oblong stretch of woods on Isaac Baker's property. A small section of the woods jutted westward from the main wood lot for approximately 300 yards, terminating at the turnpike. Nadenbousch threw two companies forward toward the woodline, while the other half of his command stayed behind the wall that lay 400 yards south of the jutting arm of trees. This area east of the turnpike and west of the old Front Royal Road consisted of a low plain without hills; therefore, Colonel Kimball could easily see the action developing on that flank.[26]

Colonel Carroll pushed three companies of the 8th Ohio along the low eastern plain; Companies F and G marched in the advance line while Company K followed in reserve. Carroll observed the Confederate cannons fall back beyond the woods as the Federal infantry advanced toward them. The 8th Ohio companies joined three companies of the 67th Ohio (A, F, and I) who had been picketing the area since early morning. Before the two forces linked, the 67th Ohio received some fire through the woodline in their front. This was the jutting arm of woods that ran from the main wood lot and tapered to the turnpike. Carroll's men were at the northern edge of the treeline and Nadenboush with his skirmish companies lined the woods less than 100 yards south of the Federal infantry.[27] (See Map 4A)

Moving to the front of his cautious skirmishers, Carroll rode through the obstructing trees toward the enemy force in his front. At 9:50 A.M. he led his force of 200 men into the woods where he was instantly greeted by a barrage of small arms fire from Nadenboush. The volley riddled Carroll's coat cape with bullet holes, but the Maryland native escaped unhurt. Private S. W. Drake, Company K of the 8th Ohio, was not as fortunate. He fell dead at the first volley, making him the first soldier to die in the Battle of Kernstown. Eight additional casualties were tallied as Carroll pushed his men through the arm of woods. Nadenboush ordered his reserve forward to repel the Federals while Chew's two pieces, supported by Ashby's cavalry, continued lobbing shells from the rear.[28]

Colonel Kimball, perched upon the crest of Pritchard's Hill, observed the action on the plain three-quarters of a mile to the east. Carroll needed help. Kimball sent his own former regiment, the 14th Indiana Infantry, to Carroll's support shortly before 10:00 A.M. The Hoosiers, commanded by Lieutenant Colonel William Harrow, advanced one mile and slowly moved across the Valley Pike where Harrow halted his men in a meadow, well to the north of the woods where Carroll and Nadenboush exchanged skirmish fire. Kimball's adjutant galloped to Harrow with instructions to proceed farther to support Carroll. By 10:15 A.M. the combined force of Harrow and Carroll outnumbered Nadenboush by five to one, forcing the Confederate captain to retire his command to the confines of the stone wall that bounded the southern edge of the woods. Nadenbousch rallied his men one-quarter of a mile to the south of his most advanced position.[29]

Major Harry G. Armstrong of Shields's staff, doing double duty as Shields's assistant adjutant general, witnessed the opening action and galloped back to Winchester. He informed Banks and Shields at the Seevers house that he believed there was no hostile force, save for Ashby again. Banks looked on while Shields had his attending physician scribble a note to return to Kimball.[30]

Shields handed his note to Colonel John S. Mason of the 4th Ohio. Mason's regiment camped at Berryville, but the colonel was in Winchester on Sunday morning. General Shields pressed Mason, a West Pointer, into service as a special aide to keep him informed of the events occurring four miles south of his headquarters. Mason, with note in hand, accompanied Major Armstrong to Pritchard's Hill.[31]

Nathan Kimball left no doubt that he was in charge of the division on this morning. While Ashby's command retreated to its new position, Kimball read Shields's note. Shields believed that Ashby's center was unsupported at the turnpike and that he had reinforced

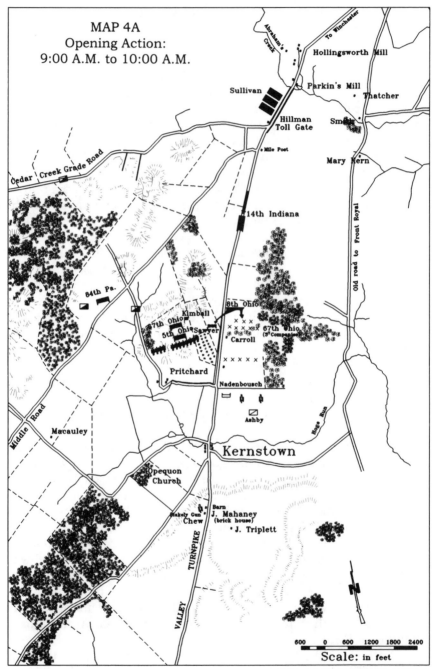

MAP 4A
Opening Action:
9:00 A.M. to 10:00 A.M.

Abraham's Creek

To Winchester

Hollingsworth Mill

Sullivan

Parkin's Mill

Thatcher

Hillman
Toll Gate

Smith

Mary Kern

Mile Post

Cedar Creek Grade Road

14th Indiana

Old road to Front Royal

84th Pa.

8th Ohio

Kimball

7th Ohio

67th Ohio
(3 Companies)

5th Ohio Sawyer

Carroll

Pritchard

Nadenbousch

Macauley

Ashby

Ross Run

Middle Road

Kernstown

Opequon
Church

Barn
Blakely Gun J. Mahaney
Chew   (brick house)

• J. Triplett

VALLEY TURNPIKE

600   0   600 1200 1800 2400

Scale: in feet

Map by Marcus D. Lemasters

his right and left on elevated ground. Shields recommended that Kimball break the enemy's center and get behind him using skirmishers supporting a column composed of cavalry, infantry, and four pieces of artillery. Shields also wanted a simultaneous charge made against Chew's guns while the center column cut off the retreat. Shields ended his message by conceding that he had no advantage of being there in person and he left the management of the force to Kimball's discretion. Shields urged his subordinate to act in the most practicable fashion because, in his own opinion, "there is no force before you but that we encountered the other day."

Despite the prodding by his injured superior, Nathan Kimball ignored the recommendation and remained on Pritchard's Hill, on the defensive, with the 5th Ohio and six companies of the 67th Ohio while the 8th Ohio, 14th Indiana, and three companies of the 67th Ohio skirmished east of the turnpike. The colonel realized that his position was strong for defense and the force he faced included infantry. Kimball incorrectly believed that his line was outnumbered at this point and that his flanks were in danger. He sent a request for reinforcements from the two other brigades of the division. Shields believed his colonel to be overly cautious, but sent orders to Erastus B. Tyler to move his Third Brigade from its camps north of town toward the tollgate. He also ordered Colonel Sullivan, commander of the Second Brigade, to support Kimball's force.[32]

The two Union skirmishing regiments gratefully received the additional reinforcements. By 10:15 A.M., as the skirmish developed between Colonels Carroll and Nadenbousch, Kimball ordered Sullivan's brigade to support his skirmish line. As Sullivan's regiments marched through Milltown, an attractive young lady stood at the gate of her residence, waved her handkerchief, and bade the men "God Speed." Sullivan collected his command, less the 5th Ohio which had already climbed Pritchard's Hill to support artillery, near Hillman's Tollgate where the previous evening's action had opened. His four available regiments (the 66th Ohio remained at Winchester on detached service) had been picketing the roads of the southern Winchester region throughout the night and would receive no rest this day. The brigade moved to the east of the pike by 10:15 A.M.: the 39th Illinois anchored the extreme left near the old Front Royal Road, followed on their right by the 62nd Ohio and the 13th Indiana. This force of approximately 1,500 effectives covered one-half a mile and advanced with a distance of nearly one mile between them and the two and one-half skirmishing regiments in their front. Although constantly exposed to shot and shell from Chew's battery, Sullivan's brigade suffered few casualties this morning.[33]

The Union cavalry, under Colonel Thornton F. Brodhead, was also called into action. Approximately 700 Federal horse soldiers organized in fourteen companies from western Virginia, Maryland, and Pennsylvania were available for service this morning. [Companies A and C of the 1st Ohio Cavalry were still en route from Paw Paw and would not reach the field until the afternoon.] Brodhead delegated the entire command to his lieutenant colonel, Joseph T. Copeland. Most of the cavalry patrolled the Romney Road, supported the Union artillery, and guarded the right flank near Pritchard's Hill. The Washington (Pennsylvania) Cavalry, a squadron commanded by Captain Andrew J. Greenfield, was sent to the Union left flank at the Front Royal Road with instructions to "watch the enemy on his right." Captain Greenfield and his thirty men patrolled the road to the left and front of the 8th Ohio skirmishers; Greenfield constantly sent messages to Pritchard's Hill concerning his observations. Suddenly, over 100 horsemen of the 7th Virginia Cavalry appeared in front of Greenfield's company. Ashby had extended the Confederate right with half of his force to flank the Federals. Approximately one third of a mile still separated the opposing cavalry, but Ashby's men closed in.[34]

Colonel Kimball countered Ashby's newest movements. He ordered Battery B, 1st West Virginia, under the command of Captain Samuel Davey, from Pritchard's Hill to the Valley Pike. Davey unlimbered his ten-pounder Parrotts between Sullivan's brigade and Carroll's skirmish line. The 5th Ohio followed Davey to support his two cannons. Taking position behind the Parrotts, the Ohioans anchored Sullivan's right flank.[35] George Neese, manning Chew's Blakely gun near the Mahaney house, well remembered Davey's opening shot:

> . . . I saw it flying in its graceful curve through the air, coming directly toward the spot where I was standing. I watched it until it struck the ground about fifteen feet in front of me. I was so interested in the skyball, in its harmless appearance, and surprised that a shell could be so plainly seen during its flight, that I forgot for a moment that danger lurked in the black speck that was descending to the earth before me like a schoolboy's innocent plaything. It proved to have been a percussion shell, and when it struck the ground it exploded and scattered itself in every direction around me, and threw up dirt and gravel like a young volcano. Some of the gravel struck me in the arm. Then I left that place instantly, as I did not have any inclination whatever to watch any more shell just then, and my gun had already retired.[36]

Additional pressure from a crack rifle company wreaked havoc on Chew's battery. The Andrew Sharpshooters, an independent rifle company recruited at Lynnfield, Massachusetts, and named after the state governor, were ordered toward Carroll's line. Over half of the company exceeded six feet in height and they carried custom-made rifles that weighed as much as seventy pounds. The guns were equipped with telescopic sights which improved their range of accurate fire to 500 yards. The sharpshooters, in addition to Davey's battery, proved to be too much for the gunners in Ashby's horse artillery; they were forced to withdraw their three cannons one-half mile south along the turnpike.[37]

Tremendously outnumbered and without adequate artillery support, Ashby withdrew the rest of his command southward. He began the morning with the impression that a mere token force was in the vicinity; Nadenbousch's reinforcements should have been adequate to secure Winchester prior to General Jackson's arrival in the afternoon. By 10:30 A.M. the scenario had changed. Ashby could see no fewer than six and one-half Union infantry regiments as well as twelve ten-pounder Parrotts positioned on the high ground north of the Confederate skirmish line. He saw Nadenbousch getting flanked on his left and Sullivan's brigade in heavy massing columns through the woods in the rear. Ashby ordered the infantry captain to withdraw, first to the road that connected the turnpike with the paralleling Old Front Royal Road at Kernstown, then an additional mile to high ground still east of the pike. Nadenbousch suffered ten casualties within his command during the hour-long skirmish and retreat. Federal casualties were equal in number; all were in Carroll's command.[38]

Captain Nadenbousch made extraordinary efforts to prevent his wounded from falling into the hands of his adversary. While withdrawing from Kernstown, Nadenbousch came across the wounded Lieutenant Thomas Link, Company H, who suffered from a crippling thigh bone fracture. Nadenbousch, with the help of other infantry, hoisted Link upon his large bay to remove him from the field. Members of the 8th Ohio closed in and one member of Colonel Carroll's force, Lieutenant A. H. Nickerson, unhorsed Link by firing at the party that aided the injured soldier; the remaining Confederates around Link fled the field to avoid capture. Nickerson was certain he wounded the man that tried to save the injured Southern lieutenant. Helping Link to a house at Kernstown later that day, Nickerson inquired as to the name of the officer he wounded. Over a quarter of a century later, the remorseful Union veteran apologetically described the event in a letter to a member of the Stonewall Brigade—"I fired at the party in the excitement of the occasion (it was my first battle)"—and he sought the name and outcome of the man he wished he never wounded. Nickerson apparently never received an answer to either question.[39]

The Federals cautiously pursued Ashby's retreating skirmishers. Colonel Carroll moved his command into the village of Kernstown and sent word to his lieutenant colonel, Franklin Sawyer, to send an additional company from the western side of the turnpike to assist in the pursuit. Sawyer complied, removing Captain William Kenney's Company B to join his colonel's command. At this juncture, the synchronized movements under Carroll and Sawyer disintegrated and the 8th Ohio's colonel lost sight of Lieutenant Colonel Sawyer's five skirmishing companies of approximately 220 men. Colonel Carroll, with eight companies from the 8th and 67th Ohio consisting of forty to fifty men in each unit, advanced his command to grassy fields south of Kernstown and halted his men there. Sullivan ordered his brigade to close the distance between his men and the regiments of Kimball's brigade. Sullivan halted his men at a point 200 yards to the rear of the eastern skirmish line.

In the meantime, Lieutenant Colonel Sawyer found little resistance on the western side of the Valley Pike and his men suffered no casualties. After Company B was sent across the Valley Pike to Colonel Carroll, four companies of the 8th Ohio Infantry remained under his command. Additionally, Company F of the 13th Indiana under Captain T. M. Kirkpatrick attached themselves to the skirmish flank. They had made an effort to join the rest of their regiment in Sullivan's brigade two hours earlier, but were ordered to form the right of Sawyer's skirmishers. By 11:00 A.M. Sawyer halted his men south of Kernstown in the churchyard of the old Opequon Church.[40]

Artillery limbers rolled forward to support the skirmish line to attempt to drive Ashby away from Kernstown. Captain Samuel Davey was ordered to lead his two ten-pounder Parrotts of Battery B southward on the Valley Pike past the village of Kernstown. He unlimbered his pieces across the road from the Mahaney house, where Chew had opened the contest two hours earlier. The 5th Ohio followed Davey's guns and halted in a meadow behind the battery. Lieutenant Colonel Sawyer, now to the right and rear of the two cannons, decided that Davey needed infantry support and advanced his command forty rods south from the Opequon Church to the front and west of the battery. The two regiments and the rifled guns were the most advanced Federal force, positioned on level ground covering a five hundred yard front at the southern outskirts of Kernstown. (See Map 4B)

By 11:15 A.M., Turner Ashby had become aware of the infantry and artillery moving toward him from both sides of the Valley Pike. He had his own cavalry and Nadenbousch's infantry companies under cover of a dense wood on elevated ground one and one-half miles southeast of Kernstown. One of Chew's artillery pieces was close by, while the other two guns of the horse artillery sat near the turnpike about one-half mile from Captain Davey's pieces. All three Confederate guns opened fire on Davey who quickly readied his pieces and returned fire. The air filled with shot and shell flying over the heads of both lines and shocking the 5th Ohio behind Davey into believing that a masked Confederate battery of twelve guns was playing into their ranks. Chew's twelve-pounder howitzer was the first gun to be sighted correctly and it sent a shell toward Davey's guns. The round exploded, spewing shell fragments that decapitated an artillerist and wounded a Buckeye soldier behind him. The fury had quite an effect on Captain Davey. Reasoning that the Confederate horse artillery was a stronger force than his two pieces, the young artillery officer withdrew his battery, without orders, to the rear of the Union skirmish line. Davey's first action produced a lingering effect on this overmatched artillerist; he resigned from the army ten days later.[41]

Battery B's sudden departure temporarily threw the 5th Ohio into confusion. The regiment rallied and returned to Pritchard's Hill. The crest now overflowed with Federal cannons and soldiers. Captain Lucius Robinson's Battery L, 1st Ohio Light Artillery, had rolled to the top of Pritchard's Hill shortly after the 5th Ohio and Davey's two-gun battery left the hill two hours earlier. Robinson's six guns, a mix of twelve-pounder howitzers and six-pounder smoothbores and rifled pieces, unlimbered on the knoll behind the ten ten-pounder Parrott rifles from Jenks's and Clark's batteries. The sixteen cannons on Pritchard's Hill formed a triangle and the 5th Ohio filled the center of the formation. With the 5th Ohio's return to add to the 300 artillerists already crowding the crest of Pritchard's Hill, the 67th Ohio found themselves forced out of their position as artillery support. They filed off to the west and reformed in a small patch of woods at the base of the knolls.[42]

The Union skirmishers near Kernstown found they were too far in advance of friendly artillery positions on Pritchard's Hill. Both Carroll and Sawyer were receiving artillery fire from Ashby's men in front, and unexpectedly from Daum's gunners in the rear. Unwilling to repeat the same mini-disaster that occurred during the March 18–20 Strasburg reconnaissance, where the Federal artillerists nearly killed men in their own ranks, the skirmish line on both sides of the Valley Pike withdrew north of the hamlet.[43]

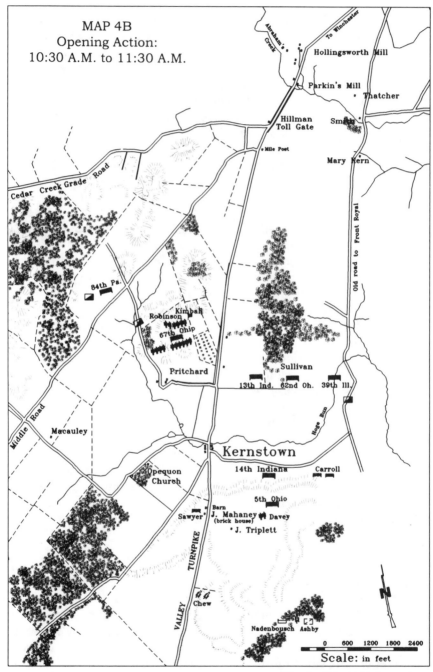

MAP 4B
Opening Action:
10:30 A.M. to 11:30 A.M.

To Winchester

Abraham's Creek

Hollingsworth Mill

Parkin's Mill

Thatcher

Hillman
Toll Gate

Smith

Mary Kern

Mile Post

Cedar Creek Grade Road

Old road to Front Royal

84th Pa.

Kimball

Robinson

67th Ohio

Pritchard

Sullivan

13th Ind. 62nd Oh. 39th Ill.

Hoge Run

Middle Road

Macauley

Kernstown

Opequon
Church

14th Indiana

Carroll

5th Ohio

Barn

Sawyer

J. Mahaney
(brick house)

Davey

J. Triplett

VALLEY TURNPIKE

Chew

Nadenbousch Ashby

0   600 1200 1800 2400

Scale: in feet

Map by Marcus D. Lemasters

By noon, no active pursuit developed against Ashby. Colonel Kimball appeared satisfied to remain in his defensive posture. A sporadic artillery exchange prevented both sides from staging any offensive action but inflicted no further damage on either line. Casualties had been light; fewer than twenty-five men fell throughout the morning action. Strategically, Ashby realized that he would need to wait for General Jackson to arrive with the remainder of the Valley District division in order for the Southerners to force their way into Winchester. On the Federal side, Colonel Kimball wanted Shields's full division at hand because he expected Ashby to receive infantry support before the afternoon was over.

Colonel Mason remained with Kimball throughout the morning. The lull allowed Kimball time to inspect and reposition his lines, but the colonel commanding chose to keep his force in its current position. Colonel Mason suggested that it would be prudent to throw some troops toward the right of their current position—presumedly referring to Sandy Ridge. Kimball replied that one of his regiments, the 84th Pennsylvania, patrolled the height. In fact, however, this regiment idled in the valley created by Pritchard's Hill and Sandy Ridge, leaving Sandy Ridge unoccupied. When Mason pressed the issue by suggesting that Colonel Kimball ride forward to inspect the ground in his front, he was told by the stubborn commander that the flanks were well protected and that he could see clearly to the front. Mason decided it was time to report the progression of action to General Shields.

General Shields had grown impatient with Colonel Kimball's direction. Colonel Mason returned to his headquarters and reported that despite Kimball's request for all available support, Mason believed that the enemy force was the same as the small one that had harassed Shields the previous evening. Shields dictated another message to his physician, Dr. McAbee, and gave it to Colonel Mason to deliver once again to Colonel Kimball.[44]

Colonel Mason returned to Pritchard's Hill at 1:30 P.M. with General Shields's directive which repeated the order sent three hours earlier. Two years after the event, Nathan Kimball remembered the message well:

> General Shields ordered me to concentrate my forces and fight the enemy on the plain, assuring me, that his force was less than mine, and that I could easily beat him there; but so confident was I from circumstances that passed under my observation on the field, that the enemy had not yet exhibited his real strength, and that it was his purpose to draw me from the strong position I held, that he might pass

my right, and, cutting me off from Winchester, capture the whole command; that I disobeyed his orders and remained in my first position and on the defensive. . . .[45]

A severe overestimation of the force in his front generated Kimball's recalcitrance. Although it was true that what he faced throughout the morning was larger than the previous evening's skirmish force, the four Stonewall Brigade companies added merely 150 infantrymen to Ashby's cavalry, giving the Southerners 450 soldiers to battle two Union brigades. This huge disparity in strength was apparent to Shields's aides, but not so to Nathan Kimball. He resolved to remain in his defensive stance and committed an act of insubordination to achieve that goal.

As erroneous as Kimball's judgement was, his decision was vindicated by developments on the field. Shortly after noon, he became aware of movements occurring approximately two and one-half miles in his front near Bartonsville. He studied the developments for the next one and one-half hours. Shortly after receiving (and refusing) Shields's order, Kimball saw soldiers massing in Barton's woods west of the Valley Pike and south of Opequon Church. This force did not belong to Ashby, for his command was still held in check several hundred yards east of the turnpike. The massing columns represented the "real strength" that had made Kimball apprehensive. General Thomas J. Jackson and his Valley District division had arrived at Kernstown.

The lull was over.

Chapter Five

"An Awful Introduction"

General Thomas J. Jackson expected little resistance from the "token" Federal force in and around Winchester on Sunday, March 23, 1862. Sending Captain Nadenbousch and four infantry companies to reinforce Colonel Turner Ashby's 7th Virginia Cavalry at daybreak seemed sufficient to clear the way for the rest of his division when they reached Winchester in the early forenoon. Stonewall Jackson and his thinned division departed from their Cedar Creek camps starting at 7:00 A.M., nearly two hours after Nadenbousch marched to Ashby's support with his skirmishers. Leading the northward march to Winchester was Brigadier General Richard B. Garnett and the Stonewall Brigade, followed by Colonel Samuel V. Fulkerson's two-regiment brigade, and Colonel Jesse Burks's brigade in the rear. Five batteries of twenty-four cannons joined their respective brigades on the march. A member of the Liberty Hall Volunteers noted that the men marched leisurely with "merry hearts" and expected to be in Winchester by nightfall. One of the gunners recalled that "none of us dreamed of a battle," as the Winchester area was expected to be void of Federal troops by the time they arrived there.[1]

Five hours and twelve miles later, General Jackson delivered his 3,300 infantry and artillerymen to Bartonsville, where the Opequon Creek crossed the Valley Pike five miles south of Winchester. Waiting for the rear of the column to close up the ranks, the men felt and heard the rumbling of the dueling artillery less than two miles away—near the village of Kernstown. General Jackson quickly realized that his plans had fallen apart. The "token" force, apparently greater in strength than anticipated, contested Ashby's movements toward Winchester and prevented his reinforced command from reoccupying Stonewall's former base of operations.[2]

Realizing that a continued march on the turnpike risked un-needed exposure, General Jackson ordered his command to file off to the west of the road. A dirt lane bisected this area approximately one mile west of the turnpike and connected Bartonsville with Kernstown. Between this back road and the Valley Pike lay the fields and woods of "Hanover Lodge," Joseph Barton's estate. The woods enveloped the road one mile northwest of Barton's house. On the northern side of this road, the woods widened and were bordered by wooden fences, finally terminating one-half mile south of Opequon Church. Jackson ordered his men into the wooded area south of the Barton farm, where the treeline resembled the shape of a boot, the heel facing east and the toe pointing south. At this point the men loaded their weapons, took regimental roll calls, and awaited the division commander's next orders.[3] (See Map 5A)

As his men filed off to the west of the turnpike near Bartonsville, General Jackson rode forward with his two aides, Lieutenants George Junkin and Sandie Pendleton, to reconnoiter the landscape near Kernstown. Observing the Federal cannons on Pritchard's Hill, Jackson "regarded [the Federals'] position in front too strong to be forced with my command, but believed it could be done by turning his right."[4] Jackson was ignorant of the enemy strength exposed to Ashby throughout the morning. Remarkably, he never conferred directly with his cavalier upon arriving on the field; therefore, Jackson was unaware that at least six and one-half regiments, approximately 3,000 Federal troops, were exposed to and fought against Ashby during the previous four hours.

Stonewall rode back toward his division resting in Barton's Woods. The major general realized that his division was not in prime battle readiness. What few men he had with him had trudged over thirty-five miles during the previous thirty hours in inclement weather. Furloughs, recruiting duties, and straggling reduced Jackson's effective infantry strength to 3,000 men, while his full division force, including cavalry and artillery, numbered under 3,700 effectives. The fact that it was Sunday also weighed in with the pious commander. General Jackson had two options. The most favorable one was to wait until morning, allowing him the opportunity to carefully devise a plan to defeat his adversary, while affording time both for his tired troops to rest and to receive the greatly needed militia to reinforce his command. Jackson's after-battle report explains his reasons for leaning toward a second option:

> Though it was very desirable to prevent the enemy from leaving the valley, yet I deemed it best not to attack until morning. But subsequently ascertaining that the Federals had a position from which our forces could be seen, I concluded that it would be dangerous to postpone it until the

next day, as re-inforcements might be brought up during the night.[5]

Stonewall Jackson's conclusion contradicted General Johnston's stated mission for him as commander of the Valley District: ". . . keeping so near the enemy as to prevent him from making any considerable detachment to reinforce McClellan, but not so near that he [Jackson] might be compelled to fight."[6] By exposing a large infantry force to Colonel Kimball's commanding position on Pritchard's Hill, Jackson could accomplish this mission without engaging his tired soldiers in battle. If Federal reinforcements were subsequently brought up during the night, Jackson would have met his objectives by removing Union troops from McClellan's support without risking the further reduction of his already thinned ranks. However, Stonewall Jackson apparently considered the liberation of Winchester as important as luring Union troops to concentrate their forces against him. He gave up Winchester without a fight eleven days earlier; now he had the opportunity to rout, what he considered to be, an inferior force and reclaim his original base of operation.

General Jackson took the disposition of his men into consideration as well. Upon returning to Barton's Woods, he rode through the ranks of the Stonewall Brigade. He reasoned that since his troops "were in good spirits at the prospect of meeting the enemy, I determined to advance at once."[7]

A council of war was out of the question as far as General Thomas J. Jackson was concerned. Stung by his subordinates' defeat of his plan to surprise Banks with a night fight on March 11, Jackson turned laconic concerning his exact intentions at Kernstown. Rather than discuss any portion of his battle plan with General Garnett, Colonels Fulkerson and Burks, or Turner Ashby, Stonewall chose not to reveal his intentions for any specific movement. Instead, the commanding general would send orders, without explanations, to his brigade and regimental commanders chiefly through his two aides, Lieutenants Sandie Pendleton and George Junkin. Stonewall's secretive nature in battle would become the hallmark of his generalship for the rest of his military career, and Kernstown marked the site of origin for Jackson's inscrutable behavior in battle.

Jackson's off-the-cuff battle plan materialized by 1:30 P.M. Apprehensive about the possibility of Federal skirmishers hiding in Barton's Woods, Stonewall instructed Colonel Fulkerson to take his brigade and scour the woods north and west of his position and

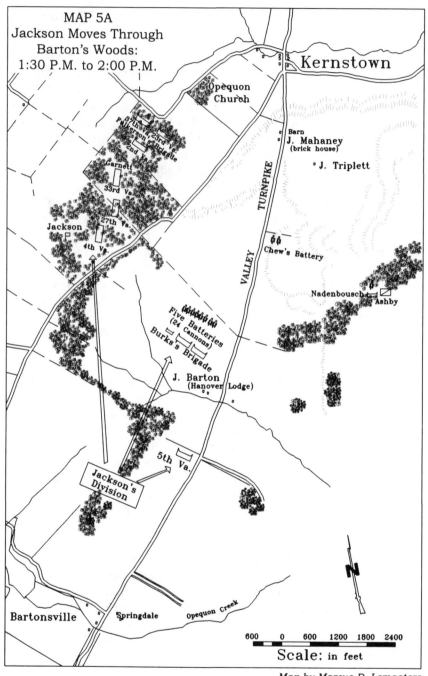

MAP 5A
Jackson Moves Through
Barton's Woods:
1:30 P.M. to 2:00 P.M.

Kernstown

Opequon
Church

Barn
J. Mahaney
(brick house)

J. Triplett

37th Va. 23rd Va.
Fulkerson's Brigade
2nd Va.

Garnett

33rd Va.

Jackson

27th Va.

4th Va.

VALLEY TURNPIKE

Chew's Battery

Nadenbousch
Ashby

Five Batteries
(24 Cannons)
Burks's Brigade

J. Barton
(Hanover Lodge)

5th Va.

Jackson's
Division

N

Bartonsville   Springdale   Opequon Creek

600   0   600   1200 1800 2400

Scale: in feet

Map by Marcus D. Lemasters

clear it of any force that may exist. Fulkerson took the 23rd and 37th Virginia to accomplish his superior's request.[8]

After Fulkerson moved out, Stonewall realized the colonel's small command of 600 officers and men required support. Jackson called on his former brigade for the extra manpower. He first directed General Garnett to place one of his five regiments in reserve. Garnett instructed the 5th Virginia to form behind a stone fence that connected the Valley Pike with the heel of Barton's Woods, one-half mile to the west of the road. Additionally, General Jackson ordered him to send another regiment to support Fulkerson's undersized command. Garnett selected the 2nd Virginia Infantry, Colonel James W. Allen's regiment, for this duty as this unit was the leading regiment of Garnett's command. Allen recalled Company G, under the direction of Major Frank B. Jones, from skirmish duty 300 yards north of the regiment. Jones returned the men, passing in sight of his home of Careysbrooke, which was east of the Valley Pike, one mile south and east of Kernstown. The 2nd Virginia, without the three companies still with Ashby's force, moved quickly northwestward and caught up to Fulkerson's men within one mile of Bartonsville. Stonewall detained Major Jones to use as an additional staff officer, realizing the major's familiarity with the vicinity would be valuable that afternoon.[9]

Within minutes of sending the 2nd Virginia toward Fulkerson's men, General Garnett received a third order from Jackson's aide, Sandie Pendleton, this time to send the remaining regiments of his brigade to follow on the route of Allen's regiment. Garnett placed the 33rd, 27th, and 4th Virginia regiments in marching column and sent them off. Having delivered his superior's message, Pendleton rode to the reserve position occupied by the 5th Virginia at the stone wall running perpendicularly westward from the Valley Pike.[10]

General Jackson used Pendleton to informally restructure his division on the field. All of the batteries, to this point, had operated

Major Frank B. Jones, 2nd Virginia Infantry (From a Pre-war Photograph)
Courtesy of Miss Louisa Crawford Collection, Photograph by Ben Ritter

under the jurisdiction of the brigade commanders. Jackson altered this chain of command by detaching the artillery from the infantry and leaving it in reserve for disposal at his own discretion. Lieutenant Pendleton informed Colonel Fulkerson of this change prior to his movements, but he never informed General Garnett about the plan. Pendleton placed all reserve artillery pieces in front of the 5th Virginia at the stone wall. The three batteries from Garnett's first brigade—Captain William McLaughlin's Rockbridge Artillery, Captain James Waters's West Augusta Artillery, and Captain Joseph Carpenter's Alleghany Artillery—were the advanced cannons on the field. These sixteen guns occupied the heights in an open meadow, north of Hanover Lodge. They were joined by the remaining eight cannons in Burks's and Fulkerson's brigade (Hampden Artillery and Danville Artillery) and were used to guard the left of the Ashby's line against Carroll's skirmishers east of the Valley Pike. This reserve was never seriously threatened, but instead witnessed the waning artillery duel between Daum's gunners and Chew's battery a mile to the north. To these unengaged artillerists, the unfriendly exchange in their front forebode battle and imminent death. One of the Rockbridge gunners witnessed the effect this had on his comrades' consciences; they discarded well-worn packs of poker cards and withdrew their un-worn pocket Testaments to prepare them for what well might be their "Judgment Day."[11]

Jesse Burks's infantry regiments brought up the rear of the column when they left Cedar Creek. They were ordered in reserve to support all of the artillery pieces near the Valley Pike between Bartonsville and Kernstown. One regiment, the 345 soldiers of the 48th Virginia, guarded the division supply trains several miles south of Bartonsville. This left Colonel Burks with only two regiments (the 21st and 42nd Virginia) and one five-company unit (1st Virginia "Irish" Battalion) on the battlefield—a total available force of only 760 effectives.[12]

After Stonewall sent his lieutenant to organize his reserve force, he moved with his former brigade through Barton's Woods toward the leading elements of Fulkerson's two regiments. (See Map 5A.) General Garnett rode near the head of the Stonewall Brigade when he was approached by a staff member who informed him that his rear regiment in the column, the 4th Virginia, was repositioned to the left of the column by General Jackson himself. This represented the second incidence of micromanagement of Garnett's brigade by its former commander (the first being the removal of the three artillery batteries from Garnett's jurisdiction).[13]

At 2:00 P.M. Fulkerson completed his scouring of Barton's Woods and reached the open land approximately 500 yards south and west of Opequon Church. The treeline here was bounded by a dirt road that crossed the Middle Road nearly three-quarters of a mile to the west, and then ran across the center of Sandy Ridge. To the east of Fulkerson's men the road turned sharply northward and ran above the Opequon Church where it gently curved eastward and terminated at the point where Hoge Run bisected the Valley Pike near the Beemer Tavern. Colonel Fulkerson sent an aide to the rear to find General Jackson and inform him that he had completed the brief reconnaissance without incident.[14]

Samuel Vance Fulkerson had been Thomas J. Jackson's choice for leading his brigade in division movements, owing to Stonewall's personal trust and affection for the colonel. The thirty-nine-year-old Fulkerson's military accomplishments to this point had been neither spectacular nor disappointing. The former lawyer and Mexican War veteran was promoted to colonel of the 37th Virginia the previous May. Most recently, Jackson tagged Fulkerson to head the tiny brigade of two regiments. Fulkerson's leadership skills were still green; his command had seen very little action prior to Kernstown, having been stationed in the mountainous terrain of western Virginia where he faced off against Union generals George McClellan and William Rosecrans. He had been part of Brigadier General Robert Seldon Garnett's command and was present when that officer became the first Confederate general to be killed in battle at Corrick's Ford. Transferring to Jackson's Valley District at the end of 1861, he now shared an equal responsibility, if not rank, with General Richard Brooke Garnett, the first cousin of his former superior officer. Stonewall had been pleased with Colonel Fulkerson's accomplishments and held him "in the highest estimate." The subordinate officer was moving on a steady track for Jackson's recommendation to receive a general's star.[15]

General Jackson received the report, spurred his horse "Little Sorrel" through the woods toward the front of the column and arrived at Fulkerson's side within minutes. At the same time Federal artillerists on Pritchard's Hill turned their pieces from south to southwest and fired at the massing column that had caught their attention moments earlier. Only 1,200 yards separated the opposing forces, and Daum's gunners let Jackson know that his men were not invited to stay in their front. As Federal projectiles arced toward Barton's Woods, Jackson hastily studied the enemy's position.

Stonewall enjoyed a clear view to Pritchard's Hill. The sky was clouded as it had been throughout the previous week, but no evidence of fog or mist impeded his line of sight. The afternoon temperature approached fifty degrees and raining artillery fire easily made this the warmest part of the day.[16]

Jackson let the opposing gunners know that he had no intention to remain idle. He scanned the field in his front, ascertained that Pritchard's Hill represented the Federal right flank, and immediately ordered Colonel Fulkerson to "turn" the batteries ensconced on the hill. Notwithstanding the shot and shell from sixteen cannons opposing him, Stonewall Jackson intended to concentrate an infantry force to take out the cannons by turning their right flank.

Under a canopy of menacing Federal projectiles, Colonel Fulkerson placed his two regiments in column by divisions with the 37th Virginia in front and the 23rd Virginia in the rear. Fulkerson galloped to the head of the column and wheeled around to face his men. Raising his hat, Fulkerson called out, "Men, follow me." The front companies of the 37th Virginia tore down a section of a plank fence that bordered a field in front of them and advanced northward directly toward the western edge of Pritchard's Hill, guided on the left by a parallel fence. After their advance carried them 200 yards, the 275 rank and file of the 33rd Virginia launched from the woodline, led General Richard Brooke Garnett.[17] (See Map 5B)

Brigadier General Garnett held the honor of second in command since he, along with Major General Jackson, were the only generals on the field. Despite this distinction, the Stonewall Brigade leader was incredulous at his superior's secretive nature this day. General Jackson had interfered with Garnett's brigade structure and movements over the past two hours without explanation. Once Garnett reached the edge of the woodline, he was instructed to support Colonel Fulkerson who had already set his regiments in motion. Garnett received the order, not through Jackson himself who was within 100 yards of him, but instead via Lieutenant Junkin. The aide directed Garnett to support Fulkerson, but never told the general what Fulkerson's orders were. This lack of communication later induced Garnett to complain about being "kept in as profound ignorance of [Jackson's] plans, instructions, and intentions, as the humblest private in the army."[18]

The Federals on Pritchard's Hill stood in awe as Fulkerson's two regiments and the 33rd Virginia approached the base of the knoll on which they stood. An Ohio private noted that they marched up steadily, in column, with colors flying in the breeze. Another Buckeye complained that all the artillery behind him failed to slow down their progress. The 67th Ohio, who had rested in a patch of woods to the west of the Union artillery, returned to the crest of Pritchard's Hill to counter the threat. Most of the 8th Ohio moved to the rear of the artillery pieces and regrouped behind the summit. Lieutenant Colonel Philip Daum grew uneasy as the enemy column of nearly 1,000 men approached within 500 yards to the right of his position. Believing the visible column was two to three times greater than its actual strength, he repositioned his former battery, now under the command of Lieutenant Jenks, to fire at Fulkerson and Garnett. Daum fumed when several of his artillerists abandoned their pieces in fright. He returned the men at the point of his sword and forced them to remain at their guns, threatening to cut the head off any man who deserted his position.[19]

The 84th Pennsylvania, with their Michigan cavalry support, added their numbers to the Pritchard's Hill batteries. Colonel Murray advanced his regiment from their position west of the Middle Road just as Fulkerson and his brigade launched their attack from the border of Barton's Woods. They reformed on the slope below the cannons. Three and one-half Union regiments (the 84th Pennsylvania, the 67th Ohio, the 5th Ohio and Sawyer's battalion of the 8th Ohio) presented a convincing show of force to counter the Southern assault. The infantry support watched Daum's gunners lower their pieces and find their range. The artillery tore into Fulkerson's column. A Michigan horseman who advanced with the 84th Pennsylvania was exhilarated to see "our noble gunners give the serried ranks of the enemy a sweeping discharge of grape and canister." An Ohio infantryman noted, "As we looked down upon them, we could see our shells knock them right and left." A German member of Jenks's battery insisted that "every gun spit fire and perdition with such magic quickness among the ill-fated mass of human beings and horses."[20]

Fulkerson acknowledged the ferocity of the artillery fire from the moment his two regiments advanced from Barton's Woods. Slowed by the marshy ground and rail fences, Fulkerson turned his men obliquely to the left, exposing his right flank to Daum's guns. His brigade worked frantically to overcome these obstacles, all the while exposed to an artillery fire so heavy that Fulkerson described it as one "that might well have made veterans quail." A shell exploded over Company E, 37th Virginia, killing three men and injuring two others. Even more members from Company D and I succumbed to artillery fire. Lieutenant G. A. Neal was hobbled with a thigh wound; his brother was felled with both of his thighs damaged. Company F attracted the most enemy fire. No fewer than twenty-four of its members fell, nearly half suffered from multiple wounds. The 23rd Virginia, marching behind the 37th Virginia, became equally exposed when Fulkerson turned them to the left and suffered one dozen casualties. Altogether, Fulkerson's brigade tallied eighty-four killed and wounded men at Kernstown. Most of them fell victim to the Federal batteries on Pritchard's Hill.[21]

Unable to turn the cannons by direct assault, Fulkerson aimed his men toward a small grove of trees on the Union right flank. This

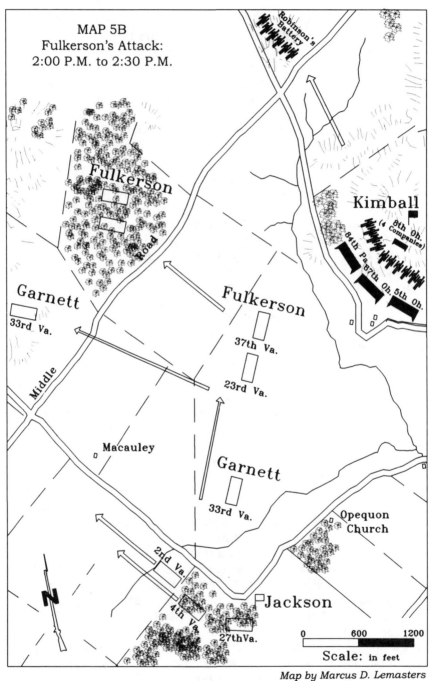

MAP 5B
Fulkerson's Attack:
2:00 P.M. to 2:30 P.M.

Robinson's Battery

Fulkerson

Kimball

8th Oh.
(4 Companies)

84th Pa.

67th Oh. 5th Oh.

Fulkerson
Road

Garnett

33rd Va.

Fulkerson

37th Va.

23rd Va.

Middle

Macauley

Garnett

33rd Va.

Opequon
Church

N

2nd Va.

4th Va.

Jackson

27th Va.

0   600   1200

Scale: in feet

Map by Marcus D. Lemasters

was the same patch of timbers that the 67th Ohio rested in half an hour earlier. Fulkerson's objective was to place the trees between his brigade and the Federal guns. As he worked to save his soldiers, Union artillerists called for three-second fuses to destroy Fulkerson's brigade. Daum's cannoneers opened gaps in the column, but the Southerners closed the breaks and continued forward. Fulkerson noted that as his men attempted to overcome both natural and man-made obstacles, they were harassed by the enemy who threw shot and shell into his column "with great rapidity." An Ohio infantryman supporting the Federal batteries on the hill could not help but be impressed by the persistence of the Virginians. Witnessing the Confederates push onward as shell and canister cut them down by platoons, he declared, "Their bravery was heroic—'worthy of a better cause'—and commanded the admiration and respect of all who witnessed it."[22]

Fulkerson never reached his destination. While the ten rifled cannons of Clark's and Jenks's batteries played upon Fulkerson's ranks, Lieutenant Colonel Daum checkmated his opponent's movement by redeploying the six cannons from Captain Lucius Robinson's Battery L, 1st Ohio Light Artillery, from their initial position near Kimball's headquarters to open ground 500 yards west of Pritchard's Hill. Robinson unlimbered his guns on a small knoll directly across the gate to Pritchard's lane west of the Middle Road. These artillery pieces now commanded the ground to the west of the cluster of trees that Fulkerson initially believed would protect him. Without options, Colonel Fulkerson led his brigade to a larger skirt of woods at the base of Sandy Ridge. The 23rd and 37th Virginia scampered across the Middle Road (One Federal described their movement as "a perfect stampede"). Upon entering the woods, Fulkerson complained of becoming "much annoyed" by the incessant rain of Daum's and Robinson's shells, but he lost only one man here as timber shelter allowed him to protect and rest his men and await orders. The colonel also expected his promised reinforcements to be close at hand.[23]

Those reinforcements never reached Fulkerson's column. General Garnett and the 33rd Virginia advanced over the same path that Fulkerson had created toward Pritchard's Hill, keeping approximately a 200-yard gap between them. After Fulkerson bore to the left, Garnett steered his small column to follow in the same course, but while Jenks's Parrotts played into the ranks of the 23rd and 37th Virginia, Garnett and the 33rd Virginia became easy targets for Clark's battery less than 500 yards away. The general noted the Federal infantry posted below their guns and witnessed the placement of Robinson's guns to the west of the Pritchard's Hill artillery.

Realizing that to continue his course guaranteed doom, he ordered the 33rd's colonel, Arthur Cummings, to move his command obliquely to the left. The 33rd Virginia safely crossed the Middle Road and took cover in the fields at the eastern base of Sandy Ridge. The patch of woods that Fulkerson entered and the low ridge between his position and Pritchard's Hill protected Garnett from Federal artillery. General Garnett and the 33rd Virginia were now 300 yards south and west of Fulkerson's brigade at the base of Sandy Ridge.

From his new position, General Garnett made two discoveries. He determined that Colonel Fulkerson's orders were "to attack the Federal batteries." The redeployment of Union artillery and infantry support rendered these instructions impracticable. Garnett considered the situation precarious; uniting Fulkerson's brigade with the 33rd Virginia provided the attacking force with fewer than 900 soldiers—too small a force to assault infantry and artillery. Colonel Cummings concurred and suggested that the force be taken back to its original position in Barton's Woods. General Garnett sent his staff aide, Lieutenant S. C. Williams, to Fulkerson to communicate his perception concerning the futility of their position. Garnett's decision was solidified by his second discovery: the remainder of his brigade did not move with the 33rd Virginia to support Colonel Fulkerson's troops.[24]

A convoluted system for transferring orders developed between Garnett and his regimental commanders. By his own admission, Garnett had become too preoccupied with observing enemy movements and conducting the 33rd Virginia's movements to organize the rest of his brigade to fulfill General Jackson's orders to support Colonel Fulkerson. He neglected to leave instructions with his regiments before he led the 33rd Virginia from the woods. Jackson's decision not to tell his brigadier what Colonel Fulkerson's orders were left Garnett guessing at the importance and strength of his intended support. Since Garnett had witnessed Jackson positioning Stonewall Brigade regiments during their initial move through the Barton's Woods, he expected Stonewall to continue this practice and personally direct each regiment to move as he saw fit. However, General Jackson had not personally directed Garnett's rear regiments since moving them through Barton's Woods.[25]

From a slight rise on cleared ground one-half mile south of Opequon Church, Stonewall Jackson watched the insufficient support following Fulkerson toward Pritchard's Hill. He sent Major Jones to the woods to find Garnett and order him to move the rest of his brigade to support Fulkerson. Jackson then ordered Sandie Pendleton up from the artillery reserve and sent him to the three remaining Stonewall Brigade regiments to find out why they had

Kernstown Battlefield, 1885
This eastward view is from General Garnett's and the 33rd Virginia's position after they unsuccessfully attacked Pritchard's Hill. The post-battle houses in the left midground are at the base of Pritchard's Hill. The white houses in the upper right are in the village of Kernstown. The clear background terrain is the area east of the Valley Turnpike.
U.S.A.M.H.I.

not also supported Fulkerson. Jones and Pendleton asked the three remaining colonels if General Garnett was with them; to a man they denied seeing their brigadier. Jones returned to Jackson. When asked again by Stonewall where General Garnett was, Jones replied that it appeared Garnett crossed over the Middle Road with the 33rd Virginia. Jones heard the word "impossible" in Stonewall's disgusted response.[26]

At this point Pendleton ordered the remaining regiments to support Fulkerson's advance. At 2:00 P.M. the 2nd Virginia received the three companies that had served with Ashby during the morning skirmish. Captain Nadenbousch delivered Companies D, H, and I to Colonel James W. Allen, increasing the regiment's strength to 310 officers and men. Nadenbousch lost only ten men during the morning action, but the rest of his command was exhausted from their active morning of marching and fighting. Colonel Allen deployed Company B as skirmishers to the right of his regiment and marched the rest of his command westward toward Sandy Ridge to the rear of Fulkerson's command.[27]

The 4th Virginia was next to follow. Company I, the Liberty Hall Volunteers, joined the regiment while it moved forward to the northern woodline. The college company had held rearguard duty in charge of the division wagons in the morning. Dissension overtook the ranks when the company realized a fight was developing and they were likely to miss it. Captain Henry Morrison took his men from the wagons on his own volition and quickly marched his troops to rejoin their regimental comrades. Although the Liberty Hall Volunteers' movement violated General Jackson's order, a company officer reasoned, "the idea of guarding a train whilst a battle was in progress was repugnant to their chivalrous spirits." The 48th Virginia, of Burks's brigade, remained as the sole force to guard the supply wagons.[28]

The college company extended the 4th Virginia's left at the woodline. Colonel Charles Ronald's command, fully united, still numbered fewer than 250 men as it prepared to move. Amidst an avalanche of artillery fire from the elevated Union guns one-half mile in their front, Colonel Ronald redeployed the 4th Virginia in column by divisions to support Garnett and Cummings. Ronald's horse became unnerved by shot and shell that crashed into the timbers surrounding it. The ungovernable animal threw Ronald off its back, disabling the colonel and forcing him to relinquish the 4th's command to Major Albert Pendleton (no direct relationship to Sandie) for the rest of the day.[29]

General Jackson sent orders for the 4th Virginia to move. The regiment advanced westward at about the same time the 33rd Virginia, three hundred yards in front of them, changed direction from north to west in an attempt to support Fulkerson. Watching the shells explode like rockets and bounce with graceful curves around him, an officer in the Liberty Hall Volunteers admitted, "But for the danger, the scene would have been beautiful." Prior to this movement, Lieutenant John Lyle of the Liberty Hall Volunteers looked to his right to see General Jackson sitting on his horse nearby. Lyle noted "his countenance was pale and shewed anxiety. But there was a set about his jaw that boded no good for the foe. . . . He was stripping his front almost bare of troops to hurl the bulk of his small force on the right flank of the enemy. . . . It was a time to look pale and anxious."[30]

Lyle's reminiscences correctly interpreted Thomas J. Jackson's intentions, although the division commander appeared to alter his plan before his orders had been carried out by Fulkerson and Garnett. From the woodline south of Opequon Church, Stonewall modified his strategy when Daum's redeployment of Federal artillery thwarted Fulkerson's and Garnett's attack. The 2nd and 4th

Virginia had begun parallel movements well to the rear of the 33rd Virginia, but it was becoming obvious to Jackson that his infantry could not turn the Union batteries without artillery support. Therefore, Sandy Ridge held the key to Confederate success. Because the military crest of this unoccupied ridge was 100 feet higher than that of Pritchard's Hill, Southern artillery would have a commanding advantage over the Union guns if enough of them could be concentrated there. This deployment depended on three factors: a successful diversion created on the Federal front and left flank, a rapid rearward movement of Confederate batteries from their reserve positions to Sandy Ridge, and adequate infantry support to protect the Southern guns from harassment or capture.

Shortly after 2:00 P.M., General Jackson created a diversion. He sent Lieutenant Junkin to Colonel Turner Ashby to order the 7th Virginia Cavalry commander "to threaten the front and right." Ashby received these orders from his retreated position one and one-half miles south of Kernstown, east of the Valley Pike. Burks's brigade and the remainder of the Confederate artillery extended the cavalier's left across the turnpike. Ashby's command had been greatly reduced when Nadenbousch's infantry was ordered to return to their respective regiments. Additionally, two cavalry companies (seventy men), under the command of Major Oliver R. Funsten, were ordered to the western base of Sandy Ridge (the intended Confederate left flank) where they occupied a knoll that rerouted the Opequon Creek from east to south. This left Ashby with 220 horsemen and Chew's three-gun battery. These men were tired and their horses were in poor condition.

Turner Ashby had been deceived concerning Federal infantry strength prior to the battle, but his subsequent actions during the afternoon at Kernstown accentuated the dash and daring that eventually earned Ashby his general's star. Ashby faced off against the equivalent of five Union infantry regiments east of the turnpike. Leaving two cannons to bear on the enemy's front, Ashby took his remaining gun and advanced farther east to flank the unsuspecting Federals on their left. Rather than merely threaten the Federal left as were his orders, Ashby prepared to assault his adversary.[31]

As Ashby's movements commenced, the Confederate cavalrymen flushed a fox out of its hiding place. The frightened animal dashed toward the Federal lines, chased by Lieutenant Thaddeus Thrasher of Company G, a Maryland unit recruited from Baltimore County. The playful officer chased the bounding fox through fields and across rail fences until he wandered near the Union skirmish lines. Fortunately for Thrasher, his excursion transpired between 2:00 and 2:30 P.M., an inactive period for the Federal left flank. The

Union skirmishers approved of this non-threatening action during their respite; they cheered Thrasher instead of firing upon him. The lieutenant abandoned the chase, returned to his command and asked Ashby to allow him to lead his company in the impending flank charge as he had already "reconnoitered" the ground. Colonel Ashby approved Lieutenant Thrasher's request and Company G led the movements toward the Federal left.[32]

Colonel Carroll remained wary of Ashby's movements in his front. Since forced back by Southern artillery in their front and their own artillery behind them, the five 8th Ohio and three 67th Ohio companies under Carroll's command had been inactive for nearly two hours. The men rested in position north of Kernstown. To their right stood the 14th Indiana whose right flank anchored at the Valley Pike. Directly behind these two units rested three regiments of Sullivan's brigade. Two cannons covered the low plain in front of the 13th Indiana, the regiment on Sullivan's right flank. The total infantry force numbered approximately 2,300 men. Thirty Pennsylvania horse soldiers continued to guard the Front Royal Road on the far left of the Union skirmish line.

At 2:30 P.M. Colonel Kimball discerned Ashby's movements and accordingly sent a message to Lieutenant Colonel Harrow to "look well to the left for an attempt of the enemy to turn that flank." Harrow adjusted his line and rode to Colonel Carroll and repeated Kimball's warning. Carroll responded, "I am looking out carefully for that." Carroll detached one company of the 8th Ohio to guard the east side of the Old Front Royal Road. Carroll then called Captain Andrew J. Greenfield of the Pennsylvania cavalry to him to discuss the deployment of his troops.

Before Carroll's and Greenfield's conference ended, Ashby launched his attack. At the head of his regiment, he charged his horsemen toward the leaderless Federal cavalry company. Ashby's horsemen marveled at the transformation that overtook their commander in battle. Normally quiet and taciturn in camp, he became animated and aggressive, shouting to his men with his unique expressiveness: "Drive them boys! Drive them!" Mounted on his white charger and leading his men forward, Ashby was ubiquitous and reckless, bounding rail and stone fences, exhorting his men the whole while. His ostentatious display that afternoon dominated camp discussions for days afterward.[33]

The bewildered Pennsylvanians scattered as Ashby pushed his men toward the infantry skirmish flank. Lieutenant Thrasher hurled Company G at the 8th Ohio skirmishers. Carroll quickly sent two more companies to assist his flank. These men opened fire upon Ashby's men for the third time in less than twenty-four hours, forcing his men back toward their original line. When the smoke cleared five dead horses, two Union infantrymen, and seven dead and wounded Confederate cavaliers lie strewn on the ground. Among them was the body of Lieutenant Thaddeus Thrasher—killed by the same men who had cheered him moments earlier.[34] (See Map 5C)

Jackson continued his diversion west of the Valley Pike and directly in front of the cannons on Pritchard's Hill. While Ashby engaged Union skirmishers east of the turnpike, Jackson detailed Frank Jones to the artillery reserve near the road. Major Jones sent two pieces of Carpenter's battery to Jackson's position on the high ground south of Opequon Church. The former infantry company ("Alleghany Roughs," Company A, 27th Virginia) of forty-eight men rode their six-pounder Tredegar smoothbore iron guns approximately three-quarters of a mile northwest through Barton's Woods. Sandie Pendleton joined the battery as did the five companies of Captain David B. Bridgford's 1st Virginia "Irish Battalion," which was sent to support the guns.[35]

General Jackson ordered Captain Joseph Carpenter to unlimber his guns on a modest elevation at the right angle formed by the dirt road that connected the Valley Pike at Kernstown with the Middle Road. At a distance of 1,000 yards from Federal infantry, Carpenter's battery fired its first shots in battle, aiming for Union skirmishers who were taking cover in Pritchard's barn below their guns. According to the battery's historian, the first shot hit its mark, crashed through the door of the building, and scattered the Federal soldiers "pell-mell to the four winds." The cannoneers were proud of their hit, as was the ever-observant Stonewall Jackson who clapped his hands and exclaimed "Good, good!" The two guns fired nine more rounds until the Federal skirmishers retreated to the rear of their main line.[36]

The two active Confederate batteries (Carpenter's and Chew's) left a lasting effect on Federal soldiers who to this point had never been exposed to deadly artillery fire. A member of the 5th Ohio, perched on Pritchard's Hill, recounted the harrowing effects of being marked as a target for enemy cannons to his father three days after the battle:

> I have heard tell of dodging shell and cannon balls before, but I think I did my share that day. A few seconds after the report of their guns, we could hear the shell or ball coming with a peculiar shrill whistle, becoming more distinct as they neared you, until whiz-z-z-ip, it would pass. By keeping a sharp lookout, as they were coming direct towards us, we could see them coming and thus be enabled to

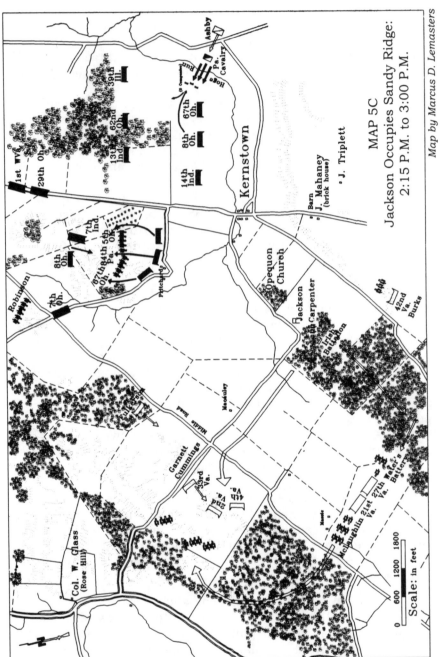

MAP 5C
Jackson Occupies Sandy Ridge:
2:15 P.M. to 3:00 P.M.

Map by Marcus D. Lemasters

Kernstown

Ashby
Hoge
Pa. Cavalry
Opequon Run

39th Ill.
29th Oh.
1st W.Va.
13th Ind.
62nd Oh.
67th Oh.
8th Oh.
14th Ind.

Robinson
7th Oh.
8th Oh.
87th Oh.
84th Pa.
5th Oh.
7th Ind.
Pritchard's

Opequon Church

Jackson
Carpenter
Irish Battalion

42nd Va.
Burks

Barn
J. Mahaney
(brick house)

• J. Triplett

Fulkerson
Garnett
Cummings

Middle Road
Macauley

33rd Va.
2nd Va.
4th Va.

McLaughlin
21st Va.
27th Va.
Waters's Battery

Col. W. Glass
(Rose Hill)

Scale: in feet
0   600   1200   1800

get out of the way. But when the whole volleys came, we would throw ourselves flat upon the ground and "trust to luck." When a solid shot would strike the earth and bounce, it would make a noise like throwing flat stones against the wind. Thus we were compelled to watch and dodge all day with nothing to eat, and no sleep the night before.[37]

Stonewall feinted on two fronts to mask the transfer of two additional batteries of artillery with infantry support westward to Sandy Ridge. Jackson had exhibited great skill in employing artillery in both the Mexican War and in early Civil War battles. Eight months earlier he had converted a sure Southern defeat into a memorable victory on Henry Hill near Bull Run by concentrating three batteries of thirteen cannons, supporting them with his brigade, and subsequently earning his *nom de guerre* and his commission of major general. At Kernstown, Jackson underestimated Union artillery power and subsequently stalemated four of his infantry regiments, but he had separated all the artillery batteries from their respective brigades for good reasons. It was time to use his cannons to dislodge the Federals from their defensive position.

Immediately after he sent Carpenter's battery to General Jackson, Major Jones escorted the Rockbridge Artillery toward Sandy Ridge. Captain William McLaughlin reported to Jackson to receive direct instructions. Jackson urged the battery leader "to occupy a hill on the left with the least possible delay. . . ." McLaughlin returned to his moving battery as did the 21st Virginia of Burks's brigade. Jesse Burks ordered the infantry regiment to support the eight guns both to and on the ridge. Lieutenant Colonel John M. Patton led the 21st Virginia this day and counted 270 officers and men present for duty. The 27th Virginia also joined the cannons as they traversed the rolling ground within Barton's Woods. The infantry and artillery exited the woodline and entered a low, marshy treeless plain to the east of the Robert Massie house. Heavy rains over the previous weeks drenched Massie's fields to the extent where some portions of the ground resembled a swamp more than farmland.[38] (See Map 5C)

Stonewall's diversions struck during McLaughlin's advance. The artillery course was turned southward to keep them away from Federal cannons. Nevertheless, the eventual Sandy Ridge deployment force became conspicuous targets for Daum's gunners on Pritchard's Hill, one and one-quarter miles to the north. Shot and shell greeted the unsuspecting artillerists and Southern infantrymen as they advanced toward the wooded confines of Sandy Ridge. Artillery Private Ed Moore, who joined the service less than one week earlier, was halfway across the field talking to a comrade when a shell exploded over their heads. The powerful concussion forced the two young men to their knees. Moore remembered the weakening effect this event produced as he and his mates began to feel that they were "going in." The 21st Virginia suffered two casualties from the exploding metal landing all around them. Patton directed his men to double-quick their pace; within minutes his command bolted across the Middle Road and reached the wooded base of their destination.[39]

Daum's artillery enjoyed great success with their long-range fire upon the Rockbridge Artillery. One shot found its mark on McLaughlin's seventh piece, breaking off the trunion of one of the battery's two rifled cannons. The damage was not discovered until the artillerymen unlimbered the gun. Once they successfully "ran the gauntlet," as one artillerist described the harrowing advance, the Virginians crossed the Middle Road. Then the Rockbridge artillerists passed through some protective timbers and turned northward, scaling Sandy Ridge along a ravine. The 21st Virginia advanced to the west of the battery during the ascent.

Members of the 27th Virginia pulled down a segment of a rock fence that traversed the entire ridge. The eight cannons of the Rockbridge Artillery rolled through the gap and entered a ravine in a cleared field. A perpendicular stone fence ran northward from the east-west wall here. The infantry and artillery passed to the west of the wall which separated them from the high cleared ground of the ridge. McLaughlin ordered each detachment to punch a gap into the rock fence; once completed, each gun was rolled to the top of the ridge. (See Map 5C) Confederate artillerist W. H. Byrd and new gunner O. P. Gray felt safer in these confines compared to moving in more open fields; however, incoming shells thrown by Daum's gunners introduced the advancing force to the terror ahead. One shell exploded on the stone wall immediately after the Virginians ran their pieces through it, scattering rock and debris in all directions. The second Federal hit was the most memorable. This shell passed completely through one of the off-wheel horses that pulled the third piece of the battery, tore the leg off Private Byrd, then burrowed into Byrd's horse. The shell exploded within the animal, turning the horse "to atoms." Flying shrapnel mangled another horse and severed the foot of Private Gray. A large shell fragment finally struck a stump near the ranks of the 21st Virginia where it spun like a top until one of the infantrymen pounced on it and took it along as a trophy. The white horse leading the gun was not struck but was so covered with blood and red gore that it resembled a bay. Ed Moore, who was one of many who would never forget the moment, considered the whole experience "an awful introduction."[40]

Captain McLaughlin ordered caisson horses to be transferred to the disabled third piece. This Tredegar iron gun would be delayed until the new horses could be hitched to pull the cannon into position. Here McLaughlin learned of the trunion damage to one of his rifled pieces. This gun could not be used at all, leaving the battery with only six cannons. The 21st Virginia stayed below the crest with one detached company lying prone on the brow to protect the artillery. Within minutes of McLaughlin's deployment another Pritchard's Hill shot "horribly mangled" John Wallace, a reserve Rockbridge gunner who was holding the battery horses in place forty yards down the hill.[41] One mile separated the Rockbridge Artillery from the Federal batteries on Pritchard's Hill.

While McLaughlin was experiencing difficulties with Union artillery near the crest of Sandy Ridge, General Garnett managed his problems on the slope below. Twenty minutes had passed without the return of Lieutenant Williams, Garnett's aide, who had been sent 300 yards north and west to find Colonel Fulkerson. (The staff officer had wandered into Union territory and was captured.) Garnett and Colonel Cummings could wait no longer; together they rode to the woods to where they saw Fulkerson enter. They found the colonel and argued their case to him concerning the futility of attacking the reinforced Federal right. Fulkerson informed General Garnett that he was awaiting orders. Garnett told the colonel his intentions of returning the 33rd Virginia to the main body and convinced Fulkerson he needed to do the same. The two brigade leaders moved back their respective commands 200 yards southward along the foot of Sandy Ridge. Garnett looked up to see the Rockbridge Artillery unlimbering its cannons on the treeless military crest of the ridge. He also witnessed Stonewall Jackson leading infantry support toward the crest. Garnett and Fulkerson turned onto the ridge, where Garnett reunited the 33rd Virginia with the 2nd and 4th Virginia near the southern base of the hill.[42]

By 3:00 P.M. McLaughlin instructed his men to unlimber his six functioning pieces and fire upon the Federal batteries one mile northeast and 100 feet below their position. His temporarily disabled iron gun was rehitched and rolled to the left of the battery. Although the Rockbridge Artillery consisted predominantly of smoothbore cannons, the distance was within the effective firing range of their two rifled pieces and the high ground aided the trajectory of the howitzer and bronze smoothbores lobbing solid shot toward their opponent. Captain Waters's West Augusta battery found its way on to the height a few minutes later; Major Jones directed their deployment 300 yards north of McLaughlin's position. Shortly afterwards, Carpenter's iron guns reached the crest, escorted by

General Jackson and the 27th Virginia. These guns unlimbered on the left flank of Waters's battery and extended the artillery line northward. Stonewall Jackson successfully repeated the feat he accomplished at Manassas. Thirteen Confederate cannons commanded the Union artillery below them.

The 21st and 27th Virginia were the only infantry units available to support the artillery on Sandy Ridge. The 2nd and 4th Virginia remained at the southern base of the ridge while the 33rd Virginia, 23rd and 37th Virginia climbed the ridge from their eastern positions. Stonewall's plan had changed from one of direct assault to one that relied on artillery power to force the Union guns off their knob. General Jackson decided to keep some infantry in advance in hopes of attaining the Federal rear. To accomplish this, he sent his northernmost available regiment, the 27th Virginia, forward in advance of Carpenter's battery. Jackson then returned to his artillery line to observe the disruption it created on Pritchard's Hill.[43]

Colonel Mason and Major Armstrong continued to assist Colonel Kimball on Pritchard's Hill. Neither had reported to Banks nor Shields in Winchester since very early that afternoon. Mason was still annoyed that Kimball had not heeded his warning about occupying Sandy Ridge. During a respite, he had explained the situation to Major Armstrong who laughingly responded, "Perhaps Colonel Kimball will say to you, as McClellan did to Lander, that you are too suggestive." Mason muttered again that Kimball better occupy the height before the enemy opened a battery upon them. Within minutes, all on Pritchard's Hill became aware that it was too late to do so.[44]

The Union high command in Winchester was oblivious to Jackson's movements four miles south of them. General Banks and the injured General Shields remained at the Seevers house. Both were confident that no serious action was developing near Kernstown. General Banks's attention focused on Williams's division which departed Winchester over the last two days. Feeling that his former division would be delayed in reaching Manassas, Banks explained to Shields that he needed to report to General McClellan for further instructions. Shields, feeling no anxiety over his own division, concurred. Banks headed toward Harpers Ferry to board a train to Washington. He left Winchester at 3:00 P.M.[45]

On the battlefield, Colonel Nathan Kimball realized by 3:00 P.M. that he had made a grievous error in neglecting Sandy Ridge. The Rockbridge Artillery blanketed his headquarters with shot and shell. Within thirty minutes two Federal artillerymen and thirteen horses lay dead on the knob. Notwithstanding their earlier successes, the remaining Union gunners could not return an effective converging fire on Jackson's flank position. Robinson's battery, to the west of Pritchard's Hill, was not spared the devastation. After watching a well-placed Southern shell sever the head of one of his gunners, a lieutenant assessed the enemy artillery salvos as "the hottest fire that it has ever been my experience to witness."

The infantry support was rendered useless. The soldiers were forced to hug the hillside and lay flat on their bellies as the Southern projectiles rained over their heads and tore up the ground around them. A soldier in the 84th Pennsylvania, guarding the Parrotts of Jenks's battery, described the effect as "equal to any bull plough." The 67th Ohio hid their flag; however, being in full view of the Southern gunners, this movement did not prevent shells from bursting close by and kicking dirt upon the infantrymen. Members of Company E, 8th Ohio, threw themselves to the ground as soon as they saw one of the first approaching shells arching toward their position behind the Union artillery. The shell exploded, throwing soil in all directions, but hurting no one. Realizing the favorable outcome, the Buckeyes arose and answered their close call with a good round cheer.[46]

The Seevers House, Winchester, Virginia, ca. 1900
Generals Banks and Shields stayed here during the Battle of Kernstown.
Banks departed this house for Harpers Ferry at 3:00 P.M.
Courtesy of Ben Ritter

Nathan Kimball had nothing to cheer about. As the opening salvos from his adversary's new and dominating line greeted his headquarters, Kimball had already devised a plan to neutralize Stonewall's position. He was resolute in his intentions, proclaiming "I must take that battery!"[47]

The complexion of what to this point had been primarily an artillery duel was about to change for good.

Chapter Six

"THE MOST VIOLENT THUNDER"

"There is now and then a man in the army who has a little humanity," wrote an officer in the 29th Ohio in March 1862. "Tyler is one of them."[1]

Kernstown was redemption time for Erastus Barnard Tyler. Born in Ontario County, New York, but raised in Ravenna, Ohio, where he spent most of his childhood, Tyler received a formal education at Granville College. He graduated in 1845 and entered the business world, working for the American Fur Company. This afforded Tyler the opportunity to explore and hunt in the wilderness regions of Ohio, Pennsylvania, Kentucky, Tennessee, and Virginia. He had also joined the Ohio militia and rose to the rank of brigadier general by the outbreak of the war in April 1861. The militia experience aided Tyler; he was commissioned colonel of the newly formed 7th Ohio Volunteer Infantry on May 7, 1861, beating future U.S. President James Garfield in the election for the post. Tyler quickly earned the prestigious commission by successfully safeguarding $40,000 in gold at Weston shortly after his regiment was sent to the western Virginia theater in June.[2]

Despite the promising introduction to his military career, Colonel Tyler's fortunes turned sour later that summer. On August 13, General Rosecrans ordered Tyler and his regiment to Cross Lanes to guard Carnifex Ferry, the only passable section of the Gauley River for several miles in that segment of the Kanawha Valley. Colonel Tyler sunk several flatboats in the river and returned his men to their crossroads camp. Neglecting to post pickets on the roads leading from Carnifex Ferry, a confident Tyler and his men were cooking corn for breakfast on the morning of August 26, when they were suddenly ambushed by spirited Confederate troops led by Brigadier General John B. Floyd, who had raised two of the sunken flatboats and crossed the river with approximately 2,000 men. Major John Casement of the 7th Ohio managed to rally most of Tyler's regiment and eventually took the men to Charleston. The embarrassing disaster left Tyler with a loss of 132 men, over 100 of whom were captured and sent to Richmond.[3]

Tyler survived Cross Lanes with minimal repercussions in the press; in fact, he continued to increase the size of his command. In January he was promoted to brigade command and continued with the responsibility through March, but he had yet to receive the corresponding rank. Although it appeared inevitable that Tyler would be commissioned brigadier general, other officers of the 7th Ohio, now a part of Tyler's brigade, openly questioned Tyler's leadership abilities; they still blamed the colonel for the Cross Lanes fiasco.[4] Like Colonel William G. Murray of the 84th Pennsylvania, Erastus Tyler needed to prove himself in battle to his men. At Kernstown Colonel Tyler was one month away from entering the fourth decade of his life. The manner in which he handled his brigade this day could determine if he would celebrate his fortieth birthday as a brigadier general or a civilian.

Tyler's five-regiment brigade of approximately 2,300 effectives had been active, but not engaged, throughout the morning; they were the only portion of Shields's division that was not exposed to Stonewall Jackson by 2:00 P.M. Tyler had spent the morning with his troops at Camp Shields three miles north of Winchester. The men had barely finished eating their late breakfasts when Tyler received Shields's order to take his men south of Winchester and support Kimball's already-engaged regiments. This did not surprise the soldiers for they could hear the desultory cannonading six miles to the south. Tyler's infantry

Colonel Erastus B. Tyler, Commanding Third Brigade, Second Division, Fifth Corps, Army of the Potomac
U.S.A.M.H.I.

regiments—the 7th Ohio, 7th Indiana, 1st West Virginia, 110th Pennsylvania, and 29th Ohio—packed three-days' rations into their haversacks and were moving by 11:00 A.M.[5]

Tyler's men marched three miles southward from camp on the
Martinsburg Pike and re-entered Winchester. The soldiers spirit-
edly sang "John Brown's Body" to pace their march. A member of
the 7th Ohio echoed the sentiments of many in the brigade by describing what he witnessed in passing through the town:

> That march through the streets of Winchester remains in
> memory as one of the most weird and unnatural scenes wit-
> nessed during the war. The resident population remaining
> at home were substantially all women and children. From
> the time of our first occupation until now they had kept
> indoors and secluded. They were bitterly hostile to us, our
> cause, our people and institutions. Charleston, South Caro-
> lina, could not furnish a female and juvenile population
> imbued with more bitter sentiments towards the North and
> her soldiers than this city. As our brigade marched through
> the streets, the artillery firing became more rapid and heavier;
> the sky was overcast and a gloom seemed to be over every-
> thing except those rebel women and children. They went
> out on the sidewalks, on their verandas or looking out from
> open windows or doors, dressed in their best or gayest ap-
> parel, as if for a holiday. Not only that, but their faces, lan-
> guage, and conduct showed them to be in a holiday frame of
> mind, too. Numerous were such greetings from them as:
> "We're going to give General Jackson and his men supper
> here tonight." "Take your last look at Winchester, you Yan-
> kees," etc.[6]

Tyler's brigade escaped the civilians and passed southward toward the foreboding sights and sounds of a deadlier enemy. The men
reached Hillman's Tollgate by 1:30 P.M. From here the command
temporarily split up: the 7th Ohio and 7th Indiana climbed the northern portion of Pritchard's Hill and supported the Union artillery engaged with Jackson's force in front. The 1st West Virginia and 29th
Ohio advanced farther up the Valley Pike to support the left flank of
Clark's battery. The 110th Pennsylvania was held in reserve on the
Cedar Creek Grade Road near the Valley Pike intersection.[7]

The heretofore unengaged regiments of Tyler's brigade took their
positions while General Jackson was carrying out the flanking movements with his artillery. The advantage of Jackson's position was
noted by Tyler's command for they received Confederate artillery fire
within half an hour of reaching their positions. The 1st West Virginia

and 29th Ohio became too exposed and were subsequently ordered to return to the rear to join the 110th Pennsylvania. The Pennsylvanians were also uncomfortable in their reserve position. A continuous barrage of Southern artillery forced the regiment to fall to the ground to let the shells pass over, rather than through, their ranks. The 7th Ohio was repositioned from Pritchard's Hill to the knoll across the Middle Road where Robinson's battery exchanged rounds with the Rockbridge Artillery on Sandy Ridge.[8]

Colonel Tyler rode to Colonel Kimball's side shortly after Tyler's regiments moved onto the field of battle. Fulkerson's attempt at turning the batteries had been stymied during the previous hour; however, both Union commanders witnessed Jackson's flank movements through the leafless woods. Kimball realized his adversary's intentions and discussed deployment options with Tyler even before Jackson's artillery reached its destination. After the Confederates announced their success with solid shot from their cannons, Kimball finalized his plan with his subordinate.[9]

A soldier in Tyler's former regiment noted a smile on the face of the fully bearded and slightly balding colonel as he rode toward their position west of the Middle Road. In a low but far-reaching voice, Tyler pointed toward the Confederate artillery on Sandy Ridge and announced, "Men, I am ordered to take that battery with my brigade. I need not ask you if you will do it, for I know you will. Remember that you belong to the Seventh. Now put on your bayonets!" The golden opportunity had finally arrived for the 7th Ohio to clear the slate of their previous setback. As the men filed to the rear, they roared their new oath of inspiration: "Cross Lanes"—the two words that had haunted Tyler and the 7th Ohio for nearly seven months.[10]

Nathan Kimball took the responsibility to send an entire brigade to capture the Southern batteries; in doing so, he signalled a change of command structure. Kimball had been the acting commander since the previous evening, but all requests for reinforcements had been relayed to the ailing General Shields in Winchester. Shields's efforts to dictate the battle from his sick bed had been nullified by Kimball on two occasions during the morning and early afternoon. Shields still was under the false belief that only Ashby's cavalry opposed his troops until he received a rare message from Colonel Kimball between 3:00 and 3:30 P.M. The message was not a request for more troops, as had been the case a few hours earlier, for nearly all the available troops in the Winchester vicinity had already reached the front. General Shields became aware for the first time that Jackson was on the battlefield.[11]

As the 7th Ohio and 7th Indiana marched to rejoin the rest of the Third Brigade at the Cedar Creek Grade Road behind Pritchard's Hill, Colonel Kimball readjusted his First Brigade's infantry positions. Lieutenant Colonel Franklin Sawyer's four-company battalion of the 8th Ohio replaced the 7th Ohio as the supporting force for Robinson's battery west of the Middle Road. The remaining companies of the 8th Ohio, under the direction of Colonel Carroll, stayed east of the Valley Pike. Two of the three companies of the 67th Ohio remained under Carroll's jurisdiction, while Company A joined the main regimental body on Pritchard's Hill. Kimball's former regiment, the 14th Indiana, also crossed the turnpike and joined the Pritchard's Hill force; this regiment was aggravated by Chew's artillery, who took every available opportunity to throw shells into the ranks of exposed infantry regiments.

The 84th Pennsylvania was the only regiment of Kimball's brigade that remained unengaged. These eight companies supported Jenks's West Virginia battery, while the 5th Ohio fronted Clark's U.S. battery. Once Tyler's brigade departed, Kimball counted his artillery support west of the Valley Pike to equal five regiments of thirty-nine companies.[12]

Kimball's juggling of troops became necessary because he, like Jackson, commanded an undersized division. Three Union regiments in the division were absent on special duty to guard other towns of the Federal-occupied Lower Valley. Additionally, several companies and portions of companies had been detached for similar duty while many company and regimental officers were in their home states recruiting men for their understrength ranks. Scores of men lay sick in camp hospitals, worn out by the unaccustomed heavy marching in the frigid, wet weather of the previous month. General Shields's March 17 division report listed over 9,500 infantry soldiers of an aggregate force of 14,000 as available for duty in the Lower Valley; however, Nathan Kimball was left with only 6,000 men available to fight Stonewall Jackson six days later at Kernstown.[13] (See Appendix B)

Despite his two-to-one infantry advantage over his opponent, Colonel Kimball believed the available Southern infantry force to be at least equal in size to his own command. Kimball's decision to send Tyler's full brigade, representing over one-third of his available force, to suppress the Confederate artillery accentuated both the dominance that Jackson's cannon positions enjoyed over his own as well as the premium Kimball placed on neutralizing them to ensure the safety of his own defensive ground.

Tyler collected his brigade on the Cedar Creek Grade Road and marched them westward by 3:15 P.M. Tyler's force, in addition to his five infantry regiments, received support from approximately 350 Union cavalry. Eight companies of horsemen (three from the 1st Michigan, three from the 1st West Virginia, and two from the 1st Ohio Cavalry) followed Tyler's advance. Their march carried them beyond the John Bell farm and a gate that stood between the two parallel ridges. Nearly one mile later, Tyler's men filed into an orchard, halted, and stripped themselves of their overcoats, blankets, and other superfluous non-battle material—"laid our cloth off," as one soldier described it—leaving hundreds of the garments littering the field. The men occupied the northern slope of Sandy Ridge, having passed through a narrow valley bisected by the Cedar Creek Grade Road. The advance beyond the ridges kept Tyler's men out of the sight of Jackson's forces, but the Federals could hear the Southern artillerists playing into the Pritchard's Hill ranks.[14]

Sandy Ridge stood over 900 feet above sea level at its topographical crest and it ran in a southwest-northeast direction, extending over four miles with a maximum width of three-quarters of a mile. It consisted of a series of peaks and swales; the Cedar Creek Grade Road advantageously ran through one of these hollows. The ridge was heavily wooded at its northern and southern extremities by cedars, locusts, oaks, and other indigenous timbers of Frederick County. Jones Road, bounded by shoulder-high stone walls on both sides, defined the western perimeter of the ridge by running south from the Cedar Creek Grade Road for one and one-half miles before turning sharply eastward through the ridge and terminating at the Middle Road. Opequon Creek flowed southward through the same valley as Jones Road. At the point where the road turned eastward, the creek continued southward. Its most distinguishing feature was Neal's Dam, a mill pond one-half mile south of the road. Many men of the Stonewall Brigade knew this area well; it had been a popular recreation site and hunting area before the war. The region south and west of the dam was wooded by the same types of trees that sprung from the limestone soil on the ridge.

The middle section of the ridge, an area 1,500 yards both north-south and east-west was cleared by cultivation, except for an 800 x 300-yard wood lot in its center. Strawstacks dotted these pastures. This area was dominated by the Glass farm, owned by 51st Virginia Militia Colonel William W. Glass. The Glass buildings stood on the western side of the ridge facing Jones Road. The Glass farm, known locally as "Rose Hill," had been owned by the Glass family since the post-Revolution period. William Wood Glass was born at Rose Hill in 1835, lived on the estate in 1862, and became the sole owner of the property when his father died that year.[15]

Limestone outcroppings were numerous throughout the northern Shenandoah Valley and Sandy Ridge was no different. Either

William Glass or a not-so-distant ancestor put the stone to good use and built stone walls throughout the property. The Glass house was boxed in by walls on three sides and a rail-fence-lined farm lane that terminated at the junction of two stone walls 200 yards west of his property. An isolated wall extended eastward from the northeast corner of this box for 400 yards. South of the Glass farm, two parallel walls ran west to east and stood approximately one-quarter mile apart. The southernmost wall, 1,000 yards long, separated cleared fields from heavy woods and was the only wall that traversed the entire ridge. A segment of this wall had been torn down to allow Jackson's artillery to pass through. Three additional north-south walls sprang from each east-west structure. Another stone wall had been constructed on the southern border of the road that connected the Middle Road with the Valley Turnpike. This road extended across the center of Sandy Ridge, terminating at Jones Road where the Opequon Creek nearly meets the road one-quarter mile south of the Glass house. A 400-yard stone wall bordered the road beginning at the junction of this road and the Middle Road and extending to the military crest of Sandy Ridge. A latticework of rail fences intertwined between the stone walls. (See Map 6A) By 3:30 P.M. Southern artillery and two infantry regiments dominated the cleared center of Sandy Ridge with additional Virginia foot soldiers at the southern base. In the woods, three-quarters of a mile to their front, Colonel Tyler's Union brigade prepared to scale the height from the Cedar Creek Grade Road.[16]

The heavily wooded terrain of Sandy Ridge forced Colonel Tyler to realign his brigade into massed column by divisions before moving them forward. This placed the regiments in a compact formation five divisions deep. Each division consisted of two double-lined companies with intervals between each company in the line and between each division. The regimental color bearer stood in the center of the regiment between the two companies that comprised the third (middle) line of the column.[17]

Tyler wanted to prevent his ranks from separating during the advance into the woodline and ordered his brigade to align in similar fashion as the regiments composing it, one behind the other. The 7th Ohio spearheaded the flanking attack on the batteries. Behind them, also in column by divisions, marched the 7th Indiana, followed by the 1st West Virginia, 110th Pennsylvania and 29th Ohio.[18] This column presented an unusual formation of twenty-five double-ranked lines, stacked one behind the other, with a brigade front of two double-lined companies. The front division, Companies B and H of the 7th Ohio, consisted of ninety soldiers in a double line (forty-five men wide). Tyler found the formation necessary to

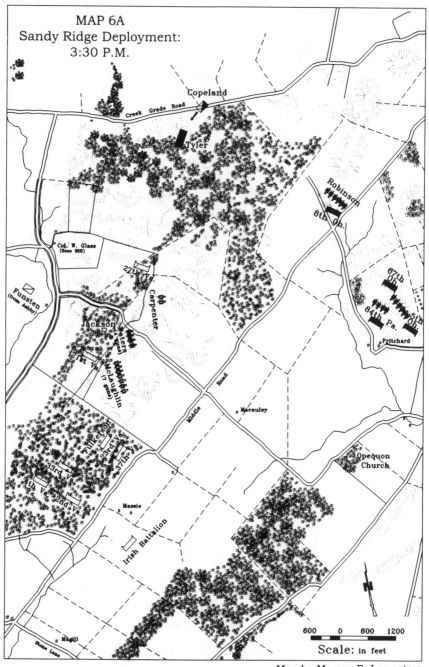

MAP 6A
Sandy Ridge Deployment:
3:30 P.M.

Copeland

Tyler

Robinson

8th Oh.

Col. W. Glass
(Rose Hill)

67th
Oh.

27th Va.

Carpenter

5th
Oh.

8th Pa.

Funsten
(from Ashby)

Jackson

Waters

Pritchard

1st Va.

McLaughlin
(7 guns)

Road

Macauley

Middle

Fulkerson

23rd Va.

37th Va.

Opequon
Church

33rd Va.

4th Va.   2nd Va.

Massie

Irish Battalion

Magill

Stone Lane

600   0   600   1200

Scale: in feet

Map by Marcus D. Lemasters

move his men through the woods; however, the column was rarely used in battles as it was an awkward formation to deploy into line of battle. Tyler believed that the formation carried little risk and he had ample opportunity to reform the line once his brigade reached the Southern artillery positions.

Tyler ordered his men into the woodline. His brigade angled into the woods, marching in a west-by-southwest direction to assure an entry behind the Southern guns. Lieutenant Colonel Joseph T. Copeland's eight cavalry companies formed the rear of Tyler's formation. Their mission was to charge the Virginia infantry once the artillery was captured by Tyler's infantry.[19] The brigade and regimental officers remained on horseback and advanced slowly with the infantry. A foot soldier near the front of the column turned to look at its formation as it moved toward battle:

> Not a word was spoken, save for the low uttered commands of the officers; the beautiful colors flying to the breeze, and seeming to defy all earth in their pride and power; the step as regular as though the column were moving through the streets of a city, to the music of a band. The Colonel moved along the line and cautioned his men to aim low, stand their ground, and victory would be theirs—this, while a scout was sent over a slight eminence to observe the position of the enemy. . . .[20]

The scout, Sergeant Lew R. Davis of the 7th Ohio, returned in a few minutes and conferred briefly with Colonel Tyler who subsequently ordered the brigade to turn to the left and march due south. Tyler then sent out his skirmishers, Companies A and G of the 1st West Virginia Infantry. Additional skirmishers included a portion of the 1st West Virginia Cavalry and the 1st Michigan Cavalry. They fanned out on the flank of the infantry skirmishers to locate any hostile force that existed in the woods.[21]

Not everyone in Tyler's brigade seemed to have his attention focused on the flank movement. The 110th Pennsylvania had earned a reputation as poachers from their dubious activities during the previous reconnaissance to Strasburg. Lieutenant Colonel Clark of the 29th Ohio, marching in the rear of the Pennsylvanians, was stunned to observe the continuation of the trend in this advance toward the cannons. He watched one of the soldiers of the 110th Pennsylvania tucking an old hen under his arm. The bewildered and somewhat disgusted Clark had no idea where the man found the bird or why he was carrying it at this particular moment.[22]

Lieutenant Colonel Philip Daum also took part in this advance. The Federal chief of artillery had a vested interest in Tyler's movements because the survival of his cannons on Pritchard's Hill depended on Tyler's success. Daum removed two howitzers from Robinson's battery and repositioned those guns farther north on the slope of Sandy Ridge. He planned to move these guns and the rest of the battery again once Tyler achieved a position strong enough to flank the Confederate artillery on Sandy Ridge. The impetuous Prussian officer rode his gray charger along Tyler's advancing line, offering encouragement and advice. "Now poys," the European instructed, "Shtay mit your ranks and I'll support you mit a pattery!"[23]

At 3:55 P.M. Tyler's skirmishers discovered a hostile force. Thirty-one members of the Shriver Greys, Company G of the 27th Virginia, mirrored the movements of the opposing Federal skirmishers in their front. This Confederate company had been recruited by Daniel Shriver of Wheeling (West) Virginia, a pro-Union city that most of Shriver's men still called "home." This company endured hardships and made sacrifices that exceeded any other unit on the field, owing to the torn feelings of loyalty that existed in Wheeling. While many of their comrades from other companies of the 27th Virginia enjoyed furloughs or recruiting service in their respective home towns, the Shriver Greys no longer had a home that they could safely visit. Communication with relatives was difficult; any letters that passed through to the Wheeling vicinity were heavily censored. During the most rabid first few months of the war, the uniforms of the Shriver Greys were manufactured by a sympathetic Wheeling tailor who was required to secretly prepare the garments.[24]

In one of the classic ironies of the battle, the infantry fight on Sandy Ridge opened between pre-war acquaintances when the Shriver Greys clashed with Company A, 1st West Virginia—another group of soldiers recruited from Wheeling. Company G of the Federal regiment was close at hand as well. At a distance of 125 yards, the Greys fired the first rounds, which sailed high over the heads of the two Federal companies. One of the bullets smacked into the packed front of Tyler's brigade which was to the rear (north) of their skirmishers. The unfortunate recipient was Private Frederick Groth of the 7th Ohio, who marched in the front division of the column. He fell dead in the woods, becoming the first infantry casualty on Sandy Ridge.[25]

For Lieutenant John Buford Lady of the Shriver Greys, this skirmish became personal. The twenty-one-year-old former nail cutter was born in Washington County, Pennsylvania. His parents had moved him at a young age to Wheeling, Virginia, where he was raised with five younger brothers and a sister. When war became inevitable, John Buford split with his Union-supporting family, joined Captain Shriver's company, and was felled by a Federal bullet at

Manassas during the first battle of Bull Run. Lady recovered in Richmond and returned to his company before the close of 1861 and embarked upon the winter campaign of 1862 as a commissioned officer in his company.

It is not known if John Buford Lady realized he was firing upon his former neighbors during that early spring afternoon on Sandy Ridge, but even if he was aware of everyone he faced, the presence of the skirmishers would not have interested him as much as the massed column they screened. For in that column marched the remaining eight companies of the 1st West Virginia, including Company E—also recruited from Wheeling. Two members of that company were present and prepared to fight: Privates David and Columbus Lady—the two teen-aged brothers of John Buford Lady. The "Brother's War" thrived at Kernstown.[26]

The Shriver Greys welcomed support from Captain Robert Dennis's Company E of the 27th Virginia, but after a few minutes of exchanging volleys, the opposing skirmishers returned to their respective units. The Confederate skirmishers rejoined the 27th Virginia of the Stonewall Brigade which was about 400 yards west of the batteries it supported, and advanced in a northeasterly direction. Though suffering from severely depleted ranks, this regiment boasted superior leadership at Kernstown. They were led by Colonel John Echols, a mountain of a man at six feet four inches and 260 pounds. Acid-tongued Andrew Jackson Grigsby served as lieutenant colonel. Major Elisha Franklin ("Bull") Paxton completed this trio of regimental officers who eventually excelled as brigade and division commanders during subsequent engagements of the war.[27]

The apparent objective of the 27th Virginia was the Federal batteries, particularly the cannons of Robinson's battery farthest to the right (west) of the Union line.[28] The previous successes of General Jackson's men had not escaped Stonewall's memory. Only eight months earlier Jackson earned his nom-de-guerre when the 33rd Virginia of his brigade temporarily captured two Union cannons on Henry Hill. In keeping with his desire to turn the Union right, Jackson

**Colonel John Echols,
27th Virginia Infantry**
U.S.A.M.H.I.

ordered Colonel Echols to advance his men from the Confederate
batteries to disrupt the Federal line with the force of only one undersized regiment. Ironically, the opposing forces on Sandy Ridge
moved with similar objectives: to neutralize the enemy's artillery;
however, the distinction between these objectives was the size of
the forces sent to accomplish their task. While Colonel Kimball committed thirty-five percent of his available force to take out Confederate batteries, General Jackson tried to achieve a similar result
with a force one-twentieth the size of Kimball's.

The unexpected presence of Tyler's brigade on Sandy Ridge
ruined Jackson's plan. The 27th Virginia had just crossed the northernmost east-to-west stone wall when Companies E and G returned
to the regiment from the north. One of the skirmish officers provided Colonel Echols with information the giant Staunton lawyer
had not anticipated—five regiments were advancing toward them.
Colonel Echols realized he was in danger of having his isolated regiment annihilated. He was forced to fight a large enemy brigade with
only 200 guns on his side.[29]

The quick-thinking Colonel Echols gave his regiment every
advantage possible to withstand the pending maelstrom. He ordered
his men to fall back several yards southward to the protection of
the shoulder-high stone wall.[30] The wall appeared to be a perfect
defensive barrier. It rested on one of the many spurs that dominated the Sandy Ridge landscape. Echols then instructed his men
to level their muskets, aiming toward the woodline 150 yards in
front of them. The spring season was less than four days old; therefore, the leafless trees did not conceal the 2,000-plus force approaching them. From this protected position the Virginians waited for
their targets with nervous excitement.

Echols and his regiment were forced to engage the enemy without adequate support. The 27th Virginia was so far removed from
the Confederate artillery that General Garnett, the 27th's brigade
commander, had been unaware of their location when he scaled
Sandy Ridge. General Garnett had led the 33rd Virginia onto the
height less than one-half hour earlier. The four regiments of his
brigade were scattered on the ridge; the 2nd and 4th Virginia were
south of the 33rd Virginia, while the 27th Virginia was out of
Garnett's view. Prior to the brief skirmishing, Colonel Echols had
sent Lieutenant Colonel Grigsby to find General Garnett and obtain
support. The regimental commander realized that without timely
reinforcements, he faced destruction by a much larger force.[31]

Just as Echols's skirmishers returned to his regiment, the 1st
West Virginia skirmish companies fell back to the main body of
Tyler's brigade. The massed-column-by-division formation crested
the peak of one of Sandy Ridge's many hillocks and had begun to

descend toward a ravine in a clearing. The Confederate artillery was audible as the guns spewed forth destruction 500 yards to Tyler's front and left. Despite the skirmish that occurred minutes earlier, Colonel Tyler chose to remain in his long, thin column.

The head of Tyler's column reached the woodline on the descent from the spur at 4:00 P.M. From here, the brigade commander could see the ravine at the bottom of the hill, beyond which began the ascent of another hill—its crest dominated by the stone wall. Echols's Virginians bobbed up and down from behind the wall approximately 150 yards away. The left flank of the Confederate artillery, represented by Carpenter's Tredegar iron guns, reoriented their muzzles toward the infantry line and began loading shot, shell, and canister to cut down the flanking Federal brigade.

Bad luck cursed Tyler and his brigade during their advance. Had the column marched seventy yards more westerly, they would have freed themselves from the crests and ravine that obstructed their progress. The ground at the western side of the ridge was nearly level and allowed quicker passage of massed troops. Tyler also would have better concealed his flanking approach to the Confederate batteries and would have come directly in their rear without a significant loss of valuable time. Even if noticed and opposed

Sandy Ridge, 1885
This photograph shows the stone wall that the 27th Virginia protected themselves behind. The view is looking north. The Glass farm can be seen in the far left side of the picture.

U.S.A.M.H.I.

by the 27th Virginia, the Union regiments should have easily and swiftly overrun their outmatched foe on this portion of the field and ended the battle—and perhaps have destroyed Jackson's Valley District army—that very afternoon.

Notwithstanding the adverse terrain features in their front, the Federal flanking force enjoyed a tremendous manpower advantage with a brigade that outnumbered one regiment by over ten-fold. Experienced commanders in this situation would have quickly deployed their regiments into double battle lines to sweep their foe from the field. Colonel Erastus Barnard Tyler was a courageous and amiable officer; however, he committed a grievous judgment error that cost the Federals an easy victory over a dispersed and outnumbered opponent. Without redeploying his troops from their cumbersome marching column, Tyler rode to the front of his men and yelled, "Charge Bayonets!" With that order the massed column pulsed forward. The first two regiments in Tyler's column, the 7th Ohio and 7th Indiana, launched from the woodline and charged to within 100 yards of their foe, the Buckeyes filling the air with redeeming shouts of "Remember Cross Lanes!"[32]

Colonel Echols and the veterans of the 27th Virginia greeted their opponent with a unified volley of flaming musketry and taunted them by chanting "Bull Run" at the top of their voices. Carpenter's iron guns supported the lone infantry regiment by belching rounds of shot and canister from their flanking position on the eastern crest of the ridge. Echols's men spread out in such a way to appear larger in size than their actual strength of 200 men, rank and file. The Southerners were also helped by Tyler's premature order to attack without previously deploying his regiments in a battle line. The 27th Virginia enfiladed the flanks of Tyler's narrow charging column, firing into the front of the packed bluecoats. A Hoosier soldier later admitted, "Being in column by divisions, we were in bad shape for such a galling fire."[33] (See Map 6B)

The Confederate fire devastated the Union brigade. As the front of the column reached the ravine, it was hit by lead flying from three directions. A member of the 7th Ohio described the opening volley as "a most terrific roar of musketry." The Confederate artillery rounds shook the earth around them and "tore through the solid ranks of the command with fearful certainty." In a common impulse, the Union soldiers of the twin 7th regiments halted and hugged the earth; many of their comrades would never rise again. Orderly Sergeant A. C. Danforth was one of the first to fall. While in the ravine on the right of the line, Confederate bullets penetrated his mouth and heart. He reeled under the shock, gasped a few seconds as he struck the ground, and perished. His death chilled

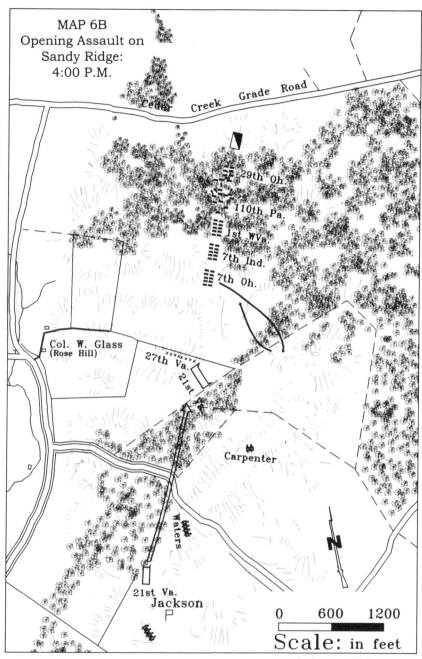

MAP 6B
Opening Assault on
Sandy Ridge:
4:00 P.M.

Cedar Creek Grade Road

29th Oh.

110th Pa.

1st WVa.

7th Ind.

7th Oh.

Col. W. Glass
(Rose Hill)

27th Va.

21st

Carpenter

Waters

21st Va.
Jackson

N

0   600   1200

Scale: in feet

Map by Marcus D. Lemasters

all those around him, but it was the deafening explosion of artillery and small arms fire that disturbed the Federals the most.[34]

Within seconds of the first Confederate fire, the officers in Tyler's brigade ordered their men to fire and charge. The front-line soldiers responded with a shout, picked themselves up, and charged once again toward the stone wall. For a second time, a devastating volley greeted their ranks and stalled them.[35]

Private G. K. Covert of the 7th Indiana was much more fortunate than Sergeant Danforth. Earlier that day Covert had fought with a company mate for possession of a tintype of a home-town girl. Covert won the fight and placed the picture in his left breast coat pocket which also contained his New Testament. A bullet struck him in the chest during the opening of the infantry fight, knocking him to the ground with what should have been a mortal injury. However, the bullet had passed through the Bible, struck the tin plate of the picture that was behind it and glanced harmlessly away. Although the young soldier never married the girl, Covert could always claim that she saved his life.[36]

The devastation that the opening Confederate fire inflicted on the front of the column rippled through to the back. The rearward regiments flinched at the swarm of bullets that whistled by their faces and thudded into the surrounding trees, peeling branches from trunks and filling the air with showers of bark and twigs. The artillery blasts crashed above them to intensify the noise. Debris of metal and wood rained down upon them. The Southern resistance stymied the stunned column's forward movement and the troops awaited orders that would get them out of their predicament.[37]

The 110th Pennsylvania had earned their reputation for poor discipline through fighting among themselves, excessive drinking, and raiding citizens' supplies. They were under the dubious leadership of Colonel William D. Lewis and marched as the next-to-last infantry regiment in the column. When the opening fire struck the front of the column, the Pennsylvanians knew exactly how to remove themselves from a potentially dangerous situation. The poorly disciplined mob of approximately 300 men fell to the ground with the rest of the column, and panic set in. When ordered to charge again, most of the regiment jumped up and fled rearward, passing through the ranks of the 29th Ohio which temporarily set that regiment into confusion. Although many of the Buckeyes managed to reform, The Irish Philadelphians and country boys from central Pennsylvania took cover behind trees several yards to the rear. The other regiments of the division considered the 110th Pennsylvania to be the "black sheep" of the division and would never forgive the Keystoners for this act of cowardice. Lieutenant Colonel Clark of the 29th Ohio noted that the 110th Pennsylvania "broke and scampered like sheep at the first fire" and wondered if the chicken thief he had seen moments earlier had managed to salvage his booty while on the run.[38]

The loss of the Pennsylvanians reduced the brigade's effective fire by nearly 300 men. Additionally, six companies of the disrupted 29th Ohio stayed in reserve in the woods. The four right-hand companies of the Buckeye regiment moved forward, firing at will, aiming at Southern heads that periodically bobbed above the stone wall and woodpiles.[39] Tyler's brigade now numbered fewer than 1,800 participating members.

Lieutenant Colonel Philip Daum was incredulous at the effects of the Virginia fire on Tyler's brigade. Minutes earlier he had been shouting words of encouragement to the bluecoats as they moved through the woods, but those words turned to derision and anger. After watching the 110th Pennsylvania break ranks, the chief of artillery denounced the whole brigade as a sorry lot of "tammed militia."[40]

Colonel Tyler worked desperately to remove his men from their awkward column by divisions. He passed along orders for a left-flank deployment, on line of first division, to place the front of his command into an effective battle line. By this time the Federals had returned fire, intensifying the volume created by the close-range fighting. Most of the men could not hear their officers over the rattling musketry. There were others that could hear, but they refused to move in line of first division since the front two companies were in the ravine—just eighty yards from the enemy.

Captain George Wood of Company D commanded the second division of the 7th Ohio. He left-faced his two companies of approximately ninety men, waved his sword over his head, and bellowed to his men to follow him toward a hillock to the left and front of the first division. Soldiers in the rear divisions of the 7th also sped for the hill. The captains tried to get their men to stop firing and form ranks, but most of the volunteers found themselves fighting promiscuously as clusters from different companies.[41] Regimental and company officers realized that the battle was escaping their control as the men chose to fight "on their own hook." Lieutenant Colonel William Creighton led the 7th Ohio in the front of the column and found it futile to shout orders to men who could not hear him. Early on, Creighton's horse was shot and became unmanageable; this helped the six-foot-three-inch officer to discover the best way to help his men. Leaping from his injured charger, Creighton snatched up a wounded soldier's Enfield rifle, rushed forward, and ordered his soldiers to follow. He spent the rest of the day fighting side by side

with his men. Creighton's selfless display earned his men's respect
and a colonel's commission.[42]

Thus far, Colonel Echols and the 27th Virginia had accomplished a tremendous feat with the help of Carpenter's battery. Aided
by the confusion and poor deployment of their adversary as well as
their own spirited fighting, they had successfully held back a brigade for nearly five minutes. Nevertheless, Echols realized he needed
immediate help. Scores of Federal soldiers had knocked down a rail
fence and were beginning to flank his right. They were in position to
force him from the stone sanctuary if reinforcements could not reach
him. Echols gallantly held his
men in line but his large frame,
conspicuously elevated on a
white horse, presented an inviting target for the Union soldiers.
A bullet from the 7th Ohio struck
Echols near the left shoulder and
forced him to leave the field with
a broken arm. Lieutenant Colonel Andrew Jackson Grigsby took
over the regiment, but the spirit
of the Virginians waned with the
loss of their leader. They began
to fall back under the withering
fire and flanking movement of
Tyler's brigade to a position fifty
yards south of the stone wall.[43]

With no time to spare, the
27th Virginia was reinforced by a
regiment that was not in the
Stonewall Brigade. The 21st Virginia of Burks's brigade had been
the only other infantry regiment

**Lieutenant Colonel William
Creighton, 7th Ohio Infantry**
U.S.A.M.H.I.

on Sandy Ridge when Echols's men were ordered to advance toward
the Northern batteries. They stayed near General Jackson and the
Rockbridge Artillery when the initial crash of musketry was heard to
the north and west of their position. Stonewall immediately ordered
Lieutenant Colonel John M. Patton to move the 21st Virginia forward
and support Echols "in case he was driven back." At that moment
General Jackson had no idea about the size of the force that had
clashed with the 27th Virginia.

At 128 pounds, Lieutenant Colonel Patton appeared the an-
tithesis of Colonel Echols in size, but became his equal in spirit and
leadership on Sandy Ridge. He threw his regiment into line on the

first company and marched them to the aid of the 27th Virginia. They arrived five minutes after the action opened, just as many of the men of the 27th were falling back from the stone wall. Patton brought 270 men to the wall. They were fired upon by the left flank of Tyler's brigade. A 7th Ohio soldier confessed to the awe he felt in observing their precision of advance, but was disgusted at the sight of "that detestable 3 striped flag" and earnestly fired his first cartridge into their ranks. Patton ordered a return fire; their volley proved to be too much for the few scores of 7th Ohio soldiers that had flanked to the east. With no signs of support coming to their aid, the Union soldiers on the left of Tyler's massed column returned toward the center of the formation. Seeing their right flank supported and the Federal flanking maneuver successfully repulsed, the retreating soldiers of the 27th Virginia rallied to their original positions behind the stone wall on Patton's left. The two Southern regiments, from different brigades, fought well together but could not expect to hold off four times their number indefinitely.[44]

Colonel Erastus B. Tyler agonized over the failure of his left flank deployment. Five minutes after the engagement began, he realized his brigade had turned into a cumbersome, unmanageable mass of soldiers because of the intermixing of men from different companies and regiments. Although the Confederate force behind the stone wall seemed formidable, they could still be dislodged by the proper deployment of his soldiers. Tyler now focused on his right flank. By extending his right, he could seize the advantage by flanking the Confederates and challenging the artillery positions from the rear. The flank move would relieve the pressure from his harried brigade's front and allow the brigade to form into a battle line and concentrate a more effective fire.

Tyler called upon Colonel Joseph Thoburn and the 1st West Virginia to take the Confederate left flank. Thoburn received his orders and placed his hat on the tip of his sword. Raising the sword high in the air, he turned toward his men and barked, "Come on, Boys!" Approximately 150 men of the 1st West Virginia answered their bearded Irish commander and followed him toward the wall.[45]

At approximately 4:10 P.M. Thoburn and his compact command left the protective woodline and skirted across the open fields toward the western portion of the wall. Less than 100 yards to their right stood a perpendicular wall that extended northward from the western end of the wall which the Confederates were protecting. The Union Virginians met no resistance as they crossed the flatter land to the west of the main attack. The main stone wall, now only 100 yards from their reach, was unprotected on this western flank. The 1st West Virginia had the opportunity to be the heroes of the day and they responded with a mad dash toward the wall.

To the surprise of Thoburn and his men, approximately 500 Confederates appeared within their line of sight and rushed to the same destination. This was the 23rd and 37th Virginia—Colonel Fulkerson's brigade—who, to this point, had already had an active day between the two contested heights of Sandy Ridge and Pritchard's Hill. By 3:30 P.M. Fulkerson and his men had been marching southward along the eastern side of Sandy Ridge when they saw General Jackson above them moving the artillery pieces to the cleared heights of the ridge. Fulkerson led his men to the center of the ridge and within minutes of hearing the opening of the infantry exchange had them moving to support the 27th and 21st Virginia. Placing his command in line under the cover of some timber, Fulkerson and his men soon attracted heavy fire from the 7th Ohio but escaped without casualties. Once the Southerners approached the left flank of the stone wall, they could see Thoburn and his men rushing toward the same destination.[46]

Thoburn and his 1st West Virginia lost the race. The leading elements of the 23rd and 37th Virginia reached the wall first and trapped their Federal foes in the open field, now only forty yards in front of them. The Confederates instinctively laid their percussion-fired smoothbores on the fence and, with cool precision, fired at point-blank range into Thoburn's regiment. The result proved devastating. Years after the event, a company officer in the 37th Virginia remembered the moment by writing, "I do not know if I ever hurt anybody during the war or not. If I did, it was probably on this occasion."[47]

Colonel Joseph Thoburn led at the head of his men when the Confederates opened upon his regiment. Two bullets tore through his coat cape and pants without striking flesh. A third bullet dug into Thoburn's upper arm, shattered the bone, and knocked him off his feet. Thoburn attempted to direct his men from his prostrate position, but the charge's momentum died when he received his wound. The injured colonel crawled to the rear on his hands and knees where he was helped to the safety of the woodline.[48]

Several members of the 1st West Virginia refused to give up the field without a fight. As soon as Fulkerson's men opened on them from the front, these Federal Virginians leaped over the perpendicular wall that skirted their right. They now flanked the Confederates, but Colonel Fulkerson saw to it that his enemy would not threaten their position. He judiciously placed the 37th Virginia, under Colonel Robert Preston Carson, at the junction of the main stone wall and the perpendicular wall and ordered him to dislodge the Federals from their front. Carson complied and within minutes the 1st West Virginia was driven from the field, temporarily leaving one stand of colors on the ground. Six men from the 1st West Virginia lay dead on the field; twenty more soldiers were wounded in the aborted flank movement. Fulkerson's timely arrival saved the Confederate left flank. This section of the stone wall would not be threatened again for two hours.[49] (See Map 6C)

Although the regiments of Tyler's brigade had failed to maintain their flank extensions near the stone wall, they slowly pulled themselves out of the packed column and reformed in clusters closer to the rear woodline, where the men took advantage of limestone outcroppings and trees to protect themselves from the growing Confederate line in front of them. The 7th Ohio, in front, was relieved by this deployment in their rear. The Buckeyes had suffered tremendously from the Confederates facing them, from their own men behind them, and from unintentional self-inflicted wounds. Men in the front companies fell with buckshot wounds delivered from close-range smoothbore fire. One member of Company H accidently ran his ramrod through his hand while he

**Colonel Joseph Thoburn,
1st West Virginia Infantry**
Theodore Lang, Loyal West Virginia from 1861 to 1865 *(Baltimore, Md.: The Deutsch Publishing Co., 1895).*

was nervously loading his rifle. Friendly fire had also taken its toll on the 7th Ohio. Corporal Seldon Allen Day of Company C was nervously loading and firing when a sergeant fell at his side. Day was convinced the shot was fired from the rear. He was not surprised since the slope of the hill to the north of the ravine behind him was not steep enough for the rearward regiments to fire over the heads of the front ones. Corporal Day inched forward and was able to fire from within a few yards of the wall; he was hidden in a gully behind a jutting chunk of limestone in front of the wall. Although the natural rifle pit protected him from enemy fire, Federal bullets from the rear tore up the ground all around him.[50]

A mere ten minutes elapsed between Tyler's opening assault upon the 27th Virginia and Fulkerson's successful repulse of the

1st West Virginia. At 4:10 P.M. the Confederate line at the stone wall consisted of the 37th Virginia and 23rd Virginia on the left, with a gap where the ridge and wall spurred upward. On the high ground stood the 27th and 21st Virginia. These four regiments numbered nearly 1,000 men and covered approximately 350 yards, but the spurring ridge isolated Fulkerson's men from Grigsby's and Patton's Virginians. Timely reinforcements were critical to hold the line even though the disorganized Federals in front of them had only a two-to-one advantage. Military doctrine dictated that this disparity favored the Southerners in their defensive position, but the gaps needed to be filled to assure a successful defensive stand.

General Richard Brooke Garnett galloped to the scene. Garnett had led the 33rd Virginia onto Sandy Ridge at 3:30 P.M. where the men shied away from Daum's gunners as they scaled the height. This did not prevent the Union artillery from continuing to menace them. A shell thrown from Pritchard's Hill passed between the legs of Elijah Hartley of the 33rd Virginia and exploded, tearing the unfortunate Virginian to pieces and terrifying his company mates advancing with him. Lieutenant Colonel Grigsby found Garnett at the base of a spur below the Rockbridge Artillery positions at 3:45 P.M. and told the brigadier that the 27th Virginia was ordered by General Jackson to support Carpenter's cannons, but now was separated from the rest of the Sandy Ridge force and was "in advance." (Grigsby and Garnett had been at West Point together over twenty years earlier, and though not in the same graduating class, the two were cordial to each other. Grigsby claimed a better military relationship with Garnett than with any other field officer.) The lieutenant colonel had made his brigadier aware for the first time of the location of his leading regiment.[51]

Prior to the infantry fight, Captain McLaughlin had descended from the military crest where his artillery stood and asked General Garnett to look at the advancing columns of Union infantry along the Valley Pike. Together, Garnett, Grigsby and McLaughlin rode to the top of the hillock where they watched Colonel Jeremiah Sullivan's Federal brigade driving Ashby southward beyond Kernstown, with the very real possibility of reaching the rear of the Confederates' Sandy Ridge position. While observing the advance of the enemy, the three officers were startled by the sporadic volleys of the Shriver Greys as they engaged Colonel Tyler's skirmishers.[52]

While Garnett and Grigsby rode toward the sound of the skirmish fire, a much heavier discharge of musketry greeted their ears. Realizing that the 27th Virginia had become engaged with the enemy, Garnett quickly called upon the other available regiments of his brigade to move to Colonel Echols's support while Grigsby continued

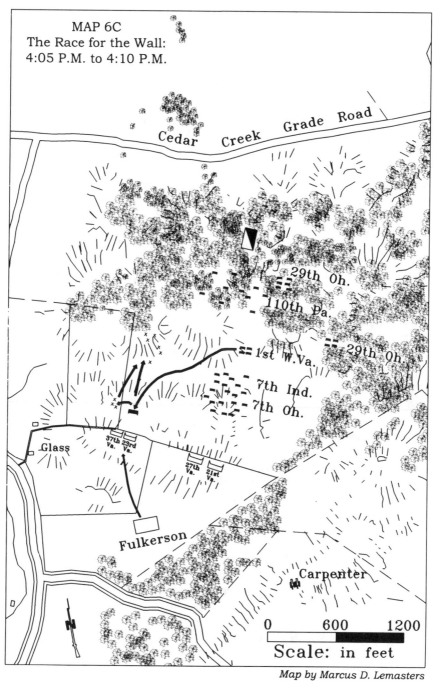

MAP 6C
The Race for the Wall:
4:05 P.M. to 4:10 P.M.

Cedar Creek Grade Road

29th Oh.

110th Pa.

1st W.Va.

29th Oh.

7th Ind.

7th Oh.

Glass

37th
Va.

23rd
Va.

27th
Va.

21st
Va.

Fulkerson

Carpenter

0   600   1200

Scale: in feet

Map by Marcus D. Lemasters

toward the stone wall to reunite with his troops. Once again, Garnett personally led the 33rd Virginia to support the engaged regiments, while the 2nd and 4th Virginia began to advance from their rearward positions on Sandy Ridge.

The 33rd Virginia was formed in line of battle, but Garnett kept them at the southern edge of a field that dominated the area behind the stone wall. The regiment remained a few hundred yards to the rear of the engaged force for a few minutes because General Garnett did not believe the 21st and 27th Virginia could hold their position for any appreciable length of time. He reasoned the 33rd would be more effective in receiving the Federals as they advanced across the field. He apparently did not know that Fulkerson was engaging the 1st West Virginia on the low ground to the left of the 21st and 27th Virginia. Two officers of the 27th Virginia, Lieutenant Colonel Grigsby and Major Paxton rode to the rear and explained to Garnett that they were holding the Federals but desperately needed reinforcements. The brigadier sent the 33rd Virginia forward, and they took position on the spur to the right of the 21st Virginia at 4:15 P.M.[53]

The 4th Virginia was the next Confederate regiment to arrive at the stone wall. They had fewer than 250 men and were led by the regimental major, Albert Pendleton, after Colonel Charles Ronald was injured by his horse in Barton's Woods. General Garnett and the regiment's adjutant, Lieutenant James H. Langhorne, assisted Pendleton in bringing the 4th to the contested ridge spur. Langhorne had to swallow his misgivings about Pendleton's leadership abilities to help the major; he had earlier believed that the late Colonel James Preston would have been extremely disappointed "if he had known that such a man as Capt. Pendleton would hold and 'field office' in his loved regiment." At first the 4th Virginia, fighting from behind trees and limestone ledges, engaged the Federals from a position well to the rear of the stone wall. General Garnett then directed the regiment to fill the gap at the stone wall line; they rushed forward to the new position. Most of the men crowded the spur to the left of the 27th Virginia. To their left the spur dropped abruptly to the lower ground where Fulkerson's regiments stood at the western edge of the wall. Two companies of the 4th Virginia occupied the depression of the ridge created by the spur; the Liberty Hall Volunteers (Company I) took position to the right of the 23rd Virginia with the Pulaski Guards (Company C) on their right. These companies were isolated from the rest of their regiment and brigade on the high ground above and to the right, completely out of their line of sight.[54] (See Map 6D)

By 4:30 P.M. the Confederates had stalemated Tyler's brigade. The Southerners packed 1,200 men at the stone wall while Tyler's initial 2,000-plus-man brigade had been severely reduced by casualties, confusion, and cowardice. The 110th Pennsylvania could not yet be rallied and remained well to the rear in the woods. The other four regiments had suffered significant casualties, most of which were received in the first ten minutes of action. By this time Colonel Tyler had belatedly taken his men out of their cumbersome marching formation, but he had no more than 1,700–1,800 remaining soldiers to contest the Virginians behind the stone wall. The dispositions of the troops prevented any attempt to organize them for an assault. Tyler's brigade was not arrayed in an organized battle line; instead, his men were dispersed along a 400-yard front that occupied ground from as close as twenty yards in front of the wall, to as far as 500 yards in the rear. Those farthest to the rear protected themselves in the trees, while the close-up men hid in terrain swales or behind thickets and limestone outcroppings. Cohesion was nonexistent as many fought—oftentimes without officers' orders—as clusters from different companies and regiments.

There was no finesse whatsoever in this fight. The two sides traded blows like boxers throwing telegraphed punches at each other in the center of the ring. Captain J. F. Asper (7th Ohio, Company H), leading the front division, proudly wrote, ". . . every man fought with the determination and will that could not be made to quail."[55] A private in Company F of the 7th Indiana, fighting the Confederates from the ravine approximately eighty yards from the wall, was awestruck at the scene which surrounded him:

> The battle was on in all its fury. The woods were soon enveloped in smoke. First on one side and then the other a comrade was seen to yield up his life for the sake of his country; the crashing of shells shot and canister through the trees has left an impression on my mind that can never be effaced. By the indomitable pluck, coupled with the ignorance of the danger of our situation, and by utilizing every stone, stump and tree as a shield from the enemy's fire, it became, as it were, a free-for-all. The regiments mixed up through and through each other, but never ceased to get rid of our 60 rounds of cartridges as fast as we could load and shoot.[56]

Lieutenant Colonel John F. Cheek commanded the 7th Indiana this day. (Colonel James Gavin was absent attending to private business.) Cheek had his horse shot out from under him early in the action, then lost the services of the regiment's major, Benjamin C. Shaw, when that officer's terrified horse threw him against a tree and severely wounded him. Cheek's adjutant, David Lostutter, also suffered an injury early on but gamely continued to assist the regiment as did many of the company officers of the 7th Indiana.[57]

Despite their best efforts, most Union regimental and company officers could not organize their men, but this did not prevent them from fighting and suffering casualties. Several, taking Lieutenant Colonel Creighton's cue, grabbed rifles and fought beside their men. Many led on foot after their horses were shot out from under them. Major John Casement of the 7th Ohio was fortunate to survive the battle. He stayed on his horse at the head of his men and suffered no wounds, although eleven bullets riddled his coat. Company F's Captain Albert C. Burgess of the same regiment suffered a fluke injury. He was commanding a two-company division of the regiment and was walking backwards in front of his men when he stumbled over a fallen soldier; as he fell his legs flew over his body and a bullet struck him in the foot, splitting the bone in his ankle. Burgess cut out the lead with his pen knife and kept it as a souvenir. He considered himself lucky—the bullet would have struck him in the back had he remained upright.[58]

Confusion reigned on both sides of the stone wall between 4:00 and 5:00 P.M. on Sandy Ridge. Disorder had prevented Tyler's regiments from eliminating Confederate artillery fire, and a similar degree of disarray impeded Confederate effectiveness. Southern regiments intermixed, resulting in confusion and disorder. Several factors contributed to the muddled organization of the defense line. The abrupt terrain forced regiments to crowd on the western portion of the stone wall. These soldiers were better protected than they would have been had they crouched behind the more open eastern segment of the wall. Regiments had entered and continued to enter the fray piecemeal. Their officers sometimes received orders through General Jackson, other times through their respective brigade commanders, and also at times through the men from neighboring regiments.

Captain David B. Bridgford and his five-company Irish Battalion suffered tremendously from the lack of cohesion which had thus far dictated the Battle of Kernstown. The battalion numbered 187 officers and men when they advanced down the Valley Pike as part of Jesse Burks's Second Brigade late that morning. General Jackson had ordered them to support Carpenter's battery near Opequon Church, assuring Bridgford and his men that they would be separated from the other regiments they had camped and trained with. At 3:30 P.M. Sandie Pendleton delivered Jackson's order for the battalion to proceed to Sandy Ridge in the rear of McLaughlin's Rockbridge Artillery and report to Colonel Burks. They arrived in less than half an hour and milled about behind the battery with the 33rd and 4th Virginia. Their brigade commander was not on the ridge; Burks had remained near the Valley Pike with the 42nd

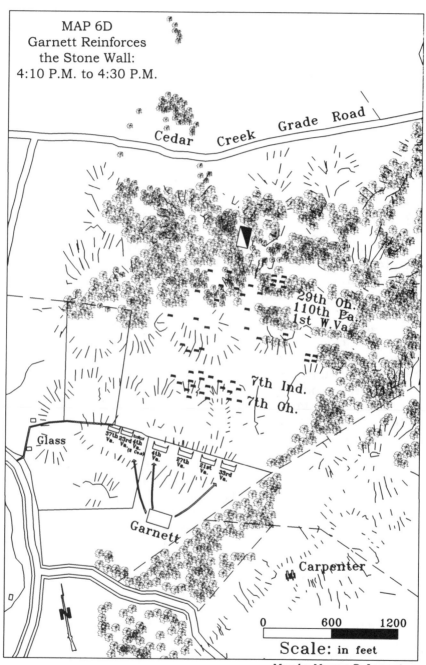

MAP 6D
Garnett Reinforces
the Stone Wall:
4:10 P.M. to 4:30 P.M.

Cedar Creek Grade Road

29th Oh.
110th Pa.
1st W.Va.

7th Ind.
7th Oh.

Glass

37th 23rd 4th
Va. Va. Va. (2 Co.s)

4th
Va.

27th
Va.

21st
Va.

33rd
Va.

Garnett

Carpenter

0   600   1200

Scale: in feet

Map by Marcus D. Lemasters

Virginia and the artillery reserve. At 4:00 P.M. Captain Bridgford heard the infantry fight open several hundred yards in front of him and sent a lieutenant to find Colonel Burks so they could obtain their orders. Unable to locate him, the lieutenant reported instead to General Jackson. Stonewall instructed the officer to tell Captain Bridgford to lead the battalion forward into action.

The Irish Battalion proceeded forward with the 4th Virginia and in rear of the 33rd Virginia. They crossed over the rolling wooded terrain of Sandy Ridge until they reached the cleared field that was dominated by the stone wall line at its northern edge. While General Garnett placed the 4th Virginia into the battle line, Lieutenant Colonel Grigsby of the 27th Virginia rode to the rear to find support for his regiment's right flank. Grigsby grew concerned when several members of Lieutenant Colonel Patton's 21st Virginia retired from the line. He bypassed Bridgford and the battalion's chain of command and delivered his orders (probably laced with his penchant for profanity) directly to the men comprising the left wing of the confused unit.

Before Captain Bridgford could give any orders, he watched in surprise as over half the battalion advanced to the left of the 27th Virginia. At this point Bridgford temporarily lost control of his command. Two companies, C and E, advanced at the right flank of the battalion and knew nothing of Grigsby's orders. Instead of joining the rest of the unit at the stone wall, they moved to the right toward the eastern segment of Sandy Ridge near the artillery. Bridgford and most of his men remained at the wall and did not communicate with the two displaced companies for the remainder of the battle.[59]

By 4:45 P.M. the 2nd Virginia arrived, the final regiment available on Sandy Ridge to enter the battle. Colonel James W. Allen's regiment of 310 men included the three exhausted companies that had fought with Captain Nadenbousch throughout the morning action. The 2nd Virginia had been delayed in its advance because it received orders from two different sources. They had climbed Sandy Ridge with the 4th Virginia before 4:00 P.M., but Allen had held the regiment in the woods at the southern base of the height while he alone rode forward to receive instructions from General Garnett. When Allen returned, Major Frank B. Jones ordered him to take the regiment forward. The one-eyed colonel complied with Jones's directions and brought his regiment into the rear of the engaged Confederates in line by the right flank. By placing his men to the right of the 33rd Virginia, he linked these men with the two misplaced companies of the Irish Battalion on his right.[60] (See Map 6E)

With both sides pinned down, the 3,500 Union and Confederate soldiers contesting for Sandy Ridge filled the air with a crescendo of small arms fire which resonated for miles around. The forces near the Valley Pike at Kernstown had not fired at each other since 3:30 P.M. Their activity was very light in terms of intensity and casualties. Most were taking part in their first battle-sized engagement and had never heard, nor were expecting, the noise that greeted their ears. One of Chew's young artillerists, upon hearing the opening of the infantry fight over one mile to his west, exclaimed, "My God, just listen to the musketry!" A member of the 8th Ohio opposing Chew's artillery east of the Valley Pike claimed to see smoke rise from Sandy Ridge and to hear the men roar while they were firing. Still another member of the 8th Ohio described the infantry fight raging one-half mile west of him as "the most violent thunder" he had ever heard.[61]

The citizens of Winchester agonized at the sounds of battle four miles south of town. Mrs. Cornelia McDonald had heard general cannonading before, but this day was different because she could hear it "thunder louder and louder, and [come] nearer and nearer." At 4:00 P.M. the cannons appeared to stop, but were replaced by "the most terrible and long continued musketry. . . not volley after volley, but one continued fearful roll. . . ." Many attempted to observe the battle from their roof tops; others scaled an obstructing hill south of town to view the developing contest. Despite being surrounded by Union pickets on the hill, the Reverend B. F. Brooke could not control his excitement and prayed out loud, "Oh Lord, help Jackson!" Another citizen noted that "the suspense was terrible and anxiety and distress marked on every countenance." To these citizens, not knowing what was occurring south of them was just as fearful as being in the middle of it.[62]

For the soldiers in the middle of the maelstrom, the thought of being in Winchester would have seemed like heaven. The sight of bloodied comrades falling around them, the choking smell of sulfurous smoke, and the deafening sounds of close-range musketry affected them for years to come. One of Tyler's soldiers, firing from behind a tree, claimed the action as "the most fearful firing you ever dreamed of," and noted that his tree had seventeen bullet holes in it. From his position on the opposite side of the wall, Major Frank Jones described the fight as "the most terrific fire of musketry that can be imagined."[63]

General Thomas J. Jackson, a veteran of the Mexican War and the largest land battle of the eastern war to date at Manassas, was also dumfounded by the severity of the infantry fight on Sandy Ridge. He admitted to a friend five days after the event, "I do not recollect having ever heard such a roar of musketry." The ever-adapting Valley District commander no longer entertained thoughts of defeating the Federals by getting in his opponent's rear or turning his flank. "I became satisfied that we could not expect to defeat the enemy,"

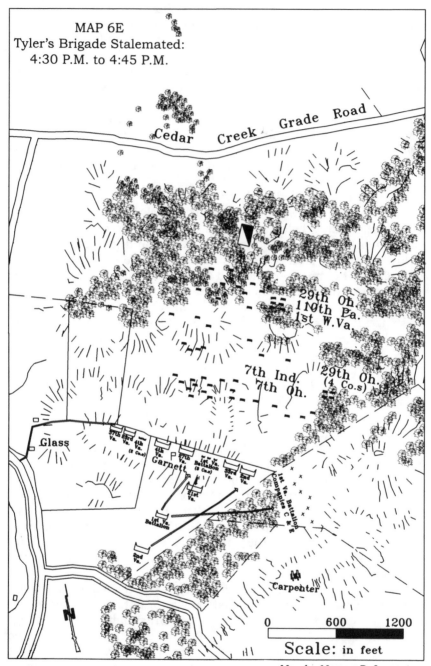

MAP 6E
Tyler's Brigade Stalemated:
4:30 P.M. to 4:45 P.M.

Cedar Creek Grade Road

29th Oh.
110th Pa.
1st W.Va.

7th Ind.   29th Oh.
7th Oh.   (4 Co.s)

Glass

37th 33rd 4th
Va. Va. Va.
(2 Co.s)

4th P 7th
Va. Va.
(3 Co.s)

1st Va.
Battalion
(2 Co.s)

3rd
Va.

2nd
Va.

Garnett

31st
Va.

3rd Va.
Battalion

1st Va. Battalion
Companies C & E

2nd Va.

Carpenter

0   600   1200

Scale: in feet

Map by Marcus D. Lemasters

Jackson admitted over four months later, "and that our safety consisted in holding our position until night and drawing off under the cover of darkness."[64]

With the arrival of the 2nd Virginia at the wall, General Jackson's 1,700 infantrymen and two cannons had negated Tyler's surprise attack and provided his other two batteries ample protection to continue suppressing the Federals' Pritchard's Hill artillery. Stonewall still held three unengaged regiments and two batteries of artillery in reserve. Alternatively, Tyler's brigade was going nowhere, bogged down in their slugfest with the Confederate line at the stone wall. With less than two hours of daylight remaining, Stonewall Jackson appeared destined to accomplish his new goal. His opponents on Pritchard's Hill would have limited time to devise a plan to disrupt his objective, and then they would have to carry it out with a force essentially reduced by over one third because of the hindrance of Tyler's brigade.

Colonel Nathan Kimball would have to commit more troops to Sandy Ridge if he expected to win the day.

Chapter Seven

"We Won't Retreat"

Colonel Nathan Kimball realized by 4:30 P.M. that he was in jeopardy of losing the fight. Stationed on Pritchard's Hill for seven hours, he had witnessed the battle shift from a skirmish and an artillery duel on his immediate left and front, to a full scale infantry fight one mile to his right. Colonel Tyler had been engaged for half an hour but had produced only smoke and noise. The unthreatened Confederate artillery continued to send shot and shell toward Colonel Kimball from the eastern crest of Sandy Ridge, making Pritchard's Hill a very uncomfortable location for Union headquarters.

General Shields continued to lay incapacitated at the Seevers house where he had become aware, merely one hour before, that his division was fighting a battle-sized engagement. After sending orders to concentrate Colonel Tyler's and Sullivan's brigades south of town in the morning, Shields had no direct involvement with the action. He could send no more troops to the field, although one regiment, the 66th Ohio, and a few detached companies from other units remained as a provost guard in Winchester. One regiment of the division (7th West Virginia) was at Martinsburg, ten miles to the north, and another detached regiment (4th Ohio) was stationed at Berryville, ten miles east of Winchester.[1]

General Shields's lone afternoon action as division commander was to send an aide to recall one of General Alpheus S. Williams's brigades from its movement out of the Valley. Williams had remained west of the Shenandoah River with one brigade since Saturday night, March 22. The brigade had been unable to cross after the bridge at Castleman's Ferry gave way from the weight of the division trains. Shields delivered a note on Saturday night requesting Williams to take the brigade to Berryville. By midafternoon on March 23, a staff aide returned to General Williams and found him at the riverbank again; this time his note from General Shields exhorted him to bring the brigade to Winchester. General Williams put his regiments in motion, mounted his horse, and with a cavalry escort quickly rode toward the battle. He would not arrive until it was over.[2]

Aside from locating more troops, General Shields was powerless to aid Colonel Kimball at Kernstown. Kimball had controlled Union deployment since the morning action and used the periphery staff with him to assist his engaged troops. Two of his aides, Colonel John Mason and Lieutenant Matthew Greene, rallied stragglers who attempted to leave the battlefield. They also directed confused and incoming troops into the positions that other regiments had previously taken.[3]

Colonel Kimball shored up his communication system. Realizing that transferring messages by aides on horseback was too time consuming, he accepted the offer from Lieutenant William W. Rowley of the 28th New York Infantry, the acting signal officer for the Fifth Corps, to set up a series of signal stations to speed up the delivery of messages between officers on the field. Lieutenant Rowley stationed flagmen on a quickly constructed signal station behind the Union artillery on Pritchard's Hill. Another station delivered messages from Colonel Sullivan's wing, east of the Valley Pike. An additional station with flagmen was perched on Bower's Hill, a dominant elevation that stood between Pritchard's Hill and the city of Winchester. Kimball also requested Lieutenant Rowley to send a signalman to the Seevers house to provide direct communication with General Shields.

Six stations were in place and working at the time of Colonel Tyler's flank attack; however, an attempt to place a signal station in the rear of Tyler's brigade was met with heated resistance by the Virginia force at the stone wall. The flagman's horse was shot through the neck during the opening moments of the infantry fight and the signalman, Private Oliver S. Temple, was added to the ever-growing casualty list when he was shot through the right forearm while attempting to set up the Sandy Ridge signal station. Temple's superior, Lieutenant David Taylor, realized his function as a signal officer had just been negated by Southern musketry; he subsequently volunteered his services as an additional aide to Colonel Tyler for the remainder of the afternoon. The other stations worked superbly, allowing Kimball to transfer orders and information rapidly to his subordinates and to communicate directly with General Shields, who was finally convinced that a force greater than Turner Ashby's cavalry and horse artillery contested his division south of Winchester.[4]

The lack of a signal station near the point of Tyler's attack did not prevent Colonel Kimball from receiving information concerning the deployment of the Third Brigade. Shortly before 4:30 P.M., Lieutenant Colonel Daum and other staff members returned to Pritchard's Hill from Sandy Ridge and updated the commanding colonel about Tyler's situation. Kimball was already aware of the bad news they carried—Colonel Tyler's flank attack had stalled hundreds of yards short of its goal. Kimball had become painfully aware of another problem that impeded success. Robinson's six-gun battery had fired 240 rounds of ammunition at Jackson's men; Clark and Jenks had used more than that. After continuously hurling shot and shell for nearly seven hours, all of the Union artillerists were running dangerously low on ammunition.[5]

These realities left Nathan Kimball with an important decision to make. Five infantry regiments consisting of thirty-nine companies surrounded his headquarters on Pritchard's Hill. This 1,600-man force consisted of most of Kimball's own First Brigade and the 5th Ohio of Colonel Jeremiah Sullivan's Second Brigade. Colonel Sullivan also had three and one-half regiments on the low plain east of the Valley Pike, an infantry force of nearly 2,000 men. With only two hours of daylight remaining, Nathan Kimball could either attempt to remain on Pritchard's Hill or strip his left and commit more troops to Sandy Ridge to remove the Confederate threat from the hills west of Kernstown.

Lieutenant Colonel Philip Daum delivered Kimball's decision to Lieutenant Colonel Franklin Sawyer, who was still in separate command of four companies of the 8th Ohio. They had been active skirmishers west of the Valley Pike throughout the morning and had been recalled to support artillery on Pritchard's Hill early in the afternoon. They subsequently redeployed to support Robinson's guns west of the Middle Road, replacing the 7th Ohio who had moved out to lead Tyler's flank movement shortly after 3:00 P.M. Sawyer and his men found themselves closer to the Sandy Ridge battle arena than any other unengaged troops

Lieutenant Colonel Franklin Sawyer, 8th Ohio Infantry
U.S.A.M.H.I.

of Shields's division; therefore, the men were not surprised to receive Sawyer's order to load and fix bayonets in preparation for a charge. The approach of Lieutenant Colonel Daum toward their position determined the fate of this battalion of the 8th Ohio for the rest of the afternoon.

The artillery chief ordered Sawyer to charge the enemy's position on Sandy Ridge. Sawyer counted 188 non-commissioned officers and privates under his command—a meager force, indeed, to be expected to charge uphill against infantry and artillery. Most of the 8th Ohio still remained under Colonel Carroll's control east of the Valley Pike and were unavailable to reinforce him. Daum pointed toward the line of march that Sawyer's force was expected to take. They were to advance from the knoll, and through a patch of woods that obstructed their view of Tyler's attack above them. The 8th Ohio's intended point of engagement represented the new Federal left flank on Sandy Ridge.[6]

Lieutenant Colonel Sawyer dressed his lines, reined his mount toward the destination point, and led his men forward at the double-quick as cannonballs crashed through the trees and musket balls whizzed by them. The rounds sailed harmlessly above the infantry force as they advanced half a mile to a rail fence on the downslope of the northeastern face of the ridge. Ahead of them was the contested stone wall, about 500 yards away.

The falling late afternoon sun deceived the advancing bluecoats into believing that the Southerners firing at them from behind the stone fence wore black uniforms. While most of Sawyer's men remained behind the rail fence, the Buckeyes of Company C advanced to within 250 yards of their adversaries and fired upon them from an exposed knoll in front of the wall. Colonel Allen's 2nd Virginia stuck them in the front, while skirmishers from the 2nd and the Irish Battalion hit the Ohioans on the left flank, forcing them from the knoll. (See Map 7A) Private John Stough, who with his pie-eating partner David Lewis had become the targets of the first shots of the battle during the morning, fought alongside his friend until a bullet pierced Stough's skull and killed him. Several other company mates fell around him, and the knoll was deemed untenable. Company C returned to Sawyer and the remaining three companies of his command.[7]

Sawyer noted that his battle line struck the enemy at a right angle to Tyler's brigade line. His men nearly demolished the rail fence that fronted them, an unfortunate consequence for the soldiers because their position now afforded them little protection. Confederate skirmish fire forced Sawyer to order his battalion to refuse their left to counter the flanking fire that devastated his men.

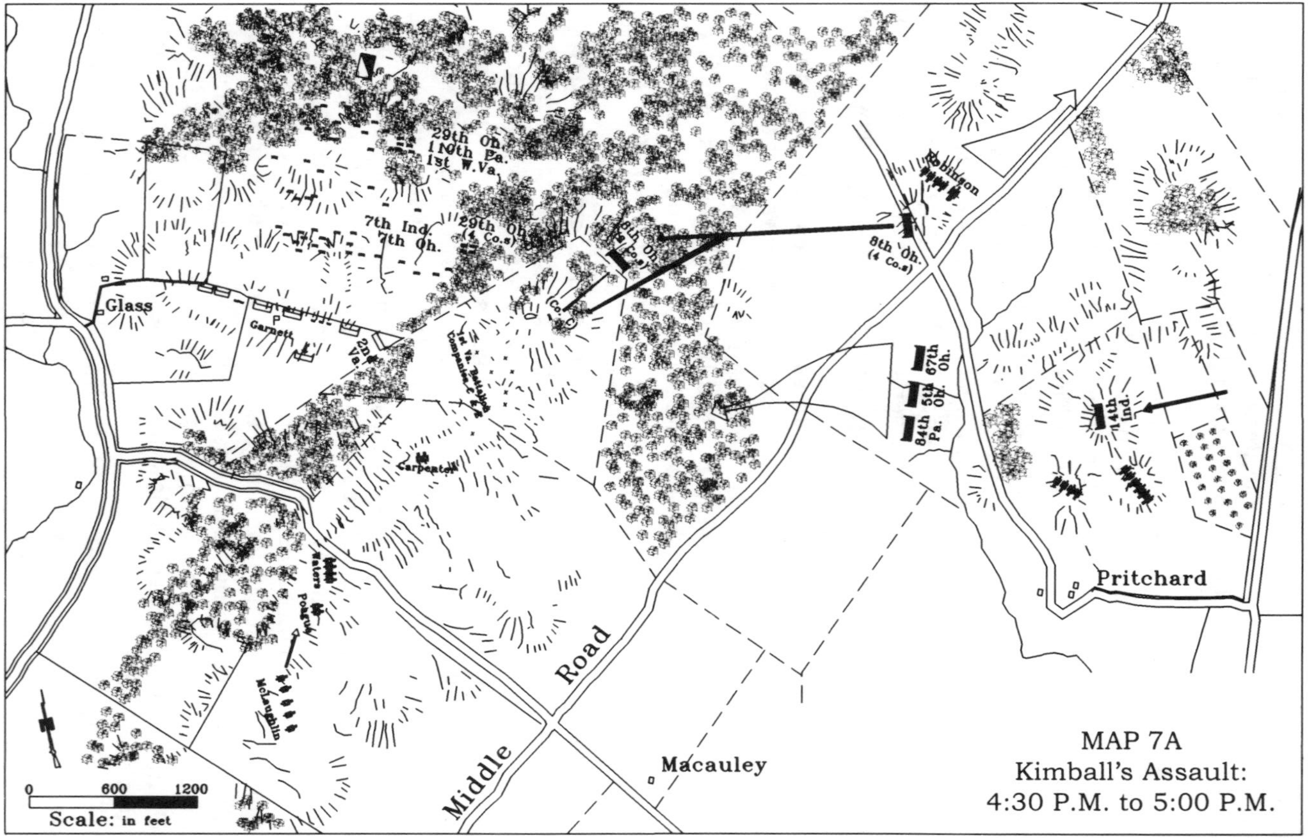

MAP 7A
Kimball's Assault:
4:30 P.M. to 5:00 P.M.

Map by Marcus D. Lemasters

Pritchard

14th Ind.

Robinson

8th Oh.
(4 Co.s)

84th Oh.
5th Oh.
67th Oh.

Macauley

Middle Road

8th Oh.
(4 Co.s)

(Co. ?)

29th Oh.
110th Pa.
1st W.Va.

29th Oh.
(4 Co.s)

7th Ind.
7th Oh.

1st Va. Battalion
Companies, ?

2nd Va.

Garrett

Waters
Pogue

McLaughlin

Glass

0   600   1200
Scale: In feet

His troops, in textbook fashion, pulled the left flank of the unit back from the main line which formed a right angle on the flank to repulse the force confronting it. The four 8th Ohio companies still were no match for the strong Confederate defense, but the company officers refused to give up the contested field. Lieutenant Alfred T. Craig, commanding Company E, was found lying on the field, bleeding profusely from a bullet wound. When his men attempted to carry him to safety, Craig refused to be moved. He pointed to his wound and, attempting to rally his men, asked them if they would avenge his injury. His men responded in the affirmative, but only twenty-two of them were still standing.[8]

Sawyer afterwards remembered that the fighting was so close as to be "almost hand to hand, some of the men discharging and clubbing their muskets." His casualty list confirmed his claim. Twelve Buckeyes died during the assault, while an additional twenty-eight men lay wounded, victims of the savage fight on the slope during the early moments of their engagement. The rapid loss of more than twenty percent of Sawyer's strength forced him to give up the attack, hold his position, and wait for support.[9]

Additional Ohio regiments moved to Sawyer's aid. The 67th Ohio was supporting Jenks's battery in front of Colonel Kimball's command post on Pritchard's Hill when the order came to attack Sandy Ridge. The regiment's colonel, Otto Burstenbinder, was under arrest and awaiting a court-martial, leaving Lieutenant Colonel Alvin C. Voris in charge. Voris counted seven companies under his charge for the afternoon; Companies F and I remained with Carroll's skirmishers east of the Valley Pike and Company G was detailed in Winchester for guard duty.[10] Voris's companies moved out simultaneously with the 5th Ohio and 84th Pennsylvania, clearing much of the infantry support from the silent batteries on Pritchard's Hill.

Lieutenant Colonel Alvin C. Voris, 67th Ohio Infantry

U.S.A.M.H.I.

The 67th Ohio scaled Sandy Ridge to the left of the 8th Ohio, turning the Union line sharper

to the south and shaping the angle of the Federal formation. The
terrain caused the 67th to lose control of its formation during the
advance. Taking advantage of a depression on the Sandy Ridge slope,
Voris rectified his battle line in the woods while what he deemed a
"hurricane of iron" stormed all around his men. The Buckeyes then
rushed forward for 400 yards, advancing much closer to the Confederate line than the 8th Ohio could maintain with their undersized battalion. Originally marching toward the Confederate artillery positions with the 84th Pennsylvania, Voris now turned his
men obliquely to the right. They assaulted the eastern end of the
same stone wall that Tyler's men had unsuccessfully contested for
the previous hour. According to Colonel Voris, his men struck the
line 200 feet from the wall and obliquely left of the 29th Ohio, the
regiment on the left flank of Tyler's brigade.[11] (See Map 7B)

The 67th Ohio faced off against Colonel Allen and the 2nd Virginia infantry of the Stonewall Brigade. The Virginians had taken
their positions to the right of the 33rd Virginia just moments before
the Union's second wave of attacks advanced to Sandy Ridge. Allen's
formation was hampered by the rugged terrain near the stone wall.
The right-hand companies managed to reach the wall, but the left
flank was impeded by thick undergrowth at the eastern end of the
wall and by the rapid fire of the Ohio regiments in front of them.
Union soldiers formed and fired within speaking distance, but this
did not intimidate Allen's regiment. "We marched up to within 25
paces of their line, and planted ourselves," raved Captain Samuel
J. C. Moore, noting that the 2nd Virginia's position now overwhelmed
their opponent. The 2nd Virginia forced the 67th Ohio back from
its original point of attack and held it at bay from their protected
position.[12]

The seven 67th Ohio companies numbered approximately 350
men on Sandy Ridge. They opposed a force of Confederates whose
volleys wreaked havoc in their ranks; however, the new regimental
commander proved a much worthier leader than his predecessor.
Seeing his men falter under the withering fire from the 2nd Virginia, Voris dismounted and cheered on his men by telling them to
do their duty. Voris realized that his regiment struck too far to the
right (north), exposing the left flank of his men to a devastating
counter fire from the right end of the Confederate line. According to
67th Ohio Captain Marcus Spiegel, Voris corrected his awkward
position when he "took the flag [to the left flank], called for the boys
to rally around it, and soon we were in position to play upon the
enemy with fearful effect." Voris appeared unfazed at the several
close calls he had survived; his overcoat bore the mark of several
bullets and his belt had been torn off by a shell fragment earlier in

the afternoon. "I cannot say enough in praise of Colonel Voris," wrote one of his soldiers days afterward, "His men are all proud of him, and would follow him if they knew that death awaited them; such is the proud respect and confidence we have in him."[13]

Perched on the brow of the ridge fifty yards away from the stone wall, Voris's 67th Ohio took heavy casualties. Company officers emulated their leader's inspiring courage and led their units with reckless bravery. Captain H. B. Ford of Company B sprung forward from the rail fence and barked, "Follow me, boys!" A Confederate bullet entered his mouth and severed his spine, killing him instantly. An additional forty-five members of the 67th Ohio filled their home-town newspaper casualty lists. Xenophon Wheeler, wounded in the leg, was the only member of Company G to become a casualty, a surprising result considering the company was detached at Winchester to guard the army stores and never had been called into action. Private Wheeler stole away from his company during the morning when he heard the rolling thunder of artillery, and found himself fighting with the 13th Indiana and 8th Ohio during the morning skirmish. Eventually hooking up with his own regiment, Wheeler afterwards considered the battle as "the most enjoyable day of my army life." He fortified his courage on Sandy Ridge by believing a calculation he had heard that it required 600 pounds of lead to kill one man in battle. His army days ended when a Southern bullet tore into his thigh, forcing Wheeler to forever distrust that calculation.[14]

The ferocity of the infantry fire that poured into the eastern end of the wall was at least equal to that experienced earlier at the center and western portions. In Company G, Corporal Bushrod C. Washington of the 2nd Virginia fell with a wound in the back of his head. Told to go to the rear, the wounded soldier replied, "Not so long as I have a drop of blood left in my body will I cease fighting for Virginia!" His brother, Sergeant George Washington of the same company, ran to the corporal's side and assisted him in loading his musket. The Washington brothers continued the collaborative effort until George Washington caught a bullet in his side, incapacitating the team for the rest of the afternoon. Fifteen-year-old Private George Burwell of the same regiment also drew a great deal of attention from his comrades. The lad had achieved an admirable reputation at Manassas for capturing a Federal captain, but now he was overcome with disappointment on Sandy Ridge. Try as he might, he could not remove a jammed ramrod from his musket. Burwell, who was captured before day's end, was last seen by a comrade bellowing because he could not get another shot at the "Damned Yankees." Private F. Whiting of Company C received a bayonet wound in the eyelid—one of the few wounds from this outmoded weapon that was recorded during the war.[15]

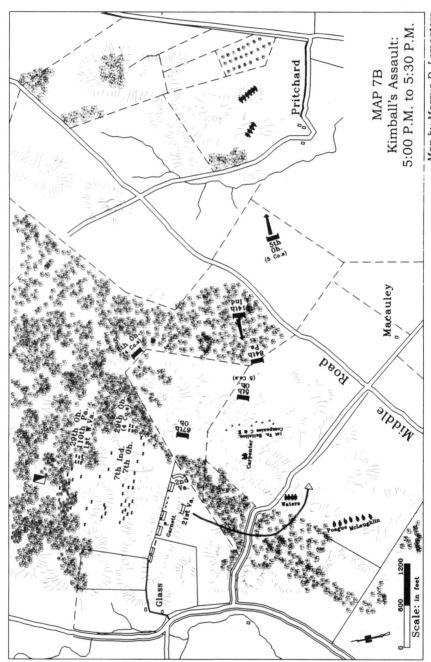

Glass

Garnett

21st Va.

2nd Va.

7th Ind.
7th Oh.

29th Oh.
110th Pa.
1st W.Va.
29th Oh.
(4 Co.s)

67th Oh.

8th Oh.
(4 Co.s)

5th Oh.
(5 Co.s)

84th Pa.

14th Ind.

5th Oh.
(5 Co.s)

1st Va. Battalion
Companies C & E

Carpenter

Waters

Poague McLaughlin

Middle Road

Macauley

Pritchard

MAP 7B
Kimball's Assault:
5:00 P.M. to 5:30 P.M.

Map by Marcus D. Lemasters

Scale: In feet

0   600   1200

Regimental flags routinely gauged the viciousness of battle because they were conspicuous targets for the opposition. At Kernstown, the 2nd Virginia proved this point to the highest degree. Sergeant Ephraim B. Crist of Company A carrying the colors for the regiment when they entered the Sandy Ridge fight. Early in the action he was shot in the head while brandishing the standard and killed instantly. Lieutenant J. B. Davis of Company K picked up the fallen colors and bore them until he was knocked down by a spent ball. At that point, Lieutenant Richard H. Lee of Company G raised the flag and kept his men in line of battle, rallying them around the colors.[16]

Private George Burwell, 2nd Virginia Infantry
Courtesy of Clarke County Historical Association

Lieutenant Lee took his new role seriously and it was likely that he instigated the most surreal moment of the battle. The new standard-bearer jumped over the wall and stared defiantly at soldiers on the right flank of the 67th Ohio who were standing and firing away at the 2nd Virginia from a point less than seventy yards away. The Virginian dared the Buckeyes to come on. The men of the 67th Ohio were astonished. They ceased firing for a moment or two, shouting down the line, "Don't shoot that man; he is too brave to die." After a few minutes they decided that this respite had gone on long enough and ordered the Virginian to return to his side of the wall. The color-bearer saluted his hospitable opponents, jumped over to the Confederate side of the wall, and the firing resumed.[17]

A severe left leg wound took Lieutenant Lee out of the action as the third color-bearer of the 2nd Virginia. A fourth man grabbed the standard before it touched the ground but he fell with a mortal wound, as did many of his regimental mates surrounding the flag. At this point the 2nd Virginia line wavered from its heavy losses. Colonel James W. Allen—his reputation tarnished by his temporary loss of sight at Manassas—refused to suffer a second setback in consecutive battles. In an inspiring moment, he lunged from his horse, picked up the fallen colors, and bore them to the wall. The remaining 250 members of the regiment still standing rallied around their one-eyed colonel. Fourteen bullet holes perforated Allen's flag and the flagstaff was shot in two, but the colonel had succeeded in restoring his line and the faith and trust of his men with his leadership on Sandy Ridge. Other members of the army were also impressed by Colonel Allen's act. "Colonel Allen fought like a man," assessed Captain Samuel J. C. Moore. Sandie Pendleton, who had earlier derided Allen as a coward, now praised the officer for leading his men "as gallantly as any man could."[18]

The Confederate right faced off against a new Federal regiment. The 5th Ohio advanced to the left of the 67th Ohio between 4:30 and 5:00 P.M., led by Lieutenant Colonel John Halliday Patrick. A native of Edinburgh, Scotland, Patrick took over the command of the 5th Ohio when its colonel, Samuel Dunning, was placed on special duty. Patrick found himself leading men in battle against the greatest of odds.[19]

The strength of the 5th Ohio dwindled even before it engaged the Confederates. Nathan Kimball suffered a moment of indecision that would hamper Patrick and his men for the rest of the afternoon. Watching the 5th Ohio, the 67th Ohio, and 84th Pennsylvania descend at the double-quick toward Sandy Ridge, Kimball surveyed the scanty infantry force remaining on Pritchard's Hill and quickly ordered the 5th Ohio to be recalled. A bugler announced the commander's new instructions as the Ohioans reached the Middle Road. Marching by the right flank, only the rear companies halted and returned to Clark's battery positions; the front companies either did not hear or did not understand the bugle call and continued their march toward Sandy Ridge. Shortly after entering the woods at the base of the contested hill, Lieutenant

Lieutenant Richard H. Lee,
2nd Virginia Infantry
Courtesy of Clarke County
Historical Association

Colonel Patrick turned to his men and, with jaw-dropping surprise, realized he was leading a battalion-sized command.[20]

Patrick encountered other difficulties in his advance. The 84th Pennsylvania had initially supported his left flank at the foot of Sandy Ridge until they recoiled under enemy fire, leaving the Buckeyes unprotected on both their left and right flanks. Patrick improvised with his force, formed them in line of battle, and quickly drove the Confederate Irish Battalion skirmishers back through the woodline in his front. Patrick fearlessly rode in front of his regiment, exhorting his men to "keep cool," "hold your ground," "stand solid," and "every man do your duty." The Westerners did not falter for Patrick knew exactly what strings to pull to keep his men moving. "Remember Cincinnati, your homes, and your country!" he shouted as the 5th Ohio emerged from the woodline. The woods ended at the brow of the hill at a small open field near the military crest of the ridge. When the 5th Ohio companies emerged from the trees, they were struck by the right of the Confederate line, including the 2nd Virginia on their right and the two Irish Battalion companies in their front and on their left. Waters's and Carpenter's iron guns spewed shot and shell from the rear of the infantry line slightly to the front and left of the Ohioans. Captain Carpenter's pieces had been pointing in the direction of Tyler's brigade for most of the afternoon. Carpenter ordered his artillerists to load with canister to pour a close-range devastating fire on the incoming Federal infantry. But the 5th Ohio and 67th swiftly closed in, forcing the battery to withdraw before Carpenter's orders could be executed. The cannoneers limbered and pulled the guns toward the southern extension of Sandy Ridge. The battery escaped without human casualties, but they did lose one wheel and two horses.[21]

With their left flank unprotected, the 5th Ohio tried to stand its ground against a withering fire that ripped through the ranks like a swarm of angry bees. Within minutes the 67th Ohio on their right fell back, allowing the right-hand companies of the 2nd Virginia to focus their attention on the 5th Ohio. The Confederates pummeled the right flank of the battalion until the 67th Ohio was able to reform and rally. The five companies of the 5th Ohio held their ground and returned approximately forty volleys from a distance of less than seventy yards. The color company became the most sought-after target and the flags of the 5th Ohio bore testimony of the action. The flagstaffs of both the national and state flag were broken in several places. The national flag was riddled by forty-eight bullets while the regimental flag took ten bullets.[22]

Unfortunately for Lieutenant Colonel Patrick, his men around the colors also attracted a disproportionate share of lead. Within half an hour he lost fifty men, more than one-fifth of his force. Two color bearers were cut down by the right flank of the 2nd Virginia minutes after the Ohioans entered the open field. Two more bearers seized the flags and were instantly gunned down. Captain George B. Whitcom, a Cincinnati native, rushed to the colors after watching them fall for the second time. Whitcom raised one of the flags over his head with one hand and was drawing his pistol with the other when a bullet smashed into his face. The gallant officer was dead before he toppled forward with the flag he had tried to save. Two corporals picked up the prized flags and held them for the rest of the afternoon. The Confederates in front of the 5th Ohio, many from the aggressive Irish Battalion companies, rushed forward to within ten yards of the Buckeyes and, at this point, the bullets whizzed through the air around all of them in a manner that a lieutenant described as "hissing snakes."

Patrick held his men in their positions as he met a new and entirely unexpected threat—fire from the rear. Were they flanked by the enemy? Patrick discerned that the fire came from a friendly source, the 14th Indiana. Nathan Kimball had sent his former regiment to reinforce the undersized attacking force that had left Pritchard's Hill one-half hour earlier. Patrick ran toward the Hoosiers and shouted that they were firing on their own men. He then instructed the Indiana adjutant to take his regiment farther to the left. When the adjutant, Lieutenant Robert Catterson, asked Patrick where the enemy lines were, the Ohio officer quickly explained that there was no such thing as battle lines here but, if the Hoosiers advanced through the woods on the left, he guaranteed Catterson that he would see "plenty of sesech." At this point Lieutenant Colonel Patrick returned to the 5th Ohio as support approached his unprotected flank. Colonel Murray had finally brought the 84th Pennsylvania up to reinforce the left of the 5th Ohio.[23]

For an officer who needed to prove his leadership in battle to prevent a subordinate mutiny, Colonel William Gray Murray was faced with a serious command control problem. His regiment was severely understrength. Many officers were detached on recruiting service while men were removed from their companies by an order on March 22 that placed several privates on special duty. Of the nine undersized companies available to him, Company I inexplicably stayed in camp at Winchester rather than look for their regiment late in the morning and subsequently fielded only three men in the fight. All told, Colonel Murray could count only 255 men on Pritchard's Hill when he received his orders to charge the Southern batteries.[24]

Making matters worse for Murray were the formidable obstacles impeding his advance. The 84th Pennsylvania had moved at the double-quick from Pritchard's Hill with the 5th and 67th Ohio; the Pennsylvanians represented the left flank of the Union attacking force. They formed into line of battle and entered the woods on the Sandy Ridge slope. While the 67th Ohio and 5th Ohio moved westward toward the Confederate infantry line, Colonel Murray obliqued his men more to the left and exited the woods facing southwest toward the cleared portion of the military crest of Sandy Ridge. Once in the clearing, he found the ninety members of the Irish Battalion a formidable and deceptive force. Likely hearing the 5th Ohio shout back to the 14th Indiana to quit firing on their own men, several Irishmen of the 1st Virginia Battalion mimicked the cry to the Pennsylvanians who were attempting to clear them from the smoke-filled ridge. The ruse worked to perfection; Murray's men, thinking they were firing into bluecoats, "were struck with horror and amazement, and instantly desisted," as one member of the regiment described the incident. A deadly volley greeted the 84th Pennsylvania and knocked down several men. With their difficulties in driving the Irish Battalion from their front, they lagged back from the flank of the 5th Ohio who faced less resistance in their advance.[25]

At 5:15 P.M. Murray and his men reached the cleared field near the military crest of Sandy Ridge, where they found themselves in a precarious predicament. Directly in their front were the consolidated Irish Battalion skirmishers who had embarrassed the Keystone Staters moments earlier. Behind the Irishmen on the military crest, the ominous cannons of Waters's West Augusta Artillery poured shot and canister onto the eastern slope of Sandy Ridge. Adjutant Thomas H. Craig, the only other regimental officer with Murray that afternoon, described what faced the regiment:

> They held a strong position on the edge of a wood, behind rocks and hillocks, with an open space of about 40 yards between us. We were exposed to a withering fire from the front and a galling cross-fire from the left, where a force was posted behind a stone fence about 100 yards from our flank, while the battery from an elevation in the rear kept pouring a deadly discharge of . . . canister.[26]

The stone fence that Craig described on the left front of the 84th Pennsylvania was not the one that Tyler, Garnett, and Fulkerson's men were contesting, but another east-west wall that lined the road which traversed the center of Sandy Ridge. This wall was 400 yards long and stood nearly 500 yards south of the eastern terminus of the wall which most of the Confederate infantry protected.[27]

This stone wall also had Southern troops behind it. By 5:00 P.M., much of the 21st Virginia had rallied from their original position at the center of the main east-west wall in response to Kimball's new threat to the Confederate right flank. Lieutenant Colonel John Patton had saved the day earlier in the afternoon by assisting the 27th Virginia just as that regiment was about to be dislodged from its position by the 7th Ohio. Seeing the new threat on the right, Patton, Captain F. D. Irving and Sergeant-Major Mann Page gathered all the men they could find who still had ammunition and ordered them to move to the unguarded wall. Patton acted without orders, relying on military instinct to strengthen the weakened portion of the line. He found his regiment's new position to be advantageous. The men enjoyed a commanding position on the flank of the luckless 84th Pennsylvania who were now fully exposed in the field in their front. Private John Worsham of Company F, 21st Virginia, noted that many men in his company kneeled behind the fence, at first. When their advantage became clear, everyone in the company fired in a full standing position; some men were caught up in the excitement of the moment and mounted the wall, "loading and firing until every cartridge was shot away."[28]

The infantry and artillery fire from two fronts savaged Colonel Murray's regiment. All the remaining members of the 84th Pennsylvania hugged the earth to protect themselves from the deadly fire that pounded them from forty yards away. Colonel Murray's horse was shot out from under him and it hobbled to the rear. Adjutant Craig's horse was killed by enemy fire. Several men used the dead animal as a breastwork to protect them from the devastating volleys fired by the Virginians.

Like those of the 2nd Virginia and the 5th Ohio, the color company of the 84th Pennsylvania and their standards became conspicuous targets. Shortly after Captain Whitcom fell in the Ohio regiment, a similar scenario transpired around the flags of the Pennsylvanians to their left. Patrick Gallagher, Company E, captained the color company and was a loyal home-town friend of Colonel Murray. Earlier that morning he had sent a brief letter back to his family in Hollidaysburg, explaining to them a premonition of his death. In the early moments of engaging the Confederates on Sandy Ridge, a bullet pierced his brain and fulfilled his prophecy. The color sergeant and four color bearers were also shot down. Finally, Sergeant Thomas Gouldsberry, one of only three men from Company I on the field, grabbed the fallen standard and ran to the front of his regiment, shouting defiance at the Virginians who were well within hearing distance. The intrepid flag bearer escaped unhurt, but he counted thirty-one bullet holes in his flag at the end of the day.[29]

Colonel Murray watched in horror as over a third of his command melted away. Company C went into the battle with twenty-two men and now had only four; the lieutenant commanding the company escaped the casualty list although he was bruised on the thigh by a shell fragment, received a flesh wound on the other leg, and had his blanket shot from his shoulder and his cap from his head. Company B's overzealous lieutenant advanced his men ahead of the remainder of the regiment to within thirty paces of the Confederates and proceeded to lose twelve men there. Private Isaac Bennett of Company B raised his gun to fire but was knocked head over heels when a Confederate musket ball entered the muzzle of his Belgian rifle. It passed down the barrel and welded itself onto the unfired bullet.[30]

Through it all the gray-eyed colonel behaved valiantly. His six-foot muscular frame was conspicuously at the head of his regiment, and he constantly moved along the line barking instructions and encouragement to prevent his men from faltering.[31] Murray's inspiring presence held his men in their positions, although many of the Pennsylvanians suffered from slight wounds and withered from the effects of close-range artillery. The colonel turned to his adjutant and exclaimed, "We can hold this place no longer. We must either advance or retreat, and we won't retreat!" With those words, orders went through the ranks to prepare for another charge. Murray intended to attack Waters's battery. Adjutant Craig passed the orders to the company commanders and returned to Murray's side. The colonel turned toward his foe and, "with a voice that was heard above the roar of the battle," he ordered his men to charge.

Colonel Murray lifted his sword above his head and stood in front of the bullet-riddled colors to lead his men forward. A member of the Irish Battalion had other ideas and sent a well-aimed shot at the Irishman from Pennsylvania. The bullet struck the embroidered bugle in Murray's cap and drove the "84" into his forehead. Murray's body toppled back into the folds of his flag, marking the colonel as the highest ranking officer to die at Kernstown and settling the issue of leadership with his conspiring subordinates once and for all. Ninety-one other Pennsylvanians fell during the short encounter, making the 84th Pennsylvania the hardest suffering Union regiment with a loss of thirty-six percent in less than forty-five minutes of fighting.[32] (See Map 7C)

Most of the remaining 84th Pennsylvania withdrew in disorder toward the wooded base of Sandy Ridge. Several clung to the hillside and waited for support. Only a few minutes passed before the

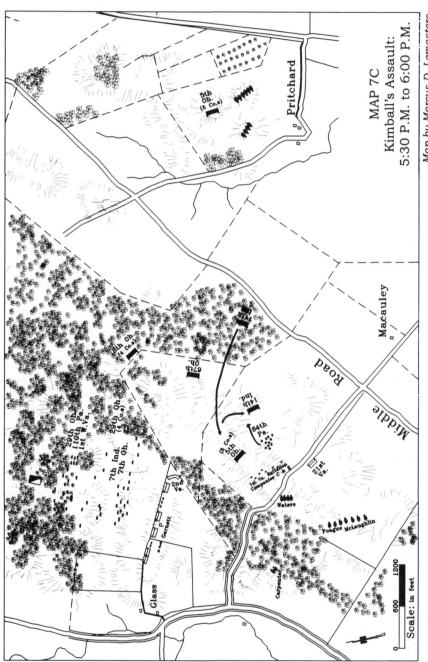

MAP 7C
Kimball's Assault:
5:30 P.M. to 6:00 P.M.

Map by Marcus D. Lemasters

Scale: in feet
0   600   1200

heads of the 14th Indiana appeared at the woodline. The Hoosiers had finally found the left flank of the Federal line and were ready to go in.[33]

The 14th Indiana, active throughout the morning as skirmishing support for Colonel Carroll, had somehow suffered no casualties. Led by Lieutenant Colonel William Harrow, the regiment was held in reserve on Pritchard's Hill under the eye of their former commander, Colonel Nathan Kimball. At approximately 5:00 P.M. Kimball ordered Harrow to advance his regiment to Sandy Ridge, pointing with his hand the direction the Westerners were to take, and telling Harrow to move as rapidly as possible and to fall in on the left of the Union line.[34]

The thirty-nine-year-old William Harrow was entering his second month as a regimental commander. Like Abraham Lincoln, Harrow was born in Kentucky and practiced law in Illinois. He was living in Knox County, Indiana, at the outbreak of the war and initially captained a company in the regiment he was now leading into battle for the first time. The lieutenant colonel would eventually ascend to lead a division in battle later in the war; however, Harrow's notorious "troublesome nature" did not endear him to his men and resulted in several resignations prior to the war's end. Captain Elijah H. C. Cavins of Company D suggested the cause of Harrow's adverse personality was linked to his penchant for the bottle: "On the day of our Winchester Battle, our Lt. Colonel Harrow was so drunk he didn't know anything." The accusing subordinate claimed, "A great many say that it takes a good deal of whiskey to get his courage up to the sticking point."[35]

Despite the possible handicap of being led by an inebriated officer, most of the 14th Indiana were prepared to make a good account of themselves. Although they considered themselves veterans of the western Virginia campaign of 1861, the battle they were entering was, by far, their biggest. Some of the men had a personal interest in their adversary. In Company D, Henry Scott was entering the contest against his "rebel" uncle, while Virginia-born John F. Stamper realized he was fighting as a Hoosier against a Confederate regiment his brother had enlisted in. Members of other regiments attached themselves to the 14th Indiana. Captain J. E. Gregg of the 8th Ohio was one of them. Unable to find his company and regiment after the battle began, Captain Gregg joined the Hoosiers and, with no command to lead, fought as a private with the rest of the Indianans.[36]

At the outset, the Westerners had moved in a solid column at the double-quick and crossed the little meadowed valley between the two heights. They escaped injury despite a continuous rain of canister and shell from the Rockbridge Artillery; the shells had sailed too high. As the Hoosiers climbed a fence and entered the wooded foot of Sandy Ridge, the bullets "rattled like hail" in the treetops and some soldiers were slightly wounded by the spent balls glancing from the tree limbs above. Unable to distinguish friend from foe on the smoke-encased height, the Hoosiers had advanced in the rear of the 5th Ohio where they threw their errant shots toward the backs of the Ohioans before working their way to the left flank at 5:45 P.M.—the approximate time of Colonel Murray's death.

Harrow formed his regiment, 450 men, in line of battle. The right-hand companies lined up 300 yards in rear of the 84th Pennsylvania while the left battalion extended on the Federal flank to the point where it was directly in front of the 21st Virginia. The right flank of the 14th Indiana fought a battle of nerves prior to charging the Confederate line. They witnessed the panic-stricken remnants of the 84th Pennsylvania flying through their ranks to find the safety of the rear. Many Indianans shuddered when the litter carriers bore the uncovered body of Colonel Murray through the ranks of Company C, his brain tissue protruding from his opened skull. The sight of the devastated Pennsylvanians produced a lasting effect on many of the Indiana boys; some refused to go into the contest and suffer the same fate. "Several of each company failed to go into the fight who were not sick and not detailed on other duty," complained Captain Cavins, adding "Severe punishment will be inflicted upon them."[37]

Most of the available Hoosiers desired only to inflict punishment upon their adversaries. The 14th Indiana received their orders, deployed into line of battle, and marched up to the cleared field as deliberately as if on drill. The regiment entered the clearing and witnessing a scene which moved a soldier on the left wing to write:

> We were soon at the top—when a scene presented itself that I never will forget. Immediately in front of our whole lines, at a distance of perhaps 80 or 90 yards, was a long wreath of blue smoke settled over a low stone wall—out of this a fire flashed constantly. Between our line and this wall the dead and wounded lay in heaps, while clustered around the stars and stripes, a few heroic blue jackets still fought desperately—some standing, some kneeling, and others lying at full length; but all apparently determined to die right there.[38]

The Hoosier had witnessed the remnants of the 84th Pennsylvania who were taking their colonel's proclamation—"We won't retreat"—to heart, even though fewer than fifty remained on the hillside. Another Indiana soldier, Corporal James H. Simpson, saw the ring of smoke decorating the stone wall, Adjutant Craig's dead horse to the front of it, and one lone soldier hugging the earth behind the carcass with scores of dead and wounded scattered around him. Simpson described the scene as one that came nearer to his boyish ideas of a battle picture than anything he had yet seen. He also knew that if the regiment stayed in the withering fire without charging or retreating, it would be destroyed within ten minutes.[39]

The 14th Indiana loosed a volley, but stayed in place on the brow of the hill. The Confederates sent back a devastating fire which knocked down several of the Westerners. The air thickened with bullets which, to one man, sounded like the dusting of carpets with rods as they crashed into the Hoosier soldiers. What impressed many was the odor of gunfire, "not the sulfurous discharge in particular, but rather the peculiar scent of lead in violent friction."[40] Without orders to move, the 14th Indiana faced the possibility of suffering the same fate as the Pennsylvanians. With total darkness less than one hour away, the successful repulse of the 14th Indiana could secure Sandy Ridge for General Jackson and his division and enable them to withdraw from the field under the cover of nightfall.

In a battle that registered countless individual heroic acts, a man named Paul Truckey swung the momentum of the contest in favor of the Federals. He was neither a regimental nor a company officer. This most unlikely hero was a thirty-four-year-old carpenter-turned-private in Company G of the 14th Indiana, a unit recruited from the town of Vincennes. Truckey was a descendant of the first French voyageurs that inhabited his hometown, the former Post Vincent, Indiana. The soldier appeared uninspiring with a slim, lithe build on a five-foot-six-inch frame and an awkward French accent, but his subsequent action in this battle would be admired by others in the regiment for decades to come.

As his company and regimental mates fell around him, Paul Truckey sprang in front of his battle line, waved his Enfield rifle over his head, shouted, "Come on, boys!" and darted "headlong after the rebels as a dog would chase a rabbit, loading and firing as he went." Truckey's ostentation electrified his regiment. Several members in both wings of the 14th Indiana picked up his momentum and yelled the order to charge, the left attacking the stone wall and the right going for Waters's guns. The men in the ranks responded with a "Hoosier Yell" and surged forward, the right flank advancing over the dead and wounded Pennsylvanians at a quicker pace than the left battalion facing the stalwart Virginians behind the stone wall. The right wing was led by its adjutant, Lieutenant

Robert F. Catterson, on horseback. The horse was gone within seconds, but Catterson continued to lead on foot.[41]

The 14th Indiana would stay on Sandy Ridge, the first Union regiment to take the offensive against the right flank of Jackson's division which was now stretched to the limits by more than two hours of continuous fighting and mounting casualties. Two other Union regiments were fast on their way to support the attack. Meanwhile, as General Garnett and his Virginians clung to their positions, Stonewall Jackson prepared to bring on all available reserves to preserve the Southern stronghold on Sandy Ridge.

The Sandy Ridge fight had raged for two hours; men alone had been unable to decide the contest. With the sun setting behind the Allegheny Mountains and dusk enveloping the Shenandoah Valley, nature and time would exert their influences on the outcome.

Chapter Eight

"But Enough of This"

General Richard Brooke Garnett inspected his infantry line as the sun dipped west of Sandy Ridge. His men had held their positions, but Garnett realized that their performance could not continue for much longer. Two factors remained strongly in his favor. Total darkness was less than one hour away, and the western end of the stone wall, held by Fulkerson's brigade and portions of the 4th Virginia, appeared safely secured by the stalwart Southerners. Since repulsing Colonel Joseph Thoburn and the 1st West Virginia two hours before, this portion of the Confederate line had barely been challenged.

The brigadier had no jurisdiction over the left portion of the line. Most of Garnett's brigade defended the spur of the ridge which separated them from Fulkerson's men and the two 4th Virginia companies on the left flank. Although the divided forces knew of each other's presence, the uneven terrain prevented them from being able to see each other. General Garnett's problems existed in the center and on the right. The awkward terrain prevented him from stretching out his line; therefore, he had packed the equivalent of four small regiments of 1,000 men behind 800 feet of available rock barrier. Men from the 33rd Virginia and the 2nd Virginia had intermixed while other segments of regiments lapped each other to exploit the available protective space.[1]

General Garnett need not have worried about his crowded line because the events of two hours of continuous infantry fire were thinning his ranks. The Virginians, firing downhill, had a tendency to fire high while the Federals found their marks more frequently owing to their uphill volleys. More than 150 men fell to Northern rifle

173

fire during that time, and no reserves were yet available to replace them. The progression of battle surprised the men as to how nefarious they could become. An Ohio soldier explained to his father two weeks afterwards about the inescapable evil that overtook him in the midst of the Sandy Ridge fight:

> In the excitement of battle I could aim at them when only forty or fifty yards from me, as cooly as I ever did at a squirrel. But now it seems very much like murder. They would throw up their hands and fall almost every time we would get a fair shot at them, and we would laugh at their motions and make jest at their misfortune. I don't nor can't imagine now how we could do it. The fact is, in battle, man becomes a sinner and delights in the work of death. And if his best friend falls at his side he heeds it not, but presses on eager to engage in the wholesale murder.[2]

Garnett was also losing soldiers to other factors. Some had decided that their hearts were not in the fight and they slipped to the rear. Others were leaving the ranks for more legitimate reasons. By 5:30 P.M., the 27th Virginia had exhausted its ammunition and other regiments who entered the line later were getting close to the same predicament. After it was all over, General Jackson would proudly note the "noble instances . . . of their borrowing [ammunition] from comrades, by whose sides they continued to fight, as though resolved to die rather than give way"; however, many of the Southern soldiers were well past the point of successfully finding bullets in the cartridge boxes of fallen comrades. Uninjured officers and men were seen milling in the rear of the line. When Lieutenant Elliott Johnston, one of Garnett's aides, asked the men why they weren't fighting in the front line, the standard response was, "I haven't a round in my cartridge box—what can I do?"[3]

The musketry from the Southern side of the wall had slackened considerably, so Garnett attempted to hold his men in line with inspiration. He rode through the ranks of each of the four Stonewall Brigade regiments engaged on Sandy Ridge (the 5th Virginia was still in reserve), encouraging his men to "aim low and pick [your] men." Lieutenant Colonel Grigsby was impressed by his superior's display of valor, noting that General Garnett "stood coolly and calmly surveying everything that was going on" earlier in the day when heavy enemy fire was storming all around him. Grigsby was equally inspired by the way Garnett "bore himself most gallantly throughout that field."[4] The right of the Southern line had been extremely hard-pressed, but for a while it appeared that the danger had passed. The 8th Ohio, 67th Ohio and 5th Ohio had been successfully held in check on the flank and posed no imminent threat. Despite all of his efforts to hold his line, the approach of the 14th Indiana against the extreme right became the impetus of doom for Garnett and the Confederates on Sandy Ridge.

Garnett had been aided by Lieutenant Colonel Patton's foresight to strengthen the Confederate right flank after Kimball's reinforcing regiments were ordered to take out the Confederate batteries. The 84th Pennsylvania Volunteers, after the loss of their colonel, were overawed by Patton's men and the Irish Battalion, except for several stubborn bluecoats who clung to the hillside. The Pennsylvanians had changed the direction of the battle and the 5th Ohio companies also advanced in that direction. No longer was infantry attacking infantry. Murray and his men had been after the Southern batteries, and although they had been repulsed, they had steered the 14th Indiana toward their line of attack. Federal reinforcements, led by the 13th Indiana and more distantly the 62nd Ohio, were fast approaching Sandy Ridge.[5]

The Southerners' immediate problem lay with the 14th Indiana. This was the first full-sized regiment to participate in Kimball's second wave of assaults (the other four regiments totaled only twenty-three companies). The 14th had attacked the extreme right of the Confederate line 500 yards behind the right flank of the 2nd Virginia. The 8th Ohio, 5th Ohio, 67th Ohio, 84th Pennsylvania, and 14th Indiana had participated in piecemeal attacks. No brigadier coordinated their assaults on Sandy Ridge (Nathan Kimball never delegated the command of his brigade after he took over Shields's division). These assaults extended the Federal flank and wore down the right side of the Confederate line. The Indianans were not exchanging volleys anymore but had pushed forward in a charge, led by the reckless valor of Private Truckey. The clever soldiers of the two Irish Battalion companies, the only men available to fill the gap between the 2nd Virginia and the 21st Virginia, attempted to stall the Hoosiers' momentum with the same ruse they pulled off against the Pennsylvanians one-half hour earlier. "Don't fire," the Irishmen shouted through the drifting battle smoke, "you are firing on the 84th Pennsylvania!" This time the trick failed; the few men remaining from Murray's regiment called for the 14th Indiana to ignore the plea and come on. The Pennsylvanians instructed the Indianans to fire over their heads and to drive the Virginians away.[6]

The right-hand companies of the Hoosier regiment fired six rounds and then smashed against the pesky Irish Battalion companies. The effect was devastating; the heavily outnumbered Confederates reeled under the weight of the Indianans' momentum and many of the men broke to find safety in the rear. The company commanders would not allow it and attempted to rally their men. Captain Joseph P. Thom kept his Company C men in the front until an enemy bullet tore through his right hand. A second round smacked into the officer's breast. Thom was lucky—a small copy of the New Testament became his guardian angel. It absorbed the bullet and saved his life. The injured captain relinquished his duty to his second in command, Lieutenant William L. Randolph, who kept his men in line.

Captain James Young Jones commanded the Richmond recruits of Company E of the battalion; they were fighting their first battle. In the 1850s Jones had given up the medicine profession for a military career and had spent time in Europe in hopes of procuring a commission in the French army to aid that country's fight against Austria. Now witnessing his first battle on American soil, the young officer despaired at the sight of his comrades facing potential defeat. Jones moved to the front of his men and jumped on a stump while the 14th Indiana was rapidly closing in around him. Captain Jones waved his sword over his head and bellowed at his men to move forward. A bullet struck him across his face. The gallant officer was last seen by his men toppling off the stump, his sword still in his hand.[7]

Pushed out by the Federals, the Irishmen fell back, exposing Waters's cannons to capture. At the same time, the "Hoosier Yell" resonated from the left side of the 14th Indiana as the line charged over the dead and dying through a storm of leaden hail. They headed toward the stone wall which protected Lieutenant Colonel Patton and the 21st Virginia. Patton noted that a galling cross-fire peppered his men as both wings of the 14th Indiana closed in to within twenty yards of his line. Patton could hold no longer, but he did not have to make the decision to withdraw. "The day was pretty well spent," he wrote matter-of-factly in his report, "when an aide of the general commanding ordered me to retire with the regiment."[8]

General Garnett was not at the right of the line when the 14th Indiana acted on their own initiative, but his decision to withdraw had not come a moment too soon. The brigadier, focusing more on the problems with the center of his line, despaired at the success of a Federal cavalry demonstration on the left—a charge that apparently succeeded in capturing several exhausted Confederates who quit the ranks and had attempted to leave the field.[9] General Garnett quickly weighed his options and decided that he could not risk the loss of part of his artillery nor endanger his transportation. His line was weakened by the loss of men and scarcity of ammunition; the brigadier also believed that he was heavily outnumbered. At 6:00 P.M., as the 14th Indiana swarmed toward the Confederate right, Garnett sent Lieutenant Elliott Johnston to Lieutenant Colonel Patton, ordering him to withdraw. The order did not come too soon as far as the 21st Virginia was concerned. After the 14th Indiana reached the wall, one of the soldiers claimed the Southerners "were scattered and fled in all directions" while another Hoosier stated they fled "pell mell" from the wall.[10] (See Map 8A)

General Jackson remained at the southern portion of Sandy Ridge, oblivious to the fact that his troops had started to withdraw from the stone wall. Stonewall realized his division's position had become tenuous and was apprehensive about the possibility of his troops becoming overwhelmed by Federal reinforcements. In the event that his infantry would be forced back, Jackson ordered Captain McLaughlin to have a portion of his battery face westward into the field behind the rest of the battery. Jackson instructed his artillerist to sweep the space after the Southern infantry crossed it to slow any Federal pursuit. He also detached a company of cavalry under Major Funsten's command from the Glass farm and ordered it to charge the western portion of the field should the enemy attempt to cross it.[11]

By 6:00 P.M., General Jackson witnessed the first signs of defeat when scores of men passed by him making their way to the rear. Though aware that the possibility of withdrawal existed, Stonewall was still surprised at the sight of his men giving up the fight with darkness so close at hand. He stopped a member of the 21st Virginia and asked him where he was going. When Stonewall heard the soldier's reply that all his ammunition was shot away and no more rounds were available, the general rose in the stirrups of Little Sorrel and exclaimed, "Then go back and give them the bayonet!"[12]

General Jackson had not anticipated a protracted infantry fight of such magnitude; consequently, he failed to have a reserve ammunition supply available for his troops. The division wagons stayed near Newtown, approximately four miles south of Sandy Ridge. He realized that for two hours his infantry had engaged the bluecoats in "almost a continuous roar of musketry." His men had depleted their forty to sixty rounds of ammunition, but Stonewall expected them to stay and fight with bayonets. He had already taken steps to rectify his supply and manpower deficiencies. One-half hour earlier, Jackson had ordered Major Frank Jones to bring up the reserve infantry at the Valley Pike.[13]

During the crucial point of the battle, when Nathan Kimball sent the First and Second Brigade regiments to the contested height, Stonewall remained near the southern portion of Sandy Ridge, from where he sent Sandie Pendleton eastward to estimate the size of the Federal force opposing him. Pendleton posted himself in front of the Rockbridge Artillery, a position with a spectacular view of Kimball's

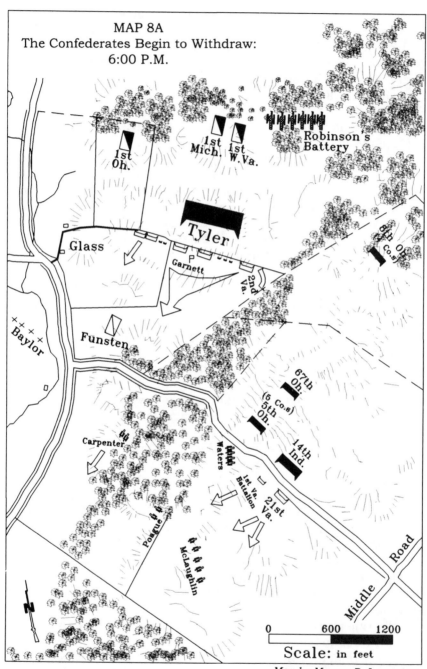

MAP 8A
The Confederates Begin to Withdraw:
6:00 P.M.

1st
Oh.

1st
Mich.

1st
W.Va.

Robinson's
Battery

Glass

Tyler

Garnett

2nd
Va.

6th Oh.
(2 Co.s)

Baylor

Funsten

67th
Oh.

(6 Co.s)
5th
Oh.

14th
Ind.

Carpenter

Waters

1st Va.
Battalion

21st
Va.

Poague

McLaughlin

N

Middle Road

0   600   1200

Scale: in feet

Map by Marcus D. Lemasters

and Sullivan's brigades but an interposing tree line prevented the lieutenant from observing the strength of Tyler's brigade. Viewing two-thirds of the available Union force and estimating the size of the unseen Third Brigade, Pendleton returned to his superior with a stunning overestimate of the numbers of bluecoats facing off against the Virginians. When Stonewall heard Pendleton's tally of over 10,000 men, he responded, "Say nothing about it, we are in for it."[14]

The force that Sandie Pendleton scanned from the Rockbridge Artillery position was essentially the same-sized force that Stonewall himself observed about two hours earlier when he helped position the artillery pieces on the cleared plateaus that commanded the Federal cannons on Pritchard's Hill. Nathan Kimball had no new forces to add to his command after this time; therefore, Pendleton misled his superior with an estimate that was nearly three thousand men higher than the Union force available. Jackson refused to withdraw in the face of the enemy; therefore, the division chief prepared to strengthen his force to hold on to Sandy Ridge until darkness enveloped the field.

Contrary to earlier incidents of micromanaging his division, Stonewall Jackson uncharacteristically exhibited a detached posture with his front-line troops; he chose to stay in a rearward position to aid in feeding reinforcements into the line once they arrived on the ridge. Those reinforcements may not have been as necessary had the division commander been at the stone wall to shift most of the unengaged left-flank troops from Colonel Fulkerson's brigade— over 500 men—to the heavily pressed Confederate right where Colonel Allen and Lieutenant Colonel Patton were losing ground against the reinforced Federals. Despite the lack of direction in the Confederate battle line, the timely arrival of the 5th Virginia, 42nd Virginia, and 48th Virginia could negate the disparity in strength and momentum by providing more than 1,000 fresh troops (and their 40,000 bullets) to hold the line until nightfall.[15]

Colonel William H. Harman waited at the Valley Pike with his 5th Virginia Infantry, by far the largest Stonewall Brigade regiment with over 450 men. The reserve role provided them a much needed respite after marching thirty-five miles. Three hours of rest arguably made this regiment the strongest of all the Southern units on the field. Three companies of the 5th Virginia were recruited from Winchester and the surrounding environs of Frederick County; they had the opportunity to free family and friends from Federal occupation.

Although his foot soldiers were veterans, Colonel William Harman was relatively new to command. The thirty-four year old was a native of the Shenandoah Valley, born in Waynesboro. Harman was a Mexican War veteran and a practicing Commonwealth attorney for Augusta County at the outbreak of hostilities in 1861. Because of his military experience, he was commissioned as lieutenant colonel of the 5th Virginia, second in command to Colonel Kenton Harper. But Harper had resigned from his command shortly after the victory at Manassas when General Jackson refused to allow him to take leave during an inactive period for the army to visit his dying wife (She passed on without her husband at her bedside). Harman had taken over the regiment on September 11, 1861.[16]

At 5:45 P.M., Harman watched the fast-approaching Major Jones and realized his regiment's reserve role had ended. Jones halted his overworked steed and relayed Stonewall's instructions to Harman to bring up the 5th Virginia. Jones also found Colonel Jesse Burks, the commander of Jackson's Third Brigade, who protected the artillery reserve and commanded the regiments protecting it. Burks's command was entirely split up—although the 42nd Virginia was with him at the Valley Pike, the 21st Virginia and Irish Battalion had gone to Sandy Ridge over two hours earlier, and the 48th Virginia was two miles in the rear guarding the supply wagons between Bartonsville and Newtown. He was ordered through Major Jones to bring the rest of his command up to Sandy Ridge. Burks complied, sending an aide galloping up the Valley Pike to find Colonel Campbell of the 48th Virginia while he personally advanced westward with the 42nd Virginia and Pleasants's battery of four guns. Burks moved at the double-quick with his command marching by the right flank.[17]

Unfortunately for the Southern infantry and artillery on Sandy Ridge, the reserves were called upon too late. The 21st Virginia was forced from the wall by 6:00 P.M., resulting in the loss of the Confederate right flank. The Irish Battalion was scattered, exposing Waters's West Augusta Artillery cannons to a front and flank fire. The 14th Indiana was joined on their right flank by the 5th Ohio, who tenaciously hung on to their positions and were now seeking to exploit their advantage. Both Union regiments wanted the Southern guns. Captain James Waters did not wait for withdrawal orders. He ordered his ninety men to extricate the four pieces from their exposed position and pull them from the battlefield. Three guns were safely removed. Sergeant Charles S. Arnall limbered the fourth piece—a twelve-pounder iron cannon—when a wheel artillery horse was killed by rifle fire delivered from fifty paces. When the animal toppled on its side, the cannon did likewise. Arnall ordered his cannoneers to right the gun and carry it off with his three remaining horses, but the swift approach of Lieutenant Catterson's wing of Indiana soldiers and the five 5th Ohio companies, along with the 67th Ohio on their right, changed Arnall's mind. He cut the other three horses loose, leaving the toppled cannon for the Hoosiers and Buckeyes to claim as their prize.[18] (See Map 8B)

Colonel Arthur Cummings received General Garnett's orders and withdrew his tired 33rd Virginia from the stone wall. Portions of the 33rd were intermingled with the left flank of the 2nd Virginia. They withdrew together, leaving the right wing of the 2nd Virginia without protection on either flank. To the immediate left of the 33rd Virginia fought the remaining three Irish Battalion companies, captained by David Bridgford. Bridgford's Irishmen had replaced the 21st Virginia one hour earlier when Lieutenant Colonel Patton transferred his men to the right of the Confederate line. The unit's color-bearer planted the flag on the spur of the ridge between the 27th Virginia on their left and the 33rd Virginia on the right. Three companies of the battalion fought around its colors for approximately one hour. Bridgford believed it was 6:30 P.M. when he received orders to withdraw (it was probably twenty minutes earlier than that), but his men continued fighting as skirmishers. The Irish captain could see the far and immediate right of the line falling back in what Bridgford considered to be "great confusion." After the Irish Battalion withdrew, the 27th Virginia followed suit. Being the first regiment engaged in the fight, Lieutenant Colonel Grigsby's men were in no position to question the withdrawal orders—they had no ammunition.[19]

The Sandy Ridge terrain split the 4th Virginia into two unequal wings. Most of the regiment occupied the spur of the ridge with the 27th Virginia. This battalion withdrew from the field with Grigsby's men, leaving two companies in the gully where they remained with Colonel Fulkerson's two regiments at the far western portion of the wall. These separated fighting units were oblivious to the mass withdrawal that had commenced on the spur above to their right, unaware that their entire force on the crest was leaving except for the right wing of the 2nd Virginia.

Tyler's brigade was well aware of the events occurring in their front. They witnessed the slackening fire from the Southern side of the wall and realized that the Confederates' ammunition was becoming scarce. The 7th Ohio's ammunition was also nearly expended after loading and firing for nearly two hours in the ravine. At this point, most of the 7th Ohio withdrew from the front and were replaced by Colonel Buckley and his 29th Ohio.[20] Captain Myron Wright, commanding one of the divisions of the 29th Ohio (Company D and I), fought gamely for over an hour after having received a shrapnel wound through his lower leg. Shortly after moving forward, he

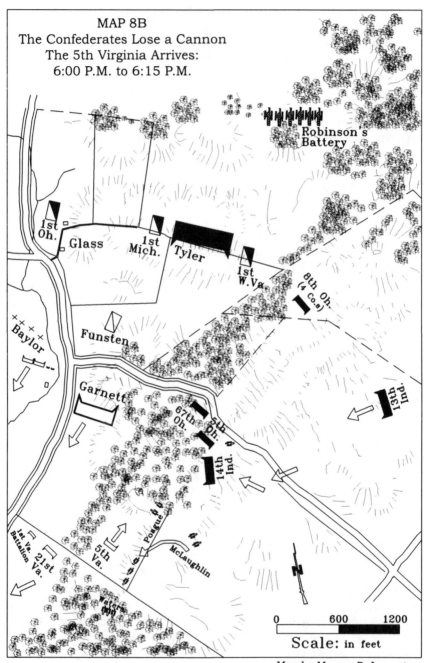

MAP 8B
The Confederates Lose a Cannon
The 5th Virginia Arrives:
6:00 P.M. to 6:15 P.M.

Robinson's
Battery

1st
Oh.

Glass

1st
Mich.

Tyler

1st
W. Va.

8th Oh.
(4 co.s)

Baylor

Funsten

13th Ind.

Garnett

67th
Oh.

5th
Oh.

14th Ind.

Poague

5th
Va.

McLaughlin

1st Va.
Battalion Va.

21st
Va.

Waters

N

0   600   1200

Scale: in feet

Map by Marcus D. Lemasters

noted the wound had been aggravated and was bleeding profusely. He signaled to Colonel Buckley for help. The colonel detached Lieutenant W. P. Williamson to relieve him.

Wright saluted Lieutenant Williamson upon his arrival and announced, "To you I entrust my command." When Williamson asked for the reason, Wright pointed to his wounded leg, and the lieutenant took over. He held the helm for less than five minutes. Moving his two companies approximately 100 yards forward, Williamson advanced at the front of the regiment where his towering form became an inviting target, and he was killed instantly by infantry fire.[21]

Had Lieutenant Williamson survived a few minutes longer, he would have witnessed what most soldiers in the war rarely got the opportunity to see—the rout of the enemy. Corporal Seldon Allen Day of the 7th Ohio noticed the Southerners withdraw from their lines. Day had enjoyed his natural rifle pit where he could safely engage in close-range fire. When he ran out of ammunition, he slid feet first down to the ravine where he replenished his minié ball supply from the cartridge boxes of fallen soldiers, then he returned to the spur he had occupied previously. Shortly after 6:00 P.M. Day saw the Virginia infantry retreating from the stone wall, dodging behind woodpiles and running through the cleared fields to the wooded southern portion of Sandy Ridge. Realizing what was occurring, he turned toward his comrades below him, and waved his cap over his head, shouting, "We have got them started! Come on, come on!"[22]

Corporal Day unnecessarily encouraged the regiments of Tyler's brigade, for all of them moved on impulse to catch their retreating foe. Even the men in the 110th Pennsylvania had recovered from their "skeddadle" which plagued them two hours earlier and were now prepared to take part in exploiting the rout. They were encouraged by the omnipresent Union artillerist, Lieutenant Colonel Philip Daum. The Prussian cannoneer was back on Sandy Ridge positioning Robinson's battery near the eastern crest to rake his adversary with its fire. After unlimbering his cannons, Daum moved to the western side of the ridge, forcing stragglers back to the line at the point of his sword. He then found Colonel Lewis and pleaded with him to get his regiment in line and charge the enemy's works. Lewis placed the 110th Pennsylvania by rear rank and ordered them to advance by the left half wheel to follow the Federal regiments on his right over the wall.[23]

Tyler's men surged and scrambled over the now-undefended stone wall where so many of their mates had lost their lives, and chased after the Confederates retreating through the open field in front of them. Additional "friendly" casualties were taken here, including a 7th Ohio lieutenant who became badly bruised when he fell from a fence in the initial moment of the chase and was trampled by his own stampeding men. Notwithstanding the fluke injuries, it was a spectacular and exhilarating moment for the Federals. Corporal Day shook hands with two of his Company C mates, Privates Orlando Worcester and Thomas Dickson, all vowing to stick together after the retreating enemy. Regiments from Tyler's brigade intermixed with the 14th Indiana, 67th Ohio, and 5th Ohio which impeded the pursuit. Many were awestruck to see Confederate soldiers throw down their weapons to lighten themselves in their flight.[24]

But not all of the Confederates were retreating. Fulkerson's brigade—the 23rd and 37th Virginia—and two companies of the 4th Virginia remained behind the gully portion of the stone wall, ignorant of the rout generated to their upper right. This segment of the line was separated from the rest of the division by steep terrain and never received orders to withdraw. They heard the Federals cheer, foreboding trouble on their flank. Lieutenant John Lyle of the Liberty Hall Volunteers was puzzled after watching Fulkerson's two regiments fall back on his left without seeing serious pressure in their front. Within minutes another company officer returned from a reconnaissance and explained that the remainder of the

Kernstown Battle at Sunset
This unrealistic view (no lines of battle existed) is drawn from near the 84th Pennsylvania's position, facing west.

Alfred R. Waud

regiment and brigade had withdrawn. At that moment an enfilading fire greeted the Virginians from the spur on the right. The Federals had flanked the unsuspecting Confederate companies and were close to cutting off their retreat. With few options available, the men of Fulkerson's brigade retreated across the Glass farm at the western base of Sandy Ridge, followed by several members of the 4th Virginia. Looking back toward the stone wall, members of the Liberty Hall Volunteers were vexed at the sight of the stars and stripes waving over their former position.[25]

Fulkerson's brigade and the 4th Virginia were not the only victims of confusion and poorly delivered retreat orders. Colonel Allen of the 2nd Virginia held the right end of the wall at the eastern portion of Sandy Ridge and never received the order to retire. His regiment was the only Confederate force still defending the line. Allen watched Tyler's bluecoats scale the wall to his left and realized he was now unsupported. The colonel ordered his men to withdraw, but for many, it was too late. Forty-two officers and men of the 2nd were captured. An additional forty-two men were wounded, including nine men who fell into Union hands when the rapid sweep prevented them from being carried to safety. Included in the latter were the Washington brothers, who, though injured, fought together for nearly an hour. Bushrod C. Washington was attempting to carry his more seriously injured brother George from the field when Federal cavalry swept over them, capturing both soldiers and ending their fight for Southern independence. With the six men killed in the action, the 2nd Virginia suffered ninety-eight casualties for a loss of thirty percent.[26]

At 6:15 P.M. General Jackson, waiting for his reserves to arrive, incredulously witnessed his division streaming rearward. At precisely the same time, Colonel Harman of the 5th Virginia reported to Stonewall, announcing that his regiment had arrived. The 42nd and 48th Virginia were still en route. Jackson welcomed the arrival of his largest regiment. He ordered Harman to take his command forward to support the engaged troops. Major Frank Jones, who led the 5th Virginia to the ridge, rode ahead of the regiment toward the front.

Stonewall detached one member of the 5th Virginia to perform a special duty for him. Hugh Barr, a drummer in Company A, had been born and raised in Winchester and had made a name for himself in 1859 when he beat the rally in the streets of his home town to call out troops to repel John Brown's insurrection at Harpers Ferry. Near the southern edge of Sandy Ridge, General Jackson pulled Barr from the ranks and ordered him to beat a rally again—this time to recall the retreating Valley District troops. Barr's drumbeats mixed into an air already filled with cracking gunshots and booming artillery. Stonewall's attempt at rallying his troops failed; however, Barr earned the sobriquet that the twenty-two-year-old man would carry for the remainder of his life: "The Drummer Boy of Kernstown."[27]

Unfortunately for Colonel Harman and unknown to General Jackson, the Confederate troops were nearly all in retreat. Harman had advanced approximately 200 yards from his point of contact with General Jackson, toward what he described as a "terrific fire of cannon and musketry" when the omnipresent Major Frank Jones rode to him and ordered the 5th Virginia to halt and to occupy a wooded ridge to the left of their advance. The position of the 5th Virginia was 150 yards behind the Rockbridge Artillery on a neighboring spur near the center of the ridge.

Major Jones delivered the order from General Garnett whom Jones had met while he was riding forward and the brigadier was riding rearward. Jones reported that he was bringing the 5th Virginia to the front, but Garnett informed him that they could be of no benefit against superior numbers without the presence of the main body. Garnett found Harman in the woods where his subordinate told him that he had been ordered forward by General Jackson but was ignorant of the ground in his front. Garnett repeated to Harman what he had told Major Jones—that the most the 5th Virginia could be expected to do was to cover the retreat of the Virginia division. Garnett employed the tactics reminiscent of the Duke of Wellington against Napoleon nearly half a century earlier. He instructed Harman to place his regiment in line of battle in a clearing below the wooded crest of a spur running parallel and one-quarter mile to the rear of the original stone wall line. Here the reserve force waited in seclusion to ambush the pursuing Federals.[28]

Hugh Barr (1839–1885), "The Drummer Boy of Kernstown". Photo Taken ca. 1880.
Courtesy of Ben Ritter

The troops approaching Harman's Virginians included the right wing of the 14th Indiana, five companies of the 5th Ohio, and an equal number of companies from the 67th Ohio. This force of 700 to 800 men were buoyed by their success against the Confederate right flank and had entered the woods seeking additional battle prizes to add to the cannon they had already captured. The rejuvenated 110th Pennsylvania, 300 strong and the only other organized body of Federal troops in pursuit, approached from the west, chasing their opponents across the open fields of Sandy Ridge. The other four regiments of Tyler's brigade and the handful of companies from Kimball's brigade were so disorganized at the stone wall that they could not execute an effective pursuit. Many men fell out of the ranks to tend to their wounded and the injured Confederates.[29] The 13th Indiana began to scale the eastern slopes of Sandy Ridge; they would be the last organized Union regiment to enter the fray.

Small clusters of companies from Tyler's brigade also conducted a southerly pursuit. Major John Casement of the 7th Ohio spurred his sorrel mare in front of some of his troops and urged them forward. "Who will go with me into that battery?" he shouted with zeal. Corporal Day and a few men from Company C, caught up in their leader's enthusiasm, heartily responded, "We will!" Getting the answer he expected, Casement led the men eastward toward the enemy cannons. Reaching the crest, he found the overturned limber and twelve-pounder cannon of Waters's battery, already overrun by the Hoosiers and Buckeye's of Kimball's and Sullivan's brigades. After surveying the captured piece, Major Casement attempted to gather the scattered force around him to lead them southward. He was still in rear of the organized forces advancing toward Jackson's fleeing division.[30]

At this point the rout bred confusion, as described by Captain Elijah H. C. Cavins of the 14th Indiana:

> The Confederates fell back in great disorder, and we advanced in disorder just as great, over stone-walls and over fences, through blackberry-bushes and undergrowth. Over logs, through woods, over hills and fields, the brigades, regiments, and companies advanced, in one promiscuous, mixed and uncontrollable mass. Officers shouted themselves hoarse in trying to bring order out of confusion, but all their efforts were unavailing along the front line, or rather what ought to have been the front line. Yet many of the brave Virginians who had so often followed their standards to victory, lingered in the rear of their retreating comrades, loading as they slowly retired, and rallying in squads in every ravine and behind every hill—or hiding singly among the trees. They continued to make it very hot for our men in the advance.[31]

Captain Cavins's description underscored the obstacles that lay in the Federal advance. Although two Confederate batteries were forced to withdraw, four pieces of Captain William McLaughlin's Rockbridge Artillery remained unlimbered on commanding ground 300 yards south from where the 21st Virginia was overrun by the 14th Indiana. Another cannon, a twelve-pounder howitzer, had previously been withdrawn after its gunners complained to Captain McLaughlin that the piece did not have sufficient range. McLaughlin allowed the frustrated artillerists to take cover behind the stone wall at the foot of the spur on which they were positioned. The other two pieces of McLaughlin's battery were commanded by Lieutenant William T. Poague. This officer had earlier run his two bronze six-pounders to aid Waters's battery, but McLaughlin ordered them withdrawn when General Jackson sent the captain orders to prepare for a Federal breakthrough. Poague placed his cannons near some straw stacks at the eastern edge of the field that fronted the 5th Virginia, pointing northwest. Poague ordered the guns to be loaded with canister to sweep the field should Federal infantry attempt to cross it. Although four pieces of Rockbridge Artillery were not concealed, Poague's guns were tucked behind the straw stacks while the 5th Virginia lay in the woods behind the brow of the hill— a perfect ambush for the oncoming bluecoats. The sun disappeared from the clouded sky to better conceal the Confederates in the field below the woods.

At 6:15 P.M. McLaughlin was surprised by retreating Confederate infantrymen streaming behind him. The left wing of the 14th Indiana had crossed the stone wall previously occupied by the 21st Virginia and was advancing and firing at them from about 250 yards in their front. McLaughlin extricated his battery in good order starting at the left (north). Each canister-loaded cannon turned to the left, fired its iron load at the Westerners, and then was wheeled through one of the gaps in a stone fence where it was pulled to safety along the same path used for the advance three hours earlier. The Hoosiers buckled temporarily under the Confederate fire. They recovered after the last gun withdrew and prepared to continue their advance.[32]

Only Poague's two bronze pieces remained, exposed to troops closing in on three sides. The 14th Indiana and portions of the 110th Pennsylvania, 5th Ohio, and 67th Ohio approached from points west and north while the 13th Indiana from Sullivan's brigade scaled Sandy Ridge and closed in from the east. Determined to follow their orders, the gunners ignored the torrent surrounding them. The 110th Pennsylvania appeared on the field first. The Southern artillerists opened upon them from a distance of 150 yards, killing eight men outright, wounding thirty-eight others, and forcing the Pennsylvanians back into the woods. But Poague kept his pieces there too long. The Federal infantry closed in, forcing the artillerymen to quickly limber and take their guns into the woods and down the hill. The men escaped, but one of the wheel horses was injured by three bullets. There was no time to replace the lame animal and it was forced to help pull the gun to the rear.[33] (See Map 8C)

The guns rolled toward the woods just beyond the field where the 5th Virginia was patiently lying in front of them. Colonel Harman rode forward to the crest of the wooded spur where he saw a field with straw stacks in his front and a heavily wooded hill beyond it. Elements of retreating Confederates were fast approaching on his left, and coming directly in front of him were two regiments of Federal infantry. Harman returned to his men of the 5th Virginia on the downslope in the back field and prepared for the onslaught. The colonel watched the opposing infantry cross the brow in the shadows of the approaching darkness and ordered his men to open fire. His command responded with alacrity; the simultaneous discharge of 350 muskets flashed into the woods, sending a storm of lead directly at the unsuspecting Hoosiers and Buckeyes. "I do not think it possible for so many bullets to fly without hitting everybody," wrote a surprised Indianan who added, "and I fully expected to feel the sting of one every minute." This soldier escaped injury; however, five company officers and both color bearers of the 14th Indiana dropped with bullet wounds. Another soldier picked up the grounded flags and also was shot down. Finally, a private bore both colors defiantly to the front of the woodline while a section of the regiment took advantage of boulders and trees to keep the 5th Virginia in check.[34]

While contesting the Indianans on his center and right, Colonel Harman observed another regiment attacking the left flank of the 5th Virginia. Colonel William Lewis had rallied his regiment for a second time and, in his words, chased after the retreating enemy by "driving them like sheep before us" until he smashed against Harman's concealed line. Harman felt overwhelmed by the new threat and after watching his center and left give way; he rode along his lines and ordered his men to cease firing. He retired his colors farther to the rear and reformed his line around them.

By retiring his regiment, Harman inadvertently exposed one of Poague's guns. The six-pounder was hauled by the team with the horse that had been shot near the straw stacks minutes earlier. The wounded animal fell dead across the pole before it reached the safety of the woods, disabling the gun. As Poague's men frantically attempted to hitch up a replacement, a platoon of 200 members of

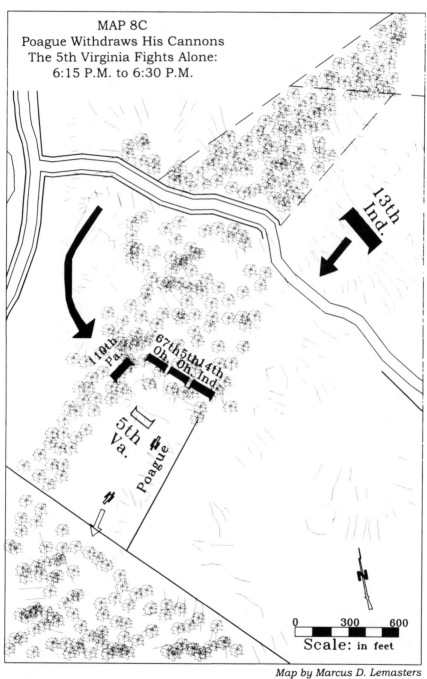

MAP 8C
Poague Withdraws His Cannons
The 5th Virginia Fights Alone:
6:15 P.M. to 6:30 P.M.

13th
Ind.

110th
Pa.

67th 5th 14th
Oh. Oh. Ind.

5th
Va.

Poague

0   300   600

Scale: in feet

Map by Marcus D. Lemasters

the 14th Indiana formed a battle line in the woods, howled another "Hoosier Yell," and charged the panicked artillerists. Poague could see that the dead artillery horse could not be replaced in time, so he ordered his gunners to cut loose the other horses and ride them to safety. The Hoosiers swarmed over the disabled cannon after wounding one Southern sergeant and two cannoneers, and killing two more horses and wounding three others. (See Map 8D) George Reintzel, one of the Rockbridge artillerists, was run over by one of the retreating limbers. The captured cannon was a special prize for the Northerners. Eight months earlier it had stood on Henry Hill as part of a Federal battery where it was captured during the Battle of Manassas.[35]

The other members of Poague's section retired to safety, but McLaughlin's command suffered dearly this day. In addition to several slaughtered horses and the lost cannon, McLaughlin lost four men with mortal wounds, eight men with lesser wounds, and two others captured. Privates Charles and Henry Gay were unscathed, although they may have had regrets about the decision they made earlier that day. The Gay brothers had wakened that morning as civilians and enlisted in the battery at the village of Kernstown, not knowing that their services were required immediately.[36]

The Westerners that captured the cannons accomplished a second goal. They now threatened the flank of Harman's new line, forcing the colonel to retire his command a second time. The 5th Virginia retreated toward the confines of another stone wall. This wall bordered thick woods south of it and ran in an east to west direction, traversing the southern end of Sandy Ridge approximately 1,000 yards south of the stone wall that the other regiments of the Stonewall Brigade had contested earlier. The 5th Virginia jumped behind this wall and fought alone as it had for the previous fifteen minutes. The time had passed 6:30 P.M. and the ridge had become ominously dark. Portions of four Union regiments, numbering 800 men, swarmed toward the remaining 400 Virginians, threatening to flank and capture the regiment. As they crossed the field, Lieutenant Colonel Voris shouted to his 67th Ohio, "Boys, if we don't drive them from these woods, we shall have to go to Richmond or the devil. Let them have it." Men of the 5th Virginia, not believing the wall provided enough protection, began to fall back farther in the woods surrounding them. Harman did not think he could hold his position much longer because he could see the enemy cavalry thundering toward to his left flank.

With no time to spare, the 5th Virginia was saved by a regiment from another brigade. The 42nd Virginia, led by their former regiment and current brigade commander, Colonel Jesse Burks,

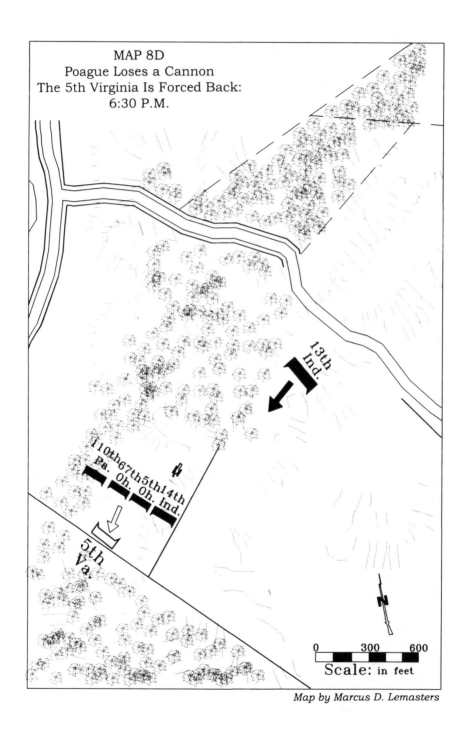

MAP 8D
Poague Loses a Cannon
The 5th Virginia Is Forced Back:
6:30 P.M.

13th
Ind.

110th 67th 5th 14th
Pa. Oh. Oh. Ind.

5th
Va.

0   300   600
Scale: in feet

Map by Marcus D. Lemasters

arrived at the scene at the double-quick. Burks's attached battery was under the command of Lieutenant James Pleasants; these guns also wheeled in the rear of the 42nd Virginia as it scaled the low rise of Sandy Ridge's southern base. With heavy action raging in their front, a staff guide (probably Lieutenant Junkin) delivered General Jackson's orders to form on the right of the 5th Virginia.

General Jackson remained south of his retiring division, frantically riding toward clusters of retreating soldiers and exhorting them to reform and advance. Stonewall was livid to see his second in command, General Garnett, accompanying some of the troops to the rear without displaying any apparent concern over the predicament. Jackson rode up to his subordinate and dressed him down, demanding to know why he was not rallying his men. Garnett replied that he had done so until he was hoarse. Garnett then collected some of the retiring soldiers of the 5th Virginia, brought them in line with the remainder of the regiment and 42nd Virginia, and advanced them all to the wall. In the meantime, Stonewall rode to Lieutenant Pleasants and ordered him to withdraw his battery to protect it from capture.[37]

The 42nd refused its right flank to counter the enveloping Federals by moving their front forward on one of the interior companies. Together, the two regiments numbered approximately 700 men and temporarily held their opponents in check. The 42nd Virginia nervously fired its first rounds without effect. Their lieutenant colonel, Daniel Allen Langhorne, determined that his men's initial volleys were too hurried. Langhorne made the necessary adjustments and noted that his men soon fired "with becoming deliberation." They succeeded in driving back the left flank of the 14th Indiana. The mix of Federals from the 5th Ohio, 67th Ohio, 110th Pennsylvania, and 14th Indiana flattened themselves on the ground, lying on their backs to load, then whirling around to take a quick and poorly aimed shot at the tree- and wall-protected Virginians. It appeared at first that the Southerners could hold their line indefinitely until Colonel Burks, looking through the shadows, saw that his refused right flank was in trouble. A new regiment was rapidly advancing to the east of the 14th Indiana.[38]

The oncoming Federal regiment was the 13th Indiana, under the command of twenty-eight-year-old Lieutenant Colonel Robert Sanford Foster. Foster had taken command of the 13th Indiana after Colonel Jeremiah Sullivan was promoted to brigade command. A former Indianapolis tinner, Foster's military role appeared to suit him well. Members of his command marvelled at his inspiring leadership. One private described him as "a soldier by instinct," adding "a braver man never drew a sword." Throughout March 23, Foster had been "as cool and unconcerned as on dress parade." Foster and his regiment had supported Union artillery until ordered to attack Sandy Ridge at 6:00 P.M.[39]

Ironically, the 13th Indiana received its second opportunity to salvage the Union army. The first test—at Sir John's Run Depot on January 4—had been a farce. At Kernstown, the fully armed 13th Indiana readied themselves to erase the previous incident from the annals of their history. Included in the ranks of Foster's Hoosiers on Sandy Ridge was "Hamlet," the commander's black servant, who grabbed a rifle when the 13th Indiana went into battle and fought with the enlisted men.[40]

"We started on the run and made the two miles in less than no time," boasted a proud member of the 13th Indiana, who noted their arrival near the point of conflict coincided with several members of the 14th Indiana falling back 200 yards into the woods on their right. Foster halted his men, then galloped up to the 14th Indiana where he was briefed on the enemy's position. Foster could see the 42nd Virginia enveloping the left of the stalemated 14th Indiana. The lieutenant colonel returned to his command near the edge of the woods, looked his men in the eyes, and ordered his command to "Charge Bayonets!" Foster's men marched forward in line of battle with arms at "right shoulder shift." According to one of the Hoosiers, "the bullets from the enemy were fairly making music as they struck and glanced from our bayonets."

Lieutenant Colonel Robert S. Foster, 13th Indiana Infantry
U.S.A.M.H.I.

A company officer of the 14th Indiana marvelled at the 13th moving to their support "sailing up like a great ship with colors flying." The advance covered 200 yards; the 13th left over thirty of their own laying on the ground as they charged up to the faltering left flank of the 14th Indiana. Foster ordered his men to return fire once they advanced to within 100 yards of the stone wall which protected the 5th and 42nd Virginia. They poured at least three volleys into the 42nd Virginia, overwhelming the regiment and shifting the momentum of their stand for a final time. The 14th

Indiana rallied on the right of the 13th Indiana, allowing Foster to confidently order a second advance: "Forward! Charge Bayonets!" Both Hoosier regiments hollered the "Hoosier Yell" and drove the 42nd from the wall, loading and firing as they walked southward. Lieutenant Colonel Langhorne's horse was shot out from under him and it slid down the hill on its back. Nathaniel and Noah Scales, fifteen-year-old twin brothers in the 42nd Virginia, fought side by side to stem the Federal tide until Nat was mortally wounded. Captain William Baylis Rector of Company I stayed within thirty steps of the 13th Indiana until he was mortally shot in the head. Colonel Burks, suffering from a hernia, ordered his command to retreat. What remained of the 5th Virginia saw their support driven back forcing them to also retreat through the woods. Both Confederate regiments took a devastating pounding; the 5th Virginia was thinned by sixty-six casualties in their forty-five minute engagement; the 42nd Virginia tallied an appalling seventy-two battle losses in approximately twenty minutes.[41] (See Map 8E)

The time approached 7:00 P.M. Despite breaking the last infantry line, Lieutenant Colonel Foster deemed it too dark to pursue the Virginians. Not wanting to risk friendly fire casualties, Foster ordered his command to halt. He found that his tired regiment had little support except for the remnants of the 14th Indiana and scattered squads from other commands that mingled near the southern foot of Sandy Ridge.[42]

This advanced command captured one more prize that evening. Corporal Seldon Day of the 7th Ohio had been following behind the 13th Indiana's advance in search of his regiment. Sporadic firing flashed in the darkness around him and Day could see a few horsemen in front of him, one ahead of the others. The young corporal walked up to the closest horseman to ask where his regiment was. Day noted that the officer was a Confederate. Knowing the Southerner believed the Ohioan was also a Confederate, Day pushed the muzzle of his rifle to the man's breast and ordered him to dismount. The surprised officer protested, claiming he was not there to surrender but had inadvertently wandered into enemy territory. Day asked the Southerner who he was and learned, in addition to his name, that his prisoner was a member of General Jackson's staff.

Two members of the 13th Indiana, Bob Owens and Lee Frazier of Company B, trailed their regiment and came across the Confederate officer just as Corporal Day ordered him off his horse. After a brief debate between the captors, the Confederate officer surrendered and the three Federals led him into the woods to find a commissioned officer to deliver their captive to. They came across the 13th Indiana's lone surgeon on the field and the three soldiers asked the harried doctor what to do with their prisoner. "Go to Hell with

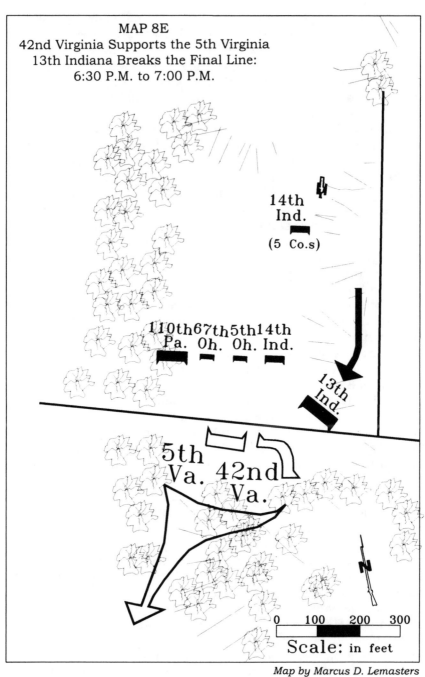

MAP 8E
42nd Virginia Supports the 5th Virginia
13th Indiana Breaks the Final Line:
6:30 P.M. to 7:00 P.M.

14th
Ind.

(5 Co.s)

110th 67th 5th 14th
Pa. Oh. Oh. Ind.

13th
Ind.

5th
Va. 42nd
Va.

0   100   200   300

Scale: in feet

Map by Marcus D. Lemasters

him! I have got men dying all over this field," came the physician's curt reply.

The three soldiers soon found Colonel Robert Foster and delivered the captive to him. Foster could see the man was a staff officer and asked Corporal Day what his name was. Day responded, "Lieutenant Dunken of Jackson's staff." At that moment, the disgusted prisoner quickly corrected the misinformed Ohioan and emphatically spelled out his name: "J-U-N-K-I-N." Earlier that afternoon, Lieutenant George Junkin had playfully commented "Those fellows seem to be mad at us," as Federal shells exploded around him. Now "those fellows" had captured him, ingloriously ending Junkin's career as a member of Stonewall Jackson's celebrated staff.[43]

General Garnett escaped the embarrassment that had befallen Lieutenant Junkin and bluntly admitted that darkness had saved Jackson's division from suffering considerably more losses than they had already received. He and some regimental officers were able to organize and rally elements of their routed force approximately 500 yards south of the last stone wall. By doing so, the officers withdrew the remainder of the 5th Virginia in comparatively good order along with the 42nd Virginia. These regiments had been weakened considerably, but their stand had allowed enough time for their comrades to escape a mass capture. Still, the organized withdrawal of the 5th and most of the 42nd Virginia stood in stark contrast to the remainder of the routed army that retreated before them. These elements streamed along the roads that filtered toward a lane which linked the Middle Road with Bartonsville. The night became especially dark; the moon was in its final quarter and cloud cover obstructed its meager light. General Jackson and his defeated division guided themselves along the double stone wall-lined lane in the darkness, passing in front of the Magill house and heading toward the safety of Barton's Woods in the distance. A detached portion of the 42nd Virginia, the last Southerners to leave the field, had fallen back scattered, disorganized, and separated from the more organized units of the regiment until a feeble Union pursuit united them at the edge of the woods. They repulsed the half-hearted assault and joined the main body of infantry in their withdrawal.[44] No Federal cavalry pursued Jackson's division as it streamed down the lane to the Valley Pike beyond Barton's Woods. Stonewall later learned what had kept the Union horse soldiers occupied.

Union cavalry in the East received heavy criticism for their poor performance throughout the first half of the Civil War. Southern horsemen were much more experienced and, at times, had literally run circles around their overmatched Federal counterparts.

The Battle of Kernstown represented one of the few exceptions during the early war in which Union cavalry outperformed their Southern counterparts. Throughout the morning and early afternoon of March 23, the Federal cavalry force had remained stagnant while Turner Ashby and half of his 7th Virginia Cavalry dueled Federal infantry and artillery. Lieutenant Colonel Joseph Copeland, with eight companies of 350 men from Ohio, western Virginia, and Michigan, supported the rear of Tyler's brigade in a solid column by companies and waited for the infantry to break the Confederate line in hopes of sweeping over the retreating Southerners. Shortly after 6:00 P.M. their opportunity arrived.

Between 6:00 and 7:00 P.M., as Jackson's infantry retreated from Sandy Ridge, Federal horsemen deepened the wounds inflicted by the Northern infantry upon the Valley District soldiers at Kernstown. Copeland ordered his men to charge as soon as he saw the Southerners break from the wall. Major Benjamin F. Chamberlain of the 1st West Virginia Cavalry galloped breathlessly to a squadron of Ohio horsemen who had been observing the battle from an open knoll toward the right of the Federal battle line. Chamberlain delivered Copeland's order to the Buckeyes, then listened in surprise when an officer asked where to go. Chamberlain responded, "Off to the right—there—anywhere! Go in Captain! Charge on them!" Chamberlain then disappeared from their view to bring on his own men.[45]

Captain A. D. Menken, Company C, 1st Ohio Cavalry, took over and hollered, "File off from the right by fours—Charge!" The Ohio squadron surged forward, then they reconnoitered eastward, looking impatiently for a gap in the shoulder-high wall to charge through. They rode nearly to the western edge of the wall where Fulkerson's brigade had just withdrawn. The Ohioans filed through the opening and then charged toward the fleeing enemy in the distance. "Like a bolt of hot lightning our red caps tore through the strip of woods," boasted a Buckeye, "and fell upon that motley army of confused and retreating traitors." These cavalry companies were closing in on the 23rd and 37th Virginia who were retreating southwestward. (They had received the withdrawal orders too late to move directly south along the ridge.) Members of the 4th Virginia, 33rd Virginia, and other Stonewall Brigade soldiers headed in the same direction. Many were generally familiar with the area, having hunted there prior to the war. Their destination was the "Big Woods," a stand of timber southwest of Neal's Dam which offered concealment from the enemy's horsemen and also the opportunity to rejoin the rest of the division on the Valley Pike near Middletown.[46]

The Federal cavalry quickly closed in on the fleeing Southern infantry with little resistance, even though nearly one-half of Turner Ashby's 7th Virginia Cavalry had been placed near the Glass house to prevent this from happening. The Confederate horsemen on the left flank of Jackson's line were under the direction of Major Oliver R. Funsten who had been stationed there with four companies of 140 men since 4:00 P.M. Between 5:30 and 6:00 P.M., Major Funsten received Stonewall's order to move some of his command to the rear of the infantry to protect them in the event that Jackson's infantry was driven from the field. Funsten complied with the order by personally leading two companies to Sandy Ridge while leaving (what he considered to be) a strong picket force on an elevated knoll in the rear of the Glass house to the west of Jones Road. Funsten provided extra protection before he left this force by placing an additional twenty men, under the command of Captain George Baylor, between the knoll and Sandy Ridge, covering a distance of 800 yards. George Baylor was new to his command. He had transferred from the 2nd Virginia Infantry to Ashby's cavalry only three weeks before the battle.

By coincidence, Major Funsten's shift to Sandy Ridge coincided with the charge of the 1st Ohio Cavalry squadron toward the routed infantry. With the exception of a brief repulse of Federals by Captain George Sheetz's Company F, Funsten's position on Sandy Ridge accomplished little. By the time Funsten returned to his original left flank position, he was astonished to learn that despite his precautionary efforts, the Union cavalry had somehow slipped through his forty horse soldiers and now were on his left and rear. Major Funsten reorganized his force to drive back a second wave of Northern pursuers, but the inability of his pickets to hold off an overwhelming force of Federal cavalry prevented him from thwarting the disaster that developed behind him.[47]

The Confederate infantry was spent after their tortuous marches and two hours of intense battle. The fight had exhausted their ammunition and their bodies. The fleeing force that headed toward Neal's Dam was ill-prepared to fend off a rejuvenated Federal pursuit. The Big Woods was never reached for more than 100 fresh Union horses carrying zealous armed riders thundered down and quickly surrounded a significant portion of Jackson's retiring army. (See Map 8F) There was no means to stop them. One Southern soldier described the harrowing experience of attempting to outrun armed cavalry:

> I started on the trail of the regiment, but a dash of cavalry across that route forced a change to the right. I kept going. Bullets would hit men about me with a thwack that sounded

like an impact with oilcloth on a frosty morning. They sang about the ears like a swarm of angry bees; they whizzed between my legs; they grazed my person, and knocked the dirt from under my heels as they lifted in flight; but I kept going. . . . It has always puzzled me why an enemy will shoot so persistently at a fellow that is running himself to death to get out of his way.[48]

The limits of human capabilities appeared to be exceeded as the Southerners desperately attempted to escape capture. Martin Miller, a soldier in the 33rd Virginia, was shot in the back of the neck as he ran down the gentle slope of Sandy Ridge. The bullet exited near his windpipe. The momentum of the blow lifted Miller into a somersault before he crashed to the ground. Several comrades retreating with Miller considered his injury fatal but were astonished to hear the wounded man declare he was alright. After helping him to his feet, the small band escaped (Miller needed only six weeks to recover from the injury). A member of the 37th Virginia suffered a similar experience when a Federal bullet penetrated his head from behind the ear and exited near his nose. Like Miller, the private rose up on his hands, ignored the blood spurting from his face, escaped, and recovered.[49] At least forty-four others in the 37th Virginia were not so lucky. These men were captured, adding to the dozens of soldiers killed or wounded in front of Pritchard's Hill. The 113 total losses in the 37th Virginia exceeded any other regiment on the field. (See Appendix C)

Colonel Fulkerson, along with several regimental and company officers, gathered stragglers on leveled ground near the William Glass property, where he ordered the men to halt and form a hollow square to repulse the cavalry—a textbook infantry tactic rarely employed in battle. Although at least three regiments were mixed together and fewer than ten men were present from any one company, Colonel Fulkerson calmly aligned in the battle formation with a fast-approaching enemy cavalry pursuing them. Fulkerson completed two sides of the square when two regiments from Tyler's brigade advanced on the ridge east of the formation and threw a flank fire into the Southerners, permanently disrupting the formation. Colonel Fulkerson quickly ordered the men to "make as fast as they could" to the Big Woods southwest of their position.[50]

The Northern cavalry enjoyed little opposition from the tired Virginia infantry. They trapped the Confederates near the dam and captured them individually or in disorganized clusters. Lieutenant Randolph Barton of the 33rd Virginia suffered the humiliation of capture when several Ohio horsemen surrounded him with pistols and carbines, then ordered the Winchester native to surrender his

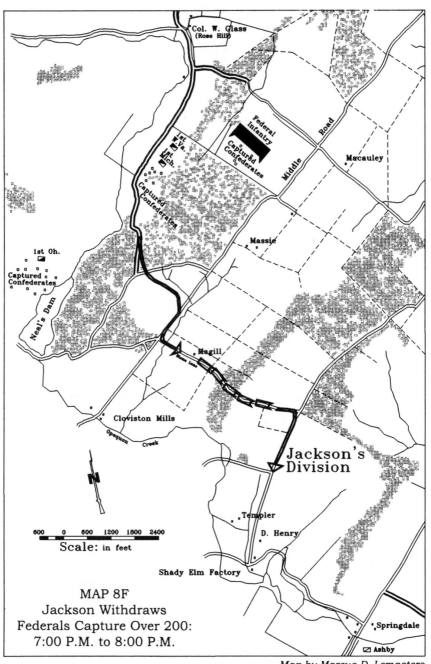

Col. W. Glass
(Rose Hill)

Federal
Infantry

Captured
Confederates

Middle Road

Macauley

1st
Va.

Rt.
Ich.

Captured
Confederates

Massie

1st Oh.

Captured
Confederates

Neal's Dam

Magill

Fence Lane

Cloviston Mills

Opequon Creek

N

Jackson's
Division

Templer

D. Henry

600   0   600 1200 1800 2400
Scale: in feet

Shady Elm Factory

MAP 8F
Jackson Withdraws
Federals Capture Over 200:
7:00 P.M. to 8:00 P.M.

Springdale

Ashby

Map by Marcus D. Lemasters

dress sword to them. Lieutenant John Lyle of the 4th Virginia's Liberty Hall Volunteers, who so vividly described the experience of being shot at by charging cavalry, found a remnant of his company and felt some relief as they closed in on the safety of the Big Woods which was less than half a mile in front of them. Cursing shouts to halt emanated from behind. Lyle turned around to witness the blue-clad cavalry swarming toward them. The Virginians wheeled and fired, then sprinted toward the woods, but they could not outrun the horses which quickly surrounded them. Lieutenant Lyle refused to surrender his sword and tried to snap it in half by placing the point to the ground and smashing the blade with his foot. The muzzle of a Federal pistol in his face and the admonition, "If you break that sword, I'll shoot you," persuaded Lyle to alter his plan and he surrendered it.[51]

The Union cavalry continued to collar retreating Virginians and now were within reach of capturing their first battle flags. Lieutenant James H. Langhorne, adjutant of the 4th Virginia, seized the 4th's standard from the ensign and attempted to rally his men around it earlier during the retreat. With all these efforts failing, Langhorne and Colonel Fulkerson, both slightly injured, rode obliquely to the right of their retiring infantry to seek safety. They rode at an "easy gallop" around the flank of Federal infantry, but Langhorne felt he was too spent to continue with the standard. He came across two members of his regiment who assured him that they could save the flag. Langhorne relinquished his mare to the two soldiers and gave one of them the flag with orders to tear it up if they thought its capture inevitable. Langhorne removed the top rail from a fence in front of his horse and slapped the animal's backside. The horse cleared the fence with both riders and the flag on its back and carried them to safety.

Most of the tired Southerners offered no resistance to the swarming Union cavalry and stuck their bayonets into the ground as a sign of uncontested surrender. But Lieutenant Langhorne refused the inevitable, preferring to risk his life rather than capitulate. Surrounded by nearly a dozen Buckeyes from Company A, 1st Ohio Cavalry, young Langhorne stood his ground and threatened the first horsemen that approached him. The fearless Southerner weighed merely 115 pounds by one Federal's estimate, but with rigid determination he exchanged pistol shots with a couple of Ohio horsemen until his gun misfired. He still refused to surrender. Instead he drew his sword and lunged at the men surrounding him, but was knocked down by a point-blank shot in his side as ten more Northern horsemen circled around him. Langhorne raised himself halfway from the ground, threw his sword at the trooper who shot him, and attempted to reload his pistol to continue the battle. Additional bullets from the closed-in cavalry finally disarmed the weakened Virginian. The gallant but injured officer pulled a ring from his finger, handed it over to one of the Federals and announced, "Send this to my mother and tell her I died rather than surrender."

Langhorne survived the encounter, surprising himself as well as the soldiers who captured him. The Union cavalryman who traded pistol shots with Langhorne told his sister six days after the battle that the Confederate "is a desperately brave man." The courage of the young Virginian so impressed the Ohio cavalrymen that one was moved to state twenty-seven years later that Langhorne was the bravest man he ever knew, adding that he "never before or since has seen a man in the midst of panic and rout rise so entirely above it and be so absolutely fearless as this young Virginia soldier."[52]

The 1st Ohio Cavalry was not alone in scooping up Southern prisoners. The Michigan and West Virginia units of Lieutenant Colonel Copeland's command also met with no resistance while scattering fleeing infantry on Sandy Ridge. They were so dominanting that several members of the 14th Indiana momentarily halted their pursuit and "stood in admiration" as Copeland's men dashed in advance of the infantry. The 1st West Virginia Cavalry was particularly successful. Led by Major Chamberlain and Captain William Carman, the western Virginians claimed the capture of two Confederate captains, four lieutenants, and 115 privates. One of the captains was Lewis P. Holloway of the 27th Virginia, Company C. Like captured officers Lyle and Barton, Holloway was forced to relinquish his sword. He ceremoniously delivered the blade to Captain Carman, saying, "I fought you while I could. I surrender myself a prisoner."[53]

Shortly after 7:00 P.M. total darkness and unfamiliarity with the terrain prevented Copeland from aggressively pursuing Jackson's division. The large number of Confederate prisoners also occupied much of his command. With a loss of nine men, all in the 1st West Virginia, the 350 Federal cavalry captured more than 200 Confederates. Additional scores of wounded and dead soldiers also fell into Union hands. Major R. Morris Copeland, assistant adjutant general of the Fifth Corps, rode over Sandy Ridge as the small arms fire faded along with the daylight. During his brief reconnoiter, he made a quick estimate of the dead and wounded and also ordered the field to be cleared of the discarded Southern muskets and equipment. As volunteers stacked the muskets in the dark, Copeland rode to the Seevers house in Winchester and reported the battle results to General Shields.[54] Copeland then informed the United

States War Department concerning the day's events. By 8:00 P.M., the telegraph office in Washington, D.C. received the first message of the entire day's activity:

> *Winchester, Va.*
> *March 23rd*

General R. B. Marcy,

    I have just come in from the very front of the battle three miles out. A complete victory over Jackson (and six thousand). Taken two guns and caissons. Killed at least one hundred and wounded twice as many. Our loss large, not over 150 killed and wounded. Our men did well. Took a great many muskets. The enemy in full retreat.

> *R. M. Copeland*
> *A.A.G.*[55]

Major Copeland overestimated Stonewall Jackson's strength and underestimated the number of Union casualties, but he also underscored the severity of Jackson's losses. By 8:00 P.M. General Jackson and his weary soldiers had safely crossed Opequon Creek at Bartonsville. Stragglers eventually streamed into his severely thinned ranks, but enough men were unaccounted for to convince all who were present to understand that the day had indeed been fought with tragic consequences. It appeared that nearly one-quarter of the force that entered the battle in the morning was missing. Some would find their way to the ranks by morning, but many were in Federal hands—both alive and dead. Several who safely left the field marveled that their entire force was not captured.[56] A bewildered Confederate rode up to some Stonewall Brigade infantrymen resting at the edge of a wood. After being assured that he had ridden up to Southern troops in the darkness, the disheartened and weary horseman could only mutter over and over again, "We've lost the day; we've lost the day."[57]

Stonewall Jackson ordered his men to bivouac near the Valley Pike south of Newtown. Ashby's cavalry took up defensive ground on the elevated terrain south of Opequon Creek, but would receive no challenges. Nearly everyone seemed sure of this. Captain Chew echoed their sentiments by announcing, "Boys, this battle is over."[58]

General Jackson did not appear daunted that evening by his defeat. Several members of Carpenter's battery cooked their day's only meal over a campfire made from fence rails near the Valley Pike north of Middletown. An unabashed artillerist saw General Jackson passing by them and asked him to share supper with them. Jackson accepted the soldier's offer and thanked him for the invitation. Stonewall took a portion of the cooked meal, sat on some rails beside the soldier who invited him, and dined with his men in front of the warm fire. The boy, apparently without fear of reprimand, spoke up again saying, "General, it looks like you cut off more tobacco today than you could chew." Stonewall turned toward the soldier, smiled and replied, "Oh, I think we did very well."[59]

Most of the members of Jackson's division did not share his sentiments that cold night. After reaching the safety of the Confederate campgrounds, Rockbridge Artillery member Ed Moore entered a small woodlot to warm himself at a crackling fire prepared by infantrymen. The evening was as memorable as the day to Private Moore, whose mind was branded with the memories of the black cooks piteously asking survivors where "Marse George" or "Marse Charles" was, and the whereabouts of others, then seeing the answer on the sorrowful faces of their masters' comrades in the flickering firelight. Devout members of the Valley District army maintained that provoking a fight on the Sabbath sealed their fate. "I trust we may never more have a Sunday fight in which we are the attacking party. . . ," complained Captain Samuel J. C. Moore, "I don't know what General Jackson was thinking of when he made the attack on that day." Major Frank Jones assisted other officers in organizing their commands, then rode to his mother's home of Vaucluse (near Middletown) where he spent the night. He recounted the results of the day in his diary and closed the entry by writing, "O, sad work was this for the blessed Sabbath: may the Lord forgive our sins for they are many, and may peace once more shine upon this distracted country."[60]

The Federal soldiers, in victory, initially shared the sentiments of Major Jones in defeat. Most were ordered to lay on their arms on the cold March soil of Sandy Ridge. The heat of battle had given way to a cold evening; the temperature had dipped to forty degrees, providing additional discomfort to fatigued soldiers. No campfires were permitted, and to make matters worse, no blankets or supper were provided the hungry, cold, and weary victors. The pitiful wails of the wounded, crying for water, mothers, wives, or sisters permeated the air around the Northerners to add more unpleasantness to their evening.[61]

The ambulance corps removed the wounded from both sides and took them to Winchester. Parties were detached from each company and spent the night searching for wounded soldiers to load into the ambulance wagons. For most on the field the truly devastating effects of a battle would become clearer at daylight, but these search parties became the first witnesses to the horrors of war. "I tramped and hunted over the woods all night until daylight . . . .," lamented a surgeon from the 7th Ohio, "Often I stumbled over dead bodies and fell down. Oh, what a sight, legs smashed, heads torn off, faces mangled, arms shattered, pools of blood, bowels protruding, and every conceivable mutilation." A member of the 29th Ohio studied the faces of the dead and described his observations to his father: "Some seemed to have died in the greatest agony, others wore a smile even in death. . . ." But Samuel List of the 7th Indiana Infantry saw no smiles that night. "Oh, it was a horrible sight to see the poor fellows lying there, some dead and some wounded, the principle part of them were shot through the head," he explained, adding, "The rebels were hard looking cases sure. One lay by the stone fence, wounded in the head. He begged us as we passed him to shoot him, but enough of this."[62]

"But enough of this"—Monday's morning light would force the rest of Shields's division to utter the same four words.

Chapter Nine

"THE MOST ESSENTIAL FRUITS OF THE BATTLE"

The citizens of Winchester endured an uncomfortable Sunday night on March 23, impatiently waiting for Monday morning to arrive with information on the results of the previous day's battle. No definitive news reached the inhabitants that bloody Sunday even though much effort was expended to do so. Crowds of men and boys climbed the hills south of town to view the battle, but they were disappointed to find that they could not get nearly close enough to see the forces. Harry and Allan McDonald, two sons of the former 7th Virginia Cavalry colonel, Angus McDonald, somehow worked their way closer to the action. Sitting on a fence south of Winchester late in the afternoon, the boys became unnerved at the sight of a severed head rolling near their position and they wisely retreated back to town.[1] The civilians in Winchester remained "in the dark" that night.

As the early morning light of March 24 finally permeated Winchester and the Lower Valley, Mary Charlton Greenhow Lee and her sister-in-law Laura Lee awoke in their Market Street home to the frantic gesticulations of their next-door neighbor, Frances Jones Barton, who had entered the house in an obviously distressed state. Mrs. Barton had three sons in Jackson's army and two of the Lee's nephews were also soldiers in the Valley District force. Mrs. Barton sadly announced that Jackson had been defeated and forced to retreat from the field. She also told the Lee sisters that the ground was covered with the dead and wounded, the town was filled with injured and dying men, and that everyone with a loved one in the army should prepare for the worst. The churches, the courthouse, and other public buildings were filled with prisoners. Mrs. Barton wished to search these buildings for her boys; she told the Lees they might find their nephews there as well.

The widow Mary Lee and her sister quickly dressed and left their home to find the streets teeming with men and women on similar missions. The Lee women eventually pushed their way to the provost marshal's office where they secured a pass to visit the prison. The harried provost marshal had not yet completed the list of captured Confederates but he willingly allowed the ladies to visit the prisoners. Mrs. Lee met Lieutenant George Junkin, Jackson's aide, who told her that General Jackson had been deceived concerning the number of Federals engaged. Eventually the Lee sisters found their nephews, Bob and Willie Burwell, safe in jail. Mrs. Barton and another neighbor found their sons safe as well. All of them appeared relieved the boys were captured for they now knew the young men were alive and uninjured.[2]

The provost marshal's completed list identified 234 Confederate prisoners who were deemed healthy enough to transport to Baltimore. The list did not include the wounded who occupied the public buildings that were not already overflowing with healthier prisoners. General Garnett's aide, First Lieutenant S. C. Williams, joined Lieutenant George Junkin as the two most prized captures of the day—division and brigade staff officers. Additionally, three captains and seven lieutenants spiced the list of twelve commissioned officers that now belonged to the Federals.[3] For two hours many of the Winchester and Frederick County soldiers received food and greetings from family members until the time arrived to send them to a temporary prison in Baltimore. Their final destination would be Fort Delaware, a new northeastern prison that awaited its first "guests."

At 2:00 P.M. the captives were marched under guard up Market Street to the Winchester and Potomac Railroad depot off Clarke Street in the northern section of town. The Federal officers leading the men away were stunned at what they saw on Market Street. Rather than witnessing a sad procession of defeated soldiers being led from the town they had tried to liberate, the prisoners marched in fine spirits, cheering for Jeff Davis and the Confederacy, and yelling their good-byes to the citizens on the street side. The residents responded by treating the boys as heroes by waving their handkerchiefs, cheering for them, and passing provisions into their lines. One of the ladies of Winchester rushed onto Market Street with a basket load of fresh biscuits which the hungry soldiers devoured. She then took the empty basket, raised it over her head, and cheered lustily. The ladies exchanged hearty banter with the prisoners all the way to the depot. One of the Federal officers, taking exception to the parade-like atmosphere, postured to one of his captives, "Well, Sesech, we have got a pretty good crowd of you here." "Yes," replied his prisoner, "but we left a damned good receipt for them on the hill yonder."[4]

The Confederate prisoner knew exactly what he was talking about for the horror displayed on the Kernstown battlefield was beyond the capacity of most people's imaginations. What confronted the burial details on Sandy Ridge shocked all of the soldiers who were forced to work there. It was the first major battle for many of them and, to a man, they hoped they would never witness anything like the post-battle Kernstown terrain. The ground on both sides of the wall was littered with the wounded and the dead. Most of the Confederate corpses had bullet holes through their heads; the Federals had fallen with wounds through their lower bodies. "Mangled remains of horses and men were to be seen in every direction," stated a private, claiming "In many places the enemy were lying so thick that one could walk for rods by stepping from one body to another." A shocked physician from Indiana believed that nearly every sprout of vegetation on the ridge was cut by small arms fire. He also was astounded at the sight of "blood, hats, clothing, and every conceivable kind of equipments" he saw strewn over the battlefield. Near the southern portion of the ridge, a severed, naked foot dangled conspicuously from a tree limb.[5]

The citizens were not allowed on the field for at least twenty-four hours so as not to impede the removal of casualties. Rumors and complaints sped through the town that many men died on Sandy Ridge from neglect, but it appears that removal of wounded to Winchester was swift. Only the dead remained on the field by Monday afternoon.

While the wounded were taken into town, burial details were formed to inter the dead. "The battle was bad enough," remarked a Pennsylvania soldier, "but this was worse. The men were buried in their great coats, blankets, etc., and without coffins as there were none to be had." The men of Company I of the 84th Pennsylvania dug a forty-foot trench six feet wide and four feet deep. In it they laid eighty-four Confederate bodies. One member of the company claimed the dead Southerners were found on a piece of ground "4 rods long and 30 rods wide."[6] Their burial site became well known to every visitor on Sandy Ridge thereafter.

The Federal dead were not buried on Sandy Ridge; instead, they were interred at a vacant lot on the east side of town. Most were privates and non-commissioned officers. The remains of commissioned officers were taken from Winchester to their home states in boxcars. Colonel William Gray Murray's body was transported to Harrisburg, Pennsylvania. Murray was not only the highest ranking officer to sacrifice his life at Kernstown, he also was the first Pennsylvania colonel to die in a Civil War battle. His funeral took place at Harrisburg. Subsequently, his body was sent to his home town of Hollidaysburg where Murray was buried next to his wife. Prominent wounded Federals, like Colonel Joseph Thoburn of the 1st West Virginia, were sent to their home towns to recover from their injuries.[7]

David Hunter Strother left Berryville after hearing details of the battle and arrived in Winchester on Monday afternoon. He immediately rode out to Kernstown to visit the battlefield. Scaling Sandy Ridge, Strother jotted down in his daily journal the scene that greeted his eyes:

> The fences were torn down and the ground marked with artillery wheels where the Federal troops had first taken position. A dead horse or two were visible and the body of a soldier with the top of his head blown off lay protected by a rail pen. Crossing a field and a wood I came upon an open ridge where marks of artillery wheels and another body of a United States soldier lay. Near here a picket guard lay by the fire and beside them upon a rail trestle lay fifteen dead Federalists. In a thicket and rock break about two or three hundred yards distant the Confederate dead lay. Entering the break I observed the bushes and trees cut to pieces with musketry in a manner terrible to witness. Here within a very small space lay forty bodies of the Confederates. The bodies lay among the bushes and the trees just as they fell, and were without exception shot through the head with musket balls. The sun had set and the dull red light from the west fell upon the upturned faces of the dead, giving a lurid dimness to the scene that highlighted its ghastly effect.[8]

Strother reconnoitered the ridge after the wounded were removed. Despite the available houses and farms close to the field at Kernstown and the Frederick County area surrounding it, nearly all the wounded were transferred into Winchester. Every available public place was seemingly turned into a hospital. The courthouse, Union Hotel, vacant banks and churches housed them. The presence of more than 400 wounded soldiers (totaled from both sides) taxed the city's supplies. The first two post-battle days were especially uncomfortable for everyone. Soldiers from both sides writhed in agony on floors intermingled with corpses and there were few comforts in the manner of pillows and blankets. Banks's Fifth Corps medical director blamed the lack of cooperation between the quartermaster and commissary departments as the chief reason for the discomfort, deflecting responsibility from his medical officers. He also cited the shortage of medical supplies as a handicap to his department's abilities. Dr. William S. Vohn complained about the "miserable track" that constituted the B & O line as a major impediment to receiving supplies from Washington. This Ohio surgeon, experiencing his first post-battle duty, found that Kernstown offered a textbook lesson in distinguishing battle wounds. "Very few injuries are reported by shells; and still fewer by bayonets," he wrote, continuing his observations. "Of bullet wounds there is every variety—Enfield, Minie, musket and rifle balls of all descriptions, from the pea or squirrel rifle, to the heaviest bore of buckshot." Dr. Vohn rated the Enfield rifle as the most dangerous small arms, for this weapon tore holes into the flesh "large enough to put a silver dollar in, smashing bones like straws."[9]

The Union casualties were initially tallied at 590 (118 killed, 450 wounded, and 22 missing). At least sixty men on the injured list suffered mortal wounds and would perish over the next few weeks. Most of the missing found their way back to their ranks; very few soldiers were unaccounted for.[10] Nearly one out of every ten Federal infantrymen engaged in the battle was injured or killed. (See Appendix C)

Eight commissioned Federal officers lost their lives at Kernstown; twenty-five others were wounded. One of the latter, thick-lipped Captain Myron T. Wright of the 29th Ohio, wrote his father from his sick bed on March 25. After explaining the circumstances surrounding his wounding, Wright described his inhospitable hospital surroundings to his family:

> Excuse my poor writing for my nerves are not in the best condition for writing, especially in my present position. There were two men from the 7th Ohio brought into my room after I came here. One of them died last night and the other cannot live till morning. Thus you see it is not the most desirable spot on earth for a wounded man to pass the nights of eternal length, amidst the groans and shrieks of dying men and those suffering from amputation; but it is only a phase in war, and we are all willing to acknowledge that war cannot be carried on without some loss of life and comfort. But that is one of the specifications in our contract, and we are not disposed to complain at all. My wound has only added one more line to the column of accounts I have to settle with the Confederate Government, and I hope to be able in a few weeks to resume my position for that purpose.[11]

Captain Wright admitted that he received good care despite the lack of supplies for the injured. The ladies of Winchester did all they could to ease the pain of the wounded—no matter what color coat they donned. "The ladies were hurrying to feed the poor creatures, friends and enemies alike," claimed Laura Lee, who worked herself until she felt like she was nearly dead from exhaustion. Cornelia McDonald spoon-fed lemonade to a dying Federal soldier at the court-house, then came across a task that she was not up to performing. A surgeon called her over to his side and then uncovered the face of Captain James Y. Jones, the gallant leader of Company E, Irish Battalion. He was last seen by his men on Sandy Ridge exhorting them forward with his sword held high until a bullet knocked him from the stump where he attempted to rally them. The bullet destroyed the captain's face; it struck him from the side, taking away both of his eyes and plowing out the bridge of his nose. His wound still oozed blood and the surgeon wished Mrs. McDonald to clean it. She tried to say "yes," but felt too faint to perform the task. Captain Jones must have realized the awful appearance his countenance displayed. He raised his finger, pointed to his temple, and said, "Ah, if they had only struck *there* I should have troubled no one."

As Mrs. McDonald tried to run to the door, she brushed against a pile of amputated limbs which convinced her she was not made to be a nurse. Another woman walked into the courthouse and took care of Captain Jones's wound. The officer lost all lucidity through the day; by the time David Hunter Strother came across him that night, he described the Southern captain as "delirious at intervals, and raved about forming his company and charging."[12] Mercifully, Captain James Y. Jones died three days later.

The engagement in which Captain Jones and over 300 other American soldiers gave up their lives was called "The Battle of Winchester" by the Union soldiers and "The Battle of Kernstown" by the Confederates; it was the largest fight seen east of the Allegheny Mountains since the Battle of Manassas eight months earlier. Because of the battle's ferociousness that interrupted months of inactivity in the East, news-starved correspondents flocked to Winchester to visit the battlefield and interview participants. By Tuesday, March 25, citizens and reporters were allowed on the field. Soldiers remaining from regiments held at Winchester were more than willing to provide the reporters with a tour. Captain Robert Horrell of the 84th Pennsylvania showed a New York reporter the spot where his regiment fought and where Colonel Murray died. Horrell told the correspondent that "a monument subscription should immediately be set on foot for Colonel Murray and the heroes of the Eighty-fourth, and the name of every one who participated in this terrible struggle should be inscribed upon the monument in letters of gold."[13] Horrell conveniently neglected to inform the newsman that shortly before the battle he co-authored the letter sent to Colonel Murray and Governor Curtin of Pennsylvania requesting Murray to resign.

The newspapers printed early statements taken from the telegraph lines. The source of most of those early telegraphs, Brigadier General James Shields, remained in Winchester nursing his fractured arm (it did not require amputation after all) while the majority of his division chased after General Jackson and his men beginning the day after the battle. General Banks had returned to Winchester on Monday morning, March 24, and with Shields's men and most of Williams's available division, pushed on to Strasburg by Monday evening. Shields's initial post-battle statements inflated Confederate strength to 15,000, a five-fold increase over the actual size of Jackson's division. He fully expected his superior, General Banks, to destroy the Southerners. In a dispatch reminiscent of what he sent Colonel Nathan Kimball on the day of the battle, Shields advised Banks, "I would respectfully suggest if our men can stand it, that they be hurled down the turnpike. . . I feel anxious to know whether there is any chance of capturing their artillery and baggage and of making more prisoners." General McClellan also believed his corps commander would bag Jackson and his men. He instructed Banks to resume his aborted movement to Manassas, ". . . the very moment the thorough defeat of Jackson will permit it." McClellan then notified Colonel Jonas P. Holliday, who commanded the 1st Vermont Cavalry at Poolesville, that the enemy that fought Shields at Winchester "will probably be disposed of to-day." Just in case, McClellan ordered the Vermont horsemen into the Valley to assist his force there.[14]

Union confidence was premature; in General Banks's case, it was nonexistent. Prior to departing Winchester that morning, Banks scribbled what he believed to be his final letter to his wife. "I go out this morning and may not see you again," Banks wrote her, "No one but myself can know how much I have loved you. . . . Tell the dear children how much I have loved them and to stand by their country always. Good Bye." Banks soon realized he had little to fear on the late afternoon of March 24; the opposing forces found themselves in nearly the same positions as they were six days earlier. Federal artillery lined up on the northern bank of Cedar Creek while the Rockbridge Artillery, supported by the 27th Virginia, took position near the southern bank of the waterway. The bridge between them had been destroyed by Ashby's men on March 18. The Southerners would not be captured this day, nor would General Banks be killed in battle. Wilder Dwight, a lieutenant colonel in Banks's corps, summarized the experience in a letter to his wife, "The lees and flatness of the sparkling goblet of victory are all we taste. Jackson and Ashby are clever men. We are slow-w-w!"[15]

Knowing that Jackson eluded him again, a frustrated Banks ordered his gunners to fire a few rounds across the creek. For four members of the 27th Virginia, the desultory volley was catastrophic. An incoming shell landed in the midst of the supporting regiment and exploded, killing the quartet instantly and wounding several others. A member of Chew's horse artillery came across one of the wounded soldiers, finding him with a leg nearly severed above the knee and literally on fire near his wound. The artillerist extinguished the flames and propped the injured man against a fence. The infantryman handed his rifle over to the gunner and said, "Here, take my gun and don't let the Yankees have it." An ambulance eventually carted the soldier off to safety while the remainder of Jackson's force retired to Woodstock for the evening. From there, General Jackson informed his wife of his repulse the previous day, telling her that "Our God was my shield. His protecting care is an additional cause of gratitude."[16]

On Tuesday morning, March 25, Jackson sent a dispatch to General Johnston requesting 400 rounds of Parrott ammunition. This was only his second note to Johnston since the battle; the first briefly described his repulse, but added that it may have accomplished something good by detaining Federal troops into the Valley. Jackson and his command then leisurely retired eight miles to the familiar grounds of Camp Buchanon, near Red Banks. While Jackson and his men slowly retreated up the Valley, General Johnston, in turn, relayed Jackson's information to Confederate President Jefferson Davis. Johnston then let Stonewall know that if the Federals pushed him beyond New Market, Johnston would send reinforcements from his position near Gordonsville.[17]

Jackson soon learned that the Federals were not aggressively pursuing him. Banks moved into Strasburg on the morning of March 25, sent his cavalry pickets toward Woodstock, then did little else for the rest of the day. While in Strasburg, brothers Clegg and John C. Robertson of the 1st West Virginia soon learned that their rebel brother, Sergeant William Robertson of the Shriver Greys, 27th Virginia, was one of the Confederate victims of the artillery fire the previous night. Dr. Henry Capehart of the 1st West Virginia Cavalry had been a friend of Robertson's father in Wheeling prior to the war. The surgeon came across Robertson first, immediately recognized him, and asked him if there was any message to send back to his father. The mortally wounded officer—both legs were severed by a shell—said to Capehart, "Well, Doc, tell—the old man—I died—game!" The renegade son perished before a final reunion with his siblings could take place.[18] The last moment they spent together turned out to be two days earlier, when the brothers had stood approximately

100 yards from each other in their respective skirmish companies which fired the opening rounds on Sandy Ridge.

While Banks vacillated at Strasburg, General Shields began to analyze the events that led to his division's victory. Perhaps realizing that he could manipulate the factors that produced the favorable outcome, the politician in Shields overtook the general. He informed the assistant adjutant general of the Fifth Corps, Major R. Morris Copeland, that he wanted to prepare a report of the battle. Claiming he could not wait for accurate details, Shields planned to produce a "very short and plain" summary of action of the day's events. He also wanted to establish an ammunition depot at Strasburg. Shields also issued Special Orders Number Eighteen, detailing provost forces at Winchester, Berryville, and Charlestown, as well as reinforcements for protecting the B & O Railroad. The Union victory at Kernstown assured the safety of the railroad while it was being repaired. The immediate consequences would be realized four days later. On March 30, the B & O Railroad opened for through traffic between Wheeling and Baltimore for the first time in ten months; 3,800 cars passed over the Harpers Ferry bridge on the first day.[19]

Although Shields had yet to issue an official report, his version of the fight was unveiled when he wrote to his friend in Washington, California Democratic Senator Milton S. Latham, to describe how he won the great battle that the papers were already reporting. In the letter, Shields shamelessly told his friend that his reconnaissance of March 18 and 19 found Jackson in a position where he was likely to get reinforced. Shields then claimed to have deliberately marched his command north of Winchester to fool Jackson into believing that the town was evacuated. Shields claimed that he saw signal fires lit to inform Stonewall that Winchester had been evacuated. When Ashby attacked on the afternoon of March 22, Shields continued to embellish upon his fictional strategy by informing Latham that he repulsed Ashby by deliberately exposing only a few of his regiments to "increase their delusion." Shields claimed that he knew the enemy was reinforced in the morning on the day of the battle, but was unsure of their strength until he unmasked them by ordering his batteries to fire into the woods where they were concealed. He then stated that he ordered Tyler's flank attack and the reinforcements that eventually forced Jackson from Sandy Ridge. Shields ended by boasting that his strategy of deception resulted in the victory and that he planned to resume command when he was healthy enough to ride in a buggy. Hinting at a favor he wanted his political friend to perform, Brigadier General Shields complained that he still lacked the sufficient rank "to do that service to the country that I hope and feel I am capable of."[20]

Shields sent orders to his subordinates to write their battle reports. Regiment and brigade commanders prepared their official reports in response to the hasty request. Realizing that the reports would be printed in the papers and would be seen by their superiors, the authors carefully chose their words to make their activity on the day of the battle come off in the best possible light.

Colonel Erastus B. Tyler understood the power of the official report. With one strike against him for his questionable performance at Cross Lanes the previous August, Tyler knew that detailing his deployment on Sandy Ridge could be military suicide. Rather than admit he had attacked with his men in a close marching column, Tyler omitted any reference to the formation description in his report to General Shields. He stretched the truth in a separate report addressed to Nathan Kimball, claiming he deployed his regiments in a line with each regiment in double-column by divisions. This claimed formation stood in contrast to letters written home by several men in the ranks who described one deep column that approached the stone wall. Tyler easily explained how his five-regiment battle line was unable to sweep away the 200 men of the 27th Virginia—he stated that they were opposed by nine Confederate infantry regiments rather than one. The report was accepted without question. Erastus B. Tyler not only stayed in command of his brigade, on May 14 he was promoted to brigadier general for his leadership at Kernstown.[21]

Only two of Tyler's regiments, the 7th Indiana and 110th Pennsylvania, filed official battle reports. Colonel William D. Lewis proudly described how he charged his regiment into the flank of the enemy and drove them from the stone wall. This contrasted sharply with the multitude of letters from participants in other regiments who denigrated the 110th Pennsylvania for fleeing at the first volley fired from the stone wall. Although it appeared the 110th successfully rallied at the end of the day, Colonel Lewis's misleading account placed too much importance upon his regiment. Lewis had the report returned to him by one of Colonel Tyler's aides with the order that the regimental commander revise it because of its "informality in address and incorrectness in facts stated." Whatever Lewis lacked in regimental leadership he made up for in aggressive marketing. He quickly detailed his regiment's action to Governor Curtin and never modified the report. It eventually was filed into the *Official Records* without revisions.[22]

The two participating regiments from Sullivan's brigade, the 5th Ohio and the 13th Indiana, both submitted reports. Lieutenant George H. Whitcamp filed a detailed account of the 5th Ohio's part in the battle, taking care to mention at the end of it that the regiment was unjustly sent on picket duty when other regiments were more rested. Bothered by declining health and considering himself unfit for duty due to "personal private reasons," Whitcamp resigned two days after filing his account.[23] The 84th Pennsylvania was the only regiment in Kimball's brigade that did not submit a report. The hard-hit unit's highest ranking officer who fought and survived the battle was its adjutant, Thomas Craig, who did not realize that the responsibility for filing his regiment's report rested on his shoulders. (He filed his report twenty-seven years later.)

The most fanciful report was filed by Captain R. C. Scribner, aide-de-camp and acting inspector general of the Fifth Corps, who General Shields sent to help Colonel Mason reconnoiter the area on the day of the battle. The German aide claimed that he faced six of Ashby's cavaliers at the end of the day, and "was forced to use my sword to kill one of them." He showed off a hole in his hat and claimed it was made by the soldier he subsequently killed. Staff officers believed that Scribner shot a hole in his own hat—"it was the most cheapest part of his clothes"—and they sent a formal complaint to General Shields. Scribner enhanced his story later by telling others that three Southern horsemen were killed by him alone. Scribner's report found its way into the newspapers. A disbelieving soldier with known artistic ability drew a satirical sketch of Scribner's fabricated performance. Scribner, also a master of self-promotion, borrowed the sketch from the artist, rubbed out its ridiculous elements, and sent it to the elite *Harper's Weekly*. They subsequently published the sketch, providing Scribner with the last laugh at the expense of the artist who drew it.[24]

Colonel William D. Lewis,
110th Pennsylvania Infantry
U.S.A.M.H.I.

Back in Winchester, the overworked ladies nursed the wounded for five days. On the night of March 28, the normal evening silence was broken by the arrival of an unwelcome visitor. Secretary of State William H. Seward showed up as Shields's guest when he visited Winchester with his son and daughter, and the wife of Secretary of War Edwin Stanton. Two regiments escorted the party from the railroad cars through the streets of Winchester as a band filled the air with martial music. On Saturday the Sewards toured the battlefield escorted by cavalry, much to the disgust of the town's inhabitants. "The town looks desolate and is further polluted by the footsteps of Mr. Wm. H. Seward," wrote John Peyton Clark in his journal entry of March 29. Kate Sperry was more derisive in her diary entry for that day: "To think our soil should ever be desecrated by the tread of such black-hearted villians!" she complained. A more welcome contingent would enter Winchester three days later. Dorothea Dix and her corps of nurses were scheduled to arrive to relieve the townspeople of the burden of caring for the unmanageable throng of wounded.[25]

General Shields did not join the Sewards on the battlefield on March 29. His injuries had debilitated him so much that he sent two letters to Secretary of War Stanton asking to be relieved of active field command. Still unable to leave his bed, Shields spent the day alone to write his official report. It repeated the account detailed in his letter to Senator Latham three days earlier. This report, contrary to his stated intentions, was neither "very plain" nor "very short." Although he correctly placed his division's strength at 6,000 infantry, 750 cavalry, and twenty-four pieces of artillery available on the day of the battle, Shields continued with the tall tale that he relayed to Senator Latham that he defeated an opponent over 11,000 strong. Shields claimed that Jackson never used a large reserve, and continued with his fabled luring of the Confederate general into battle by deliberately hiding his division three miles north of Winchester.

Shields shamelessly credited himself for every phase of action that led to the victory. He specifically stated that *he* ordered Tyler's attack after Colonel Kimball sent him a dispatch "requesting directions as to the employment of infantry." Shields closed his report by stating that Kimball "executed my orders in every instance with vigor and fidelity," thus denying that deserving officer of the credit he deserved. Shields commended Colonel Tyler's performance, assuring that colonel of receiving an undeserved general's star.[26]

Shields's report was instantly plucked from the telegraph lines, as was his letter to Senator Latham; both were published in newspapers throughout the North. The Northern papers, starving for battle victories to write about, hailed the colorful Irishman as a hero. The attention heaped upon Shields was done so at the expense of his chief subordinate, Colonel Nathan Kimball. Shields's semi-fictitious report was carefully worded to make it appear that he knew exactly what his division faced throughout the day of the battle when, in fact, Shields had no idea that Jackson's full division contested his men until after 3:00 P.M. Shields's battle report kept Kimball's performance in obscurity and strongly suggested that

Kimball's role was similar to that of an aide delivering his superior's orders to the men.

Colonel Kimball stewed over initial newspaper battle accounts even prior to the publication of Shields's report. Writing to his friend J. J. Cravens from Strasburg shortly after receiving newspaper accounts of the battle, he credited the three Indiana regiments for significantly helping the Federals in winning a battle that generated infantry fire "heavier and deadlier than in but few battles of modern times." But Kimball was definitely displeased at what he considered patent misstatements of his role in the battle that were appearing in print. "I had full command and planned and directed the movements of the entire fight in person. . . .," Kimball complained, "You will not wonder, therefore, that I am annoyed at seeing the garbled and false accounts that have appeared in the newspapers. . . ." Kimball told his friend that he also wrote a similar letter to another influential Hoosier living in Washington. He ended his letter by telling Cravens that he looked forward to actions of the Indiana Congressional Delegation to appoint him brigadier general. They succeeded in April.

Not surprisingly, the publication of both Shields's report and his letter to Senator Latham frayed the tempers of Kimball, his fellow brigade and regimental commanders, and his friends back home. "That letter of Shields is a disgrace to the soldier and the man," fumed a friend back in Indiana upon seeing the Latham letter in print. The friend also informed Kimball that the people of Indiana knew Kimball's real role in the battle and assured the beleaguered commander that "the government by this time is well aware to whom the credit is due."[27]

The men in the ranks also felt indignant at the injustice given Nathan Kimball's performance in the newspaper accounts of the battle. A soldier corresponding to a Cincinnati newspaper regretted what he considered to be a "studied effort on the part of some persons in the army to refuse to 'Caesar the things that are Caesar's.' This brilliant victory was won by our forces under Colonel Kimball. The honor is his, and he should have accredited to him what his merit deserves." "The Hoosier soldiers love Col. Kimball," boasted a member of the commander's former regiment, "and they will not sit sleepingly and see one laurel torn from the hero's brow." Another Hoosier soldier vented his disgust at faulty newspaper reports that failed to acknowledge Kimball and then he haughtily announced, "So long as Colonel Kimball leads the forces of Shields's Division, all will go well; naught will be lost for the want of prudence, forethought or sagacity; which qualifications, together with great determination and true bravery, so greatly distinguish him."[28]

Most of the regiments of Shields's division sat still near Strasburg on March 26–29, affording the rank and file the opportunity to write letters home describing their role in the great battle that came off three days earlier. The letters demonstrated their flair for the dramatic—"I might say that it was a miracle that I escaped injury"—their humbling by the intensity and devastation of the battle— "I never want to get into a harder one"—and their willingness to mock the performances of others in the division— "The 110th Pennsylvania ran like dogs from a few shells that burst near them." Additionally, the Westerners of Shields's division felt they were better fighters than their opponents and showed little respect for Jackson and his division. Although the sobriquet of "Stonewall" frequented the newsprint both North and South for several months prior to the battle, the Federal soldiers evidently were ignorant of the title given to Jackson and his brigade until prisoners from that unit were interrogated after the battle. Even then, the name failed to stick with many of Shields's Westerners. (One soldier naively reported to his home town that his regiment faced off against the "Stone Fence Brigade".) Some of the Northern participants claimed that they bestowed the name "Stonewall" upon Jackson and his men in derision to highlight the fact that the bluecoats forced them to retreat from the stone wall on Sandy Ridge.[29]

The object of the Union soldiers' disdain appeared to have little ammunition to fire back at their slander. From January 1 through March 23, 1862, Major General Thomas J. Jackson suffered through an inauspicious debut as an independent commander. Few bright spots shone during those eighty-one days to justify Stonewall's promotion and additional responsibilities, but now Jackson's fortunes appeared to be turning for the better. His losses at Kernstown had indeed been substantial—once his regimental officers compiled their official reports, Stonewall would know for certain how severe—but his division had survived. Although a sizable force was collecting north of him, Jackson appeared to be out of immediate danger and he knew he could always move quicker than his adversaries.

While Banks remained inactive twenty miles north of him, General Jackson took several of the necessary steps needed to strengthen his division. On the morning of March 27, Stonewall sent for Jed Hotchkiss, the young New York cartographer who had briefly met him two days before the Battle of Kernstown. Jackson chatted with Hotchkiss at his headquarters, a stone house at Narrow Passage, about his previous experience as a surveyor and cartographer in the western Virginia campaign of the previous summer. Jackson then announced to Hotchkiss, "I want you to make me a map of the Valley from Harper's Ferry to Lexington, showing all the points of offence and defence in those places. Mr. Pendleton will give you orders for whatever outfit you want. Good morning, Sir."[30] Hotchkiss became Stonewall's acting topographical engineer and was added to the nucleus of a staff that would provide Jackson with excellent service throughout the remainder of the campaign. Though Lieutenant George Junkin was captured, Jackson had Chief Engineer Lieutenant James K. Boswell, Medical Director Dr. Hunter McGuire, Quartermaster Major John A. Harman, Commissary Chief Major Wells J. Hawks, and Assistant Adjutant General Lieutenant Sandie Pendleton in the fold.

Hotchkiss's service became valuable immediately. He notified Jackson that the area around Narrow Passage was not strong for defense, so Stonewall moved his division up the Valley to the old grounds at Camp Buchanon on March 28. The weather turned from clear and pleasant to miserable—"cold and cheerless" as described by one officer—and it started to rain again as it had done for several days during the early part of the month.[31] Despite the inclement weather, the mood displayed in camp appeared far from dispirited.

In defeat, Jackson's soldiers displayed as little regard for the Union soldiers as the Federals did to the Virginians in victory. Although there were some who admitted the apparent results immediately after the battle—"We have had a severe fight today and are pretty badly whipped"—the return to their comfortable campgrounds near Mount Jackson and a few days of hindsight changed the Southerners' views on the battle. Sandie Pendleton described the battle to his mother as "a harder fight than Manassas," but firmly believed that they would have whipped the Federals if they had 1,000 more men. "It was a terrific fight and our men all behaved like heroes," wrote Alexander Boteler, Jr., a young cannoneer with the Rockbridge Artillery. Boteler revelled in how his cannons devastated the enemy: "our canister scattered them like scared sheep, and made them all run, all that was left of them, like so many ——— Yankees!" Major John A. Harman claimed that Turner Ashby told him that the enemy was injured a great deal in the battle; Harman surmised that if the Federals attempted to attack them when the Confederates were reinforced, "we will whip them badly." The Confederate prisoners also displayed pride rather than chagrin or remorse in their performance at Kernstown. Twenty-year-old Lieutenant James Langhorne of the 4th Virginia perhaps deserved the most recognition. He was captured by the Federals after taking three bullets and saving his regiment's flag from capture. Langhorne was justifiably pleased with his accomplishments. Writing home to his parents after transferring from a Baltimore prison to Fort Delaware, Langhorne proudly chirped, "I am a jail bird now but a happy one, for I have done my duty."[32]

Despite their wagons remaining packed to facilitate a quick retreat if Banks decided to advance, the carefree demeanor of the Southern soldiers surprised their officers. Major Paxton, 27th Virginia, explained to his wife that he believed 15,000 Federals fought them near Winchester and were prepared to chase them toward Staunton. "To you this would seem exciting," he wrote, "yet the soldiers sit around in squads, laughing and talking as if they enjoyed the sport." "For the last two days we have had a cold rain and our suffering has been great," complained Major Frank B. Jones to his wife at the end of March. "Our men stand out in the rain and sleep in the wet, yet they are cheerful and hopeful beyond belief." General Jackson, enjoying his familiar headquarters at Israel Allen's house, wrote his wife explaining the demeanor of his men. "My little army is in excellent spirits. It feels it inflicted a severe blow upon the enemy."[33]

Jackson's little army also shared a better opinion of their commander and of themselves. The regiments from Loring's division appeared to be losing their animosity toward Stonewall and the brigade they once called "Jackson's Pets." This transformation took its genesis at the Battle of Kernstown. On two separate occasions regiments from each unit fought well together against tremendous odds. First it was the 21st Virginia, one of Loring's former units, coming to the aid of the 27th Virginia, a Stonewall Brigade regiment, at the beginning of the fight on Sandy Ridge. The 21st's commander, Lieutenant Colonel John M. Patton, was notified by one of Colonel Echols's subordinate officers that he unintentionally slandered the 27th Virginia in his March 26 report when he described his men as coming up to Echols's support in case he was driven back, adding "this occurred very soon." Seeing the injustice done to a regiment Patton's men no longer despised, the commander took pains to carefully word an amended portion of the report to read "Meantime the troops who fell back, rallied. . . ."[34] Patton's diplomatic skills improved the stung feelings of the 27th Virginia.

The other time two regiments from Loring's and Jackson's former commands shared side-by-side battle action was at the close of the Sandy Ridge fight when the 42nd Virginia extended the right of the 5th Virginia to hold back the Federal advance long enough for Jackson's command to retreat in the fast-approaching darkness. Colonel Harman of the 5th Virginia carefully worded his report of battle, written March 27, to compliment Loring's former unit: "The gallant Forty-second Virginia Regiment had taken position on my right and were most efficiently engaged." Other examples of detente between the two factions appeared in the soldiers' letters. A member of Fulkerson's brigade, formally in Loring's command, took exception to reading an erroneous account printed in a Richmond newspaper which described the 27th Virginia, rather than the 23rd and 37th Virginia, racing toward the stone wall against a Federal regiment (1st West Virginia). Correcting the account for the editor of the paper, the soldier went on to say, "We have no disposition to quarrel with the Stonewall Brigade about positions, feeling confident that each and all endeavored to do their duty, and that Gen. Jackson, in his report, will give all a fair share in the glory." Battle experience had improved the opinion of Loring's men toward General Jackson; although they had yet to demonstrate the tremendous respect their commander would enjoy in the next six months, they no longer hissed and hooted at him as they did after the ill-fated Romney expedition.[35]

The brigade and regimental commanders provided General Jackson with their casualty reports at the end of March; the consolidation of Jackson's division losses revealed an army that was little bigger than a brigade after the Battle of Kernstown. Only one regiment, Colonel Campbell's 48th Virginia, carried at least 350 rifles the day after the battle. (It was the only unit not engaged on March 23, 1862, but still had two men injured after they stole away from their reserve duty and entered the fight.) In contrast, the 27th Virginia counted only 140 musket-carrying soldiers, while the 4th Virginia of the Stonewall Brigade and the 23rd Virginia of Fulkerson's brigade each took 128 men off the field at the end of the day's battle. Stonewall could count only 2,400 healthy infantrymen, 270 cavalry, and twenty-three operable cannons after the engagement. His 700-plus aggregate casualties amounted to twenty-one percent of his engaged force. Additionally, two cannons were captured and two others were disabled by the aggressive Federals fighting under Nathan Kimball.

The Confederates removed 160 of their serious casualties from the battlefield. These wounded were taken to Staunton and cared for in a friendly environment. The remainder, more than 550 men, were either left dead on the field, wounded in the hands of the enemy and the citizens of Winchester, or captured and shipped off to Fort Delaware prison awaiting exchange. The latter became the most serious casualties to Jackson. The 250 captured troops would not be exchanged for the next four and one-half months while many of the wounded were able to return to the ranks in a matter of weeks. When the totals in killed and mortally wounded were tallied, nearly 140 Confederate soldiers gave up their lives at Kernstown.[36] (See Appendix C)

Despite the crippling losses sustained by the Valley District army, Stonewall Jackson took heart in watching his division strength improve almost immediately after the battle. Stragglers who had not been able to keep up with the demands of heavy marching prior to the battle rejoined their units. Furloughed officers and privates also returned to their regiments. New recruits suited up and swelled the ranks. On March 28, the Rockbridge Artillery welcomed four new members into their battery, including a young artillerist of Tidewater ancestry who was fitted with a new uniform purchased by his father. The recruit also carried his father's name—Robert E. Lee, Jr.[37]

Then came the militia. On March 29, Virginia Governor John Letcher ordered all ranks to be filled with drafted county militia, beginning April 4. Although the militia had failed him previously and might not substantially replete his ranks, Jackson hoped for a decent number of these soldiers because one-year term of enlistments in his volunteer ranks were due to expire on April 1. Although it had not yet become the law, there was widespread talk of a mandatory conscription bill that would draft all able-bodied men, including veterans, between the ages of eighteen and thirty-five. The thought of being forced into unfamiliar units had been successful in convincing many of these soldiers to reenlist in their Valley District units. These measures gave Jackson hope of returning his independent division to the strength it had seen in January.[38]

General Johnston also promised Stonewall reinforcements; this became necessary owing to the consequences of Jackson's surprise attack at Kernstown. Not only was General Shields's demagoguery alienating his allies, it was also aiding his adversary. Although he never saw any of the battle and Confederate prisoners were sent to Baltimore from only nine infantry regiments and one battalion, Shields's official report, written six days after the battle, still boasted of routing a Confederate force that exceeded 11,000 men. His inflated enemy strength estimates caused much uneasiness in a War Department that had no other direct source of information. Believing rumors that Jackson had already been reinforced with an additional 10,000 men under Major General James Longstreet, General Banks's pursuit of the elusive Stonewall had come to a halt near Strasburg on March 25. By March 27, Shields believed that the Confederates had over 30,000 men in the Valley, forcing the U.S. War Department to discuss the possibility that Jackson intended to invade the North! Three days later saw Banks's corps still resting in their camps while additional troops were being juggled to meet this phantom force of Southerners that loomed in the Valley.[39]

General McClellan's Peninsula campaign required overwhelming numbers. His original plan to have Banks cover the Washington approaches toward Centreville was wiped out in the aftermath of the Battle of Kernstown. Now Banks's corps, with an aggregate strength of nearly 20,000, lay in the Valley stretched out between Winchester and Woodstock. Additionally, Brigadier General Louis Blenker's 10,000-man division marched to Strasburg from Warrenton as reinforcements to Major General John C. Frémont's Mountain Department. McClellan also detached 3,652 "disposable" cavalry to aid Banks in the Shenandoah region. The total force in the Valley, according to McClellan's improvised plan, now exceeded 35,000 men with an additional 20,000 covering the Virginia Piedmont between the Blue Ridge and Washington—fulfilling the function that McClellan had intended for Banks.

McClellan's plan called for 18,000 additional men, under the command of Brigadier General James Wadsworth, to remain in the defenses of Washington to guard the capital. However, President Lincoln did not feel that this was enough men to protect Washington from an attack while the Army of the Potomac advanced on Richmond. McClellan's Peninsula campaign plan called upon his First Corps, a 35,000-man force under the command of Major General Irvin McDowell, to move southward from Fredericksburg while McClellan took three corps of his army up the Peninsula, thus overpowering the defenders of the Confederate capital between two converging armies toward Richmond. Citing the forced removal of Banks from Manassas to the Shenandoah Valley, Lincoln detained McDowell's corps which hampered McClellan's plan. "I do not forget that I was satisfied with your arrangement to leave Banks at Manassas Junction," the President explained to McClellan, "but when that arrangement was broken up, and nothing was substituted for it, of course I was not satisfied; I was constrained to substitute something for it myself." After McClellan complained about being "weakened by detachments to the extent of nearly 50,000 men," Lincoln allowed Brigadier General William B. Franklin's division of 11,000 to be detached from McDowell's corps and join McClellan.[40]

An informant who had been in Banks's corps for months left the Union force at the end of March, found Jackson, and provided him with heartening news. Stonewall was pleased to learn from him and easily accessible Northern newspapers that his tactical defeat at Kernstown was responsible for detaining nearly 35,000 troops from McClellan's campaign plan that he believed were essential to its success. The combination of his attack, Shields's exaggerations, and Abraham Lincoln's paranoia, effectively weakened McClellan's army to give General Johnston a chance at successfully defending Richmond. Jackson was also surprised to learn that his attack at Kernstown had been misinterpreted by the opposition. Although he simply attacked under the false notion of an understrength opponent, Jackson realized that it appeared from the Northern standpoint that he attacked for another reason, thereby disregarding Johnston's order not expose himself to the danger of defeat by getting so close to the enemy that he was compelled to fight. "It is understood in the Federal Army that you have instructed me to keep the forces now in this district and not to permit them to cross the Blue Ridge, and that this must be done at every hazard, and that for this purpose I made the attack," Jackson wrote to his superior at the end of March, clarifying, "I have never so much as intimated such a thing to any one." Though not happy at losing the battle, Stonewall was satisfied at the strategic consequences and later would write at the end of his Official Report, "I feel justified in saying that, though the field is in possession of the enemy, yet the most essential fruits of the battle are ours."[41]

Despite all the factors working in his favor during the first week after the battle, Stonewall Jackson still had problems to deal with beginning on Tuesday, April 1, 1862. President Lincoln's last-minute alterations to McClellan's plan were still two days from reaching McClellan's ears. In the meantime, McClellan communicated to General Banks from the steamship *Commodore* at Alexandria. He told his Fifth Corps commander of the new troop deployment plan and his doubts that Johnston would be able to reinforce Jackson in the Valley since the senior Confederate officer would be compelled by McClellan's advance up the Peninsula to abandon his Rappahannock defenses and concentrated his army at Richmond. Informing Banks that it was vital to "throw Jackson back and to assume such a position as to enable you to prevent his return," McClellan ordered the Fifth Corps to move on Staunton to coincide with the Army of the Potomac's march on Richmond. McClellan believed that a heavy force of 25,000 to 30,000 soldiers was necessary for this operation; therefore, Blenker would move his division to Strasburg and answer to Banks rather than to his immediate superior, Major General John C. Frémont.[42]

Banks did not receive McClellan's letter for several days, but began to move on his own initiative against Jackson on the first of the month. Sending out elements of Williams's division and Shields's division, Banks's men attempted to occupy Woodstock and push Jackson farther southward. The only force opposing them near Woodstock was Colonel Ashby's 7th Virginia Cavalry and Chew's three-gun horse artillery. By early afternoon the Federals had advanced beyond Woodstock to the village of Edinburg.

Turner Ashby had engaged the Federals daily since the day after the Battle of Kernstown and had boldly contested every inch of the Union advance, retiring on many occasions just when it appeared the bluecoats were ready to capture him. At Edinburg, only Stony Creek separated the Federals from Ashby. He ordered the bridge across the North Fork tributary burned which prevented the Federals from moving farther, but did not prevent them from firing at the Virginia horsemen. Jed Hotchkiss rode with Ashby that day and realized they had become the targets of Federal marksmen. A bullet whizzed behind the two Confederates and killed the horse of "Dixie," a boy who routinely followed Ashby. The young tag-along tumbled off the dead mount, jumped up from the ground, and began running. Ashby called "Dixie" back and instructed him to grab the dead horse's saddle and bridle. Ashby patiently and nonchalantly waited for the boy to collect his accoutrements while Federal sharpshooters peppered away at the cavalier, then he rode to the safety of the woodline. An impressed Hotchkiss wrote his wife about the incident, hoping against hope that Ashby would be preserved for he "is a noble man." An Ohio soldier across the creek watched the Southern cavalry move back and forth between two woodlines and declared, "They are a brave, dashing set of fellows, and worthy of a better cause than the one in which they are engaged."[43]

But Stonewall Jackson was becoming suspicious of his cavalry chief's leadership, particularly after receiving Ashby's battle report of the 7th Virginia Cavalry's performance at Kernstown. Ashby had mustered 600 cavalrymen in sixteen companies just six days before the battle, yet less than half that number fought at Kernstown. Although his men fought superbly east of the Valley Pike, Major Funsten's command had failed to stop Federal horsemen from apprehending over 200 soldiers after the battle. Jackson realized that his cavalry needed help in numbers and leaders to be more effective for the Valley District, and Ashby had yet to exhibit the disciplinary trait necessary to keep renegade cavalrymen in line. Colonel Ashby's previous exploits had generated a movement to promote him brigadier general. Stonewall believed that the flamboyant cavalier lacked the basic command skills to earn the commission. He vented his disapproval of Ashby when he wrote to a friend, ". . . he has such bad discipline and attaches so little importance to drill, that I would regard it as a calamity to see him promoted."[44]

Despite Stonewall's misgivings, Ashby once again stymied Banks's advance on April 1 and provided Jackson with enough time to move his division farther south the next day. Stonewall's new headquarters would once again be at Reverend Anders Rudolph Rude's house at the foot of Rude's Hill. The troops received their new orders and would execute them at daylight.[45]

Jackson made certain that one particular member of the division would no longer be joining them in a military capacity. On

April 1, Stonewall sent Sandie Pendleton to General Garnett's headquarters at Red Banks. Pendleton found him there and arrested
Garnett for "neglect of duty on March 23 at Kernstown." Jackson
had feuded with Garnett since the latter took over Stonewall's namesake brigade; now he would purge himself of Garnett as he had
attempted to do to Loring two months earlier. Garnett was stunned
at the order relieving him from command. His subordinates were
equally shocked. Many visited their disgraced leader's tent to express their astonishment and regret.

Stonewall Jackson did not share the regret. For him, removing
Garnett from command relieved him of one of the factors that he
considered to be a hindrance to his division's success. Someone
had to be held responsible for all those killed and wounded men as
well as the scores of captured Confederates and the two valuable
cannons. That someone would be General Garnett. Jackson levelled seven court-martial specifications against his luckless brigadier to assure that he be held accountable for the loss at Kernstown.
Although this punitive measure initially upset the officers of
Jackson's division, years of hindsight allowed a reevaluation of
Jackson' action. "If he erred in his condemnation and removal of
Gen'l Garnett. . .," wrote Henry Kyd Douglas in 1880, "it was an
error that the future operations and success of that army excused,
perhaps justified. It taught Jackson's subordinates what he expected
of them."[46]

Stonewall had other pressing problems to solve. The
Rockingham militia responded negatively to the governor's orders
which drafted them into the service. A large band of them took cover
in the Blue Ridge Mountains to resist the order. Jackson detached
four companies of infantry, some cavalry, and two cannons to suppress the small uprising, which was accomplished with no blood-
shed in just a few days.[47]

Then there was the Northern army he faced. The Valley District army had been reinforced to approximately 4,000 men by early
April as furloughed veterans returned to the ranks. Militia and ammunition were also finally arriving. Stonewall still requested more
men to fend off the numbers that Banks could throw against him,
but he was also concerned with the quality of troops in Banks's
army. General Jackson displayed little respect for his adversary
throughout his military career; however, the performance of the
Indiana, Ohio, western Virginia, and Pennsylvania soldiers of
Shields's division gave him pause. Writing to General Longstreet on
April 5 concerning Banks's maneuvers against him, Jackson had
thoughts of Kernstown fresh in his mind when he gave begrudging
respect to Shields's men by writing, "As Shields' brigade [sic] is

composed principally of Western troops, who are familiar with the use of arms, and embraces troops that have met with success in Northwestern Virginia, we must calculate on hard fighting to rout Banks if attacked only in front, and may meet with obstinate resistance, however the attack may be made. . . ."[48]

Despite Jackson's surprising respect, one new member of Banks's corps wanted no part of Shields's division, the Union army, or life itself. Colonel Jonas P. Holliday had transported his seven companies of 1st Vermont Cavalry to Winchester from Poolesville, Maryland. From there he advanced with General Shields (The general was recovering quickly and no longer wished to be relieved). on April 1 to Strasburg where his cavalry was ordered to support Banks. Complaining of poor firearms and horses, and disciplinary problems in his ranks, the tall and fully bearded Holliday had been depressed about his command and suffered from personal problems that plagued his thoughts for nearly three weeks. At Strasburg, Holliday decided to suffer no longer. On Saturday, April 5, Colonel Holliday rode southward toward Fisher's Hill where his command was stationed. At the stone bridge that crossed Tumbling Run, he dispatched an orderly and his bugler to tell the adjutant to join him, but this was merely an excuse to send the aides away from him. Totally alone and behind his command, Holliday rode farther with a little speed, wheeled his horse to the right on a by-road that led to the North Fork of the Shenandoah River, and dismounted at the riverbank. Holliday then drew a pistol from his belt, placed the muzzle against his forehead, and squeezed the trigger. His lifeless body tumbled backward into the river and gently floated near the men he had commanded up to just minutes earlier.[49]

Colonel Holliday would forever miss what most of Shields's division was hoping for—an opportunity to meet Jackson's men in battle again. They found out that Jackson's men had the same aspirations. A member of the 1st West Virginia Cavalry found a note purposely dropped by a member of Jackson's division, who was picketing near Strasburg before the Federals occupied the town. It read:

Camp Near Strasburg

You Yankee Devils — Come on. You will meet with a warm and most cordial welcome from the brave sons of the South. We have been trying to get you to follow us for a long time, and have finally succeeded. I have been told that you say that you are going straight through to Richmond, but if you don't see sights before you get there I'll give up. You cowardly devils, when fifteen of Sheets' men run two hundred of your brag cavalry. I think if I was old Shields, after my arm was broke and taken off, I would quit lying so. Your

own men admit that he lies like old Harry. Well, as I have to go out
picketing, I must close for the present. You will hear from me soon
again.[50]

The soldier's warning proved to be accurate. Two months later
the inevitable rematch between the two forces began with the early
morning light on June 9, 1862, near Port Republic, a town on the
South Fork of the Shenandoah River at the southern point of the
Massanutten Mountain. The status of the opposing forces there, as
well as their fortunes, were reversed in comparison to Kernstown.
Jackson's Valley District army had been reinforced by Major General Richard Ewell. At full strength they numbered over 15,000
effectives. These troops had enjoyed a campaign that had embarrassed opposing forces for the previous forty days. After losing at
Kernstown, Jackson and his men enjoyed success through rapid
maneuvers and hard-spirited fighting to come away victorious at
McDowell, Front Royal, Winchester, and Cross Keys. Stonewall Jackson, on the verge of completing a campaign that placed him among
military legends, planned to cross the river and whip Shields's men
to add another link to what since Kerntown had been an unbroken
chain of victories. Jackson's successes had been achieved at the expense of several independently operating, but hapless Federal forces
that proved to be "no contest" against his fast-moving, powerful, and
confident army.

Those hapless Federals that Jackson and his men rolled over
had never included Shields's division. Detached from Banks in mid
May and sent to General McDowell, Shields's division reorganized
into four brigades had arrived at Falmouth (across the river from
Fredericksburg) on May 22, where they were reviewed by President
Lincoln the next day. Instead of joining McDowell's men in the advance toward Richmond, the Westerners received unexpected orders to return to the Valley when General Banks was swept from
Winchester on May 25 and sent fleeing across the Potomac River to
the safety of the Maryland shore. Shields's men re-entered the Valley at Front Royal as May turned to June. Advancing up the mud-
died and winding main road of the Page Valley, two brigades of
Shields's division advanced ahead of the remaining command and
found themselves near Port Republic—twenty miles ahead of the
rest of the division. Arriving there on June 8, these two brigades,
under the commands of Colonel Carroll and General Erastus Tyler,
bivouacked that night on the morrow's killing fields. A private in
the 7th Indiana accurately predicted that the calm of the late spring
night would last only until daylight.

Though always confident, the men in those two Federal brigades were in the same fighting condition as Jackson's men had

been two and one-half months earlier at Kernstown. Numbering fewer than 3,000 men, fatigued from marching nearly 400 miles in twenty-five days, hungry and barefoot, the men in Shields's two advanced brigades faced the foreboding sight of Jackson's larger and healthier army advancing against them in the hazy June morning.[51] For the 84th Pennsylvania, the similarity between the pending fight to that of the potential disaster that faced them at Bath five months earlier must have been stupefying. This day, as on January 4, the 84th Pennsylvania and the remaining Union force were outnumbered by more than 5,000 men, lacked sufficient supplies, and faced disaster.

No military force could have been more ill-prepared to fight.

Chapter Ten

"JACKSON'S WINCHESTER FOLLY"

General Thomas J. Jackson's Shenandoah Valley campaign of 1862 closed with a climactic Confederate victory at Port Republic. It was a victory earned, once again, by concentrating a large and powerful force upon an overmatched foe. Jackson's army suffered 800 casualties in the relatively short and vicious fight, but the victory over Shields's two brigades avenged the earlier loss the Valley District army suffered at their hands. The Southerners inflicted a casualty rate of over thirty-five percent on the Federals—more than 1,000 killed, wounded, and captured. Throughout May and June, Stonewall Jackson had frustrated and mystified over 40,000 Union troops with his strategy of swift marching, surprise, and massing large forces on weaker opponents. In those two months Jackson's campaign inflicted more than 7,000 casualties upon his Federal opponents at the cost of only 2,500 Southerners.

Nearly one-third of Jackson's May and June losses fell at Port Republic. Adding these to his Kernstown casualties, the Southerners realized that nearly half of Jackson's total campaign losses— over 1,500 men—were caused by Shields's men. Inevitably, some of Jackson's people offered comparisons of the fighting quality of Shields's troops to that of other Federal armies in the Valley. Henry Kyd Douglas of Jackson's staff considered Shields's men of like mettle to Jackson's people, and criticized Stonewall for believing that he could defeat Tyler's two brigades at Port Republic as easily as he handled General Frémont's men at Cross Keys the day before. After watching an Ohio regiment change front to rear on first company while under a heavy fire early in the battle, Douglas realized that Jackson underrated his opposition by impetuously battling "an army of such troops" as Shields's men.[1]

Stonewall Jackson's victory at Port Republic demoralized an already frustrated Federal force that had marched so proudly after Kernstown only seventy-eight days earlier. This division, once united, now resorted to finger pointing and bickering about their poor handling during the past two months. They felt unappreciated after their Kernstown victory and had physical proof to attest to the claim. Kimball's brigade had marched toward Stanardsville while two other brigades fought at Port Republic. He claimed that 1,100 men in his force marched barefoot and more than 200 men were without pants! Similar lack of provisions can be claimed for the eight infantry regiments, three batteries, and one cavalry regiment that lost on June 9. That force had more than 1,000 battle losses to add to the complaint list.[2]

The fact that Tyler fought Jackson's overwhelming force without support infuriated Shields's men. Earlier, they pointed accusing fingers at General Shields as the guilty party for their sickness, fatigue, half-rations, and lack of clothes and provisions. "Shields boasts that his division can do more hard marching than any other in the service," wrote an Ohio officer in June, adding, "He, I suppose, thinks he is marching to a seat in the U. S. Senate while the soldiers are marching to their graves." Although not solely responsible for the discomfort suffered by his men, General Shields was criticized as incompetent by his soldiers for not supporting Tyler at Port Republic, thereby sacrificing his exposed force unduly. One particularly livid officer in the hard-hit 7th Indiana suggested "that the responsible General have his head decapitated."[3] Another Hoosier linked Shields's troubles with his post-Kernstown exaggerations:

> When General Shields first resumed command of this division the soldiers and men all liked him. After the battle of Winchester (23d March) and the publication of his report of that battle, wherein he gave such a glowing description of the manner in which he *fooled* Jackson,—of the *trick* he "played off" on the rebels, &c., &c., his command began to think something was wrong. When he removed his Division from New Market, they thought that something was *very* wrong, and when he sent his handfull of men, who had become completely worn out from extreme exhaustion and privations, to Port Republic *the whole Country* knew that something was wrong. . . .[4]

The news reporters assured that the whole country would harbor doubts about Shields. The newspapers, who had courted General Shields as an American hero after Kernstown, now turned on him less than three months later. "General Shields has got to be one of the most unpopular men connected with the army," graced the pages of one daily paper during the summer of 1862, while another editor nearly slandered the general when he informed his readers, "It is said that many of the officers, medical and military, nearest to the person of General Shields for some time past, have been ready to bear testimony to his insanity."[5]

The claims of the news correspondents may have been based upon comments made by officers prior to the Port Republic battle. Major R. Morris Copeland, General Banks's assistant adjutant general who aided Shields during the Battle of Kernstown, happened to be in Washington in May where he witnessed seven officers in Shields's division "using every effort to get transferred to some other command." Generals Tyler and Sullivan, and Colonels Mason and Carroll headed this contingent. Knowing that Banks had earlier predicted what was unfolding in front of him, Copeland was quick to acknowledge Banks's foresight. "General Shields has cut his own rope without any aid from you or any opposition," he wrote to Banks, "and I am compelled to admit that your theory, when one has the patience to wait, is conclusive." Continuing to explain to Banks about Shields's careless tactics and abusive behavior, Copeland relayed to Banks the officers' collective opinion: "They think he must at times be crazy."[6]

The timing of this outward dissension could not have been worse for Shields. The day after Copeland wrote to Banks, three of the complainees testified against Shields to the most influential political committee in Washington. As a result of the Union fiasco at Ball's Bluff in October of 1861, a seven-member Congressional Committee, comprised principally of Radical Republicans, was called into being in December and given the mandate to inquire into the conduct of the war. This powerful group was called the Joint Committee for the Conduct of the War and was chaired by Ohio Senator Benjamin Franklin Wade, a partisan and vindictive zealot who questioned the loyalty of West Pointers, Democrats, and those with ties to the South.[7] Unfortunately for General James Shields, the latter two applied to him. (He was a Democratic politician who had led South Carolina troops during the Mexican War.) In an unusual turn, the committee met on May 22, 1862, to investigate a Union victory rather than a defeat. Four members of Shields's division appeared before the committee to answer questions about their commander's alleged role in the Battle of Kernstown.

Three witnesses—Colonel John Mason, Dr. H. M. McAbee, and General Jeremiah C. Sullivan—had openly complained about Shields on the eve of the trial. They, along with Colonel William Harrow, painted an unflattering picture of Shields in front of the

Joint Committee, highlighting Shields's limited role in the Kernstown victory. Their testimony clearly indicated that: (a) Shields did not believe Jackson was anywhere near Kernstown on the morning of the battle; (b) Shields was unaware that Jackson was not on the battlefield until after 3:00 P.M.; (c) Nathan Kimball directed the forces on the field; and (d) no particular strategy by upper command had led to the victory. The witnesses confirmed the prevailing sentiments of the foot soldiers in claiming that the spirited fighting of the men superseded any tactics in gaining the victory on March 23.

The testimony was particularly damning because it contradicted General Shields's claims of luring Jackson into battle and then directing the winning tactics from his bed. Surgeon McAbee's testimony embarrassed Shields; he stated that the General refused to allow him to care for the wounded after the battle, insisting that the doctor remain at his bedside instead. The final questions put forward to Dr. McAbee unveiled Shields as an officer who had no right to claim responsibility for his division's success at Kernstown:

Q: "What time did he (Shields) become aware that Jackson was there in force?"

A: "I think somewhere along between 3 and 4 o'clock in the afternoon."

Q: "What did he do when he ascertained that fact?"

A: "He could send no more forces on the field, for they were all there then."

Q: "Did he assume the command then?"

A: "Not in any other sense than he had done before."[8]

Through it all, Brigadier General Shields sought a promotion. President Lincoln put Shields's nomination for major general to the Senate during the late spring of 1862. Shields apparently felt the procedure to be an inevitable formality; he signed his dispatches with the rank of major general and reportedly wore two stars on his coat. The Senate was set to vote on the nomination on July 14, 1862. By then, Shields's failure at Port Republic had been informally reviewed; this, in combination with the committee's investigation of Kernstown, determined Shields's fate. His nomination was rejected and Shields was shelved. He spent the remainder of the summer visiting his wounded troops in Washington, D.C. and lobbying in vain to be given a new command. His former division was already dispersed at the end of June: two brigades sent to the Army of the Potomac at Harrison's Landing on the Peninsula, and two brigades sent to a new army—the Army of Virginia—under the command of Major General John Pope. Strengthened and molded under Lander, fought and marched under Shields, victorious under both—the Western division was dissolved.[9]

*   *   *   *   *

Contrary to the ill fortunes of the Federals he faced during the spring, Stonewall Jackson's popularity continued to rise during the summer of 1862. Joining Army of Northern Virginia commander Robert E. Lee near Richmond in late June, Jackson's lackluster performance in the Seven Days' battles (June 25–July 1, 1862) failed to tarnish his star. By mid July, Robert E. Lee placed enough faith in Jackson to send him off on another independent operation to suppress General Pope and his Federal Army of Virginia. Jackson's command enlarged to a wing of Lee's army, three divisions numbering 22,000 men. By early August, Jackson's Confederates camped south of the Rapidan River between the towns of Orange Court House and Gordonsville.

Although comfortable in his return role as an independent commander, the ugly residue of Jackson's failed efforts at Kernstown coated him in early August. A huge reminder of Jackson's losses at Kernstown appeared on August 5, when the surviving prisoners from Jackson's previous command were finally exchanged at Aiken's Landing, Virginia, in accordance with the Dix-Hill Cartel. Some, like Captain Lewis P. Holloway of the 27th Virginia, succumbed to disease at Fort Delaware and were buried in Northern territory. Those that survived their four and one-half months of confinement either reentered the Confederate services in other units or returned to civilian life.[10]

While Stonewall Jackson won victory after victory in the Shenandoah Valley, the scapegoat for his only loss in the 1862 Valley Campaign worked tirelessly to release himself from his arrest. General Richard Brooke Garnett faced seven specific court-martial charges for neglect of duty at Kernstown. Jackson sent the charges to the Richmond War Department on April 29. Refusing to see another general with charges against him returned to command rather than be disciplined, Jackson was determined to see the charges carried through. When Adjutant General Samuel Cooper suggested in writing that Stonewall drop the Garnett affair, Jackson derisively responded, "In regard to the suggestion of releasing him from court assigning him to duty, I have only to say, that I have no desire to see the case pressed any further; but that I regard General Garnett as so incompetent a Brigade commander, that instead of building up a brigade, a good one, if turned over to him, would actually deteriorate under the command."[11]

Garnett sat in Harrisonburg in April, where he recovered enough from the initial shock of his unsuspected fall from grace to plead his case to Richmond. Complaining that Jackson's charges "blast my character both as a soldier and a man," Garnett asked for a speedy trial to vindicate himself. He soon found out that there would be no quick resolution to his problem. The court-martial required a period of military inactivity for officers to take part in the proceedings, and April and May were too active and perilous for the Confederacy to allow high-ranking officers to participate.

Garnett did the best he could to clear his name. He showed up at the War Department in Richmond on May 6 to appeal his case in person to Adjutant General Cooper. Garnett was willing to gamble away any advantage to receive a speedy hearing; he waived his right to affect the composition of the court in order to obtain immediately available officers to facilitate the proceedings. With his risky proposal as leverage, Garnett asked General Cooper to temporarily suspend the case if no board could immediately be formed so that he could reassume field command.

General Jackson, in the midst of routing Federal armies in the Valley, saw to it that Garnett was denied any special favors by the Confederate War Department. In a letter to Confederate Congressman A. R. Boteler—a Jackson partisan—written on the same day Garnett presented his proposal to Samuel Cooper, Jackson complained about what he considered to be undeserved commissions of four subordinate officers—including General Garnett. Jackson was adamant in his denunciation of the brigadier. "I wish that if such appointments are continued, that the President would come in the field and command them," Stonewall sarcastically complained, "and not throw the responsibility upon me of defending this District when he throws such obstacles in my way." Later in the month, Garnett's request to return to duty passed through the appropriate channels of the Confederacy without opposition until it reached Robert E. Lee's desk. Lee sympathized with Garnett's plight, but when he read Jackson's earlier commentary evaluating Garnett as a brigade commander, he decided that Garnett's case must go to trial before he returned to command.[12]

With a stirring rebuke to mull over, Garnett relocated to Staunton where he re-petitioned General Cooper in a sixteen-page letter specifically answering each of the seven charges placed against him. He also suggested that Jackson had embarrassed him throughout the winter and early spring by withholding plans and intentions from him. Garnett's letter apparently persuaded the Confederate War Department to suspend his military arrest on June 25. Although he was restored to temporary brigade command under Major General Daniel Harvey Hill, Garnett worked to bring his case to trial and restore his reputation. To do this, he would have to go one-on-one with General Hill's brother-in-law, Stonewall Jackson.

In June, Garnett prophetically worried that "my most material witnesses may be, from various causes, rendered unavailable to me." Within a few days of receiving permission to return to the field, three of Garnett's potential witnesses died in the vicious Seven Days' battles that turned back McClellan's Army of the Potomac from the gates of Richmond. Colonel Samuel Vance Fulkerson, Colonel James W. Allen, and Major Frank Jones were all major players in the Battle of Kernstown; but, by the end of June, they had joined Turner Ashby (killed at Harrisonburg on June 6) as memories. Other regimental leaders at Kernstown no longer held field commands. Garnett realized that the testimony of those officers was extremely valuable to his defense. So did his father, William Garnett, who sought justice to remove his son from the responsibility of what he coined "Jackson's Winchester folly." The elder Garnett aided his son by writing to the regimental officers, requesting them to provide certified statements to absolve his son from the charges against him. Richard Garnett's long-awaited trial was set to begin on July 16, but the genesis of Jackson's second campaign as an independent commander suspended the proceedings. Despite the initial disappointment, the delay allowed the accused to strengthen his defense.[13]

Garnett welcomed the positive responses from surviving witnesses. Colonel John Echols and Lieutenant Elliott Johnston sent certified statements. Notes were also taken from statements made by Colonel Harman of the 5th Virginia and other regimental officers of Stonewall Brigade units. Two other Kernstown witnesses, Colonel Cummings, formerly of the 33rd Virginia, and Colonel Andrew J. Grigsby of the 27th Virginia, offered to help Garnett by testifying before the court. General Jackson was also well aware of the united support Garnett would receive from the regimental officers. Those same commanders displayed their resentment over Garnett's arrest in April when they refused to give the complimentary greeting to his replacement, Brigadier General Charles Winder, when he took over the Stonewall Brigade on April 2. It was also known that Colonel Cummings had refused to stand for reelection in his regiment, owing to his aversion to serve under General Jackson. Cummings's testimony would not likely be helpful to the prosecution.

Stonewall found out that he would not have many witnesses whenever the court-martial convened. He had questioned several of his regimental commanders in May concerning Garnett's order to retreat and asked if they could have held on to Sandy Ridge for five minutes longer. Not one commander asked this particular question answered in the affirmative. Grigsby was the most adamant in his reply, "No Sir, they could not have stood a damned second longer." While Garnett had the support of regimental officers to bolster his defense, Stonewall would rely upon the testimony of his loyal adjutant, Sandie Pendleton, and the prestige and popularity achieved by his own accomplishments in the Shenandoah Valley to successfully convict Garnett in a military court.[14]

The written statements and official reports available to Garnett strengthened his case on nearly every specification General Jackson had used to handcuff his subordinate. It is difficult to believe that Garnett was unaware of how powerful his evidence was on the eve of the court-martial. Bolstered by the testimony promised by Grigsby and other regimental officers, Garnett's defense was prepared. Writing to former Confederate Secretary of State Robert M. T. Hunter in April, Garnett believed even then "that all the specifications, except the first one, can be *completely overthrown*" (his emphasis).[15] The evidence countered every charge:

The first two specifications Jackson levelled against him dealt with actions that developed in front of Pritchard's Hill prior to Jackson's redeployment of his artillery to Sandy Ridge. The first charge stated "that Brigadier-General R. B. Garnett after having been directed by Major-General T. J. Jackson to support Colonel S. V. Fulkerson on the day of the battle near Kernstown, Virginia, on March 23, 1862, did, after advancing with four regiments for some distance, have three of them in rear, and continued to advance with only one, and finally notified Colonel S. V. Fulkerson, he would move back this regiment, thus leaving him without any support." By the letter of the law, General Garnett was guilty of the specification, and previous to the trial he had provided a weak explanation stating that he was too concerned with the Federal artillery in his front to assure that all his regiments would follow him as he led the 33rd Virginia from the edge of Barton's Woods toward Pritchard's Hill. However, Garnett's complaint of Stonewall Jackson micromanaging his brigade (Jackson removed the artillery and realigned rearward regiments on the march through the woods) were persuasive to attest that he expected the commanding general to personally order the rear regiments from the woodline. The strongest evidence to counter the charge was Jackson's secrecy—he never told his second in command what Fulkerson's orders were and it would be difficult to discredit the notion that one regiment was adequate support for Fulkerson's two-regiment brigade, particularly when no explanation of his intentions was available.

Jackson's second specification also concerned the Pritchard's Hill action: "In this that Brigadier-General R. B. Garnett did so separate himself from his command that he could not be found by Major F. B. Jones, who was directed to give him an order." This charge loosely restated the first specification and would be unlikely to hold up in court even if Major Jones had survived to testify to the incident; the inability of an aide to locate an officer in the midst of a battle is not unusual. Interestingly, Garnett misinterpreted the location of the charge to take place on Sandy Ridge rather than in front of Pritchard's Hill earlier in the day and he had prepared his defense accordingly.

The remaining five specifications all dealt with the Sandy Ridge action chronologically; three of them smack of pettiness and impossibilities. Specification three stated "that Brigadier-General R. B. Garnett did neglect to be with his leading regiment when it went into battle, near Kernstown, Virginia on March 23, 1862." Jackson placed his subordinate in double-jeopardy with that charge, for he was accusing him of failing to be at two places at the same time. The charge referred to the 27th Virginia opening the battle without Garnett at its helm. Garnett, at the time, was already with his leading regiment—the 33rd Virginia—taking it onto Sandy Ridge when the 27th Virginia opened the fight. Garnett himself considered the charge to be frivolous, sarcastically belittling its importance when he wrote General Cooper "I am not aware of any military rule which would oblige me to occupy the position assigned." Regardless, Garnett had two witnesses from the 27th Virginia, Colonels Echols and Grigsby, to support his defense that Jackson ordered the regiment forward and Garnett could not have known where they were when they engaged Tyler's brigade.

Jackson's fourth charge against Garnett— "that Brigadier-General R. B. Garnett neglected to have a regiment in supporting distance of his leading one, when it went into action near Kernstown, Virginia on March 23, 1862"—once again places the accused in an impossible situation; i.e., if Garnett was nowhere near the 27th Virginia when Stonewall sent them from their artillery positions, how could he have the other Stonewall Brigade regiments within supporting distance of the 27th when those regiments (2nd, 4th, and 33rd Virginia) had just reunited on Sandy Ridge? Still, Garnett prepared a reasonable defense to persuade the court that he reinforced the battle line within ten minutes of the 27th Virginia's initial fight.

Jackson's fifth specification read: "In this that Brigadier-General R. B. Garnett did so neglect to post his regiments properly in the battle of Kernstown, Virginia on March 23, 1862, that they became mixed together, when they should have been kept separate." Although Garnett's report supports the charge, he had the terrain limiting features and the desperate fighting from behind the stone wall to explain why and how the intermixing occurred.

Specification six stated "that Brigadier-General R. B. Garnett did during the battle near Kernstown, Virginia on March 23, 1862, give the order to fall back, when he should have encouraged his command to hold its position." Because Jackson's charge admitted allowable discretionary decisions, it is difficult to believe that it was strong enough to result in a court-martial. Had Jackson's order been "hold your line at all cost," Garnett would have indeed been found guilty of the charge, but this did not apply here. Once again, Garnett had the testimony of his regimental commanders to provide ample evidence that his decision to leave the ridge could not be avoided. Jackson had precourt warning of the Stonewall Brigade colonels' support of Garnett after he queried his regimental commanders in May about this specification.

Jackson's final charge against Garnett was both Stonewall's angriest accusation and Garnett's most defensible response. Jackson claimed "that Brigadier-General R. B. Garnett did during the battle near Kernstown, Virginia on March 23, 1862, send an order by Major F. B. Jones, directing Colonel W. H. Harman to retreat, notwithstanding his regiment had not yet been brought into action, and should have continued to advance on the enemy, as it was doing at the time, in obedience to orders from Major-General T. J. Jackson." Garnett denied giving Major Jones the order to send to Harman and claimed that Jones also had no recollection of the order. Frank Jones was no longer alive to settle the issue; his fate was stronger support for Garnett as Jackson lacked the burden of proof in his charge. Harman was willing to testify that he never received a retreat order from Garnett, negating this charge once and for all. The specification also lacked clarity. Did Jackson expect the 5th Virginia to "advance on the enemy" when the remainder of the Confederate battle line was already in retreat? Did Stonewall consider Garnett's rearward positioning of the 5th Virginia to ambush pursuing Federal troops to be an order to retreat? As nebulous as the charge seemed to be, Garnett confidently predicted that his brigade officers' after action reports vindicated him and "argues either malice or great carelessness on the part of my accuser."[16] Richard Brooke Garnett was prepared to take on his accuser in a military court of law.

The brief inactivity of early August convinced the Confederate War Department to settle the affair. Garnett received his summons to report to General Richard Ewell's headquarters at Liberty Mills, north of Gordonsville and west of Orange Court House on the Rapidan River. Officers were available to sit in judgment of what would prove to be one of the most famous military trials in Confederate history. The reason for the trial's notoriety was due to the first witness scheduled to take the stand on August 6, 1862—Major General Thomas J. Jackson. Stonewall's subordinates would weigh their commander's testimony to decide the fate of General Richard Brooke Garnett. To intensify the drama, Garnett would fire the questions at his former superior officer who was now attempting to destroy his military career.

Garnett pulled no punches in defending his honor. Buoyed by the strength of his defense, the brigadier's objective was to discredit Stonewall and to turn the responsibility for the loss at Kernstown from himself to General Jackson. Jackson appeared unconcerned when he took the stand at Ewell's headquarters on the hazy, hot morning of August 6. He soon learned from Garnett's aggressive questioning that he underestimated the capabilities of former subordinate and faced the embarrassment of falling victim to Garnett's plan.

Stonewall Jackson opened the court-martial with a statement from the witness stand, briefly recounting the actions of March 23, 1862, that supported his seven charges against Garnett. Stonewall's initial testimony pointedly suggested that Garnett would not have rallied his men until Jackson asked him why he had not done so. Jackson's opening remarks suffered from duplicity. He ended his statement by regretting that Garnett gave the order to fall back, but Jackson also admitted earlier that he became "apprehensive that our infantry would be forced back" and, therefore, had made artillery and cavalry adjustments to prevent the enemy from pursuing the retreating Confederate infantry. In other words, Stonewall levelled a charge against Garnett that he should not have ordered a retreat, but, at the same time, he personally prepared for the inevitability of a withdrawal by redeploying his batteries and cavalry.

After Jackson finished his opening statements, Garnett attacked him with a series of questions orchestrated to show the court that Garnett was second in command on the field at Kernstown, but never had Jackson's plan of battle communicated to him. Once Jackson admitted this fact to the satisfaction of Garnett, the accused questioned his accuser about the disparity of strength between the Federals and Confederates on the field. Throughout the morning, Garnett constantly returned to the numbers engaged questions, trying to get Jackson to admit being greatly deceived into entering the fight. Jackson's reply claimed Federal strength at 11,000 and that his force engaged did not exceed 2,500. Stonewall backed off from the suggestion that Ashby was responsible for the misinformation, carefully wording his testimony not to disparage that late but still beloved cavalryman. Jackson admitted that he received similar erroneous information from a spy that led him to believe that Winchester had been evacuated the day before the battle. Garnett's strategy scored valuable points to support his contention that he was compelled to lead his men blindly against a numerically superior enemy without any sense of a battle plan to follow.

Stonewall continued to weaken his case at the hands of his well-prepared subordinate when he was cornered into stating that he gave "special attention" to Garnett's brigade artillery, but fell short of admitting that he told Garnett that he would take charge of it. Garnett was trying to convince the court that Jackson was acting as a secondary brigade commander, but when Garnett tried to get Jackson to state that he ordered only one regiment to support Fulkerson's advance through Barton's Woods, Jackson refused to fall into the trap and emphatically announced, "I am well satisfied that I did not."

Garnett quickly left all questions pertaining to the first charge against him and pursued the issue of the final two specifications. Garnett appeared offended by Jackson's opening statement that the brigadier fell back rather than rallied his men. Garnett wanted to show the court that while he was with his men at all times, Stonewall stayed in the rear. Garnett asked Jackson how far he was from the infantry when it engaged Tyler's brigade at the stone wall. Jackson's answer—"I should think about 100 yards"—was clearly a lie as far as Garnett was concerned (He wrote the word "lie" in the margin of his trial transcript to the left of this response), but he did not pursue the issue any further. The brigadier mixed his next set of questions, jumping from another strength-disparity issue, to Fulkerson's instructions, to movements transpiring the day before the battle, then back to questions concerning Fulkerson's orders. Stonewall provided brief answers to all questions, indicating that Garnett could not confuse him; but, Garnett did force him to admit, once again, that he had not provided battle-plan information to his second in command.

Garnett then attempted to illustrate that Jackson expected to turn the enemy's right by using an undersized force. Jackson admitted that the lead force was only the two regiments of Fulkerson's command, but sought to clarify his response to illustrate that Fulkerson was to be supported by the "main body of the Army." Jackson's answer likely scored more points for Garnett because Jackson, once again, provided contradictory statements. Stonewall wanted his army to support a two-regiment attack, but earlier admitted that he did not provide that attack plan to the commander who was expected to provide the support. If Garnett believed that the first charge against him was Jackson's strongest, he successfully illustrated to those who sat in judgment of him that the ambiguous orders and withheld information could explain his inability to fulfill the instructions.

Garnett's next line of questioning forced Jackson to provide a reasonable rationale as to why the third charge against him ("did neglect to be with his leading regiment when it went into battle") carried any weight for a court-martial proceeding. Jackson replied that he believed it was the officer's duty to be with his command for practical military movements and observations, but, when asked, could not cite any military law to defend his response. Garnett ended his questioning of Jackson specifically to set him up for the next day's witness. When asked by the accused if he sent messages through Lieutenant A. S. Pendleton on the battle day, Jackson replied in the affirmative. Then the court adjourned for the day. August 6 came to its inevitable close at midnight, ending a day that saw the mercury rise toward 100 degrees outside Ewell's headquarters, while tempers and activities inside must have made the heat seem unbearable.[17]

On the morning of August 9, Sandie Pendleton took the witness stand and faced a determined General Richard Garnett. Pendleton lacked confidence as Jackson's primary witness; two nights earlier he had conceded in a letter to his mother that "The case will most probably go by default in favor of General Garnett."[18] Jackson's testimony on the first day likely did little to change Pendleton's opinion. Garnett's first questions to Sandie concerned what Pendleton knew about the specifications against Garnett. He admitted he knew little about the first charge, because he was guarding the artillery pieces near the turnpike at the time. As for the second charge, Pendleton testified that he could not find Garnett after Major Jones and Lieutenant Junkin each failed to locate the brigadier. Pendleton claimed that he rode toward the eastern base of Sandy Ridge where the 33rd Virginia had advanced after failing to turn Federal batteries on Pritchard's Hill. Sandie stated that he could not find Garnett with the 33rd Virginia. Pendleton then testified about finding the 2nd and 33rd intermixed at the stone wall (the body of the fifth specification against Garnett).

Jackson had evaded the scenario of taking charge of the Stonewall Brigade artillery during the first day of the trial, so Garnett directed his questioning of Pendleton to settle this issue with the presiding court. Garnett forced Pendleton to detail his early battle responsibility of separating and guarding the artillery batteries from all the brigades. Pendleton inadvertently satisfied Garnett's persuasive question of who had taken charge of the artillery. "I believe Captain McLaughlin, being Senior Captain of Artillery, acted as a sort of Chief of Artillery," Pendleton answered, but then aided Garnett by admitting, "under General Jackson's own supervision."

Garnett then dug into Pendleton's damning remarks about being unable to find the brigadier with the 33rd Virginia. When asked if he was sure he didn't overlook the general in the midst of the regiment, Pendleton testily responded, "Yes, I certainly would have been able to recognize anyone on horseback with the regiment." The answer indicated that Pendleton did not see Colonel Cummings on horseback either, for both he and Garnett were persuading Colonel Fulkerson to move back from his advanced position. The meeting site was several hundred yards north of the 33rd Virginia—both were out of Pendleton's line of sight when he sought Garnett. However, when Garnett pressed Pendleton further about looking for the brigadier, Sandie ended this line of questioning by stating that General Jackson was planning his infantry movement and Pendleton had no time to continue "a fruitless search."

Garnett then led Pendleton into the line of questioning concerning the Confederate retreat from Sandy Ridge. Sandie remarked that when the advanced artillery pieces retired, he rode one and one-half miles to the rear to bring up the 48th Virginia but, when he returned, it was too late; the battle line had withdrawn. Garnett asked Pendleton about the timing of the artillery withdrawal, attempting to show that his infantry line lacked adequate support when the batteries left the field. Pendleton admitted that the artillery pieces withdrew in consequence of the advance of Federal infantry, but he believed this occurred prior to Confederate infantry retiring. (This may have been true for Carpenter's battery only.) Pendleton then sought to show the court that the artillery withdrawal was not an attempt to leave the battlefield, but rather one to align in a new defensive position.

The trial abruptly terminated before Pendleton could continue his testimony. General Jackson, reacting to information gathered from his intelligence system, ordered his army to cross the Rapidan River to contest the movements of Union General John Pope and his Army of Virginia who had occupied Culpeper Court House. Two days later, on August 9, Jackson's divisions defeated 12,000 men in Banks's corps of Pope's army at the Battle of Cedar Mountain.[19] Garnett never finished cross-examining his other witnesses. The dishonored brigadier never had the opportunity to present his exonerating defense. The court-martial of General Richard Brooke Garnett never reconvened.

It was mere coincidence that important military matters evolved during the trial; however, Jackson's opportunity to battle Pope was fortuitous. Had the trial continued, Jackson would likely have seen the military court acquit General Garnett of all the charges placed against him. The brigadier's painstakingly prepared defense effectively countered all the specifications against him. The court-martial's continuation could have been disastrous for Garnett's accuser. The officer most responsible for Confederate failure at

Kernstown was not Brigadier General Richard Brooke Garnett; it was Major General Thomas J. Jackson.

Stonewall Jackson had inherited many impediments as an independent commander. His isolated command was hampered by inclement weather, quarreling volunteer troops led by back-biting commanders, hapless militia, and a respectfully game opponent in General Lander and his Westerners. The Confederate Valley District commander had little to celebrate during the first three months of 1862. Withdrawing his undersized force to the safety of the Upper (southern) Valley should have provided Jackson with sufficient time to refit and reorganize his division.

But Stonewall had not allowed it. Prodded by General Johnston's suggestion to close the gap between his division and Banks's corps, Jackson complied by marching northward, but disobeyed his superior's warning to not expose himself to the danger of defeat. Stonewall had been spoiling for a fight since the night of March 11 (the date he was forced out of Winchester). Always looking for the trademark of his success, Jackson lunged at the opportunity to concentrate his larger force against what he thought was an outnumbered opponent. He did this at the expense of his unprepared and footsore men, who fought gamely at Kernstown but would be in better fighting condition if they had waited until the next morning to wage war. At face value, Jackson's decision not to wait seemed appropriate, but his concern that the Federals had already seen him and would reinforce their numbers if he chose to rest belies his objective. Drawing Federals into the Shenandoah Valley—Jackson's mission—could have been accomplished without pushing tired men into battle; however, the temptation to defeat what he believed to be three or four Union regiments would accomplish the same objective and would provide his men the morale-boosting experience of routing a hapless foe.

Stonewall Jackson jeopardized General Johnston's mission when he shunned his superior's stipulation of caution and risked his division in an impetuous fight. However, the strategic consequence was so favorable to the Confederacy that Johnston never criticized his subordinate for his overzealous actions. No evidence exists to support the notion that Jackson fought Nathan Kimball while harboring the incredible degree of foresight necessary to predict that his attack would produce the Union's misinterpretation that followed. The hordes of blue-clad troops that streamed into the Shenandoah Valley after the battle benefitted the Confederacy as a result of Federal overreaction, not from Confederate grand strategy. The Union's exaggerated response could not have been planned or anticipated.

Jackson's thinly veiled battle report casts a shadow on Colonel Turner Ashby for misleading Stonewall into fighting an opponent that outnumbered him (He confirmed this in his testimony at the trial). Had Jackson communicated directly with Ashby at noon on March 23, while the Valley District infantry rested in Barton's Woods, he would have learned that over six regiments of Federal infantry and more than a dozen cannons had contested Ashby throughout the morning. Eighteen Union cannons were employed, but Ashby might not have seen all of them. Captain Nadenbousch's official report describes Ashby seeing the "heavy columns of the enemy" while Ashby's report adds the fact that his left was threatened as well by Federal infantry and artillery. Ashby's report also states that he "learned that your [Jackson's] force had arrived," strongly suggesting that he never conferred directly with Stonewall. A brief conference with his cavalry chief could have prevented the calamity that fell upon Jackson's men due to the impetuosity of their commanding general.

Six weeks before his June 6 death at Harrisonburg, Turner Ashby registered a series of complaints about General Jackson in a letter sent, ironically, to one of Stonewall Jackson's favorite sounding boards—Confederate Congressman A. R. Boteler. Ashby's note to Boteler explained why he resigned (temporarily) his command in May. Had Garnett seen the letter, he would have used it in the trial for it specified the same complaints Garnett registered against Stonewall. Ashby resented the interference with his command and went out of his way to state: "I feel bold to announce the fact without a fear of being considered vain that for the last two months I have saved the Army of the Valley from being utterly destroyed. . . . This I have done without the aid of Gen. Jackson's command and by the want of such information from him which I considered myself entitled to. As not knowing his movements has made my dutys [sic] much more arduous."[20]

Jackson's penchant for secrecy, noted by Generals Ashby and Garnett, hindered Southern success at Kernstown. Garnett justifiably complained that, although second in command on the field, the commanding general kept him in complete ignorance of his intentions during the day. Perhaps Stonewall had not fully developed his strategy and was permitting the flow of the battle to dictate his next move. Inconceivably, however, when finally ordering movements of troops under Garnett's command, Jackson refused to communicate directly with his chief subordinate even though he was less than 100 yards from him during Fulkerson's Pritchard's Hill attack, preferring to transfer the order through his aide although he chose to speak directly to Fulkerson minutes earlier. Garnett was indeed guilty of Jackson's first specification against him, but Stonewall's trademark of withholding information from his subordinates produced Garnett's inappropriate support of Fulkerson's attack. Had Garnett known what Fulkerson's orders were, it is highly likely he would have taken extra time to make sure his full brigade moved forward rather than just the 33rd Virginia.

Jackson's orders at Kernstown also lacked clarity. Did "turn a battery" (Jackson's orders to Fulkerson) mean attack the artillery or flank it? Fulkerson did not seem clear about the specifics of his orders—he chose to attack Pritchard's Hill. (This is what Garnett believed while he was following him.) Jackson's after-battle explanations never give indication for an attack. Had he desired Fulkerson to flank the artillery rather than attack it, he should have made this clear to his brigadier.

Garnett labored in vain during his cross-examination of Jackson to embarrass Stonewall into admitting that he was surprised by the Federal strength at Kernstown. Based on Jackson's positioning on the field, he knew precisely the numbers he was up against when he led the Rockbridge Artillery onto the ridge. From the open crest where Jackson ordered the batteries to unlimber at approximately 3:00 P.M., he enjoyed an unobstructed view of the swarm of bluecoats supporting Daum's artillery pieces as well as Sullivan's brigade on the open plain east of Pritchard's Hill. More than two-thirds of the Union force that fought under Kimball that day was exposed to his view. Jackson never testified as to what fell under his gaze during the interval before the Sandy Ridge infantry fight, because it did not affect his subsequent plan to push forward infantry to outflank the Federals. But, by first separating the artillery batteries from Garnett's command, then by sending the 27th Virginia toward the woods and out of their brigadier's view, Jackson compromised Garnett's effectiveness to lead his troops that afternoon. Jackson poured salt in Garnett's wound when he charged that Garnett was not with the leading regiment that Jackson personally removed from Garnett's view.

Despite all of the mistakes made in the early phase of the battle, the Confederates had a positional advantage and should have held onto Sandy Ridge until they could withdraw under the cover of darkness. They enjoyed interior lines and although the infantry was outnumbered by five to two, military doctrine still favored the Southerners in their defensive position. But in two hours, the Virginians fled from the hill with jubilant Federals in pursuit. Three factors were responsible for this unsuspected turn of events.

The first factor was, once again, General Jackson. Stonewall handled his forces poorly once they became engaged on Sandy Ridge. He took a "hands-off" approach to the fight at the stone wall when it was his responsibility to redeploy his unengaged troops to heavier-contested areas on the height. Fulkerson's 600 men stood relatively inactive after forcing the 1st West Virginia from the western end of the stone wall. Garnett could not move them to the right of the Confederate line; he was not in charge while General Jackson was still on the ridge. It was Stonewall's responsibility to send at least one regiment to support the 21st Virginia, Irish Battalion, and 2nd Virginia on the Confederate right, where these regiments sorely needed men to repel the second wave of Union assaults. But Jackson preferred to stay well to the rear of the wall and direct the coming reinforcements into the battle line. It was an unfortunate command decision that handcuffed Confederate efforts.

Even more detrimental to the Southerners was the scarcity of small arms ammunition, a responsibility of the commanding general. Although Stonewall exhorted his men to give the Federals the bayonet and lauded his men for liberally borrowing from standing and fallen comrades, his neglect in having an ample supply of cartridges left regiments like the 27th Virginia with little choice but to withdraw from the field after their morning supply had been exhausted. "An army marches on its stomach," was one of Napoleon's familiar axioms. Jackson discovered all too painfully that an army fights with bullets, and his army had almost none left by 6:00 P.M. Garnett's propitious positioning of the 5th Virginia and subsequent darkness saved Jackson's division from a more disastrous defeat that fateful March Sunday. Inexplicably, Jackson never utilized half of his available artillery. At least ten Confederate cannons never fired a round on the battlefield. Although all of these pieces could not be expected to be squeezed onto the military crest of Sandy Ridge, Jackson had attempted to use only four of them, but they were ordered up too late. The artillery reserve could have rendered effective service for the Valley District army on the more modest elevations south of Kernstown where they could have hammered the center and left of the Union line.

The disparity in weaponry between Union and Confederate forces also factored into the outcome at Kernstown. With the exception of three regiments who carried Belgians and smoothbores, the Federals enjoyed the advantage of rifled muskets over the percussion smoothbores carried by most of the Southern soldiers that day.[21] The shotgun effect of muskets aided Fulkerson's men and the 21st and 27th Virginia during the initial stages of the Sandy Ridge fight; however, once the troops had spread out and found a position where they could carefully aim their shots, the rifles carried by the bluecoats outperformed the smoothbores. Although much of the infantry fire between the two sides was conducted within effective smoothbore range of 70–100 yards, the rifled weapons were more likely to strike their targets consistently at this close encounter. The Federals also had more powerful artillery. Fourteen out of the eighteen Federal cannons that fired rounds at Kernstown were rifled pieces. Daum's men enjoyed success at distances of greater than one mile. Conversely, only three cannons used by Jackson in the battle were rifled. Although the Southern artillery devastated Pritchard's Hill and compelled Kimball to commit most of his available force to take them out, it appears that the two rifled pieces in the Rockbridge Artillery had the greatest success (the other rifled cannon was Chew's Blakely gun). The smoothbores were so ineffective that one howitzer was limbered to the rear into a reserve position by its frustrated artillerists. Six-pounder smoothbores constituted approximately half of Jackson's available artillery force (including the reserves). Had Jackson more rifled pieces at his disposal, he may have contended more effectively with Nathan Kimball.

The final factor that was responsible for the Confederate failures on Sandy Ridge was the dogged performance of the Federal soldier. The Confederates fought valiantly, but lost on March 23 partly due to the efforts of the bluecoats. Federal high command exhibited similar lapses as the Confederates (no artillery ammunition and no unified leadership on Sandy Ridge, to name two examples). The unintentional piecemeal assaults, usually a mark of doom for an army, worked in the Yankees' favor this afternoon. Tyler's oversight in deployment ground his brigade to a halt in the first half hour, but his men continued to engage in close-range fire while reinforcements bent and extended their left during the next hour. The constant pressure of reinforcing Federal regiments strained their opponents and eventually forced the Confederate retreat. The usually maligned Federal cavalry took over from there and successfully mopped up the field, leading back scores of captured Confederates. This combined effort of artillery, infantry, and cavalry, in combination with failures of Confederate high command, produced the Union victory at Kernstown.

One of the most overlooked facets of why the Shenandoah Valley Campaign played out as it did exists in General Shields's decision not to interrogate the 234 captured Confederates immediately sent to Baltimore. Had Shields, his staff, or the U.S. War Department reviewed and evaluated the provost marshal's list of captured, they would have realized that the nine infantry regiments and one battalion could not have yielded the 11,000 Southern troops that Shields insisted had battled his division. Considering General Banks's fetish for careful and detailed documentation of all prisoners' statements, the lack of interest in these valuable Confederates remains an important and puzzling oversight with far-reaching consequences.

Despite his tactical lapses on the Kernstown battlefield, General Thomas J. Jackson profited from the misinterpretation of and overreaction to his audacious attack, and his subsequent Shenandoah Valley Campaign graces the list of all-time military endeavors and earns him respect as one of America's most perceptive and respected generals. Stonewall could also claim responsibility for the defining moment of the Battle of Kernstown, one that bears repeating. Shortly after 5:00 P.M., as Nathan Kimball sent his second wave of assailants to Sandy Ridge, Sandie Pendleton returned to Jackson from the Rockbridge Artillery positions and gave him a woefully inflated estimate of the number of Federals opposing them. Perhaps Jackson overreacted to the number "10,000," or perhaps he did not believe the naive estimate of his young aide, but instead had come to the realization that the battle was not turning in his favor. Throughout his military career Stonewall Jackson never admitted defeat in battle; he had never experienced the bitter taste of defeat before. But on Sunday, March 23, 1862, General Jackson blurted out a response to his aide that he had never had to say before, nor would he ever say again. "Say nothing about it," he declared to Pendleton, "We are in for it."[22]

Once again, Stonewall Jackson proved to be a man of his word.

Epilogue

When I was a baby I was a great admirer of military stories, now their honors seem tarnished with blood and with tears of widows and orphans. Ah no, no war for me, unless my country, and country's liberties are in danger, then conquer or die is my motto.

John G. Marsh, 29th Ohio,
to his father two weeks after the
battle of Kernstown[1]

The American Civil War had yet to complete its first year when General Jackson attacked Colonel Nathan Kimball at Kernstown on March 23, 1862. Predictably, many of the division, brigade, and regimental commanders that fought on the hills near Winchester could not endure the remaining toils of war. This was particularly true for the Confederates. By the time Richard Brooke Garnett's court-martial trial convened in early August of 1862, General Turner Ashby, Colonels Samuel V. Fulkerson and James W. Allen, and Major Frank Jones were dead—all killed in battle within three months of Kernstown. Additionally, Colonels Arthur C. Cummings, Jesse S. Burks, Daniel A. Langhorne, Robert P. Carson, and William H. Harman no longer held regiment or brigade commands in Jackson's division. Most were dropped at reorganization or resigned due to injuries or illness. Colonel John Mercer Patton of the 21st Virginia, whose exemplary performance at Kernstown prevented the Federals from flanking the Confederates on Sandy Ridge, resigned on August 8—the day after Sandie Pendleton testified at the Garnett trial)—due to impaired health affecting his digestive tract to the point where he lost thirty-five pounds. He survived his two brothers (both were killed during the war), wrote several legal books afterwards, and died at the age of seventy-two in 1898.[2] John Mercer Patton represented the midpoint of a famous military family history. His grandfather

252

was Revolutionary War General Hugh Mercer and his brother George's namesake grandson, born in 1885, would achieve the ultimate notoriety for the family for his performance in the Second World War.

The Valley District regiments were reorganized as John R. Jones's division in General Jackson's three-division wing when Robert E. Lee took his Army of Northern Virginia into Maryland in September of 1862. Colonel Andrew Jackson Grigsby, who initially led the Stonewall brigade into Maryland, took over the division at the close of the Battle of Antietam. Grigsby's rise in responsibility from second in command of the 27th Virginia at Kernstown to essentially heading the old Valley District army (as Stonewall Jackson had done at the Battle of Kernstown) seemingly assured him of receiving a general's commission. But Colonel Grigsby was snubbed for the promotion in November when General Jackson awarded the commission to Major Frank "Bull" Paxton, who subsequently took over the Stonewall Brigade. It was believed that Grigsby's tendency to be "such an awful swearer" ultimately led the pious Jackson into denying him a general's star; however, the fact that Grigsby was also an ardent supporter of General Garnett in the aftermath of Kernstown may have also played a role in Stonewall's decision process. Paxton's promotion understandably irked Grigsby. Paxton had been dropped by the 27th Virginia during their reelection of officers in May. Jackson, however, liked Paxton, a former neighbor of Stonewall and a member of the same church in Lexington. He placed him on his staff where Paxton served until November when the major superseded Grigsby to take over the Stonewall Brigade. Grigsby resigned in anger on November 19, 1862, and spent the remaining thirty-three years of his life as a civilian.[3]

In October of 1862, one of Jackson's former staffers at Kernstown attempted to get his old job back. George Junkin had been captured at the close of the Sandy Ridge fight and was transferred to Fort Delaware on April 1, 1862. Two days later Junkin's father, a minister and devout unionist, showed up at the prison with a proposal worked upon with Abraham Lincoln to release his son if he took an oath of allegiance. Reverend Junkin convinced his son to formally reject the Confederacy by informing George that his mother had taken very ill in Philadelphia and the reverend had no doubt his return to that city without George "would produce either permanent insanity, or her death." George took the oath, but upon reuniting with his mother in Philadelphia, Junkin found her in good health and realized that his father had deceived him. Four months later Junkin persuaded his father to seek to annul the oath, but he was unable to do so. George breached the Articles of

War and attempted to rejoin the Confederacy without Union clemency. He wrote General Jackson in September to explain his situation. Jackson, who was angered that Junkin had been careless enough to get captured in the first place, never doubted his loyalty; however, upon meeting Junkin in October, told him that his staff position had been filled by another Pennsylvanian, Lieutenant James Power Smith. Junkin married a Virginian in November and—in violation of his oath—rejoined the Confederacy as a captain of the 25th Virginia Cavalry. He finished the war as a horse soldier.[4]

The bloody year of 1862 closed in the eastern theater with the Battle of Fredericksburg. As 1863 opened, Federal officers who fought at Kernstown also found themselves out of the service. General Nathan Kimball received a severe leg wound while leading a brigade in front of Marye's Heights at Fredericksburg. His recuperation took him out of the army for several months. General James Shields realized he had been permanently shelved by the U.S. War Department and would never receive another field command. When sent to California by Secretary Stanton in February of 1863, Shields decided his days in the service were over. He tendered his resignation on March 28, 1863, and resided in San Francisco for the remainder of the war. Shields's chief of artillery, Lieutenant Colonel Philip Daum, found himself out of the army for suspicious reasons. The Prussian immigrant seemingly disappeared after rumors flew through his former command that he had attempted to draw pay twice for one period of service. Perhaps returning to his homeland, Daum was never heard from again.[5]

General Thomas J. Jackson rose from the depths of a dismal division command in March of 1862 to achieve Confederate immortality just one year later, owing to his summertime accomplishments at Cedar Mountain, Manassas, and Harpers Ferry. His dominating performances earned him the prestige and responsibility of leading troops that exceeded the size of his Kernstown force by nearly ten fold. Jackson saved his best for last. On May 2, 1863, with the consent of Robert E. Lee, Jackson took his corps of 30,000 men on an unprecedented march that flanked the Federal army at the Wilderness crossroads known as Chancellorsville. Jackson rolled up the flank at dusk, but, during an evening reconnaissance, Stonewall was severely wounded by his own men who fired blindly into the darkened thickets. The Confederate victory was sealed the following day, at the cost of the life of the Stonewall Brigade's handpicked commander, Brigadier General "Bull" Paxton. The victory was pyrrhic to Lee, for it permanently cost him his "right arm." Stonewall's injured left arm was amputated; pneumonia set in; and at 3:15 P.M. on May 10, 1863, Jackson breathed his last.[6] His death dealt a severe blow to an army that was fighting to secure the life of a nation.

The next day Jackson's body was taken to Richmond by railroad car and escorted to the executive mansion where it lay for public viewing. Sandie Pendleton and Henry Kyd Douglas (both members of Jackson's staff) greeted one of Jackson's former brigade commanders at the door and directed him to the coffin. The officer looked upon the face of his lifeless superior and trembled with fits of sorrow. The brigadier wept uncontrollably for a time, then took Douglas and Pendleton by the arms, led them to a mansion window, spoke a moment about how severely Jackson's death had taken him, then asked a question that could receive no answer: "Who can fill his place?" Pendleton asked the sorrowed visitor if he would help carry Jackson's coffin at the funeral and the brigadier willingly consented. Jackson's new pallbearer fought under Jackson at the Battle of Kernstown, and against him for several months afterwards. He was General Richard Brooke Garnett.[7]

Garnett had returned to action almost immediately after his suspended trial. He served in Lieutenant General James Longstreet's corps as a brigadier in Major General George Pickett's division. Garnett had led Picket's former brigade of Virginia troops at Antietam and Fredericksburg, but missed the Chancellorsville campaign to procure supplies with the division at Suffolk. When Lee moved northward toward Pennsylvania in June of 1863, Pickett's division followed by passing through the Shenandoah Valley—the site of Garnett's army troubles. The inimitable Valley dealt Garnett another unfortunate blow on June 20, when an unruly horse of one of Pickett's staff officer's kicked Garnett in the ankle as the division passed through Snicker's Gap. Two weeks later, on July 3, 1863, a still hobbling Garnett looked across the Emmitsburg Road at Gettysburg, Pennsylvania, where—in reverse of circumstances at Kernstown—the Union troops were defending a ridge behind a stone wall. Knowing that Pickett's orders were to break that line, Garnett confessed to another brigade commander, "This is a desperate thing to attempt."

The officers commanding the three divisions preparing to assault Cemetery Hill were ordered to do so dismounted; several generals and staffers were excused from the order or disobeyed it, General Garnett being one of them. He rode his bay, "Red Eye," in the charge and his men were among the first to breech the Union line. Watching the Confederates approach his front and right was Brigadier General William Harrow. Harrow had led the 14th Indiana when they broke the Confederate line at Kernstown. Now he found himself on Garnett's right flank again, this time on the defensive. Harrow

saw to it that his men would hold firm against the Southerners
storming toward their position. He had earlier ordered his men to
kill any coward that ran away from the brigade, announcing, "If you
see me running I want you to kill me on the spot." Neither Harrow
nor his men ran when Garnett's brigade stormed the angle on their
right; however, his troops played only a minor role this day on the
outcome of Garnett's command. Brigadier General Alexander Webb's
brigade was responsible for stopping the onslaught and they also
held their ground. According to two Confederate eyewitnesses, a
volley delivered by one of Webb's regiments unhorsed Garnett with
a bullet that penetrated his brain. An hour later it was all over; the
Union held and the Confederates retreated. The Battle of Gettysburg cost Robert E. Lee seventeen casualties among his generals,
six of them killed or mortally wounded. Only one of their bodies was
not recovered in the aftermath of the battle. Stripped of his sword
and other distinguishing features of his general's attire, General
Richard Brooke Garnett's body was never identified and it is believed he was interred on the battlefield as an unknown and was
reinterred with his men in a mass grave at Hollywood Cemetery in
Richmond.[8] No one knows for sure.

The Shenandoah Valley hosted a series of clashes that began
in May of 1864 and lasted until the end of the war. First came the
Battle of New Market, where a Union force was stopped in its attempt to advance southward. Leading a brigade at New Market was
Brigadier General John Echols, the former colonel of the 27th Virginia who held back an entire brigade on Sandy Ridge before being
wounded at the Battle of Kernstown. At New Market Echols opposed an army that included a division commanded by Brigadier
General Jeremiah C. Sullivan, who returned to the Valley after serving an unimpressive stint in the Mississippi Valley. Sullivan's only
bright note after Kernstown was serving under the victorious Major
General David Hunter at the Battle of Piedmont three weeks after
the Union's New Market loss; however, Hunter's subsequent
Lynchburg expedition stalled and was turned completely away when
Major General Jubal Early, commanding Stonewall Jackson's corps,
was sent to the Valley by Robert E. Lee. Echols's old command, the
27th Virginia, had returned along with the remainder of the Stonewall Brigade, a unit that was a shadow of its former self after it had
been severely reduced by a mass capture at the Bloody Angle of
Spotsylvania. The reinforced Confederates forced Hunter's army to
retreat west into the mountains of West Virginia, thus opening the
Valley for another invasion into northern territory.[9]

Although a significant number of Stonewall Brigade members
who saw action at Kernstown were about to embark upon their

third campaign north of the Potomac River, Lieutenant James Langhorne would not be joining them. Over two years earlier at Kernstown, Adjutant Langhorne had saved the flag of the 4th Virginia but was captured after a desperate and gallant fight against several Union cavalrymen. Langhorne's mind and body withered from disease contracted during his confinement. He never returned to the army after his release from Fort Delaware in August of 1862. Instead, he was institutionalized at Staunton's insane asylum for nearly two years. By early May of 1864, Langhorne had become surprisingly lucid and even found it in himself to accept religion and become baptized. Although Langhorne's intellect strengthened, his body weakened. He died at Staunton on May 31. A Lynchburg paper closed the announcement of his death with a succinct assessment of Langhorne that the Ohio cavalrymen he faced at Kernstown could not dispute: "No braver or nobler youth ever gave his life to the country or died for its cause."[10]

Jubal Early took his Confederate corps to the gates of Washington on July 11, 1864, before being turned back by reinforced Federals at the earthworks north of the city. The Confederate victory at the Battle of Monocacy, fought two days earlier near Frederick, Maryland, bought the Federals valuable hours to reinforce Washington to prevent General Early from entering the capital. Guarding the northern (right) flank of the Federal line at the battle was a brigade of Ohio 100-day men, Maryland Home Guards, and a hodgepodge of volunteer units led by Brigadier General Erastus B. Tyler. Tyler was promoted general after his questionable performance at Kernstown was never questioned. He earned his star by fighting gamely against Stonewall Jackson at Port Republic in June, and, after hard service with the Army of the Potomac through the Battle of Chancellorsville, he was ordered to Baltimore in June of 1863, to command troops manning the defenses of the city. Tyler led his troops superbly at Monocacy where they held their positions near the Monocacy River long enough for the Federal army to escape. Afterwards, General Tyler returned to Baltimore. He grew very fond of the city from his service there, lived in Baltimore for over twenty-five years after the war, and was buried there after his death in 1891.[11]

Jubal Early returned to the Shenandoah Valley in mid-July, 1864. The Federals pursued him south of Winchester where Early saw the opportunity to attack an isolated Union corps and did so on July 24, 1864. The battle took place on the old Kernstown battlefield. Pritchard's Hill rather than Sandy Ridge was the focus of this fight where hundreds of veterans from both sides found themselves fighting against each other on the same ground for the second time in twenty-eight months. Jed Hotchkiss was not at the first Battle of

Kernstown, but he directed General Stephen Ramseur's troops to the Confederate left flank during the second battle there based on his knowledge of the area gained by sketching the battlefield in October of 1862. Union Colonel Isaac Duval commanded a division that July; two and one-third years earlier he was the major of the 1st West Virginia. History did not repeat itself for the Federals in the summer of 1864; they were routed from the Kernstown field which resulted in Major General Philip Sheridan on August 7 taking over the Valley forces. In September of 1864 Sheridan routed Early's forces at Winchester and Fisher's Hill; former Jackson aide Sandie Pendleton lost his life in the latter engagement. The Union forces had now reoccupied Frederick County, Virginia. It would remain this way for the rest of the war.[12]

The first Battle of Kernstown was a unique Union victory in Stonewall Jackson's 1862 Shenandoah Valley Campaign, especially considering that the Federals won the fight with no officer on the field holding a rank above colonel. By the end of the war, eleven Union officers that fought there were commissioned as generals. Colonel Joseph Thoburn did not enjoy the prestigious promotion, although he led a division of troops for most of 1864. The colonel ascended to hold the same responsibility of a major general primarily as a result of his performance at the Battle of Piedmont on June 5, where his brigade crushed the Confederate right flank to secure the victory there. Thoburn's service kept him in West Virginia and the Shenandoah Valley for most of the war; the isolated location may have delayed any opportunity for him to be awarded a general's star. He did not survive the war to receive the fruits of his labor. Cut down at Middletown during the Battle of Cedar Creek on October 19, 1864, Thoburn expired at the home of Mary Hoover. She wrote a consoling note to the colonel's widow shortly thereafter, describing to the grieving Mrs. Thoburn her husband's last moments:

> It is with a heavy heart I sit down to drop a few lines it was the request of your dying husband. I was by his side in about ten minutes after he fell. I did all I could for him. . . . he told me that all his regret was to leave his wife and children. O, he said, how I would love to see them here. He said he was prepared for death, prepared to meet his God. He told me to give you his dying farewell, and for you all to meet him in heaven where there would be no more parting. Your husband did not die for want of care. He has paid the debt we all have to pay, and is now a bright Angel around the throne of our heavenly Father.[13]

Thoburn's body was sent to Wheeling and was buried there on October 26, 1864. Cornelia McDonald, the Winchester resident whose children experienced the harrowing sight of a severed head rolling near them during the first Kernstown battle, focused on Wheeling late in 1864 for more personal reasons—her husband was imprisoned there. The McDonalds had fled Winchester as refugees in 1863 and headed up the Valley to Lexington. Her husband Angus, the first colonel of the 7th Virginia Cavalry, was captured in June of 1864 and had been held since in Wheeling. Two weeks after Thoburn was sent back to Wheeling for burial, Angus McDonald was released via exchange and sent to Richmond. Cornelia and her children rushed to the Confederate capital to see the frail patriarch. They arrived too late; he died there on December 1. Cornelia moved her family to Kentucky. She died in Louisville, Kentucky, on March 11, 1909, forty-seven years to the day after General Jackson was forced out of Winchester.[14] Her informative diary survived with its first entry describing the night in 1862 when General Jackson retreated from Winchester, reducing her to "violent fits of weeping at the thought of being left. . . ."

The inimitable Mary Charlton Greenhow Lee would also be forced out of Winchester before the Civil War ended. Her thorough contempt for Northerners sealed her fate during the final Federal occupation of Winchester. For continuing her notorious disobedience of Federal edicts, General Sheridan exiled Mrs. Lee in February of 1865. She eventually found a home in Baltimore where she lived to the age of eighty-seven. Although Mrs. Lee apparently never returned to Winchester, her detailed war diary "came home" nearly 100 years after the war.[15]

The final Union occupying force at Winchester was the Army of the Shenandoah which policed Frederick County for four months. The brigadier general appointed to head this force, Samuel Sprigg Carroll, was an ironic choice for he was a member of the first occupying force in March of 1862 and fought well at Kernstown as a colonel. The performance of his Gibralter Brigade (two of its four regiments fought at Kernstown in Kimball's brigade) at Gettysburg helped Carroll secure a brigadier general's star the following May. The same month Carroll was severely wounded twice, first at the Battle of the Wilderness, then at Spotsylvania while commanding a brigade in Major General Winfield S. Hancock's Second Corps. Carroll was held in high regard by General Hancock, whose biographer considered Carroll "a soldier of great capacity and great fighting courage." Hancock, taking over Sheridan's Middle Military Division in February of 1865, did not hold the same opinion of General Jeremiah C. Sullivan, the Kernstown brigade commander who found himself without an assignment since the summer of 1864. "I do not want officers who my predecessor has found unsuitable after trial in an active campaign," Hancock said of Sullivan. Sullivan resigned and moved to Oakland, California, where he died in 1890.[16]

The last Civil War battle in the Shenandoah Valley was fought at Waynesboro on March 2, 1865. Brigadier General George Custer's two mounted brigades overwhelmed the Confederate line and produced chaos in the streets in the middle of town. It is said that the last man killed in the melee was Colonel William H. Harman, the former commander of the 5th Virginia whose final stand at Kernstown prevented the Valley District from suffering even more losses. It was a cruel irony for Harman—he was born in Waynesboro thirty-seven years earlier.[17] One month after Harman's death, the surviving Kernstown Confederates surrendered at Appomattox.

The American Civil War had endured three more years of valor, redemption, and sacrifice after the Battle of Kernstown. Most of the battles were larger; some, like Antietam, Gettysburg, and the Wilderness witnessed clashing armies that outnumbered the size of the Kernstown forces by greater than ten fold and single-day casualty figures that exceeded those incurred on March 23, 1862, by fifteen to twenty thousand. The fortunate ones left the service to relate the story of their army career to their children and grandchildren. Although miniscule when compared to the monstrosities of the later war, Kernstown was not diminished in the eyes of those who fought there. Several veterans considered it to be a greater fight than witnessed at the first battle of Manassas, while others stretched their claim to place Kernstown's fury over any other battle of the war.

For some, the Civil War was a stepping stone to a military career. General Carroll stayed on, serving as Acting Assistant Inspector General of the Division of the Atlantic; however his battle wounds forced him out of the service on June 9, 1869. Carroll was retired as a major general of the United States Army. He died on January 28, 1893, and was buried at Georgetown, D.C. Conversely, George Burwell, the teenager in the 2nd Virginia who cried when his ramrod jammed in his musket barrel at Kernstown, refused to accept the end of the Confederacy. Burwell joined Brigadier General Joseph Shelby and the 1,000 Confederate soldiers he pushed into Mexico to support the puppet regime of Maximillan. Burwell impressed his new leaders south of the U.S. border enough to ascend as commandant of Maximillan's body guard. Maximillan's power disintegrated when the French withdrew his support. He was captured at Queretaro, Mexico. Burwell was killed there attempting to prevent his overthrow.[18]

Some Kernstown veterans returned to their pre-war occupations or parlayed their war accomplishments into more prestigious careers. John Quincy Adams Nadenbousch switched from 2nd Virginia colonel to his old profession of Martinsburg mill proprietor. Paul Truckey, the 14th Indiana private who initiated the Hoosier attack to destroy the Confederate right flank on Sandy Ridge, returned to his home town profession of carpentry at Vincennes, Indiana—minus one leg that was amputated after receiving a severe wound in front of Bloody Lane at the Battle of Antietam. General William Harrow resumed his law practice in Indiana and then attempted to enter the world of politics. Converting from pre-war Radical Republican to the liberal movement of the early 1870s, Harrow actively campaigned for Horace Greeley's bid for president against Ulysses S. Grant in 1872. Harrow did not live to see Greeley lose his contest; he was killed in a train accident on September 27 and was buried in Mount Vernon, Indiana. The most successful transition from Kernstown veteran to politician was accomplished by Frederick W. Holliday. Then a captain at Kernstown, Holliday ascended to the colonelcy of the 33rd Virginia before a shattered arm at the Battle of Cedar Mountain ended his war career and initiated his move to public service. The Winchester native beat Jackson's confidant, A. R. Boteler, to gain a seat in the Confederate Congress which he held until the close of the war. Holliday then used his magnificent oration skills to gain popularity within the state of Virginia during the 1870s. He rolled on to win the state house in 1878 and served one term. Governor Holliday died in 1899.[19]

General James Shields eventually returned to his political career. He moved from San Francisco to Carrollton, Missouri, in 1866 where he tried his hand at farming and devoted much of his time to the lecture circuit, speaking on a variety of charitable causes such as raising money for victims of the yellow fever epidemic. During the process Shields became impoverished and returned to the political arena. The Democrat won a special election to fill an unexpired term in the U.S. Senate vacated by another Missouri Democrat. The victory earned Senator Shields his third state seat, a feat that had never been accomplished before or since. Shields also gained some relief financially when his pension was increased from thirty to 100 dollars per month. But Shields did not live long enough to enjoy the term nor the pay. While on a lecturing tour in Ottumwa, Iowa, he was stricken with chest pains on June 1, 1879, and died one-half hour later. He was buried in Carrolton, Missouri. His biographers kept the erroneous notion alive that Shields called the shots in the Kernstown victory that earned him the distinction of being the only man to beat Stonewall Jackson in battle. Twenty years after Shields's passing, William H. Condon, president of the Chicago Lawyer's Club and a former friend, published a biography of the Irishman entitled *Life of Major-General James Shields. . .*, thus awarding the brigadier with the rank the Senate denied him in 1862.[20]

During the 1880s the man in command of the victorious forces at Kernstown attempted to have his say in the matter. General Nathan Kimball recovered from his Fredericksburg wound to complete a distinguished Civil War career as a division commander that included participation in crucial Union victories at Vicksburg, Atlanta, Franklin, and Nashville. Immediately after the war, Kimball returned to Indiana where he broke up the activities of the radical Knights of the Golden Circle in southern Indiana. After serving as state legislator, treasurer, and commander of the Grand Army of the Republic, Kimball moved west when President Grant appointed him surveyor general of the Utah Territory. Settling in Ogden, Utah, Kimball was eventually appointed postmaster by President Rutherford B. Hayes.

While living in Utah, the first published accounts of the Battle of Kernstown caught Kimball's eye and ire. The first was William Allan's and Jed Hotchkiss's collaboration, *Stonewall Jackson's Valley Campaign in the Shenandoah Valley of Virginia*, published in 1880. Although the section of the book dealing with Kernstown was hailed as "the best one given to the public from any source," Kimball and many Union veterans were not satisfied at the Southern bias in the narrative. The next published account was John Imboden's contribution to Century Magazine's *Battles and Leaders* series. The 1885 piece, entitled "Stonewall Jackson in the Shenandoah," once again was a Southern-based account that miscredited Shields with the Kernstown victory; this one never mentioned the name of Nathan Kimball. Both Allan's and Imboden's accounts were points of view authored by non-participants of Kernstown.

Kimball wrote his version of the Battle of Kernstown in 1887. He corresponded with Elijah H. C. Cavins, a captain at Kernstown, who was attempting to write a regimental history of the 14th Indiana. In writing his version of the battle, Kimball took pains to cite examples of how he, and not General Shields, made the decisions on the field on March 23, 1862, that led to the Union victory. Kimball included a portion of Cavins's description of the Sandy Ridge attack in his article. The piece was published in the *Battles and Leaders* series later that year.[21]

Kimball's 1887 article was designed to settle the issue of who was commanding the victorious troops on March 23, 1862; however, two years later a former 1st West Virginia cavalry surgeon unraveled any gains made by Kimball in claiming the Kernstown victory. Brevet Brigadier General Henry Capehart wrote nine articles that were published in a weekly series by *The National Tribune*, a publication sponsored by the Grand Army of the Republic and widely read by Civil War veterans North and South. Capehart's Kernstown contribution was published March 21, 1889. In it, he credited Shields with directing the victory and heaped disproportional praise upon the 7th Ohio and the 1st West Virginia Cavalry. Capehart's piece pulled several veterans out of their post-war silence to respond to his version of the story. Their rejoinders, covered in subsequent issues of the paper, initiated a debate about who were the first Union regiments to take the stone wall. A member of the 14th Indiana claimed that his regiment and the 5th Ohio took the wall, and not the 7th Ohio as Capehart had claimed. No one appeared to entertain the prospect that two stone walls, nearly 500 yards apart, were fought over at the same time.

British officer and author Colonel G. F. R. Henderson's biography of Stonewall Jackson, published in 1898, was the last widely-read effort depicting the Battle of Kernstown. Written by a non-participant, Henderson's chapter dealing with the battle relied upon official reports and the memory of the few surviving Southern officers who still had something to say about the matter. At the turn of the century, memories of Kernstown faded with the passing of its chief participants. General Kimball died early in 1898. Most Northern and Southern regimental and brigade commanders had expired before him. In the early 1900s Kernstown made news again when General Garnett's sword turned up at a pawn shop in Baltimore. Donated to the Museum of the Confederacy in Richmond soon afterwards, the blade hangs on display in the basement of the museum while Stonewall Jackson's sword is prominently (and symbolically) exhibited one floor above.[22]

Aside from the participants' artifacts, by far the most significant and tangible evidence of the fight at Kernstown is the battlefield itself, truly hallowed ground. Veterans of both armies found it necessary to see Sandy Ridge and Pritchard's Hill, Opequon Church and Bartonsville, the cemeteries where comrades lay buried, and the stone walls over which Americans fought Americans. In the summer of 1912, the *Winchester Evening Star* covered the story of a veteran from Tyler's brigade, since removed to Tennessee, who made a special trip to visit the field where he had fought fifty years earlier. Guided by a local physician to Sandy Ridge, the old soldier was reported to recognize the boulders which had concealed Jackson's men that bloody afternoon.[23] His claim cannot be disputed for although he stood on the ground for only five hours half of a century earlier, the events of Sunday, March 23, 1862, had burned a lasting impression in his mind that time could not erase. It was a day when brother fought brother, when reputations were saved or lost, when lives were sacrificed for duty, honor and country, and when on-the-field decisions affected the results of the day and even the survival of an army. This is what they remembered; this is what they wanted everyone else to know.

In 1891, an aging veteran described "that gritty and most obstinate fight" to an audience of his peers. Well aware that the Battle of Kernstown appeared more as a skirmish in terms of numbers engaged and casualties when compared to Shiloh, Antietam or Gettysburg, the old soldier spiced his presentation with descriptions of action and anecdotes to illustrate why Kernstown veterans still gathered on the anniversary of the battle "with a pride and exuberance of glory that after acquired renown can not overshadow. . . ." He confidently closed his address with a question that he effectively rendered rhetorical with the evening's speech—not knowing, however, that little else would be spoken or printed about his topic for over 100 years. Today, the question can be repeated with the same confidence trumpeted over a century ago:

> Who will say that we may not laud this glorious battle of the boys?[24]

Appendix A

ORDER OF BATTLE
THE BATTLE OF KERNSTOWN
MARCH 23, 1862

<u>THE UNION ARMY</u>

Second Division, Fifth Corps, Army of the Potomac

Division Commander: Brigadier General James
                                    Shields (wounded), Colonel
                                    Nathan Kimball

<u>First Brigade</u> Colonel Nathan Kimball
14th Indiana   Lieutenant Colonel William
                                    Harrow
8th Ohio   Colonel Samuel S. Carroll
67th Ohio   Lieutenant Colonel Alvin C. Voris
84th Pennsylvania   Colonel William G.Murray
                                    (killed), Adjutant Thomas Craig

<u>Second Brigade</u> Colonel Jeremiah C. Sullivan
5th Ohio   Lieutenant Colonel John H.
                                    Patrick
13th Indiana   Lieutenant Colonel Robert S.
                                    Foster
62nd Ohio*   Colonel Francis B. Pond
39th Illinois*   Colonel Thomas O. Osborn

<u>Third Brigade</u> Colonel Erastus B. Tyler

7th Ohio	Lieutenant Colonel William R. Creighton
7th Indiana	Lieutenant Colonel John F. Cheek
1st West Virginia	Colonel Joseph Thoburn (wounded), Major Isaac Duval
29th Ohio	Colonel Lewis P. Buckley
110th Pennsylvania	Colonel William D. Lewis

<u>Cavalry</u>   Colonel Thornton F. Brodhead

1st West Virginia (6 companies)	Major Benjamin F. Chamberlain
1st Ohio (2 companies)	Captain Nathan D. Menken
1st Michigan (4 companies)	Lieutenant Colonel Joseph T. Copeland
1st squadron Pa. (2 companies)	Captain John Keys
Maryland Indpt. (2 companies)	Captain Henry Cole

<u>Artillery</u>   Lieutenant Colonel Philip Daum

West Virginia -- A Battery	Captain John Jenks
West Virginia -- B Battery	Captain Samuel Davey
4th United States -- E Battery	Captain Joseph C. Clark
1st Ohio -- H Battery*	Captain James F. Huntington
1st Ohio -- L Battery	Captain Lucius N. Robinson

<u>Signal Officer</u>: Lieutenant William W. Rowley, 28th New York

Absent (Detached): 4th Ohio Infantry, 66th Ohio Infantry, 7th West Virginia Infantry

THE CONFEDERATE ARMY

Valley District, Department of Northern Virginia,
Provisional Army, Confederate States of America

Division Commander: Major General Thomas J. Jackson

<u>First Brigade</u> Brigadier General Richard B. Garnett

2nd Virginia	Colonel James W. Allen
4th Virginia	Colonel Charles Ronald (wounded), Major Albert Pendleton
5th Virginia	Colonel William H. Harman
27th Virginia	Colonel John Echols (wounded), Lieutenant Colonel Andrew J. Grigsby

33 Virginia	Colonel Arthur C. Cummings

Rockbridge Artillery	Captain William McLaughlin
West Augusta Artillery	Captain James H. Waters
Alleghany Artillery	Captain Joseph Carpenter

Second Brigade Colonel Jesse S. Burks (wounded)

21st Virginia	Lieutenant Colonel John M. Patton
42nd Virinia	Lieutenant Colonel Daniel A. Langhorne
48th Virginia*	Colonel John A. Campbell
1st Virginia Battalion	Captain David B. Bridgford
Hampden Artillery *	Lieutenant James Pleasants

Third Brigade Colonel Samuel V. Fulkerson

23rd Virginia	Colonel Alexander G. Taliaferro
37th Virginia	Lieutenant Colonel Robert P. Carson
Danville Artillery *	Lieutenant A. C. Lanier

Cavalry   Colonel Turner Ashby

7th Virginia	Colonel Turner Ashby
Horse Artillery	Captain Robert P. Chew

* Present but not engaged

Appendix B

THE NUMBER OF FEDERAL SOLDIERS ENGAGED AT KERNSTOWN

General Thomas J. Jackson reported 2,742 infantry engaged at Kernstown out of an available force of 3,087. (The 48th Virginia did not participate). His numbers were derived from official reports in which all regimental commanders, except the 5th Virginia, tabulated the number of men from their regiments who fought that day. Unfortunately, one of the greatest obstacles to understanding what took place on the fields near Kernstown stems from the lack of knowledge concerning the number of Federal soldiers engaged in battle that day. No March 23, 1862, morning reports exist for companies and regiments in Shields's division and Federal brigade and division returns for Kernstown are also lacking; therefore, engaged Union strength at Kernstown must be derived from the units' morning reports for the date nearest March 23, 1862, as well as letters from company and regimental officers. The absence of consolidated Northern strength reports for the Battle of Kernstown has fostered a guessing game by historians who have written about Stonewall Jackson or his 1862 campaign in the Valley. Douglas Southall Freeman estimated Shields's division strength at 9,000 men. William Allan claimed that "at the average Gen. Shields would have had over 9,000 men present." Colonel G. F. R. Henderson claimed that Shields had 9,752 at Kernstown, including nearly 8,400 infantry. Robert Tanner believed Sandie Pendleton's on-the-spot estimate and chimes in with the highest assessment of how many troops opposed Jackson; he placed Shields's strength at 10,000 men at Kernstown.[1]

All of the aforementioned historians disregarded General Shields's estimates. Perhaps it is because the general changed his figures two times. Immediately after the battle Shields claimed the strength of his division to be "not over 8,000." Two days later the numbers dropped to "between 7,000 and 8,000 men," then his March 29 official report clarified the estimate by stating: "We had 6,000 infantry, a cavalry force of 750, and twenty-four pieces of artillery."[2] William Allan scoffed at the latter estimate, basing his own estimates on what he believed was 152 to 153 Federal companies present on the battlefield. Allan then quoted a disbelieving George McClellan who, in an April 1 letter, questioned Shields's calculations by stating "If Shields's division, leaving out the cavalry, consisted of only 7,000, the other division, under Williams, must have been over 12,000 men."[3]

It appears that those who have previously written about Kernstown, particularly Henderson, were influenced by a Federal strength report filed six days before the battle. General Shields filed a report of "the present strength and condition of my command" on March 17, 1862. This report listed an available force of 9,549 infantry, 608 artillery, and 698 cavalry for a total of 10,855 soldiers from an aggregate force exceeding 15,000.[4] Shields did not mention the fact that the force was dispersed. A significant portion of Shields's division was detached to guard other areas of the Federal-occupied Lower Valley. On the day of the Kernstown battle the following regiments were absent: 4th Ohio (at Berryville), 66th Ohio (provost guards in Winchester), and the 7th West Virginia (Martinsburg).[5] Henderson corrected his Kernstown estimates to compensate for regiments counted on March 17 but absent on March 23, 1862.

Looking only at available infantry (the portion of the army under dispute), the corrected March 17 report shows thirteen regiments with an average strength of 644 men. Assuming, as the others have done, that these regiments consisted of ten companies, then the average Federal infantry company strength was sixty-four men. However, five infantry companies were not at Kernstown: the 84th Pennsylvania had mustered only nine companies in early 1862; and another one did not participate at Kernstown. Additionally, one company each from the 67th Ohio, the 110th Pennsylvania and the 8th Ohio were on detached service.[6] The Andrew Sharpshooters were an independent company that was active on March 23; adding this unit to the available regiments results in a total of no more than 126 Federal infantry companies engaged at Kernstown.

How could General Shields claim an infantry force of only 6,000 present at Kernstown when these 126 companies, averaging 64 men each on March 17, should provide 8,000 available infantrymen on the battlefield? What the aforementioned historians did not consider was that Shields's division suffered many of the same deprivations that thinned Jackson's infantry strength to 3,000 men. Like Jackson's men, Shields's division was particularly active in the six days before the battle, marching more than forty-five miles between March 18 and March 20. The first two days the morning temperature in Cumberland hovered near the freezing mark; the third day sleet and snow greeted the Federals during a twenty-two mile march. The two quiet days before the battle were not enough to keep sick soldiers without tent shelter off the inactive list. Company K of the 1st West Virginia filed a morning report on March 22 (No other company reports were found for the rest of the division); out of a possibility of fielding seventy-eight healthy recruits to fight a battle, this company had only forty-six men available. Twenty-six members of Company K were listed as sick and six others were absent for other reasons.[7] Then there is the startling revelation provided by Colonel Jeremiah C. Sullivan, commanding Shields's second brigade. One week after the battle he complained to Banks's adjutant: "I am afraid my Brigade cannot move tomorrow. They are *absolutely barefoot*."[8] Considering the fact that Sullivan's men had been relatively inactive for five days before submitting his report, one can assume the inadequate footware hampered the effectiveness of the second brigade before the Battle of Kernstown. The other two brigades were likely affected by shoddy shoes as well.

These considerations force a re-evaluation of using the March 17 report to judge Federal infantry strength six days later. The best evidence available to disregard it entirely is provided by the 84th Pennsylvania, the only Union regiment whose strength at Kernstown was officially reported. The nine companies reportedly mustered 503 men available for duty six days before the battle. No fewer than three official sources place their engaged strength at Kernstown to be 255 men[9]—only half of the March 17 estimate! The 110th Pennsylvania fared little better. Although the March 17 report places the 110th Pennsylvania's strength at 426 men, by the best estimates of the time, they carried only 300 men onto the battlefield, "the severe marching of the few preceding days having rendered many unfit to stand in the ranks."[10] From various sources, including the *Official Records*, nine other Federal company estimates are known:

13th Indiana	1 company	30 officers and men[11]
8th Ohio	4 companies	188 officers and men[12]
7th Ohio	3 companies	130 officers and men[13]
1st West Virginia	1 company	46 officers and men[14]

Adding in the Pennsylvanians:

110th Pennsylvania	9 companies	300 officers and men
84th Pennsylvania	8 companies	255 officers and men

Total Sample	26 companies	949 officers and men
Average per company:	37 men	

This known sample represents twenty percent of Shields's infantry force that fought at Kernstown. Using this as the average for all companies at Kernstown, then only 4,662 men were present. This estimate, of course, seems unreasonably low. However, for Henderson, Allan, and Freeman to be close to the mark with their estimates of at least 8,000 Federal infantrymen, then the remaining unknown 100 companies would have to average over seventy men per unit—a number that nearly doubles the average of the known sample. This is even more unlikely, particularly considering that of the twenty-six known company strengths, the highest return shows only fifty-three officers and men. If the other 100 companies all had strengths equal to the the highest report, and the regimental officers are added to the total, then the Federals took no more (and probably fewer) than 6,300 infantry to Kernstown. This figure closely agrees with Shields's estimates.

Fortunately, another source for Federal strength has been found. A division report was filed eight days after the Battle of Kernstown, while the force lay inactive for the sixth straight day in Strasburg. Notwithstanding the casualties incurred at the battle, the respite allowed more time for sick and march-weary soldiers to rejoin their respective commands. The numbers reported omit two detached regiments that fought at Kernstown. Fortunately those two units were the 84th and 110th Pennsylvania, the only regiments whose Kernstown strengths are known. When the other units had their Kernstown casualties added to their March 31 strength, a rough estimate of their battle strength is found:

First Brigade (Nathan Kimball)[15]

Regiment	March 31 Strength	Casualties at Kernstown	Estimated Battle Strength
14th Indiana	400	54	454
8th Ohio	650	53	703
67th Ohio	426	47	473
84th Pennsylvania			255
Total for First Brigade			**1,885**

Second Brigade (Jeremiah C. Sullivan)[16]

Sullivan reported 2,577 aggregate for five regiments, four of which were engaged at Kernstown. Unfortunately, he did not break the numbers down by regiment. The average March 31 strength for his brigade would be 515 per regiment for five regiments. Multiply this average by four regiments and add the 93 casualties reported in this brigade at Kernstown will correct Sullivan's battle strength to **2,153**.

Third Brigade (Erastus B. Tyler)[17]

Regiment	March 31 Strength	Casualties at Kernstown	Estimated Battle Strength
7th Ohio	300	92	392
7th Indiana	533	49	582
1st West Virginia	500	29	529
29th Ohio	496	15	511
110th Pennsylvania			300

Total for Third Brigade **2,314**
Totals for the three brigades = **6,352**

The result achieved by this method of analysis closely agrees with the previous calculation and is a far cry from McClellan's report of over 12,000; however, it should be noted that this still is an *overestimation*. A case in point is seen with the 8th Ohio. Four of the nine companies engaged at Kernstown had a known total strength of 188 officers and men. Using the above estimate of 703 for March 31 with Kernstown casualties added would indicate that the remaining five companies carried 515 men—103 men per company! This is impossible and merely reflects that the respite allowed the sick and weary to replenish the ranks to a strength greater than what could have been present at Kernstown. Detachments were necessary to supply hospital nurses to care for the 800 wounded Union and Confederate soldiers immediately after the battle; however, the 110th Pennsylvania appears to have supplied the necessary manpower for this task.[18]

These two methods of comparison refute the estimates of Freeman, Allan, Henderson, Tanner and others who claimed the Federals carried 7,000–9,000 infantry into battle at Kernstown. A total available strength of 6,000 appears to be much closer to the truth. Adding the 750 cavalry and 600 artillerymen, Shields had a division of approximately 7,350 available for battle on March 23, 1862. Two regiments, the 39th Illinois and 62nd Ohio, did not see action and suffered no casualties in the battle. Both regiments were in Sullivan's brigade and were likely 500 strong per regiment. Therefore, the Federal engaged strength at Kernstown did not exceed 5,000 infantry against the 2,742 that Jackson reported for his force.

Appendix C

CASUALTIES AT KERNSTOWN

<u>Confederate</u>:

Official reports for the Battle of Kernstown, filed within one week of the day it was fought, list casualty figures including killed, wounded, missing and/or captured. Of the 3,500 infantry, cavalry and artillery engaged from General Jackson's Valley District, a loss of 718 was reported. This represents approximately twenty-two percent of the engaged force. Jackson's earliest reports of losses break down as follows:

Killed	80
Wounded	75
<u>Missing</u>	<u>263</u>
Total	718

Most of Jackson's "missing" were captured and sent to Baltimore the day after the battle. Banks's intelligence reports list 234 sent away on March 24; in April an additional seventeen prisoners were sent to Fort Delaware. The latter were too badly wounded to go on the first trip and were listed as wounded in the initial reports. Therefore, approximately twenty of Jackson's missing had not been accounted for. Those listed as killed were those who died on the day of the battle or very soon afterward. It can be assumed that scores of wounded eventually died from their wounds although no previous attempt at this enumeration had been made. Confederate service records and newspaper reports published within one month after the battle indicate the early casualty reports are somewhat underestimated. The following revised list, by regiment, depicts battle casualties in killed and mortally wounded, wounded, captured, and missing. All of those depicted as "wounded" list only those who were brought from the field. Those wounded and left in Federal hands are enumerated as captured or mortally wounded, depending on the consequences of their injuries. Those listed as missing are soldiers who were left on the field but apparently not sent to prison. Since many of the missing were known to be wounded, it can be assumed that most in this category died. At least two did wind up at Fort Delaware and missed Banks's initial list.

Unit	Killed and Mortally Wounded	Wounded	Captured	Missing	Total
Division Staff			1		1
First Brigade					
Staff			1		1
2nd Virginia	7	43	42	6	98
4th Virginia	10	19	44	3	76
5th Virginia	18	44	2	2	66
27th Virginia	6	15	36		57
33rd Virginia	24	16	16	3	59
Brigade Total	65	137	141	14	357
Second Brigade					
Staff		1			1
1st Virginia Battalion	8	20	18	4	50
21st Virginia	14	37	12	1	64
42nd Virginia	22	45	2	3	72
Brigade Total	44	103	32	8	187
Third Brigade					
23rd Virginia	5	12	31	4	52
37th Virginia	19	45	44	5	113
Brigade Total	24	57	75	9	165

Unit	Killed and Mortally Wounded	Wounded	Captured	Missing	Total
Cavalry & Artillery					
7th Virginia Cavalry	2	1	3	1	7
Rockbridge Artillery	4	8	1	1	14
West Augusta Artillery	—	6	—	—	6
Non-Infantry Total	6	15	4	2	27
Division Total	139	312	253	33	737
Percent of Engaged	4.2%	9.5%	7.7%	1%	22.4%

Federal:

Union casualty statistics for the Battle of Kernstown are easier to adjust compared to Confederate numbers because of low numbers of men reported as missing or captured. Officially, the Federal casualty statistics break down as follows:

Killed	118
Wounded	450
Missing/Captured	22
Total	590

These numbers include the two casualties inflicted upon the Federals the day prior to the battle. Shortly after the battle, eighteen men reported as missing returned to the ranks, reducing the division total in this category to four men. Many men suffered from minor wounds that were deemed too insignificant to report. Therefore, like the Confederate revisions, the focus on updating Federal casualties at Kernstown is to enumerate, by regiment, those soldiers listed as wounded who died from their Kernstown wounds. This tally is largely obtained from William F. Fox's exhaustive study *Regimental Losses in the American Civil War*. This work lists regiments that lost over 130 killed and mortally wounded during the war. Eight of the thirteen Union infantry regiments that fought at

Kernstown made Fox's list of "Three Hundred Fighting Regiments." The remaining units had their losses computed through a study of published regimental histories and post-battle newspaper reports. Only the casualties incurred on March 23 are reported.

Unit	Killed and Mortally Wounded	Wounded and Survived	Missing or Captured	Total
First Brigade				
8th Ohio	16	36	1	53
67th Ohio	15	32		47
14th Indiana	12	42		54
84th Pennsylvania	30	62	—	92
Brigade Total	73	172	1	246
Second Brigade				
5th Ohio	23	27		50
13th Indiana	6	36		42
39th Illinois		No Losses Reported		
62nd Ohio	—	No Losses Reported		—
Brigade Total	29	63	0	92
Third Brigade				
7th Ohio	30	52	1	83
7th Indiana	15	27		42
1st West Virginia	9	20		29
29th Ohio	5	8	2	15
110th Pennsylvania	13	39	—	52
Brigade Total	72	146	3	221

Unit	Killed and Mortally Wounded	Wounded and Survived	Missing or Captured	Total

Cavalry and Artillery

	Killed and Mortally Wounded	Wounded and Survived	Missing or Captured	Total
1st West Va. Cavalry	3	6		9
1st West Va. Light Artillery - A Battery	1			1
1st West Va. Light Artillery - B Battery	1			1
1st Ohio Light Artillery - L Battery	1	2		3
4th U.S. Light Artillery - E Battery	1	—	—	1
Non-Infantry Total	7	8	0	15
Division Total:	181	389	4	574
Percent of Engaged	2.5%	5.6%	0.1%	8.2%

Combined Union and Confederate Losses at Kernstown:

Killed and Mortally Wounded:	320
Wounded and Survived	701
Captured/Missing	290
Total	1,311

Endnotes

ABBREVIATIONS

DU   Duke University, William R. Perkins Library, Manuscript Department, Durham, North Carolina

HL   Handley Library, Archives Room, Winchester, Virginia

IHS   Indiana Historical Society, Indianapolis, Indiana

LC   Library of Congress, Washington, D.C.

MC   Eleanor Brockenbrough Library, Museum of the Confederacy, Richmond, Virginia

NA   National Archives, Washington, D.C.

OHS   Ohio Historical Society, Columbus, Ohio

OR   U.S. War Department. The War of the Rebellion: A Compilation of the Official Records of the Union and Confederate Armies. 128 vols. Washington, D.C., 1880–1901

RBGCMP   Richard Brooke Garnett Court Martial Papers, Museum of the Confederacy, Richmond, Virginia

SHSP   Southern Historical Society Papers

USAMHI   United States Army Military History Institute, Carlisle Barracks, Pennsylvania

VHS   Virginia Historical Society, Richmond, Virginia

VSL   Virginia State Library, Richmond, Virginia

PREFACE

1. James H. Simpson, "Criticizing Capehart. Who Took the Stonewall at Kernstown?", *The National Tribune,* May 9, 1889.

   E. H. C. Cavins, Letter to Nathan Kimball, June 1885, Collection M42, Box 2, Folder 4, EHC Cavins Collection, IHS.

   John O. Casler, *Four Years in the Stonewall Brigade* (Guthrie, Oklahoma: State Capital Printing Company, 1893), p. 64.

2. Brevet Major General A. C. Voris, "The Battle of the Boys," in W. H. Chamberlin, ed., *Sketches of War History, 1861–1865,* vol. 4 (Cincinnati, Ohio: The Robert Clarke Company,1896), pp. 87–88.

CHAPTER ONE

1. William J. Miller, *The Training of an Army: Camp Curtin and the North's Civil War* (Shippensburg, Pa.: White Mane Publishing Company, Inc., 1990), p. 258.

   Isaac Hooper (84th Pa.), Letter dated January 6, 1862, *Altoona Tribune*, January 16, 1862.

   Most of the letters from soldiers that were published in home town newspapers were addressed to the editors of the paper, but were written for the benefit of home town and county citizens. Unless a letter was written to a family member who subsequently submitted it to a newspaper, all referenced letters to the newspaper here and hereafter will include the name or pseudonym of the soldier and the date of his letter.

2. Richard A. Sauers, *Advance the Colors! Pennsylvania Civil War Battle Flags,* vol. 1, Capitol Preservation Committee, Commonwealth of Pennsylvania, 1987, pp. 265–266.

   William J. Miller, Personal Correspondence, 1993.

   It was not unusual for regiments to train at Camp Curtin without weapons. Target practice was rarely conducted at the training camp.

3. James I. Robertson, Jr., *Soldiers Blue and Gray* (Columbia, S.C.: University of South Carolina Press, 1988), p. 5.

   Grenville W. Dodge, "General James A. Williamson," *Annals of Iowa*, vol. 6, 1903, p. 164.

4. Thomas A. Merchant, *Eighty-Fourth Pennsylvania Volunteers, An Address* (Philadelphia: Sherman and Company,1889), p. 20.

5. "Keystone" (84th Pa.), Letter dated January 8, 1862, *The* (Philadelphia) *Press*, January 13, 1862.

   Charles M. Clark, *The History of the Thirty-Ninth Regiment Illinois Volunteer Veteran Infantry (Yates Phalanx) in the War of the Rebellion, 1861–1865*, Veteran Association, Chicago, 1889, pp. 27, 30.

   Today, the town of Bath is known as Berkeley Springs, West Virginia. It still has retained its official name of "Bath."

6. Samuel P. Bates, *History of Pennsylvania Volunteers 1861–1865,* vol. 2 (Harrisburg, Pa.: B. Singerly, State Printer, 1869), p. 1307.

   Charles Clark, *The History of the Thirty-Ninth Regiment Illinois Volunteer*, p. 52.

   "Keystone," Letter dated January 8, 1862, *The* (Philadelphia) *Press*, January 13, 1862.

   Frederick Lander, Telegram to Nathaniel P. Banks, January 5, 1862, Reel #47, #85848, George B. McClellan Papers, LC.

   The above-mentioned telegram indicated a tally of 186 fires on the night of January 5. It can be assumed that approximately the same number of campfires were lit two nights earlier. The soldier may have seen Confederate militia campfires; the rest of Jackson's division was five miles away with an obstructing hill concealing their camps.

7. Charles Clark, *The History of the Thirty-Ninth Regiment Illinois Volunteer*, pp. 34–35.

   Clark's regimental is a valuable source of information concerning the actions at Bath and Hancock, for it includes unpublished reports from regimental and company officers. Colonel Osborn's report is cited above.

8. Frederick H. Dyer, *A Compendium of the War of the Rebellion*, vol. 1 (reprint, New York: Sagamore Press, Inc., 1959), pp. 335–336.

9. William Allan, *Stonewall Jackson's Valley Campaign in the Shenandoah Valley of Virginia from November 4, 1861, to June 17, 1862* (reprint, London: Hugh Rees, Ltd., 1912), pp. 223–224.

   OR, V, pp. 390, 1026–1027.

   Allan collaborated with Hotchkiss in this acclaimed Shenandoah Valley Campaign history. The original was published by J. B. Lippincott in 1880. Allan's Southern-based history is valuable for he interviewed officers who were actively involved with the campaign; however, it should be noted that Allan did not join Jackson's staff in the Valley until after the Battle of Kernstown. Allan places Jackson's strength at 8,500, a figure derived from Jackson's February 21 report. Jackson actually had more men than that, based on a January 10 dispatch to General Joseph E. Johnston. Jackson's full command in his district was estimated at 10,766 men (including cavalry and militia, excluding artillerists), 8,745 volunteer and militia infantry were with him at Bath.

10. Charles Clark, *The History of the Thirty-Ninth Regiment Illinois Volunteer*, pp. 35–36, 39.

11. Abraham S. Miller (Confederate Militia), Letter to his wife, January 6, 1862, James Miller Collection, 1 WFCHS, Box 1, HL.

   Anonymous militia veteran, "A War Story," *Shenandoah Herald* (Woodstock, Va.), November 26, 1897.

   The reminiscences published in the *Herald* accentuate how poorly trained the militia was. The veteran remembers an incident following their poor Bath performance: "a few days afterward, the commander of the militia, desiring to keep his command in fighting trim, ordered the guns to be cleaned. In firing against an embankment, it was noticed that many of the guns could not be discharged. An examination exposed the fact that many of the command had loaded by putting the ball end of the cartridge in first."

12. William Gilham (21st Virginia), Letter to Jed Hotchkiss, November 25, 1866, Hotchkiss Papers, LC.

   "Keystone," Letter dated January 8, 1862, *The* (Philadelphia) *Press*, January 13, 1862.

   Hooper, Letter dated January 6, 1862, *Altoona Tribune*, January 16, 1862.

13. OR, V, pp. 390–391.

   Hooper, Letter dated January 6, 1862, *Altoona Tribune*, January 16, 1862.

   Alexander Read (84th Pa), Letter to Martin Watts, January 30, 1862, *The Progress* (Clearfield, Pa.), April 9, 1961.

   This informative letter was published during the Civil War centennial.

14. OR, V, p. 402.

   Charles Clark, *The History of the Thirty-Ninth Regiment Illinois Volunteer*, p. 52.

   Joseph Ward (39th Illinois), Letter to his parents, January 8, 1862, in D. Duane Cummins and Daryl Hohweiler, eds., *An Enlisted Soldier's View of the Civil War: The Wartime Papers of Joseph Richardson Ward, Jr.* (West Lafayette, Ind.: Belle Publication, 1989), pp. 3–4.

   "John" (39th Illinois), Letter dated January 6, 1862, *The Shirleysburg Herald*, January 23, 1862.

   Henry W. Talcott (13th Ind.), Letter dated June 26, 1862, *Valparaiso Republic*, July 10, 1862.

Talcott describes the weapons of the 13th Indiana as "old, altered, flint lock Muskets." They were likely muskets refitted with percussion ignition systems. They still fired musket balls.

The information about the Indianans having only two rounds is obtained from Lieutenant Colonel Orrin L. Mann's account (39th Illinois). He describes a "Major Mann" asking for Foster's ammunition. He likely refers to Major Sylvester Munn.

15. "John," Letter dated January 6, 1862, *The Shirleysburg Herald*, January 23, 1862.

   "Keystone," Letter dated January 8, 1862, *The* (Philadelphia) *Press*, January 13, 1862.

16. Read, Letter to Martin Watts, dated January 30, 1862, *The* (Clearfield) *Progress*, April 9, 1961.

   "Keystone," Letter dated January 8, 1862, *The* (Philadelphia) *Press*, January 13, 1862.

   Hooper, Letter dated January 6, 1862, *Altoona Tribune*, January 16, 1862.

   C. S. McReading (39th Illinois), Letter dated January 14, 1862, *Ohio State Journal* (Columbus), January 17, 1862.

   S. F. (84th Pa.), Letter dated January 23, 1862, *Clearfield Republican*, February 12, 1862.

   Rev. James B. Avirett, *The Memoirs of General Turner Ashby and His Compeers* (Baltimore, Md.: Selby & Dulany, 1867), p. 145.

   The drowned soldier's name was Theodore Pardee, Company I, 84th PVI.

17. Charles Clark, *The History of the Thirty-Ninth Regiment Illinois Volunteer*, p. 36.

   Jed Hotchkiss, Journal, January 4, 1862, Reel #1, Hotchkiss Papers, LC.

   Jed Hotchkiss did not participate in this campaign. The information for these journal entries were provided by other staff officers, particularly Charles Faulkner.

18. James C. M. Hamilton, *Manuscript History of the 110th Pennsylvania*, War Library and Museum, Philadelphia, Pa., pp. 5–7.

   D. R. Miller (110th Pa.), Letter dated January 20, 1862, *The Shirleysburg Herald*, January 30, 1862.

   Samuel C. Baker (110th Pa.), Letter dated January 6, 1862, *The Shirleysburg Herald*, January 12, 1862.

19. N. P. Willis, "General F. W. Lander," *Williams County Leader* (Bryan, Ohio), April 3, 1862.

   Ezra J. Warner, *Generals in Blue: Lives of the Union Commanders* (Baton Rouge, La.: Louisiana State University Press, 1964), p. 274.

   "Frederick Lander: Biographical Note," Frederick Lander Papers, LC.

   Nathaniel P. Banks, Telegram to Seth Williams, January 4, 1862 (3:10 P.M.), Reel #15, #7514, McClellan Papers, LC.

   Nathaniel P. Banks, Telegram to Seth Williams, January 5, 1862 (12:15 A.M.), Reel #15, #7525, McClellan Papers, LC.

   The two dispatches that Banks sent to McClellan's assistant adjutant general fill a time-line for Lander's travels that could not be uncovered in Lander's papers. According to Banks, Lander left Frederick for Hancock (to eventually get to Cumberland) at noon. Banks became aware of the attack on Bath at 3:00 P.M. His midnight dispatch states "He [Lander] left Williamsport at 11:15."

It appears Lander learned of the attack at Hagerstown, then rode to Williamsport, stayed there several hours to receive information and instructions, and finally arrived in Hancock during the morning hours of January 5, 1862.

20. "Frederick Lander: Biographical Note," Frederick Lander Papers, LC.

    George B. McClellan, *McClellan's Own Story* (New York: Charles L. Webster & Company, 1887), p. 190.

    Lander, Telegram dated January 4, 1862, #6497, Lander Papers, LC.

21. Nathaniel P. Banks, Telegram to Frederick Lander, January 4, 1862, #6493 and #6495 Lander Papers, LC.

22. Temperature readings, Cumberland, Maryland, January 5, 1862, U.S. Department of Commerce Weather Bureau, National Weather Records Center, Federal Building, Asheville, N.C. (hereafter cited as National Weather Records).

    Banks, Telegram to Frederick Lander, January 4, 1862, #6502, Lander Papers, LC.

    Alpheus S. Williams, Telegram to R. M. Copeland, January 8, 1862, Carton #18, Banks Papers, LC.

23. Hamilton, *Manuscript History of the 110th Pa.*, p. 11.

24. Charles Clark, *The History of the Thirty-Ninth Regiment Illinois Volunteer*, p. 46.

25. T. J. Jackson, Letter dated January 5, 1862, #6505, Lander Papers, LC.

26. Charles Clark, *The History of the Thirty-Ninth Regiment Illinois Volunteer*, pp. 46–47.

    The slang "Sesech" will only be used within a soldier's quote. It will be spelled as it is quoted throughout the text. Hereafter, all spelling and punctuation will retain the form of its original source. [*Sic*] will follow incorrect identification or spelling of proper names.

    Jed Hotchkiss, Journal, January 5, 1862, Hotchkiss Papers, LC.

    Frederick Lander, Response to General Jackson, January 5, 1862, #6661, Lander Papers, LC.

    Lander copied his response on the back of this dispatch sent to General Banks.

27. S. F., Letter dated January 23, 1862, *Clearfield Republican*, February 12, 1862.

28. Frederick Lander, Telegram to Nathaniel P. Banks, January 5, 1862, #6660–6661, Lander Papers, LC.

    Frederick Lander, Telegram to Nathaniel P. Banks, January 7, 1862, #6514–6515, Lander Papers, LC.

    Ibid, Carton #19, Banks Papers, LC.

29. Harvey S. Wells, "With Shields in 1862," *Philadelphia Weekly Times*, March 28, 1885.

    Harvey S. Wells, "The Eighty-fourth Volunteer Infantry in the Late War," *Philadelphia Weekly Times*, April 10, 1886.

30. Hamilton, *Manuscript History of the 110th Pa.*, p. 13.

31. James R. Smith, Diary, January 5, 1862, in Emily M. Leatherman, *Hancock: 1776–1976*, Hancock, Md., 1976.

    Jed Hotchkiss, Journal, January 5, 1862, Hotchkiss Papers, LC.

    Today, both churches appear to be composed of the same colored brown brick. The identity of "Brown Church" and "Red Church" is unknown. Perhaps one appeared red from a distance by how the sun shone upon it.

32. "Volunteer" (84th Pa.), Letter dated January 8, 1862, *Muncy Luminary*, January 14, 1862.

    This correspondent has been identified as Harvey S. Wells, the same soldier/author in note 29.

33. Jed Hotchkiss, Journal, January 6–7, 1862, Hotchkiss Papers, LC.

    OR, V, p. 389.

    Alpheus Williams, Letter to his daughter, February 3, 1862, in Milo M. Quaife, ed., *From the Cannon's Mouth: The Civil War Letters of General Alpheus S. Williams* (Detroit, Mich.: Wayne State University Press and the Detroit Historical Society, 1959), p. 54.

    Charles Clark, *The History of the Thirty-Ninth Regiment Illinois Volunteer*, pp. 48–49.

34. Lander, Telegram to Banks, January 7, 1862, #6514–6515, #6522, Lander Papers, LC.

35. George B. McClellan, Telegram to Banks, January 7, 1862, Reel #15, #7608, McClellan Papers; #6519, Lander Papers, LC.

    Both sources are included for they reveal that McClellan's final note—"General Lander is too suggestive and critical"—was originally enclosed in parentheses, likely indicating this was not to be sent to Lander. Banks, probably upset about the aggressiveness and tone of Lander, sent this segment of the dispatch to put the general in his place.

    McClellan's angry remarks to Lander initiated a great deal of press over the following month. Although Lander appeared much angered about it all, and went on to write derogatory poems about McClellan (see "Tardy George," #6675, Lander Papers, LC), McClellan harbored no grudges about the exchanges. Twenty-five years afterwards, McClellan said he was "obliged to check Lander rather abruptly," and attributed Lander's requests to inexperience, concluding "These occurrences did not change my feelings toward him..." (See McClellan, *McClellan's Own Story*, p. 191.)

36. OR, V, p. 404.

37. Ibid.

    Anonymous soldier of 1st West Virginia Infantry, Letter to his sister, January 2, 1862, (Wheeling) *Daily Intelligencer*, January 10, 1862.

    Although Union Virginia regiments do not officially change their name to "West Virginia" until statehood is received in June of 1863, all references to these regiments will be described as West Virginia to avoid confusion in the narrative with the Southern regiments.

38. C. J. Rawling, *History of the First Regiment Virginia Infantry* (Philadelphia, Pa.: J. B. Lippincott Company, 1887), pp. 20, 33.

39. J. H. Newton, G. G. Nichols & A. G. Sprankle, *History of the Pan-Handle; Being Historical Collections of the Counties of Ohio, Brooke, Marshall and Hancock, West Virginia* (Wheeling, W.Va.: J. A. Caldwell, 1879), p. 253.

    Population Schedules of the Eighth Census of the United States, Ohio County, Virginia, 1860, RG 29, M-653, NA, p. 338.

40. "Prock" (14th Indiana), Letter dated January 8, 1862, *Vincennes Western Sun*, January 18, 1862.

    The soldier's letters to this newspaper were published in the *Indiana Magazine of History* in 1934 (September issue, vol. 30). "Prock" was later identified as William Landon. See *Indiana Magazine of History*, vol. 35, p. 76.

"Volunteer" (7th Ohio), Letter dated January 9, 1862, *Painesville Telegraph*, January 23, 1862.

A June 1862 issue of the *Cleveland Morning Leader* identified "Volunteer" as Sergeant V. E. Smalley, Company D.

OR, V, p. 404.

Temperature readings, Cumberland, Maryland and Georgetown, D.C., January 7, 1862, National Weather Records.

The temperature was measured to be eighteen degrees in Georgetown and twenty-six degrees in Cumberland at 7:00 A.M.

41. John W. Elwood, *Elwood's Stories of the Old Ringgold Cavalry, 1847–1865, The 1st Three Year Cavalry of the Civil War* (Coal Center, Pa.: published by the author, 1914), p. 82.

Hiram Treher (5th Ohio), Letter to his parents, January 15, 1862, *Semi-Weekly Dispatch* (Chambersburg, Pa.), January 28, 1862.

Treher wrote three letters that were subsequently published in two Chambersburg newspapers. His vivid letters have recently been donated to the Ohio Historical Society in Columbus, Ohio.

42. OR, V, p. 404.

Franklin Sawyer, *A Military History of the 8th Ohio Volunteer Infantry: Its Battles, Marches and Army Movements* (Cleveland, Ohio: Fairbanks & Co. Printers, 1881), pp. 27–28.

N. N. H. (1st W.Va. Cavalry), Letter dated January 8, 1862, (Wheeling) *Daily Intelligencer*, January 14, 1862.

Anonymous soldier (5th Ohio), Letter dated January 12, 1862, *Cincinnati Daily Commercial*, January 21, 1862.

43. "Prock," Letter dated January 8, 1862, *Vincennes Western Sun*, January 18, 1862.

OR, V, p. 404.

44. "Volunteer," Letter dated January 9, 1862, *Painesville Telegraph*, January 23, 1862.

OR, V, p. 405.

"Prock," Letter dated January 8, 1862, *Vincennes Western Sun*, January 18, 1862.

Sergeant Moore (1st W.Va. Infantry), Letter dated January 9, 1862, (Wheeling) *Daily Intelligencer*, January 21, 1862.

45. O. P. H. (4th Virginia Militia), Letter dated January 14, 1862, *Rockingham Register and Virginian*, January 24, 1862.

Benjamin Kelley, Letter to Lander, January 7, 1862, #6520, Lander Papers, LC.

46. Anonymous soldier (5th Ohio), Letter dated January 9, 1862, *Cincinnati Daily Commercial*, January 16, 1862.

T. F. A. (5th Ohio), Letter dated January 10, 1862, *Cincinnati Daily Commercial*, January 14, 1862.

47. George B. McClellan, Telegram to Lander, January 9, 1862, #6698, Lander Papers, LC.

T. F. A. (5th Ohio), Letter dated January 10, 1862, *Cincinnati Daily Commercial*, January 14, 1862.

Hiram Treher, Letter to his parents, January 15, 1862, *Semi-Weekly Dispatch* (Chambersburg), January 28, 1862.

Augustus Van Dyke (14th Indiana), Letter dated February 8, 1862, Van Dyke Collections, IHS.

Elwood, *Elwood's Stories of the Old Ringgold Cavalry*, p. 86.

48. James I. Robertson, ed., "An Indiana Soldier in Love and War: The Civil War Letters of John V. Hadley," *Indiana Magazine of History*, vol. 59, no. 5, 1963, p. 203.

49. "From Gen. Lander's Division," (Wheeling) *Daily Intelligencer*, February 13, 1862.

This unsigned account was penned by *Cincinnati Daily Gazette* war correspondent Whitelaw Reid. He covered Lander's movements in January and February, 1862, under the pseudonym "Agate." Other newspapers, including the *Daily Intelligencer*, also published his accounts. (See James G. Smart, ed., *A Radical View: The "Agate" Dispatches of Whitelaw Reid 1861–1865*, vol. 1, Memphis State University Press, 1976, pp. 61–63.)

50. Monroe F. Cockrell, ed., *Gunner with Stonewall: Reminiscences of William Thomas Poague* (reprint, Wilmington, N.C.: Broadfoot Publishing Company, 1989), p. 15.

51. Dyer, *A Compendium of the War of the Rebellion*, pp. 335–336.

52. Baker (110th Pa.), Letter dated February 5, 1862, *The Shirleysburg Herald*, February 13, 1862.

53. "Keystone," Letter dated January 20, 1862, *The* (Philadelphia) *Press*, January 27, 1862.

54. Rawling, *History of the First Regiment Virginia Infantry*, p. 52.

George Wood (7th Ohio), Diary, March 4, 1862, vol. 398, OHS.

"From Gen. Lander's Division," (Wheeling) *Daily Intelligencer*, February 13, 1862.

55. Simon F. Barstow, Letter to Samuel Chase, February 4, 1862, Reel 19, #19838, Salmon P. Chase Collection, LC.

Thomas Clark (29th Ohio), Letter to his wife, February 2 & 6, 1862, Letters in possession of Marilyn Clark-Snyder, Annandale, Virginia (hereafter cited as Clark Letters).

I am indebted to Mrs. Clark-Snyder for permitting me to access her ancestral uncle's collection. Lieutenant Colonel Thomas Clark wrote home to his wife nearly every day of the campaign. The letters are a valuable source of information concerning camp life, marches and opinions about other officers.

56. Ladies of Cumberland, Letter to Frederick Lander, Dispatch #6671–6672, Lander Papers, LC.

Frederick Lander, Letter to Randolph Marcy, January 16, 1862, #85875, McClellan Papers, LC.

Thomas Clark, Letter to his wife, February 20, 1862, Clark Letters.

"Sixty-Seventh Regiment," Letter dated March 16, 1862, *Williams County Leader* (Bryan, Ohio), April 3, 1862.

Otto Burstenbinder Court-martial Case, RG 94, B1205, (VS) 1862, Box #23, NA.

57. "Prock," Letter dated February 13, 1862, *Vincennes Western Sun*, February 26, 1862.

Lawrence Wilson, *Itinerary of the Seventh Ohio Volunteer Infantry, 1861–1864, with Roster, Portraits, and Biographies* (New York: The Neale Publishing Company, 1907), p. 119.

J. Hamp SeCheverell, *Journal History of the Twenty-Ninth Ohio Veteran Volunteers, 1861–1865, Its Victories and Its Reverses* (Cleveland, Ohio: published by the author, 1883), p. 36.

McClellan, *McClellan's Own Story*, p. 191.

58. OR, V, p. 405.

Captain Marcus Spiegel (67th Ohio), Letter to his wife and children, February 17, 1862, in Jean Powers Soman and Frank L. Byrne, eds., *A Jewish Colonel in the Civil War: Marcus M. Spiegel of the Ohio Volunteers* (Lincoln, Nebraska: University of Nebraska Press, 1995), p. 40.

59. Hiram Treher, Letter dated February 15, 1862, *Semi-Weekly Dispatch* (Chambersburg, Pa.), February 25, 1862.

60. OR, V, p. 405.

Sawyer, *Military History of the 8th Ohio Vol. Inf'y*, pp. 25–26.

Whitelaw Reid, *Ohio in the War: Her Statesmen, Generals and Soldiers,* vol. 1 (Columbus, Ohio: Eclectic Publishing Company,1893), p. 930.

61. Sawyer, *Military History of the 8th Ohio Vol. Inf'y*, p. 32.

Augustus Van Dyke, Letter dated March 4, 1862, Van Dyke Collection, IHS.

Treher, Letter dated February 15, 1862, *Semi-Weekly Dispatch*, February 25, 1862.

62. Soman and Byrne, ed., *A Jewish Colonel*, p. 40.

W.S. (1st W. Virginia Cavalry), Letter dated February 28, 1862, (Wheeling) *Daily Intelligencer,* March 5, 1862.

"Younger" (1st W. Virginia Cavalry), Letter dated February 26, 1862, (Wheeling) *Daily Intelligencer,* March 5, 1862.

Ralph Haas, *Dear Esther: The Civil War Letters of Private Augier Dobbs, Centreville, Pennsylvania, Company "A," The Ringgold Cavalry Company 22nd Pennsylvania Cavalry, June 29, 1861 to October 31, 1865* (Apollo, Pa.: Closson Press, 1991), p. 60.

63. W. S. (1st W. Virginia Cavalry), Letter dated February 28, 1862, (Wheeling) *Daily Intelligencer,* March 5, 1862.

Lovejoy, *A History of Company A, First Ohio Cavalry 1861–1865* (Ohio: Washington Court House, ca. 1898), p. 51.

The copy of "Lovejoy's" history at the Library of Congress has the name "Samuel L. Gillespie" pencilled above the author's pseudonym on the title page. Lovejoy wrote a more contemporary history as a weekly correspondent for the *Fayette County Herald* (Washington Court House, Ohio) in early 1862. His 1898 book makes wide use of those accounts. Hereafter, Lovejoy's letters to the newspaper will be cited.

64. OR, V, pp. 405, 407.

65. OR, V, p. 405.

"Younger", Letter dated February 26, 1862, (Wheeling) *Daily Intelligencer*, March 5, 1862.

W. S., Letter dated February 28,1862, (Wheeling) *Daily Intelligencer*, March 5, 1862.

66. OR, V, p. 405.

W. S., Letter dated February 28,1862, (Wheeling) *Daily Intelligencer*, March 5, 1862.

67. Nancy Niblack Baxter, *Gallant Fourteenth: The Story of an Indiana Civil War Regiment* (Traverse City, Ind.: Pioneer Study Center Press, 1980), p. 76.

Elwood, *Stories of the Old Ringgold Calvary*, p. 88.

Thomas Clark, Letter to his wife, February 27, 1862, Clark Letters.

68. W. S., Letter dated February 28, 1862, (Wheeling) *Daily Intelligencer*, March 5, 1862.

69. OR, LI, pt. 1, p. 531.

Edwin Stanton, Telegram to Frederick Lander, February 17, 1862, #6571, Lander Papers, LC.

70. OR, LI, pt. 1, p. 533.

The final line of this dispatch conjures up images of Ulysses S. Grant during his period of boredom; however, this account may indicate something other than an admission to a drinking problem. Lander was very aware of his poor health. He wrote a revealing letter to Salmon P. Chase on February 8, complaining about how his earlier reprimand by McClellan was being misinterpreted. He tried to shrug off the controversy when he stated, "But as I am dying, with the rest of my health gone, I fear, for all time—why complain?" (no punctuation in original). See Chase Papers, #12872, LC.

71. Thomas Clark, Letter to his wife, February 22, 1862, Clark Letters.

72. Temperature readings, Cumberland, Maryland and Georgetown, D.C., February 1862, National Weather Records.

Coley (13th Indiana), Letter dated March 29, 1862, *Franklin Democrat*, April 11, 1862.

Nathaniel L. Parmater (29th Ohio), Diary, February 22, 1862, Mss. 246, OHS.

Frederick Lander, Telegram to George B. McClellan, #85969, McClellan Papers, LC.

73. Henry Anisansel Court-martial Transcript, RG 153, Case File #II-693, NA.

OR, LI, pt. 1, p. 539.

74. OR, LI, pt. 1, p. 544.

McClellan, *McClellan's Own Story*, p. 195.

75. George Wood (7th Ohio), Diary, March 4, 1862, vol. 398, OHS.

Thomas Clark, Letter to his wife, March 2, 1862, Clark Letters.

76. OR, LI, pt. 1, pp. 544–546.

Moore, *Rebellion Record*, vol. 4, p. 46.

S. F. Barstow, Telegram to G. B. McClellan, March 2, 1862 (5:00 P.M.), #85986, McClellan Papers, LC.

77. Wood, Diary, March 4, 1862, OHS.

George Washington Lambert, Journal, March 3, 1862, M178, Box 2, Folder 3, IHS.

CHAPTER TWO

1. Kate S. Sperry, Diary, March 2, 1862, *Surrender? Never Surrender!*, 975.5991 Sp3, HL.

2. Garland R. Quarles, *Some Worthy Lives: Mini-Biographies of Winchester and Frederick County* (Winchester, Va.: Winchester-Frederick County Historical Society, 1988) p. 108.

Jed Hotchkiss, Journal, March 2, 1862, Hotchkiss Papers, LC.

The information contained in Jed Hotchkiss's entries are taken from accounts of other staff officers until his own observations are recorded beginning in the final weeks of March 1862.

3. Byron Farwell, *Stonewall: A Biography of General Thomas J. Jackson* (N.Y. & London: W. W. Norton & Company, 1992), pp. 3, 38, 110, 117, 127.

4. Stewart Sifakis, *Who Was Who in the Civil War* (New York & Oxford: Facts on File Publications, 1988), p. 337.

    Roger U. Delauter, *Winchester in the Civil War* (Lynchburg, Va.: H. E. Howard, Inc., 1992), pp. 10–11, 13.

5. Douglas Southall Freeman, *Lee's Lieutenants: A Study in Command,* vol. 1 (New York: Charles Scribner's Sons, 1942), pp. 81–82, 733–739.

    Farwell, *A Biography of General Thomas J. Jackson,* p. 201.

6. Delauter, *Winchester in the Civil War,* p. 13.

    Thomas J. Jackson, Letter to his wife, October 14, 1862, in Mary Anna Jackson, *Life and Letters of General Thomas J. Jackson ("Stonewall" Jackson)* (New York: Harper Brothers, 1892), p. 195.

    Ibid., pp. 210–211.

7. Ben Ritter, "A Favorite Portrait of Stonewall," *Civil War Times Illustrated,* vol. 17, no. 10, 1979, pp. 37–39.

    Mr. Ritter convincingly disputed the claim that the photograph was taken in the winter. His evidence placed the timing of the photograph in October or November of 1862.

    Freeman, *Lee's Lieutenants,* p. 305.

    Farwell, *A Biography of General Thomas J. Jackson,* p. 121.

    Jackson's description is obtained from an 1856 passport application.

8. J. R. Graham, "Personal Characteristics of General Stonewall Jackson," March 12, 1895, Reel #49, Hotchkiss Papers, LC.

9. Gilham, Letter to Jed Hotchkiss, November 25, 1866, Hotchkiss Papers, LC.

10. Allan, *Stonewall Jackson's Valley Campaign,* pp. 223–224.

11. OR, LI, pt. 2, pp. 461–462.

12. Ibid, p. 462.

    Charles W. Turner, ed., *Ted Barclay, Liberty Hall Volunteers: Letters from the Stonewall Brigade, 1861–1864* (Natural Bridge Station, Va.: Rockbridge Publishing Company, 1992), p. 44.

    Arthur H. Noll, ed., *Doctor Quintard, Chaplain C. S. A. and Second Bishop of Tennessee* (Sewanee, Tennessee: University Press of Sewanee, 1905), p. 40.

    John Apperson (4th Va.), Diary, January 24, 1862, Microfilm #28992, VSL.

13. OR, V, pp. 1050, 1053.

14. Farwell, *A Biography of General Thomas J. Jackson,* pp. 220–221.

    OR, V, p. 1071.

    OR, LI, pt. 2, pp. 468–469.

15. OR, V, pp. 1068, 1080.

16. Allan, *Stonewall Jackson's Valley Campaign,* pp. 228–231.

17. William L. Wessels, *Born to be a Soldier: The Military Career of William Wing Loring of St. Augustine, Fla.* (Fort Worth, Texas: Texas Christian University Press, 1971), pp. 59–60.

OR, V, pp. 1040–1041.

18. Richard Garnett, Letter to Hon. R. M. Hunter, April 1862, Richard Garnett Court-martial Papers, MC.

Hunter was Secretary of State and Richard Garnett's cousin. Jackson's letter that Garnett alluded to was a request to replace him with Lieutenant Colonel Seth Barton of the 3rd Arkansas (see James I. Robertson, *Stonewall Jackson—The Man, The Soldier, The Legend* (New York: MacMillan Publishing, USA, 1997), p. 310). Jackson's request, written on January 10, was denied by the War Department. His complaint may have stemmed from an incident during the first days of the Bath-Romney campaign when Garnett rested his men near a roadside, Jackson rode up and asked Garnett the reason for the delay. When told they were cooking rations, Jackson responded there was no time for that. Garnett protested and claimed it is impossible for the men to march further without being fed. "I never found anything impossible with this brigade!" was Stonewall's final word (see G. F. R. Henderson, *Stonewall Jackson and the American Civil War* (reprint, New York: Da Capo Press, 1988), p. 145). Author's note: Henderson's history, written from Europe in 1898, is a secondary account of Jackson's life that took much of its information from officers' reminiscences. Henderson rarely footnoted his anecdotes; therefore, their original sources are unknown. Because many of his stories concerning Jackson's Shenandoah Valley Campaign are unconfirmed and others have been refuted, I have refrained from referencing Henderson's history in my text. I will, on occasion, refute his anecdotes concerning the Battle of Kernstown when it becomes necessary to set the record straight.

19. Robert K. Krick, "Armistead and Garnett: The Parallel Lives of Two Virginia Soldiers," *The Third Day at Gettysburg & Beyond*, Gary W. Gallagher, ed. (Chapel Hill, N.C., and London: University of North Carolina Press, 1994), pp. 95, 97, 100–101.

James Mercer Garnett, Genealogy of the Mercer-Garnett Family of Essex County, Virginia, Whittet & Shepperson, Richmond, Va., ca. 1910, pp. 35–39.

U.S. Military Academy Application Papers, 1805–1866, RG 94, M688, Roll 91, NA.

Monthly Consolidation of the Weekly Class Reports including the Conduct Roll, U.S. Military Academy, RG 94, NA.

Register of the Officers and Cadets of the U.S. Military Academy, June 1841, J. P. Wright, New York, 1841, n.p.

I am indebted to Mr. Krick's well researched essay detailing Richard Garnett's pre-Civil War career. The four sources listed above were obtained from Krick's work.

Sifakis, *Who Was Who in the Civil War*, p. 238.

20. Krick, *The Third Day at Gettysburg & Beyond*, pp. 104–107.

Nyle H. Miller, ed., "Surveying the Southern Boundary Line of Kansas," Kansas Historical Quarterly I, February 1932, pp. 107–127.

Richard B. Garnett, Letter to Honorable Secretary of War, December 22, 1857, "Applications for Army Promotions," 15W3, Row 11, Compartment 5, Shelf A, Box 59, RG 107, NA.

21. Richard Brooke Garnett, Compiled Service Record, M331, Roll 103, NA.

William B. McCash, *Thomas R. R. Cobb: The Making of a Southern Nationalist* (Macon, Ga.: Mercer University Press,1983), pp. 256, 271.

22. James H. Langhorne, Letter to his father, December 7, 1861, Langhorne Family Papers, VHS.

Langhorne's description of Garnett has enabled Robert Krick to convincingly refute a familiar photograph depicting a bearded, dark-haired and dark-eyed general, widely accepted to be that of Richard Garnett, to be of Garnett's cousin Robert Seldon Garnett (see Robert K. Krick, "The Army of Northern Virginia's Most Notorious Court Martial . . . Jackson Vs. Garnett," *Blue & Gray Magazine*, June–July 1986, pp. 30, 32). The photograph is identified as General Robert S. Garnett in the Battles & Leaders series, vol. 1, p. 134. However, Langhorne's description of a fair-complected Richard Garnett is disputed by James W. Clay, an 18th Virginia private who served as Garnett's orderly for ten days per month in 1863. Clay claims that Garnett was darker complected, ". . . his dark eyes flashing and as black as coals. He wore a black beard and hair rather long." SHSP 33 (1905), p. 29.

23. Allan, *Stonewall Jackson's Valley Campaign*, p. 229.

    OR, V, pp. 1016–1017.

24. Sperry, Diary, March 4, HL.

25. Delauter, *Winchester in the Civil War*, pp. 2–3.

26. T. K. Cartmell, *Shenandoah Valley Pioneers and Their Descendants: A History of Frederick County, Virginia from its formation in 1738 to 1908* (Berryville, Va.: Chesapeake Book Co., 1963), p. 54.

    John W. Wayland, *History of Shenandoah County* (Strasburg, Va.: Shenandoah Publishing House, 1927), pp. 262–266.

27. Population Schedules of the Eighth Census of the United States, Winchester, Virginia, 1860, RG 29, M-653, NA.

    Delauter, *Winchester in the Civil War*, pp. 1, 4–5.

28. "Union Men of Winchester," Colonel William D. Lewis Collection, 573 WFCHS, HL.

    General Thomas J. Jackson, Letter #151, March 5, 1862, Letters sent by General T. J. Jackson in 1862, Reel #49, Hotchkiss Papers, LC (hereafter cited as Jackson Letterbook, LC).

29. Julia Chase, Diary, March 3, 1862, *War-Time Diary of Miss Julia Chase, 1861–1864*, 973.78 C38, HL.

30. Major John A. Harman, Letter to his brother, March 6, 1862, Reel #49, Hotchkiss Papers, LC (hereafter cited as Harman Letters, LC).

31. OR, V, pp. 521–523.

    James T. Fairburn (Confederate soldier), Letter to his brother, March 14, 1862, Box 19, Folder #1, Nathaniel Banks Papers, LC.

    Richard L. Armstrong, *7th Virginia Cavalry* (Lynchburg, Va.: H. E. Howard, Inc.,1992), p. 21.

    Harman, Letter to his brother, March 8, 1862, Harman Letters, LC.

32. Sandie Pendleton, Letter to his mother, March 7, 1862, in W. G. Bean, ed., "The Valley Campaign of 1862 as Revealed in Letters of Sandie Pendleton," VMHB, vol. 78, 1970, pp. 327, 336 (hereafter VMHB).

33. Charles D. Walker, *Memorial, Virginia Military Institute. Biographical Sketches of the Graduates and Eleves of the Virginia Military Institute Who Fell During the War Between the States* (Philadelphia, Pa.: J. B. Lippincott & Co., 1875), pp. 21–22, 25.

34. Harman, Letter to his brother, March 8, 1862, Harman Letters, LC.

35. Statement from T. J. McVeigh, General Banks' Intelligence Reports, RG 393, entry 223, NA, p. 76.

Statement from Arthur S. Markell, General Banks' Intelligence Reports, p. 80.

Markell led a troubled life that may have been exacerbated by a drinking problem. His wife divorced him, and his children refused to communicate with him. He died a pauper on July 11, 1912. (Ben Ritter, Personal Communication; *Winchester Evening Star*, July 12, 1912.)

36. Temperature readings, Sheets Mill, Hampshire County, March 1862, National Weather Records.

Although it was a freezing morning, the temperature at Georgetown, D.C. by 2:00 P.M. that day was recorded to be sixty-five degrees.

Wm. D. Wilkins, Letter to Nathaniel Banks, March 9, 1862, Box 19, Folder #1, Nathaniel Banks Papers, LC.

"Statement of Jacob Poisel," General Banks' Intelligence Reports, NA, p. 97.

"Minutes of examination of Jacob Poisel," Miscellany of Lists and Reports, 1862, Box 79, Folder #4, Nathaniel Banks Papers, LC.

It is unknown how Poisel (spelled "Poisal" on his headstone) was treated by his neighbors in Hedgesville after his discharge. He died at the age of thirty-six years on May 31, 1880.

37. Thomas Clark, Letter to his wife, March 10, 1862, Clark Letters.

Consolidated Morning Reports, March 1–9, 1862, Carton #78, Nathaniel Banks Papers, LC.

Alonzo H. Quint (2nd Mass.), *The Potomac and the Rapidan, Army Notes From the Failure at Winchester to the Reinforcement of Rosecrans: 1861–63* (New York: Crosby and Nichols, 1864), pp. 104–105.

Pendleton, Letter to his mother, March 13, 1862, VMHB, pp. 336–337.

Harman, Letter to his brother, March 10, 1862, Harman Letters, LC.

38. John Apperson, Diary, March 11, 1862, VSL.

Pendleton, Letter to his mother, March 13, 1862, VMHB, pp. 336–337.

William Kinzer (4th Va.), Diary, March 11, 1862, Mss5:1 K6275:1, VHS.

39. Frank Jones (2nd Va.), Diary, March 11, 1862, HL.

40. James T. Fairburn, Letter to his brother, March 14, 1862, Box 19, Folder #1, Nathaniel Banks Papers, LC.

A. T. (42nd Virginia), Letter dated March 8, 1862, Lynchburg *Daily Republican*, March 17, 1862.

Thomas J. Jackson, Letters #160 & 161 to Capt. Nadenbousch, March 11, 1862, Jackson Letterbook, LC.

Julia Chase, Diary, March 11, 1862, HL.

41. Mrs. Hugh Lee, Diary, March 11, 1862, 1182 WFCHS, HL.

42. Laura Lee, Diary, March 11, 1862, Ben Ritter Collection, 12 WFCHS, Box 1, HL.

Sperry, Diary, March 11, 1862, HL.

Mrs. Cornelia McDonald, *A Diary With Reminiscences of the War and Refugee Life in the Shenandoah Valley 1860–1865* (Nashville, Tenn.: Cullom & Ghertner Co., 1934), p. 40.

43. Frank Jones, Diary, March 11, 1862, HL.

44. John Apperson, Diary, March 11, 1862, VSL.

45. John Newton Lyle (4th Virginia), *A Reminiscence of Lieutenant John Newton Lyle of the Liberty Hall Volunteers*, Charles W. Turner, ed. (Roanoke, Va.: The Virginia Lithography & Graphics Company, 1987), p. 149.

  Allan, *Stonewall Jackson's Valley Campaign*, pp. 42, 230.

  Hunter McGuire, "General T. J. ("Stonewall") Jackson, Confederate States Army. His Career and Character," SHSP 25, 1897, p. 97.

  Lyle's places the council at the Moore house, Jackson's headquarters. (Colonel Lewis T. Moore is a direct ancestor of actress Mary Tyler Moore.) Allan takes his information from Colonel John Echols, 27th Virginia, who was in attendance that night. It is assumed that Jackson's planned point of attack was Williams's division near Stephenson Depot. This was the closest Federal force to Winchester and they had an exposed flank.

46. Pendleton, Letter to his mother, March 13, 1862, VMHB, p. 337.

  Where Jackson slept that night is a matter of debate. Pendleton's letter recounts he and Jackson sitting from 3:00 A.M. until daybreak in a fence corner at the rear of the column, approximately four miles south of Winchester (the general vicinity of Bartonsville). A member of Jackson's staff believed the fence corner was near Newtown where the head of the column rested (Hotchkiss Journal, March 12, 1862, LC). I chose Pendleton's account to be more accurate as it was written less than two days after the event.

47. McGuire, General T. J. ("Stonewall") Jackson, p. 97.

  The doctor times the quote as occurring "late in the afternoon" of March 11, 1862. This is not possible as Jackson's council broke up late at night. Sandie Pendleton's letter two days later clearly notes leaving town at midnight, delivering orders to the front of the column, then joining Jackson at a fence rail at the rear of the column four miles south of Winchester at 3:00 A.M. McGuire's recollection could have taken place at midnight, however, his recollection would certainly have highlighted the fact that it was dark when the two looked toward Winchester. The fact that McGuire believed that it was in the afternoon indicates that it must have been during daylight hours. Therefore, I have placed the "last council" quote to take place in the early morning of March 12, 1862. Exactly where Jackson made his famous statement is unknown.

CHAPTER THREE

1. Averitt, *The Memoirs of General Turner Ashy*, p. 157.

  Clarence Thomas, *General Turner Ashby: the Centaur of the South, a Military Sketch* (Winchester, Va.: The Eddy Press Corporation, 1907), p. 70.

  John Lutz, Jr. (110th Pa.), Letter dated March 21, 1862, *The Shirleysburg Herald*, April 3, 1862.

  Mrs. Hugh Lee, Diary, March 11, 1862, HL.

  Subsequent to Ashby's departure from Winchester, nearly all accounts describe him astride his white (or gray) horse. Interestingly, John Newton Lyle claims to remember Ashby one week later on his black horse—". . . Ashby rode by on his famous black stallion . . ." (Turner, *A Reminiscence of Lieutenant John Newton Lyle*, p. 156)—but Lyle's reminiscences were written nearly forty years later; this long passage of time may have fogged his memory as to what date he remembered Ashby on the black horse. Lutz's account was written the same day of the event when he said, "I was out to-day to see a fine black horse that was shot from under Col. Ashby. One of his hind legs was shot off by a cannon ball."

2. Alpheus S. Williams, Letter to his daughter, March 13, 1862, *From the Cannon's Mouth,* p. 63.

    OR, LI, pt. 1, p. 746.

3. John Peyton Clark, Journal, March 12, 1862, Louisa Crawford Collection, 424 WFCHS, HL.

    Alpheus S. Williams, Letter to his daughter, March 13, 1862, *From the Cannon's Mouth,* p. 63.

    Mrs. Hugh Lee, Diary, March 12, 1862, HL.

4. John Peyton Clark, Journal, March 12, 1862, Louisa Crawford Collection, 424 WFCHS, HL.

    Sperry, Diary, March 12, 1862, HL.

    Kate Sperry's complaint is ironic, for the melody for "Dixie" was originally taken from a Northern minstrel tune. It was composed by Dan Emmet, the son of an Ohio abolitionist. (See Bruce Catton, *The American Heritage Picture History of the Civil War* (reprint, New York: Crown Publishers, Inc., 1982), p. 379.

5. Alpheus S. Williams, Letter to his daughter, March 30, 1862, *From the Cannon's Mouth*, p. 63.

    Mrs. Hugh Lee, Diary, March 12, HL.

    "Volunteer" (13th Indiana), Letter dated March 18, 1862, *Madison Daily Courier*, March 29, 1862.

    Julia Chase, Diary, March 12, 1862, HL.

    Temperature readings, Sheets Mill and Georgetown, March 12, 1862, National Weather Records.

6. Mrs. Hugh Lee, Diary, March 14, 1862.

    Garland Quarles, *The Story of One Hundred Old Homes in Winchester, Virginia* (Winchester, Va.: Prepared for the Farmers and Merchants Bank, 1967), pp. 33–34.

    Dyer, *A Compendium of the War of the Rebellion*, pp. 300–301.

    OR, V, pp. 746, 748, 750.

    Abraham Lincoln, President's General War Order No. 2, March 8, 1862, Reel #2, Edwin McMaster Stanton Papers, LC.

    The origin of the Fifth Corps is traditionally but incorrectly placed in the Urbanna campaign with General Fitz John Porter as the unit's first commander. Banks's tenure as Fifth Corps commander was short lived. The corps was discontinued on April 4, 1862, and his troops were merged into the Department of the Shenandoah and the Department of the Rappahannock. The Fifth Corps was re-created and organized provisionally on May 18, 1862. These troops saw their first action on the Peninsula, led by Brigadier General Fitz John Porter.

7. General James Shields Papers, USAMHI, Carlisle Barracks, Pa.

    Shields's date of birth has oftentimes been misplaced as 1810 (see Warner, *Generals in Blue*, p. 444), but the original family records have pre-dated it to 1806.

    Other useful sources about Shields's pre-war life include: William H. Condon, *Life of Major General James Shields* (Chicago: Press of the Blakeley Printing Co., 1900); Henry A. Castle, "General James Shields, Soldier, Orator, Statesman," *Collections of the Minnesota Historical Society*, vol. 15, 1915, pp. 710–740; and

Joseph R. Purcell, *James Shields: Soldier and Statesman* (Dublin, 1932), pp. 73–87. For a detailed book-length account about the near-duel between Shields and Lincoln, see James E. Myers, *The Astonishing Saber Duel of Abraham Lincoln* (Springfield, Ill.: Lincoln-Herndon Building Publishers, 1968), pages in the entire book.

8. OR, V, pp. 700–702.

9. "Brigadier-General James Shields," *The Philadelphia Inquirer*, March 26, 1862.

    Rawling, *History of the First Regiment Virginia Infantry*, p. 53.

    J. F. Huntington, "In the Valley: The Campaign in the Spring of 1862," *The National Tribune*, September 5, 1889.

10. "The Serenade to General Shields by the Irish Brigade," *Semi-Weekly Dispatch* (Chambersburg, Pa.), January 14, 1862.

11. OR, V, p. 749.

    W. E. C. (110th Pa.), Letter dated March 17, 1862, *Semi-Weekly Globe* (Huntingdon, Pa.), March 25, 1862.

    Mrs. Hugh Lee, Diary, March 14, 1862, HL.

    Fanny Graham, Letter to Mrs. Jackson, April 3, 1862, "Old Letters Tell of War in Winchester," *Winchester Evening Star*, January 13, 1965.

    Joseph R. Ward (39th Illinois), Letter to his parents, March 13, 1862, *An Enlisted Soldier's View of the Civil War*, pp. 8–9.

    W. C. F. (13th Indiana), Letter dated March 21, 1862, Indianapolis *Daily Journal*, March 28, 1862.

12. W. C. F. (13th Indiana), Letter dated March 21, 1862, Indianapolis *Daily Journal*, March 28, 1862.

13. John Cashner (13th Indiana), Diary, March 13, 1862, W. H. Smith Memorial Library, IHS.

    Isaac Banta (7th Indiana), Letter to his brother, March 1862, IHS.

    William S. Vohn, Letter dated April 2, 1862, *Weekly Perrysburg Journal*, April 10, 1862.

    W. E. C. (110th Pa.), Letter dated March 17, 1862, *Semi-Weekly Globe* (Huntingdon, Pa.), March 25, 1862.

    "Eugene" (8th Ohio), Letter dated March 14, 1862, *Bucyrus Weekly Journal*, March 28, 1862.

    David Beem, Letter to his parents, March 15, 1862, David Beem Collection, M151, Folder 2, Box 1, IHS.

14. "Old Town" (84th Pa.), Letter dated March 21, 1862, *Clearfield Republican*, April 2, 1862.

15. George McClellan, Letter to Edwin Stanton, March 14, 1862, Lincoln Papers, LC.

    OR, V, p. 56.

    OR, XII, pt. 3, p. 4.

16. Captain James W. Abert, Letter to Nathaniel Banks, March 24, 1862, Box 19, Banks Papers, LC.

    Abert was the engineer in charge of constructing the bridge. In this post-battle letter, he reveals that the bridge was ready on Wednesday, March 19.

    Wilder Dwight, Letter to his wife, March 15, 1862, in *Life and Letters of Wilder Dwight, Lieut.-Col. Second Mass. Inf. Vols.* (Boston, Mass.: Ticknor and Field, 1868), p. 213.

Mrs. Hugh Lee, Diary, March 13, 1862, HL.

Sperry, Diary, March 13–14, HL.

17. Henry Kyd Douglas, *I Rode with Stonewall* (reprint, St. Simons Island, Georgia: Mockingbird Books, Inc., 1987), p. 88.

Freeman, *Lee's Lieutenants*, pp. 308–309.

Charles W. Turner, ed., *A Reminiscence of Lieutenant John Newton Lyle*, p. 156.

18. Thomas, *General Turner Ashby: the Centaur of the South*, p. 70.

Sawyer, *Military History of the 8th Ohio Vol. Inf'y*, p. 38.

Wilder Dwight, Letter to his wife, March 28, 1862, *Life and Letters*, p. 221.

19. Turner Ashby Compiled Service Record, M331, NA.

According to Act #356 in Ashby's service record, the date of Ashby's commission is dated February 12, 1862. This commission may have been past-dated.

Turner Ashby, Letter to Judah P. Benjamin, March 17, 1862, Turner Ashby Papers, Chicago Historical Society, Chicago, Illinois.

20. Averitt, *The Memoirs of General Turner Ashby*, pp. 256, 272.

21. Laura Lee, Diary, March 13, 1862, HL.

John S. Mason, Testimony, May 22, 1862, Third Session of the 39th Congress, *Report of the Joint Committee of the Senate on the Conduct of the War*, vol. 3, pt. 2, no. 108, Government Printing Office, Washington, D.C., 1863, p. 404 (hereafter JCCW).

22. Ibid.

David Hunter Strother, "Personal Recollections of the War by a Virginian," *Harper's New Monthly Magazine*, January 1867, pp. 183–184 (hereafter *Harper's*).

David Hunter Strother, Diary, March 17, 1862, in Cecil D. Eby, Jr., ed., *A Virginia Yankee in the Civil War: The Diaries of David Hunter Strother* (Chapel Hill, N.C.: The University of North Carolina Press, 1961), pp. 12, 15 (hereafter Eby).

23. Mason, Testimony, JCCW, pp. 405–406.

Sawyer, *Military History of the 8th Ohio Vol. Inf'y*, p. 37.

M. D. (8th Ohio), Letter dated March 21, 1862, *The Sandusky Register*, April 1, 1862.

24. Strother, March 18, 1862, *Harper's*, p. 184.

Eby, *A Virginia Yankee in the Civil War*, pp. 15–16.

"Volunteer" (7th Ohio), Letter dated March 23, 1862, *Painesville Telegraph*, April 3, 1862.

D. Ross Miller (110th Pa.), Letter dated March 21, 1862, *Semi-Weekly Globe* (Huntingdon, Pa.), March 27, 1862.

25. George M. Neese, *Three Years in the Confederate Horse Artillery* (reprint, Dayton, Ohio: Press of Morningside Bookshop, 1983), pp. 29–30.

26. Ibid., p. 30.

Thomas D. Gold, *History of Clarke County, Virginia and its Connection with the War Between the States* (Berryville, Va.: published by the author), p. 168.

Mason, Testimony, JCCW, pp. 404–405.

Strother, *Harper's*, p. 185.

Eby, *A Virginia Yankee in the Civil War*, p. 17.

Sawyer, *Military History of the 8th Ohio Vol. Inf'y*, p. 38.

G. S. F. (1st Michigan Cavalry), Letter dated March 30, 1862, *Detroit Tri-Weekly Tribune*, April 7, 1862.

Although the term "company" correctly identifies artillery units, "Battery" is used throughout the text to prevent confusion with infantry.

27. Sawyer, *Military History of the 8th Ohio Vol. Inf'y*, pp. 38–39.

Captain Butterfield (8th Ohio), Letter dated March 22, 1862, *Bucyrus Weekly Journal*, April 4, 1862.

Mason, Testimony, JCCW, p. 405.

M. D., Letter dated March 21, 1862, *The Sandusky Register*, April 1, 1862.

28. Eby, *A Virginia Yankee in the Civil War*, p. 17.

Neese, *Three Years in the Confederate Horse Artillery*, pp. 30–31.

G. S. F. (1st Michigan Cavalry), Letter dated March 30, 1862, *Detroit Tri-Weekly Tribune*, April 7, 1862.

29. John W. Wayland, *The Valley Turnpike Winchester to Staunton and Other Roads*, vol. 6 (Winchester, Va.: Winchester-Frederick County Historical Society, 1967), p. 143.

John Apperson, Diary, March 16–March 19, 1862, VSL.

Frank Jones, Letter to his wife, March 19, 1862, Ann Cary Randolph Jones Papers, 451 THL, HL.

Elisha Franklin Paxton, Letter to his wife, March 19, 1862, in John G. Paxton, ed., *Memoir and Memorials, Elisha Franklin Paxton Brigadier-General, C. S. A.*, (New York: The Neale Publishing Company, 1907), p. 53.

30. Thomas J. Jackson, Letter to Turner Ashby, March 19, 1862, in Averitt, *Memoirs of Turner Ashby and his Compeers*, p. 400.

Pendleton, Letter to his mother, March 21, 1862, VMHB, p. 340.

31. Joseph E. Johnston, Letter to Major General Jackson, March 19, 1862, Thomas J. Jackson Papers, VHS.

This is the only contemporary evidence for Johnston describing Jackson's mission in the Valley. The word "prudence" indicates that Johnston did not wish Stonewall to hazard a battle. This is clearly stated in Johnston's memoirs (see reference note 39), but Jackson may have not interpreted it the same way.

32. Robert E. Lee, Telegraph to Joseph E. Johnston, March 20, 1862, Telegraph Book, Lee Headquarter Papers, series 2, VHS.

33. Ezra J. Warner, *Generals in Gray, Lives of the Confederate Commanders* (Baton Rouge, Louisiana: Louisiana State University Press, 1959), p. 80.

Robert K. Krick, *Lee's Colonels* (Dayton, Ohio: Morningside Bookshop, 1979), p. 66.

Frank Jones, Diary, March 20, 1862, HL.

John H. Grabill (33rd Va.), Diary, March 20, 1862, Charles Affleck Collection, 36 WFCHS, Box 2, HL.

John Apperson, Diary, March 20,1862, VSL.

34. Jed Hotchkiss, Journal, March 20, 1862, Hotchkiss Journal, LC.

Jed Hotchkiss, Letter to his wife, March 21, 1862, Reel #1, Hotchkiss Papers, LC.

Wayland, *The Valley Turnpike Winchester to Staunton*, p. 144.

Charles W. Turner, ed., *A Reminiscence of John Newton Lyle*, p. 152.

35. Frank Jones, Diary, March 21, 1862, HL.

Jacob Lemly (48th Va.), Diary, March 21, 1862, 1374 THL MMF Lemly, Jacob, HL.

J. Tucker Randolph (21st Va., Co. F), Diary, March 21, 1862, MC.

Apperson, Diary, March 20, 1862, VSL.

Jed Hotchkiss, Journal, March 21, 1862, Hotchkiss Journal, LC.

Pendleton, Letter to his mother, March 21, 1862, VMHB, p. 341.

36. Jed Hotchkiss, Journal, March 21, 1862, Hotchkiss Journal, LC.

OR, XII, pt. 3, p. 835.

Gen. Joseph E. Johnston, *Narrative of Military Operations During the Civil War* (reprint, New York: Da Capo Press, Inc.,1990), p. 107.

According to Joseph E. Johnston, he "suggested" to Jackson that his distance from the Federal army was too great; this may have prompted Stonewall to move northward toward Woodstock. However, Jackson's plan to move northward after acknowledging that a large enemy force was intending to move southward against him is consistent with his aggressive nature.

37. Lewis Owen (14th Indiana), Letter to his cousin, March 22, 1862, David Howell Collection, USAMHI.

D. Ross Miller, Letter dated March 21, 1862.

Mason, Testimony, JCCW, p. 405.

Thomas Clark, Letter to his wife, March 19, 1862, Clark Letters.

M. D., Letter dated March 21, 1862, *The Sandusky Register*, April 1, 1862.

38. Mason, Testimony, JCCW, p. 405.

James W. Abert, Letter to Nathaniel Banks, March 24, 1862, Box 19, Nathaniel P. Banks Papers, LC.

Alpheus Williams, Letter to his daughter, March 30, 1862, *From the Cannon's Mouth*, p. 65.

39. Thomas, *General Turner Ashby: the Centaur of the South*, p. 68.

OR, XII, pt. 1, p. 380.

Johnston, *Narrative of Military Operations*, p. 106.

Robert E. Lee, Telegraph dated March 22, 1862, Telegraph Book, Lee Headquarter Papers, Series 2, VHS.

Johnston's mission for Jackson in the Valley is stated in his memoirs as follows:

"After it had become evident that the Valley was to be invaded by an army too strong to be encountered by Jackson's division, that officer was instructed to endeavor to employ the invaders in the Valley, but without exposing himself to the danger of defeat, by keeping so near the enemy as to prevent him from making any considerable detachment to reenforce McClellan, but not so near that he might be compelled to fight."

40. Georgetown temperature readings, March 22, 1862, National Weather Records.

Averitt, *The Memoirs of General Turner Ashby*, p. 157.

Neese, *Three Years in the Confederate Horse Artillery*, p. 31.

Thomas J. Jackson, Testimony, August 6, 1862, RBGCMP, MC.

James E. Taylor, *With Sheridan up the Shenandoah Valley in 1864: Leaves from a Special Artist's Sketchbook and Diary* (Cleveland, Ohio: The Western Reserve Historical Society, 1989), p. 153.

G. S. F. (1st Michigan Cavalry), Letter dated March 30, 1862, *Detroit Tri-Weekly Tribune*, April 7, 1862.

John Robertson, comp., *Michigan in the War* (Lansing, Michigan: W. S. George & Co.,1882), p. 553.

41. Averitt, *The Memoirs of General Turner Ashby*, p. 159.

Neese, *Three Years in the Confederate Horse Artillery*, p. 31.

OR, XII, pt. 1, pp. 348–349, 355–356.

George Johnson, *The Battle of Kernstown, March 23, 1862, A Paper Read Before the Michigan Commandery of the MOLLUS*, War Paper No. 3 (Detroit, Michigan: Winn & Hammond Printers, 1890), p. 5.

W. L. Frisbee (46th Pa.), Letter dated March 23, 1862, *The Pittsburgh Evening Chronicle*, March 27, 1862.

42. Mrs. Hugh Lee, Diary, March 22, 1862, HL.

John Peyton Clark, Journal, March 22, 1862, HL.

"One Of The Boys" (1st W.Va. Cavalry), Letter dated March 28, 1862 (Wheeling) *Daily Intelligencer*, April 7, 1862.

43. Neese, *Three Years in the Confederate Horse Artillery*, p. 32.

"One of the Boys," Letter dated March 28, 1862, (Wheeling) *Daily Intelligencer*, April 17, 1862.

Jed Hotchkiss, Sketch of section of Valley Turnpike from Winchester to Bartonsville, Hotchkiss Sketchbook, LC, p. 4.

44. James Shields, Letter to Nathaniel P. Banks, March 22, 1862, Box 19, Nathaniel P. Banks Papers, LC.

OR, XII, pt. 3, p. 5.

OR, XII, pt. 1, p. 359.

James Shields, Letter to Milton S. Latham, March 26, 1862, James Shields Papers, USAMHI.

"Justice" (1st W.Va. Artillery), Letter to Augustus Pollock, (Wheeling) *Daily Intelligencer*, May 1, 1862.

45. H. M. McAbee, Testimony, May 22, 1862, JCCW, p. 409.

Neese, *Three Years in the Confederate Horse Artillery*, p. 32.

John Peyton Clark, Journal, March 23, 1862, LC.

46. Warner, *Generals in Blue*, p. 267.

Nathan Kimball Manuscript, Lilly Library, Indiana University, Bloomington, Indiana.

47. George Washington Lambert (14th Indiana), Journal, January 13, 1862, M178, Box 2, Folder 3, IHS.

Charles Gibson (14th Indiana), Letter to his parents, January 8, 1862, Copy at Fredericksburg and Spotsylvania National Military Park, Fredericksburg, Va.

James Oakey (14th Indiana), Letter dated March 27, 1862, *The Daily Express* (Terre-Haute, Indiana), April 5, 1862.

48. Nathan Kimball, "Fighting Jackson at Kernstown," in Robert U. Johnson and Clarence C. Buel, ed., *Battles and Leaders of the Civil War*, vol. 2 Castle, Secaucus, N.J.: Castle), p. 304 (hereafter "Fighting Jackson at Kernstown").

"Wanderee" (Huntington's Battery), Letter dated March 30, 1862, *Daily Toledo Blade*, April 3, 1862.

Frank C. Gibbs (Robinson's Battery), Letter dated March 26, 1862, *Portsmouth Times*, April 12, 1862.

S. F. Forbes (67th Ohio), Letter to his family, March 25, 1862, *Daily Toledo Blade*, April 1, 1862.

J. H. J. (8th Ohio), Letter dated March 26, 1862, *The Sandusky Register*, April 3, 1862.

OR, XII, pt. 1, p. 370.

Neese, *Three Years in the Confederate Horse Artillery*, p. 33.

49. John M. Kitchen File, Nathaniel Banks' Intelligence Reports, RG 393, Entry 223, NA.

    Sketch of Old Front Royal Road, Jed Hotchkiss Sketchbook, LC.

50. Elwood, *Elwood's Stories of the Old Ringgold Cavalry*, pp. 93–94.

    OR, XII, pt. 1, pp. 356–357.

51. OR, XII, pt. 1, pp. 385–386.

    Jackson, Testimony, August 6, 1862, RBGCMP.

52. OR, XII, pt. 1, pp. 380–381.

    Jed Hotchkiss, Journal, March 22, 1862, Hotchkiss Journal, LC.

    Jackson, Testimony, August 6, 1862, RBGCMP.

53. Frank Jones, Diary, March 22, 1862, HL.

    J. Tucker Randolph (21st Va), Diary, March 22, 1862, MC.

54. OR, XII, pt. 3, p. 836.

    William Kinzer, Diary, March 23, 1862, VHS.

    The Confederate States Almanac, and repository of useful knowledge, for 1862 (Vicksburg, Miss.: H. C. Clarke, comp.), pp. 3, 6.

    On March 23, 1862, the sun rose at 6:01 A.M.

    Georgetown and Cumberland temperature statistics, March 23, 1862, National Weather Records.

    At 7:00 A.M., the temperature was read at forty degrees at Georgetown and thirty-seven degrees at Cumberland.

CHAPTER FOUR

1. Mrs. Hugh Lee, Diary, March 23, 1862, HL.

   Quarles, *Some Worthy Lives*, p. 108.

2. Richard S. Skidmore, *The Civil War Journal of Billy Davis* (Greencastle, Indiana: The Nugget Publishers, 1989), p. 116.

3. John F. Moore (29th Ohio), Letter to L. P. Buckley, March 23, 1862, Box 19, Nathaniel P. Banks Papers, LC.

4. 84th Pennsylvania Infantry Regimental Orders and Furlough Book, RG 94, NA.

5. Samuel P. Bates, *Martial Deeds of Pennsylvania* (Philadelphia, Pa.: T. H. Davis & Co., 1876), pp. 541–543.

   Merchant, *Eighty-Fourth Pennsylvania Volunteers*, pp. 18–20.

6. William Murray, Letter to R. M. Flack, March 23, 1862, Box 19, Nathaniel Banks Papers, LC.

7. Officers of the 84th Pennsylvania Volunteer Infantry, Letter to Colonel William G. Murray, March 10, 1862, 84th Pennsylvania Regiment File, RG 19, Pennsylvania Historical and Museum Commission, Harrisburg, Pa.

   The officers did not identify themselves in this letter, but instead closed the note as follows: "(Signed by nearly four-fifths of the officers of the Regiment, and others approve, but will not sign.) The letter sent to Governor Curtin was signed by three officers, Captains R. Horrel, Crissman, and Alex. Frick, who based their arguments on the observation that Murray had not held one battalion drill during five months of service.

   Jacob Peterman, Letter to his father, March 21, 1862, private possession of David Richards, Gettysburg, Pa.

   The letters to Colonel Murray and Major Barrett were written in Martinsburg two weeks before the battle; however, Peterman told his father on March 21, that he believed Murray received his copy "this morning." Peterman told his father that he signed the letter and alluded that the other officers of his company, including Captain Flack, did likewise.

8. Mrs. Hugh Lee, Diary, March 23, 1862, HL.

   Mrs. Cornelia McDonald, *A Diary With Reminiscences of the War and Refugee Life,* p. 42.

9. OR, XII, pt. 3, p. 13.

   Kitchen's claims raises one unanswerable question: How did he know that Jackson was moving northward from Strasburg under the false impression that only a few Union regiments were in Winchester when he (Kitchen) was captured before Stonewall and his division even arrived at Strasburg on the night of March 22?

10. Jeremiah C. Sullivan, Testimony, May 22, 1862, JCCW, pp. 413–414.

    James F. Huntington, "Operations in the Shenandoah Valley, From Winchester to Port Republic, March 10–June 9, 1862," in Theodore F. Dwight, ed. *Papers of the Military Historical Society of Massachusetts,* vol. 1 *(Campaigns in Virginia 1861–1862)* (Wilmington, N.C.: Broadfoot Publishing Co., date unknown), p. 304.

    Jeremiah C. Sullivan, Letter to R. Morris Copeland, March 31, 1862, Box 19, Nathaniel Banks Papers, LC.

11. Sawyer, *Military History of the 8th Ohio Vol. Inf'y,* pp. 40–41.

12. David Lewis (8th Ohio), Letter dated March 26, 1862, *Bucyrus Weekly Journal,* April 4, 1862.

13. Rebecca A. Ebert and Teresa Lazazzera, *Frederick County, Virginia: From the Frontier to the Future, A Pictorial History* (Norfolk, Va.: The Donning Company Publishers, 1988), pp. 16–17.

    Population Schedules of the Eighth Census of the United States, Frederick County, Virginia, 1860, RG 29, M-653, NA, p. 517.

    Taylor, *With Sheridan up the Shenandoah Valley,* p. 144.

    Ibid., p. 146.

    "Volunteer" (7th Ohio), Letter dated March 23, 1862, *Painesville Telegraph,* April 3, 1862.

    Spiegel (67th Ohio), Letter to his family, March 22, 1862, *A Jewish Colonel,* p. 75.

14. 1860 U.S. Population Census of Frederick County, Virginia, p. 518.

    William Couper, *History of the Shenandoah Valley,* vol. 2 (New York: Lewis Historical Publishing Company, Inc., 1952), pp. 875–876.

Couper's history includes a list of the captured Union men taken to Strasburg, Mahaney being the fourteenth name on the list. The list was obtained from "an old wallet belonging to Joseph S. Jackson, one of the prisoners carried away. . . ."

15. Krick, *Lee's Colonels*, p. 263.

   OR, XII, pt. 1, pp. 389–390.

   Samuel J. C. Moore (2nd Virginia), Letter dated May 7, 1888, *Spirit of Jefferson* (Charlestown, Va.), June 12, 1888.

16. Avirett, *The Memoirs of General Turner Ashby*, pp. 154–155, 159.

   Jed Hotchkiss, Sketchbook, Geography and Map Division, LC, p. 4.

   Hotchkiss drew this sketch, depicting the Valley Turnpike from Winchester to Bartonsville, in October of 1862, during the aftermath of the Antietam Campaign. Although Hotchkiss was not a participant at Kernstown, he likely interviewed members of Jackson's division to mark the position of Chew's Blakely gun.

17. David Lewis, Letter dated March 26, 1862, *Bucyrus Weekly Journal*, April 4, 1862.

18. Avirett, *The Memoirs of General Turner Ashby*, pp. 154–155, 159.

   George Washington Lambert (14th Indiana), Diary, March 23, 1862, IHS.

   Jed Hotchkiss, Sketchbook, LC, p. 4.

   Hotchkiss scribbled the time of the battle's opening on this sketch. The ground is elevated behind the house, an ideal location for artillery pieces. The Mahaney house is no longer standing.

19. Sullivan, JCCW, p. 415.

20. Kimball, "Fighting Jackson at Kernstown," p. 304.

21. Sawyer, *Military History of the 9th Ohio Vol. Inf'y*, pp. 40–41.

   OR, XII, pt. 1, pp. 368–369.

22. Quarles, *Some Old Homes in Frederick County, Virginia* (Winchester, Virginia: published by the author, 1971), pp. 234–235.

23. "Sketch of the Battle of Kernstown," Reel #39, Hotchkiss Papers, LC.

   This map is the base map used in the Allan history and is the most recognizable Kernstown map as it is seen in altered forms in secondary accounts (example, Henderson, p. 181). Several errors exist in the base map: most importantly the scale of miles is set two times higher than the actual distance between points. Hotchkiss also places the Mahaney house on the wrong side of the turnpike (he inadvertently places "Jo Mahaney" at the site of the Jere Triplett house), an error he does not make in his sketchbook. Despite the errors, this map is crucial to the understanding of the Kernstown battle for Hotchkiss includes all swamps and fencelines (stone and rail) that are seen between Bartonsville and Winchester.

24. OR, XII, pt. 1, pp. 359, 370, 373.

   Neese, *Three Years in the Confederate Horse Artillery*, p. 33.

25. J. Jeff Parsons (67th Ohio), Letter to friends, March 30, 1862, *Weekly Perrysburg Journal*, April 10, 1862.

   Hiram Treher (5th Ohio), Letter to his father, March 26, 1862, *Chambersburg Valley Spirit*, April 30, 1862.

   W. C. H. (5th Ohio), Letter to his father, March 30, 1862, *Perry County Weekly*, April 16, 1862.

26. Averitt, *The Memoirs of General Turner Ashby,* p. 267

    Jed Hotchkiss, Map of Kernstown Battlefield, Reel #39, Hotchkiss Papers, LC.

    Jed Hotchkiss, Sketchbook, p. 4.

    OR, XII, pt. 1, pp. 360, 368.

27. Kenneth R. Martin and Ralph Linwood Snow, ed., *"I Am Now a Soldier!" The Civil War Diaries of Lorenzo Vanderoef* (Bath, Maine: Patten Free Press, 1990), p. 92.

    OR, XII, pt. 1, pp. 360, 368, 370.

28. Martin and Snow, *The Civil War Diaries of Lorenzo Vanderoef,* p. 93.

    OR, XII, pt. 1, pp. 368, 389.

    Captain Ogle (8th Ohio), Letter dated March 26, 1862, *Tifflin Weekly Tribune,* April 11, 1862.

    S. F. Forbes (67th Ohio), Letter to his family, March 25, 1862, *Daily Toledo Blade,* April 1, 1862.

29. OR, XII, pt. 1, pp. 360, 366, 368, 385, 389.

    William Harrow, Testimony, May 22, 1862, JCCW, p. 412.

30. Kimball, "Fighting Jackson at Kernstown," p. 305.

    OR, XII, pt. 1, p. 341.

31. William Kepler, *History of the Three Month and Three Years Service from April 16th 1861, to June 22d, 1864, of the Fourth Regiment Ohio Volunteer Infantry in the War for the Union* (Cleveland, Ohio: Leader Printing Company, 1886), p. 59.

    Mason, Testimony, JCCW, p. 406.

32. Kimball, "Fighting Jackson at Kernstown," p. 305.

33. H. E. S. (5th Ohio), Letter to his brother, March 25, 1862, *Cincinnati Daily Commercial,* April 8, 1862.

    James M. King (13th Indiana), Journal, IHS.

    OR, XII, pt. 1, pp. 372–373.

    Oscar Rudd (39th Illinois), Journal, March 23, 1862, Typescript copy at Fredericksburg and Spotsylvania National Military Park, Fredericksburg, Va.

    Charles M. Clark, *The History of the Thirty-Ninth Regiment Illinois,* pp. 73–75.

    Hiram Treher, Letter to his father, March 26, 1862, *The Chambersburg Valley Spirit,* April 30, 1862.

    Rudd's account places the 62nd Ohio on the extreme left followed on their right by the 39th Illinois. The other accounts suggest a reverse alignment. The latter seems more likely as the 62nd Ohio is called upon to attack Sandy Ridge at the end of the day, they apparently being the closest available unit. Neither the 62nd Ohio nor the 39th Illinois registered any casualties at Kernstown.

34. OR, XII, pt. 1, pp. 357–358.

    "Cosmus" (1st Ohio Cavalry), Letter dated March 31, 1862, *The* (Harrisburg, Pa.) *Patriot & Union,* April 12, 1862.

35. H. E. S. Letter dated March 25, 1862, *Cincinnati Daily Commercial,* April 8, 1862.

    OR, XII, pt. 1, p. 373.

36. Neese, *Three Years in the Confederate Horse Artillery,* pp. 33–34.

37. Massachusetts Adjutant-General's Report, January 1863, Public Document No. 7, p. 374.

The Massachusetts Register, 1862, Containing a Record of the Government and Institution of the State Together with a Very Complete Account of the Massachusetts Volunteer, Series #94, (Adams Sampson and Co., 1862), pp. 406–407.

"The Andrew Sharpshooters," Lander Family Papers, Box 1, Folder 1, Stanford University Libraries, Stanford, California.

James H. Simpson (14th Indiana), "Battle of Kernstown," *The National Tribune*, February 4, 1882.

Neese, *Three Years in the Confederate Horse Artillery*, p. 33.

38. OR, XII, pt. 1, pp. 368, 389–390.

39. Ibid.

A. H. Nickerson (8th Ohio), Letter dated April 13, 1888, *Shepherdstown* (W.Va.) *Register*, May 18, 1888.

Samuel J. C. Moore (2nd Virginia), Letter dated May 7, 1888, *Spirit of Jefferson* (Charlestown, Va.), June 12, 1888.

Nickerson was an officer in Company I, 8th Ohio. This company was not engaged at Kernstown (detached at Winchester). Nickerson likely stole away from the company to fight with his regiment. His account agrees closely with Moore's. Link died in 1874; he apparently told Nickerson who he shot, but time erased the name from Nickerson's memory, inducing him to write about it again in 1888. Samuel Moore believed that Nickerson thought he injured Captain Nadenbousch. He assured the Union veteran that this did not occur, but was unable to help him any further in his pursuit.

40. OR, XII, pt. 1, pp. 367–371.

Martin and Snow, *The Civil War Diaries of Lorenzo Vanderoef*, p. 93.

Harrow, Testimony, JCCW, p. 412.

Captain T. M. Kirkpatrick (13th Indiana), Letter to his wife, *Howard Tribune*, April 8, 1862.

41. OR, XII, pt. 1, pp. 369, 373.

Neese, *Three Years in the Confederate Horse Artillery*, p. 34.

Martin and Snow, *The Civil War Diaries of Lorenzo Vanderoef*, p. 93.

Hiram Treher (5th Ohio), Letter to his father, March 26, 1862, *Chambersburg Valley Spirit*, April 30, 1862.

W. C. H. (5th Ohio), Letter to his father, March 30, 1862, *Perry County Weekly*, April 16, 1862.

Theodore F. Lang, *Loyal West Virginia from 1861 to 1865: with an Introductory Chapter on the Status of Virginia for Thirty Years Prior to the War* (Baltimore, Md.: The Deutsch Publishing Co., 1895), p. 311.

Kimball's after-battle report places Robinson's Ohio battery east of the Pike, a claim refuted by Daum's report and other artillery accounts.

42. W. C. H. (5th Ohio), Letter to his father, March 30, 1962.

Frank (5th Ohio), Letter dated March 29, 1862, *The Cincinnati Times*, April 8, 1862.

Hiram Treher, (5th Ohio), Letter to his father, March 26, 1862.

F. C. Gibbs (Robinson's Battery), Letter dated March 26, 1862, *Portsmouth Times*, April 12, 1862.

OR, XII, pt. 3, p. 5.

J. Jeff Parsons (67th Ohio), Letter to his friends, March 30, 1862, *Weekly Perrysburg Journal*, April 10, 1862.

Shields's March 17 division report is the only available estimate of the number of artillerists who manned their guns on Pritchard's Hill. Accounting for the two cannons from Jenks's battery not used on March 23, then it seems reasonable that at noon approximately 300 Union artillerists occupied the knoll. Shields's report mistakingly identifies Robinson's battery as all smooth-bores; Gibbs's letter acknowledges that rifled and unrifled pieces were used.

43. OR, XII, pt. 1, pp. 368–369.

44. Mason, Testimony, JCCW, p. 406.

45. Nathan Kimball, Letter dated March 20, 1864, U.S. Army General's Report of Civil War Service, Roll M1098, Vol. 3, NA, p. 871.

CHAPTER FIVE

1. OR, XII, pt. 1, p. 396.

   Edward A. Moore, *The Story of a Cannoneer Under Stonewall Jackson* (Lynchburg, Va.: J. P. Bell, Inc., 1910), p. 30.

   Hotchkiss Journal, March 23, 1862, Hotchkiss Papers, LC.

   William Kinzer, Diary, March 23, 1862, VHS.

   W. G. Bean, *The Liberty Hall Volunteers: Stonewall's College Boys* (Berryville, Virginia: The University Press of Virginia, 1964), pp. 104–105.

2. Henry S. Shanklin (27th Va.), Letter to his father, March 31, 1862, MS #25688, VSL.

   Frank Jones, Diary, March 23, 1862, HL.

   John H. Worsham, *One of Jackson's Foot Cavalry* (New York: The Neale Publishing Company, 1912), p. 66.

   Richard B. Garnett, Official Report of the Battle of Kernstown, RBGCMP, pp. 1–2.

   The distance stated in Confederate accounts between their Cedar Creek camps to Bartonsville varies between twelve and fifteen miles. The actual distance between Cedar Creek and Opequon Creek crossings of the Valley Turnpike is ten miles. The campsites were likely within one to two miles of Cedar Creek. Therefore, the marching pace for Jackson's division was less than two miles per hour, a leisurely pace for tired troops who were not expecting a battle.

3. Jed Hotchkiss, Map of Kernstown, Reel #39, Hotchkiss Papers, LC.

   Jed Hotchkiss, Sketchbook, LC, p. 4.

   OR, XII, pt. 1, p. 387.

4. Jackson, Testimony, August 6, 1862, RBGCMP, pp. 1–2.

   Jackson likely stayed to the west of the pike during his reconnaissance and advanced to the heights a few hundred yards south of Opequon Church, perhaps near the Mahaney house from where Federal infantry had recently retreated. Turner Ashby's official report states "Upon falling back . . . I received your order to prepare for an advance and learned that your force had arrived." This strongly suggests that Ashby never communicated directly with Jackson; instead he likely received orders through Jackson's aides. Averitt, in his Ashby biography, makes a fleeting reference to Jackson conversing with Ashby; however, he makes it appear that this occurred later in the afternoon. No other reports link Jackson in direct conversation with Ashby—an unusual occurrence for a commanding general to neglect an active subordinate with valuable information concerning enemy strength.

It is likely that at least one of Jackson's aides accompanied him on his reconnaissance. George Junkin was a Hollidaysburg, Pennsylvania native (as was Colonel William Murray, 84th Pa.). He was a cousin of Jackson's first wife. See W. G. Bean, "The Unusual Experience of Lieutenant George G. Junkin, C.S.A." VMHB, vol. 76, April 1968, p. 181.

5. OR, XII, pt. 1, p. 381.

Thomas J. Jackson, Letter to his wife, April 11, 1862, in *Life and Letters*, p. 249.

Jackson acknowledged to his wife that he "was greatly concerned" about attacking on Sunday.

6. Johnston, *Narrative of Military Operations*, p. 106.

7. Shanklin, Letter to his father, March 31, 1862, VSL.

OR, XII, pt. 1, p. 381.

8. OR, XII, pt. 1, p. 408.

All references to time for the Battle of Kernstown will be estimated by the author. This is made necessary by the variance and discrepancies that exist in letters and reports of participants. Using all these accounts from both sides, the best estimate will be provided. For example, Jackson's arrival on the field varies between 1:00 and 3:00 P.M. Based on the time required for subsequent actions to occur and the time mentioned in reports of these actions, it is most likely that Jackson began his movements from Bartonsville at 1:30 P.M. For an excellent explanation about how time was kept (and the discrepancies existing in these methods), see Arthur Candenquist, "Did Anyone Really Know What Time It Was?" *Blue & Gray Magazine*, 8 (6), 1991, pp. 32–35.

9. OR, XII, pt. 1, pp. 387, 391.

Garnett, Report, RBGCMP, p. 1.

Richard B. Garnett, Letter to Samuel Cooper, June 20, 1862, RBGCMP, p. 3.

Frank Jones, Diary, March 23, 1862, HL.

10. Pendleton, Testimony, August 7, 1862, RBGCMP, pp. 15–16.

Garnett, Letter to Cooper, RBGCMP, p. 3.

11. Jed Hotchkiss, Sketchbook, LC, p. 4.

Pendleton, Testimony, RBGCMP, pp. 19–20.

L. (Rockbridge Artillery), "The Battle of Barton's Mills," *Lexington Gazette*, April 3, 1862.

Clement D. Fishburne, "Historical Sketch of the Rockbridge Artillery, C. S. Army, by a Member of the Famous Battery," SHSP, Vol. 23, 1895, p. 130.

12. OR, XII, pt. 1, p. 401.

Allan, *Stonewall Jackson's Valley Campaign*, p. 231.

13. Garnett, Letter to Cooper, RBGCMP, p. 5.

14. OR, XII, pt. 1, p. 408.

Jed Hotchkiss, Kernstown Map, Reel #39, Hotchkiss Papers, LC.

15. S. Bassett French, Virginia Biographies: Samuel Vance Fulkerson, VSL, pp. 218–219.

Walker, *Memorial, Virginia Military Institute*, pp. 210–216.

Douglas, *I Rode with Stonewall*, p. 64.

T. J. Jackson, Letter dated July 17, 1862, in *The Confederate Philatelist*, January–February 1990, p. 2.

16. Georgetown, D.C. temperature readings, 2:00 P.M., March 23, 1862, National Weather Records.

Strother, *Harper's*, p. 186.

The temperature at Georgetown, D.C. was recorded at fifty-two degrees at 2:00 P.M. Strother's entry for March 23 began with a one-word sentence: "Clouds."

17. OR, XII, pt. 1, p. 408.

George C. Pile (37th Va.), "The War Story of a Confederate Soldier Boy," *Bristol Herald-Courier*, January 23–February 27, 1921.

This twentieth-century newspaper feature was credited to Oliver Taylor. He apparently was the newspaperman who submitted the piece; Pile was the soldier who wrote the story.

United States Department of the Interior, Geological Survey Map, Winchester Quadrangle.

Jed Hotchkiss, Kernstown Map, Hotchkiss Papers, LC.

Garnett, Report, RBGCMP, p. 2.

All known secondary descriptions of the Battle of Kernstown leave one with the assumption that Fulkerson was not ordered to attack Union batteries, but instead was moving onto Sandy Ridge. The "Hotchkiss Map" in William Allan's campaign history may have been the original source of this misinterpretation. Fortunately, Hotchkiss's original map sketchings for the book survive in his personal collection at the Library of Congress and clearly depict the route of the 23rd, 37th, and 33rd Virginia moving due north toward Pritchard's Hill, then turning sharply westward. Both Fulkerson's and Garnett's reports confirm this. It is likely that during the final processing of the Hotchkiss maps for the Allan book, a lithographer smoothed out the route and left the impression that the two regiments of Fulkerson's brigade were heading toward Sandy Ridge the entire time. The 33rd Virginia was removed from the final version and the name "27th" Virginia was inadvertently placed where the 37th Virginia should have been. It is surprising that even without the contrary evidence that this route was never questioned. Why would Fulkerson's brigade move toward Sandy Ride on a circuitous route that placed his right flank 500 yards directly in front of Daum's artillery, when he could have simply taken the road that led from Barton's Woods directly to Sandy Ridge—five hundred yards farther south of Union artillery? The fact that Fulkerson was not initially heading to Sandy Ridge is also confirmed by the fact that his regiments were not the first Confederate infantry units to reach the heights. Jackson's report omits the entire interlude of the assault of Pritchard's Hill.

18. Garnett, Letter to Cooper, RBGCMP, pp. 3–4, 15.

19. OR, XII, pt. 1, p. 359.

Hiram Treher (5th Ohio), Letter to his father, March 26, 1862, *Chambersburg Valley Spirit*, April 30, 1862.

J. Jeff Parsons (67th Ohio), Letter dated March 30, 1862, *Weekly Perrysburg Journal*, April 10, 1862.

J. H. J. (8th Ohio), Letter dated March 26, 1862, *The Sandusky Register*, April 3, 1862.

G. S. F. (1st Michigan Cavalry), Letter dated March 30, 1862, *Detroit Tri-Weekly Tribune*, April 7, 1862.

Thomas C. Fowler (84th Pa.), "Criticizing Capehart. The Troops that Captured the Stonewall at Kernstown," *The National Tribune*, May 16, 1889.

20. Hiram Treher (5th Ohio), Letter to his father, March 26, 1862, *Chambersburg Valley Spirit*, April 30, 1862.

G. S. F. (1st Michigan Cavalry), Letter dated March 30, 1862, *Detroit Tri-Weekly Tribune*, April 7, 1862.

"Justice," (1st W.Va. Artillery), Letter to Augustus Pollack (Wheeling) *Daily Intelligencer*, May 1, 1862.

21. OR, XII, pt. 1, p. 408.

James W. Orr (37th Va.), "Recollections of the War Between the States," 1909, VSL, p. 3.

Major G. C. Coleman (23rd Virginia), Letter to his wife, March 25, 1862. Unfiled manuscript at the Museum of the Confederacy. The author is indicated to Rob Hodge of Alexandria, Virginia, for finding the Coleman letter.

"Report of the Killed and Wounded serving in the Army of the Valley of Virginia — in the engagement of the 23rd March 1862 — near Winchester Va." Thomas J. Jackson Papers, Folder 3, Mss7:1J1385:1, VHS.

The casualty list reveals the names of the killed and wounded and a brief description of the location of the injury on their bodies. Although Fulkerson's men were involved in the infantry fight later in the afternoon, the description of the wounds are more consistent with artillery casualties. Many lower body and abdominal wounds are noted. This is unlikely to have occurred behind the stone wall they fought behind later in the day (see Chapter Six). A discussion with James Tubessing, a local inhabitant who relic hunted on Sandy Ridge in the 1960s, reveals that very few bullets were found near Fulkerson's segment of the line. This is more evidence that the 23rd and 37th Virginia took most of their casualties near Pritchard's Hill rather than on Sandy Ridge.

22. OR, XII, pt. 1, p. 408.

W. C. H. (5th Ohio), Letter to his father, March 30, 1862, *Perry County Weekly*, April 16, 1862.

23. OR, XII, pt. 1, pp. 358, 408.

Frank C. Gibbs (Robinson's battery), Letter dated March 26, 1862, *Portsmouth Times*, April 12, 1862.

G. S. F. (1st Michigan Cavalry), Letter dated March 30, 1862, *Detroit Tri-Weekly Tribune*, April 7, 1862.

24. Garnett, Report, RBGCMP, pp. 2–3.

Garnett, Letter to Cooper, RBGCMP, pp. 4–6.

OR, XII, pt. 1, p. 395.

Exactly where Garnett and the 33rd Virginia positioned themselves on Sandy Ridge is open to debate. Colonel Cummings's report of the activities of the 33rd Virginia states that his regiment "crossed a ridge running northeast and southwest, and occupied by our artillery." Garnett states that he "reached the opposite side of the ridge." These statements suggest that they crossed over Sandy Ridge; however, Garnett also mentions that Fulkerson's men were 200 to 300 yards in front of him (Fulkerson rested in the woods at the eastern slope of the ridge). Sandy Ridge contained many spurs and swales. By this evidence, it appears that Garnett tucked his men in a protective area on the eastern slope of the ridge and did not cross over the crest since that would have carried him an additional 200 yards away from Fulkerson and would have separated him from the rest of his brigade.

25. Garnett, Letter to Samuel Cooper, pp. 4–5.

In the letter, Garnett stated "I thought he [Jackson] might have changed the disposition of the troops which had not come up."

26. Pendleton, Testimony, RBGCMP, p. 16.

Specification notes, RBGCMP, p. 1.

These three pages of notes were prepared to defend Garnett against each specification against him for his court-martial trial. Although the handwriting resembles Garnett's, it appears the notes were taken by his aide Lieutenant Elliott Johnston. Evidence for this is provided in the notes to specification number three: "Genl. G., Col. Grigsby, and I accompanied. . . ."

27. OR, XII, pt. 1, pp. 383, 387–390.

Frank Jones, Diary, March 23, 1862, HL.

28. John N. Lyle (4th Va.), "Stonewall Jackson's Guard, the Washington College Company, or Imperialism in the American Union," Washington and Lee University, pp. 395–396.

Charles W. Turner, ed., *A Reminiscence of Lieutenant John Newton Lyle,* p. 159.

Lyle makes several references to "archive" wagons in his memoirs. The content of the archive and supply wagons is not specifically known. It can be assumed that small arms ammunition was in one of them.

29. Charles W. Tuner, ed., *A Reminiscence of Lieutenant John Newton Lyle,* p. 158.

OR, XII, pt. 1, pp. 390–391.

Colonel Ronald stated, "The regiment numbered 203, rank and file, when the engagement commenced." He likely took morning roll in Barton's Woods, before the College company joined them; therefore, they may have taken about 240 men into the battle.

Georgetown, D.C. temperature readings, 2:00 P.M., March 23, 1862, National Weather Records.

30. John N. Lyle (4th Va.), "Stonewall Jackson's Guard, the Washington College, or Imperialism in the American Union," p. 396.

Hugh White (4th Virginia), Letter to his father, March 29, 1862 in William S. White, ed., *Sketches of the Life of Captain Hugh A. White* (Columbia, S.C.: South Carolina Steam Press, 1864), p. 79.

31. OR, XII, pt. 1, pp. 385–387, 389.

George Baylor, *Bull Run to Bull Run or Four Years in the Army of Northern Virginia* (Richmond, Va.: B. F. Johnston, 1900), p. 36.

Baylor commanded one of the companies in Funsten's detachment. His account suggests that Jackson originally intended on using twenty men from his company to support Fulkerson's attack of Pritchard's Hill ("When the call was made it was accompanied with the report that Jackson wanted the men to charge that battery. . . ."). Fortunately for the cavalrymen, Jackson changed his mind, perhaps after watching the Federals thwart his plan. Baylor continued, "Great was our relief, however, when on reporting to General Jackson, we were directed by him to take position on the extreme left. . . ."

32. Thomas, *General Turner Ashby: the Centaur of the South,* pp. 63–64.

The Thrasher story in this book was provided by J. P. West, a cavalier in Company G.

33. Avirett, *The Memoirs of General Turner Ashby*, pp. 162–163.

34. OR, XII, pt. 1, pp. 358, 360, 363, 364, 368.

 Avirett, *The Memoirs of General Turner Ashby*, p. 160.

 Eby, *A Virginia Yankee in the Civil War*, p. 25.

 David Hunter Strother was not saddened upon hearing of Thrasher's death. Strother's father was imprisoned by the Confederates earlier in the year. The elder Strother was held in a cold, wet cell for five days until finally released. He died in January, shortly after arriving home. Upon hearing of Thrasher's death on April 2, David Hunter Strother entered the following into his journal: " . . .Tad Thrasher was killed at the Battle of Winchester. He fell with two wounds. There is some poetry in this. He is the man who arrested my father and stole my guns. This account is settled."

35. OR, XII, pt. 1, pp. 399, 401, 405.

 Pendleton, Testimony, RBGCMP, p. 16.

36. C. A. Fornerden, *A Brief History of the Military Career of Carpenter's Battery: From its organization as a rifle company under the name of the Alleghany Roughs to the ending of the war between the states* (New Market, Va.: Henkel & Company Printers, 1911), p. 20.

 OR, XII, pt. 1, p. 399.

37. Hiram Treher (5th Ohio), Letter to his father, March 26, 1862, *Chambersburg Valley Spirit*, April 30, 1862.

38. OR, XII, pt. 1, pp. 396, 402.

 Shanklin, Letter, March 31, 1862, VSL.

 Frank Jones, Diary, March 23, 1862, HL.

39. Edward A. Moore, *The Story of a Cannoneer Under Stonewall Jackson*, p. 30.

 OR, XII, pt. 1, p. 402.

40. Shanklin, Letter, March 31, 1862, VSL.

 OR, XII, pt. 1, p. 396

 G. K. Bedinger, Letter to his father, April 1, 1862, Bedinger-Dandridge Family Papers, DU.

 L. (Rockbridge Artillery), "The Battle of Barton's Mills," *Lexington Gazette*, April 3, 1862.

 Fishburne, *Memoirs*, p. 131

 Worsham, *One of Jackson's Foot Cavalry*, p. 67.

 Edward A. Moore, *The Story of a Cannoneer Under Stonewall Jackson*, p. 31

 "Notae" (7th Ohio), Letter dated March 29, 1862, *Lawrenceville Journal*, April 20, 1862.

 Both artillerists died within twenty-four hours of the incident. Worsham's version of this oft-cited incident makes it appear that a member of his company pounced on the shell. This is not realistic since the other accounts clearly demonstrate that the round exploded in one of the horses. It is possible that Worsham recollects another unexploded shell that his mate carried away as a trophy.

41. Fishburne, *Memoirs*, p. 31.

L. (Rockbridge Artillery), "The Battle of Barton's Mills," *Lexington Gazette*, April 3, 1862.

Edward A. Moore, *The Story of a Cannoneer Under Stonewall Jackson*, p. 31.

OR, XII, pt. 1, p. 396.

42.　Garnett, Letter to Samuel Cooper, RBGCMP, pp. 5–6.

Garnett, Report, RBGCMP, p. 3.

In his letter, Garnett states that he saw the batteries "moving along the ridge *under which I was marching.*" (emphasis added). Garnett states in his report: "Returning with the Thirty-third it was found that Captain McLaughlin's Battery was moving along the ridge, on the west side of which the Thirty-third Regiment and Colonel Fulkerson's troops were." At first glance, this report appears to state that the infantry moved to the west of the battery (below the spur, not on it); however the wording may also suggest that the battery was on the west of the ridge along which the 33rd and Fulkerson moved. When Garnett found Fulkerson, the two may have moved their three regiments back in a westerly direction that took them west of the battery. However, Garnett's objective was to link with the rest of the brigade. He thought they were still in Barton's Woods. Therefore, the return was taking them away from the infantry. This may have been done to hide the troops from Federal artillery.

43.　John S. Bowman, ed., *The Civil War Almanac* (New York: World Almanac Publications, 1983), p. 295.

OR, XII, pt. 1, pg. 393, 396–400.

Shanklin, Letter, March 31, 1862, VSL.

According to tables of fire, the maximum range of twelve-pounders was approximately one mile with solid shot, and no more than 1300 yards (three-quarters of a mile) with spherical case shot and shell (at five degrees of elevation). The maximum range of a six-pounder was 1200 to 1500 yards, depending on the type of ammunition fired. The height of the ridges and a higher elevation may have improved the distance of fire. Rifled pieces can hit targets at distances of over one mile (2,000-plus yards), as proven by Daum's guns on Pritchard's Hill. The Rockbridge Artillery carried eight guns to Kernstown: three ten-pounder Parrotts (rifled), one Tredegar iron gun, three bronze six-pounders, and one twelve-pounder howitzer (all smoothbores) (see Fishburne, *Historical Sketch of the Rockbridge Artillery*, SHSP 23, pp. 130–135). McLaughlin claimed that a rifled piece was disabled while advancing to Sandy Ridge, Fishburne believed it was the Tredegar gun. McLaughlin's report was written six days after the battle; Fishburne's history was written thirty years after the war.

It is unknown how many cannons Captain Carpenter rolled onto Sandy Ridge. He states he brought two of his four guns to join General Jackson south of Opequon Church. Those same two pieces were taken to the height. The deployment of the other two pieces of his battery has not been ascertained. They may have stayed in reserve at the Valley Pike.

44.　John S. Mason, Testimony, May 22, 1862, JCCW, p. 407.

45.　Nathaniel P. Banks, Telegram to Seth Williams, March 23, 1862, Reel 19, #9963, McClellan Papers, LC.

Banks specifically states the time in his apologetic telegram: "I intended to report at Head Quarters to-morrow for instructions and left Winchester at 3 pm for that purpose—everyone was confident the enemy had retired."

46.　OR, XII, pt. 1, p. 359.

Frank C. Gibbs (Robinson's battery), Letter dated March 26, 1862, *Portsmouth Times*, April 12, 1862.

William Gallagher (84th Pa.), Letter to his parents, April 22, 1862, William Gallagher Pension File, NA.

J. Jeff Parsons (67th Ohio), Letter dated March 30, 1862, *Weekly Perrysburg Journal*, April 10, 1862.

J. H. J. (8th Ohio), Letter dated March 26, 1862, *The Sandusky Register*, April 3, 1862.

Gibbs's description of the decapitation of one of his artillerists is suspiciously similar to the one suffered by a member of Davey's battery witnessed by the 5th Ohio earlier in the day. Interestingly, no casualties are reported for Davey's battery, and Nathan Kimball's report states that Robinson's battery moved east of the Valley Pike in the morning. Despite these samples of contrary evidence, it is still more likely that the Robinson's battery casualty occurred at 3:00 P.M. and Davey's battery suffered a similar casualty earlier in the day. The weight of the available accounts lean in this direction, particularly from Lieutenant Gibbs who claimed that his battery occupied Pritchard's Hill "for about five hours" before the redeployment occurred. The 5th Ohio witnesses agree that the artillery casualty they saw occurred in the morning. Therefore it is most likely that both Davey's battery and Robinson's battery had members who were beheaded by Confederate artillery rounds.

47. John S. Mason, Testimony, JCCW, p. 407.

Most of the destruction on Pritchard's Hill would have been caused by the two working rifled guns of the Rockbridge Artillery. The other eleven Confederate cannons on Sandy Ridge were smoothbores. Their shots may have occasionally reached Pritchard's Hill (sometimes causing additional destruction by bouncing), but the distance between the heights limited the effectiveness of Confederate smoothbores.

CHAPTER SIX

1. Thomas Clark, Letter to his wife, March 7, 1862, Clark Letters.

2. Wilson, *Itinerary of the Seventh Ohio Volunteer Infantry*, p. 365.

   Ezra J. Warner, *Generals in Blue: Lives of the Union Commanders* (Baton Rouge: Louisiana State University Press, 1964), p. 515.

   Whitelaw Reid, *Ohio in the War: Her Statesmen, Generals and Soldiers*, pp. 831–833.

   Granville College today is known as Denison University.

3. Wilson, *Itinerary of the Seventh Ohio Volunteer Infantry*, p. 632.

   Jacob D. Cox, "McClellan in West Virginia," *Battles and Leaders of the Civil War*, vol. 1 (Secaucus, N.J.: Castle), pp. 143–144.

   W. D. S. (7th Ohio), Letter dated August 31, 1861, *Painesville Telegraph*, September 12, 1861.

4. Sifakis, *Who Was Who in the Civil War*, p. 665.

   Thomas Clark, Letter to his wife, March 28, 1862, Clark Letters.

5. S. M. (1st W.Va.), Letter dated March 29, 1862, (Wheeling) *Daily Intelligencer*, April 8, 1862.

6. John S. Cooper (7th Ohio), "The Shenandoah Valley in Eighteen Hundred and Sixty-Two," Military Essays and Recollections, vol. 5, *Military Order of the Loyal*

Legion of the United States - Illinois Commandery (Chicago: Cozzens & Beaton Company, 1907), pp. 45–46.

7. Colonel William D. Lewis (110th Pa.), Letter to Governor A. G. Curtin, March 30, 1862, 110th Pennsylvania Regiment File, RG 19, Pennsylvania Historical and Museum Commission, Harrisburg, Pa.

8. George Wood (7th Ohio), Diary, March 28, 1862, OHS.

    S. M., Letter dated March 29, 1862, (Wheeling) *Daily Intelligencer*, April 8, 1862.

    William D. Lewis, Letter to Governor A. G. Curtin, March 30, 1862.

9. Kimball, "Fighting Jackson at Kernstown," p. 306.

    William S. Young (7th Indiana), "Shenandoah Valley. Criticizing Gen. Capehart's Article on That Campaign," *The National Tribune*, April 18, 1889.

    James H. Simpson (14th Indiana), "Criticizing Capehart—Who Took the Stonewall at Kernstown?", *The National Tribune*, May 9, 1889.

    Starting in the March 21, 1889, issue of *The National Tribune*, former 1st West Virginia Cavalry surgeon Henry Capehart wrote a series of nine weekly articles covering the actions of Shields's division in the Valley. His accounts generated a flood of responses from soldiers who remembered the events of twenty-seven years earlier a little differently than Capehart did. Those responses, including the ones cited above, became a valuable source of information concerning regiment-level actions at Kernstown.

10. "Volunteer" (V. E. Smalley, 7th Ohio), Letter dated March 30, 1862, *Painesville Telegraph*, April 10, 1862.

    Wilson, *Itinerary of the Seventh Ohio Volunteer Infantry*, p. 135.

11. Dr. H. M. McAbee, Testimony, May 22, 1862, JCCW, p. 411.

    OR, XII, pt. 1, p. 360.

    Kimball's report states " . . . At this juncture I ordered the Third Brigade . . . to move to the right to gain the flank of the enemy." McAbee's testimony makes it clear that Shields was oblivious to what opposed his division until after 3:00 P.M. Although it is not known exactly what the dispatch that Shields received at this time contained, it can be assumed that the message told him that Jackson was present in force on the Union flank.

12. OR, XII, pt. 1, pp. 366, 369–370, 373.

    Neese, *Three Years in the Confederate Horse Artillery*, p. 35.

    Alexander Read (84th Pa.), Letter dated March 26, 1862, *Clearfield Republican*, April 16, 1862.

13. OR, XII, pt. 3, pp. 4–5.

    See Appendix B for strength of Union forces at Kernstown.

14. OR, XII, pt. 1, pp. 357, 359.

    Elizabeth Davis Swiger, ed., *Civil War Letters and Diary of Joshua Winters: A Private in the Union Army Company G, First Western Virginia Volunteer Infantry* (Parsons, W.Va.: McClain Printing Company, 1991), p. 31.

    William D. Lewis, Letter to Governor Curtin, p. 2.

    "Volunteer," Letter dated March 30, 1862, *Painesville Telegraph*, April 10, 1862.

15. Quarles, *Some Worthy Lives*, p. 100.

    Garland R. Quarles, *Some Old Homes in Frederick County, Virginia* (Winchester, Va.: Winchester-Frederick County Historical Society, 1990), p. 108.

16. James H. Simpson, "Criticizing Capehart," *The National Tribune*, May 9, 1889.

OR, XII, pt. 1, pp. 364–365.

Jed Hotchkiss, Cover Page, Hotchkiss Sketchbook, LC.

This page is entitled "Sketch Book of Jed Hotchkiss Capt of Top Eng . . . 2nd Corps Army of Virginia" and includes a sketch below the title. The sketch is Sandy Ridge in detail, showing all the fencing that existed on the ridge in October of 1862, the month Hotchkiss drew the sketch. Today some of the stone walls are intact; many of the rail fences have been replaced by wire fences running in the same location. The field is more overgrown today compared to 1862 and a bypass route cuts into the eastern portion of the height. Fortunately, the highway does not cut into areas where the heaviest fighting occurred.

17. Anonymous soldier (7th Ohio), Undated letter and sketch published in *Painesville Telegraph*, April 10, 1862.

18. G. B. (1st W.Va.), Letter dated March 27, 1862, (Wheeling) *Daily Intelligencer*, April 2, 1862.

William S. Young (7th Indiana), "Shenandoah Valley: Criticizing Gen. Capehart's Article on that Campaign," *The National Tribune*, April 18, 1889.

19. OR, XII, pt. 1, p. 357.

W. J. Curry, *Four Years in the Saddle. History of the First Regiment Ohio Volunteer Cavalry. War of the Rebellion—1861–1865* (Jonesboro, Ga.: Freedom Hill Press, Inc., ca. 1898), p. 236.

20. "Notae" (7th Ohio), "From Shield's Division, March 29, 1862," *Lawrenceville (Pa.) Journal,* April 12, 1862.

21. Wilson, *Itinerary of the Seventh Ohio Volunteer Infantry*, p. 131.

E. B. Howard (29th Ohio), Letter dated April 1, 1862, *Conneant Reporter*, April 9, 1862.

P. A. B. (1st W.Va.), Letter dated April 6, 1862, (Wheeling) *Daily Intelligencer*, April 15, 1862.

G. B. (1st W.Va.), Letter dated March 27, 1862, (Wheeling) *Daily Intelligencer*, April 2, 1862.

22. Thomas Clark, Letter to his wife, March 27, 1862, Clark Letters.

23. "Justice" (1st W.Va. Artillery), Letter to Augustus Pollack, (Wheeling) *Daily Intelligencer*, May 1, 1862.

Cooper, "The Shenandoah Valley in Eighteen Hundred and Sixty-Two," p. 48.

"Volunteer," Letter dated March 30, 1862, *Painesville Telegraph*, April 10, 1862.

24. OR, XII, pt. 1, p. 393.

Charles A. Wingerter, *History of Greater Wheeling and Vicinity: A Chronicle of Progress and Narrative Account of the Industries, Institutions and People of the City and Tributary Territory*, vol. 1 (Chicago: Lewis Publishing Company, 1912), pp. 199–201.

"W." (27th Virginia), Undated letter, *Richmond Daily Dispatch*, April 2, 1862.

25. Swiger, ed., *Civil War Letters and Diary of Joshua Winters*, p. 32.

P. A. B., Letter, (Wheeling) *Daily Intelligencer*, April 15, 1862.

Anonymous Soldier (7th Ohio), *Painesville Telegraph*, April 10, 1862.

Captain J. F. Asper (Co. H, 7th Ohio), Letter dated March 26, 1862, *Western Reserve Chronicle*, April 2, 1862.

26. Population Schedules of the Sixth Census of the United States, Washington County, Pennsylvania, 1840, RG 29, M-653, NA, p. 192.

Population Schedules of the Seventh Schedule of the United States, Ohio County, Virginia, 1850, RG 29, M-653, NA, p. 167.

Population Schedules of the Eighth Census of the United States, Ohio County, Virginia, 1860, RG 29, M-653, NA, p. 398.

John Buford Lady, Compiled Service Record, NA.

Rawling, *History of the First Regiment Virginia Infantry*, p. 266.

27. Warner, *Generals in Gray*, p. 80.

OR, XII, pt. 1, p. 393.

Henry S. Shanklin (27th Va.), Letter to his father, March 31, 1862, MS #25688, VSL.

John G. Paxton, ed., *Memoir and Memorials, Elisha Franklin Paxton Brigadier-General, C. S. A.*, pp. 54–55.

28. OR, XII, pt. 1, p. 375.

No direct evidence has been found to confirm that the 27th Va. was after Federal cannons. Tyler's report to Shields (cited above) states, "I afterward learned from his [Jackson's] wounded, consisting of nine infantry regiments, and on the eve of attempting a flank movement similar to ours to capture Robinson's battery." Tyler's reports will later be shown to contain inaccuracies; however, the mention of Confederate wounded explaining their mission is consistent with the 27th Va.'s position well to the west and north of the batteries they were sent to protect. Robinson's battery was somewhat isolated from the rest of the Federal artillery line. Jackson knew of their position and may have sent the 27th to take out those cannons.

29. Shanklin, Letter to his father, March 31, 1862, MS #25688, VSL.

OR, XII, pt. 1, p. 394.

Although 170 muskets were tallied in Barton's Woods, this number did not include Company H. This unit was with Nadenbousch and Ashby. According to Shanklin, a member of Captain Dennis's company informed Echols "that 5 or 6 Regts were advancing."

30. Shanklin, Letter, VSL.

31. Richard Brooke Garnett, Report, RBGCMP, p. 2.

John Echols, Statement, July 30, 1862, RBGCMP.

32. Wilson, *Itinerary of the Seventh Ohio Volunteer Infantry*, p. 135.

D. Q. Steen (7th Ohio), Letter dated March 27, 1862, *Cleveland Daily Plain Dealer*, April 8, 1862.

Young, "Shenandoah Valley," *The National Tribune*, April 18, 1889.

33. Thomas Clark, Letter to his wife, March 27, 1862, Clark Letters.

Interestingly, Clark claims the Southerners shouted "Bull's Run."

Young, "Shenandoah Valley," *The National Tribune*, April 18, 1889.

OR, XII, pt. 1, p. 400.

The precise location of Carpenter's guns during the initial phase of the Sandy Ridge fight is unknown. The placement of the battery on Map 6B was derived from a combination of Northern and Southern reports and a study of the terrain.

34. Wood, Diary, March 28, 1862, OHS.

David Bard (7th Ohio), Letter to a friend, March 28, 1862, 361 WFCHS MMF, HL.

Anonymous Soldier (7th Ohio), Letter, *Painesville Telegraph*, April 10, 1862.

Dr. Elliott Denig (7th Ohio), Letter to his father, March 28, 1862, *State Capital Fact* (Columbus, Ohio), April 12, 1862.

George Wood, *The Seventh Regiment: A Record* (New York: James Miller Publisher, 1865), p. 101.

35. S. M., Letter dated March 29, 1862, (Wheeling) *Daily Intelligencer*, April 8, 1862.

36. Richard S. Skidmore, ed., *The Civil War Journal of Billy Davis* (Greencastle, Indiana: The Nugget Publishers, 1989), p. 117.

37. Thomas Clark, Letter to his wife, March 27, 1862, Clark Letters.

38. William D. Lewis, Letter to Governor Curtin, March 30, 1862, p. 3.

Nathaniel L. Parmater (29th Ohio), Diary, March 23, 1862, OHS, p. 11.

E. B. Howard, Letter dated April 1, 1862, *Conneant Reporter*, April 9, 1862.

Thomas Clark, Letter to his wife, March 28, 1862, Clark Letters.

A telling example of how the 110th Pennsylvania was regarded can be seen in the introduction of an 1883 regimental history of the 29th Ohio. Colonel Buckley, in a brief speech designed to keep his men from straggling on an impending march, said, "Men of the Twenty-ninth, let there be no straggling on the march to-day. But if any of you do straggle take Twenty-ninth off from your caps and put on One Hundred and Tenth Pennsylvania." The regimental historian continues: "The joke on the One Hundred and Tenth Pennsylvania was fully appreciated and immensely enjoyed (a regiment noted for straggling). With roars of laughter the boys shouldered their muskets and knapsacks for another hard day's march through the pine barrens." (See SeCheverell, *Journal History of the Twenty-Ninth Ohio Veteran Volunteers*, pp. 13–14.)

39. T. S. Winship (29th Ohio), Letter to J. H. Kilborn, March 29, 1862, *Conneant Reporter*, April 9, 1862.

E. B. Howard, Letter dated April 1, 1862, *Conneant Reporter*, April 9, 1862.

40. Cooper, "The Shenandoah Valley in Eighteen Hundred and Sixty-Two," Military Essays and Recollections, vol. 5, p. 48.

41. Wood, Diary, March 28, 1862, OHS, p. 15.

Bard, Letter, HL, pp. 3–4.

42. William D. Lewis, Letter to Governor Curtin, March 30, 1862, p. 3.

Wilson, *Itinerary of the Seventh Ohio Volunteer Infantry*, pp. 131, 365.

Steen, Letter dated March 27, 1862, *Cleveland Daily Plain Dealer*, April 8, 1862.

Henry Capehart, "Shenandoah Valley: Operations in Virginia During the Year 1862," *The National Tribune*, March 14, 1889, p. 2.

43. Friends of John Echols, Letter to Jefferson Davis, April 12, 1862, John Echols Compiled Service Record, M331, NA.

Wilson, *Itinerary of the Seventh Ohio Volunteer Infantry*, p. 136.

Wood, *The Seventh Regiment*, p. 101.

"W.", Undated letter, *Richmond Daily Dispatch*, April 2, 1862.

44. OR, XII, pt. 1, pp. 402–404.

Bard, Letter, HL, p. 3.

Wood, *The Seventh Regiment*, p. 101.

John Mercer Patton, Compiled Service Record, M331, NA.

45. Swiger, ed., *Civil War Letters and Diary of Joshua Winters*, p. 32.

G. B., Letter dated March 27, 1862, (Wheeling) *Daily Intelligencer*, April 2, 1862.

S. M., Letter dated March 29, 1862, (Wheeling) *Daily Intelligencer*, April 8, 1862.

46. OR, XII, pt. 1, pp. 408–409.

Bard, Letter, HL, p. 3.

47. James W. Orr (37th Va.), "Recollections of the War Between the States," 1909, VSL, p. 3.

48. P. A. B., Letter dated April 6, 1862, (Wheeling) *Daily Intelligencer*, April 15, 1862.

"The Late Battle Near Winchester," (Wheeling) *Daily Intelligencer*, March 28, 1862.

49. OR, XII, pt. 1, pp. 346, 409.

H. J. J. (1st W.Va.), Letter dated March 28, 1862, *The Wellsburg Herald*, April 4, 1862.

The race for the wall has been misinterpreted as the initiation of the Sandy Ridge fight (see Allan, *Stonewall Jackson's Valley Campaign*, p. 57), but it occurred a few minutes after the initial repulse of Tyler's brigade by the 27th Virginia (and later the 21st Virginia). Colonel Fulkerson, in his report, mistakes the 1st West Virginia as "two regiments of the enemy," but clearly states that his arrival: "extended from the left flank of our forces, already engaged with the enemy. . . ." Subsequently, the 110th Pennsylvania has been misnamed as the regiment opposing Fulkerson (see Allan, *Stonewall Jackson's Valley Campaign,* p. 58; Henderson, *Stonewall Jackson and the American Civil War*, p. 184), but this regiment never left the woods.

50. J. F. Asper, Letter dated March 26, 1862, *Western Reserve Chronicle* (Cleveland, Ohio), April 2, 1862.

Wilson, *Itinerary of the Seventh Ohio Volunteer Infantry*, pp. 136–137.

51. John O. Casler (33rd Va.), *Four Years in the Stonewall Brigade* (reprint, Dayton, Ohio: Morningside Bookshop, 1982), p. 66.

Colonel Andrew J. Grigsby, Letter to William Garnett, July 12, 1862, G-386, RBGCMP.

Elliott Johnston, Statement, July 25, 1862, RBGCMP.

52. Elliott Johnston, Specification notes, RBGCMP.

53. Garnett, Report, RBGCMP, p. 4.

Richard Garnett, Letter to Cooper, RBGCMP, p. 8.

OR, XII, pt. 1, p. 395.

54. OR, XII, pt. 1, p. 391.

James H. Langhorne, Letter to his parents, April 3, 1862, *Lynchburg Virginian*, April 16, 1862.

James H. Langhorne, Diary, Feb. 2, 1862, Mss5:1L2654:1, VHS.

Charles W. Turner, ed., *A Reminiscence of Lieutenant John Newton Lyle*, p. 159.

John Newton Lyle, "Stonewall Jackson's Guard: The Washington College Company," pp. 397–398.

55. J. F. Asper (7th Ohio), Letter dated March 26, 1862, *Western Reserve Chronicle*, April 2, 1862.

56. Young, "Shenandoah Valley," *The National Tribune*, April 18, 1889.

57. Erastus B. Tyler, Report to Governor Morton, April 10, 1862, *Rebellion Record*, vol. 4, document 103, p. 332.

John F. Cheek (7th Indiana), Official Report: Battle of Kernstown, March 28, 1862, *Rebellion Record*, vol. 4, document 103, p. 333.

58. Joseph Molineaux (7th Ohio), Interview, *Cleveland Morning Leader*, April 1, 1862.

(Wheeling) *Daily Intelligencer*, March 29, 1862.

Cincinnati Daily Commercial, March 31, 1862.

"The Battle of Winchester: A Bloody But Glorious Record," *Cleveland Morning Leader*, March 31, 1862.

59. OR, XII, pt. 1, pp. 401–403, 405–407.

Bridgford's report claims the battalion entered the line "About 5 o'clock. . .", but states that they supported Carpenter's guns after 3:00 P.M. Both times appear to be at least one-half hour later than what the events on the field dictated; therefore, a more accurate estimate of time has been placed in the narrative.

60. OR, XII, pt. 1, 388–389.

Colonel Allen believed his regiment entered the line "about 5:00 P.M., or soon afterwards." His estimate appears to be approximately fifteen minutes later than the best estimate of his arrival. The 2nd Virginia was clearly the last Confederate regiment to reinforce Garnett's line.

61. Martin and Snow, eds., *The Civil War Diaries of Lorenzo Vanderoef*, p. 93.

Neese, *Three Years in the Confederate Horse Artillery*, p. 35.

J. H. J., Letter dated March 26, 1862, *The Sandusky Register*, April 3, 1862.

62. Mrs. Cornelia McDonald, *A Diary With Reminiscences of the War and Refugee Life,* pp. 51–52.

Mrs. Hugh Lee, Diary, March 23, 1862, HL.

John Peyton Clark, Journal, March 23, 1862, HL.

Reverend B. F. Brooke, Journal, March 23, 1862, 226 WFCHS MMF, HL.

63. Anonymous Soldier (110th Pa.), Letter to his friend, March 29, 1862, *The* (Philadelphia) *Press*, April 11, 1862.

Frank Jones, Diary, March 23, 1862, HL.

64. Thomas J. Jackson, Letter to A. W. Harman, March 28, 1862, SHSP 19, 1891, p. 318.

Jackson, Testimony, August 6, 1862, RBGCMP, pp. 1–2.

CHAPTER SEVEN

1. E. H. C. Cavins, Letter to Nathan Kimball, July 7, 1887, EHC Cavins Collection, M42, Box 2, Folder 4, IHS.

2. OR, XII, pt. 1, p. 378.

D. D. Perkins, Letter to Alpheus S. Williams, March 23, 1862, Box 19, Nathaniel Banks Papers, LC.

Alpheus S. Williams, Letter to his daughter, March 30, 1862, *From the Cannon's Mouth*, p. 65.

3. Mason, Testimony, May 22, 1862, JCCW, p. 407.

4. OR, XII, pt. 1, pp. 351–355.

   David Taylor, Official Report, April 17, 1862, RG 94, NA.

5. OR, XII, pt. 1, p. 374.

   Frank C. Gibbs (1st Ohio Artillery), Letter dated March 26, 1862, *Portsmouth Times*, April 12, 1862.

   H. E. S (5th Ohio), Letter to his brother, March 25, 1862, *Cincinnati Daily Commercial*, April 8, 1862.

6. OR, XII, pt. 1, pp. 369–370.

   Sawyer submitted the official report cited above. Nineteen years later he wrote the regimental history of the 8th Ohio. In the latter account, Sawyer claims that "Col. Clark, of Gen. Banks' staff" delivered the order rather than Daum. The official report suggests that one person delivered the order to support the battery, then Daum came over to deliver the attack directive. Perhaps Colonel John S. Clark, a member of Banks's Fifth Corps staff, delivered the first order. (See Sawyer, *A Military History of the 8th Ohio Inf'y*, p. 42). This is the only source that places Colonel Clark on the battlefield.

7. David Lewis, Letter to a friend, March 26, 1862, *Bucyrus Weekly Journal*, April 4, 1862.

   Lewis claims that his company was twenty-five yards from the enemy. He likely refers to skirmishers who approached Company C of the 8th Ohio when they reached the knoll. The knoll was several hundred yards from the stone wall.

8. Sawyer, *A Military History of the 8th Ohio Inf'y*, pp. 42–43.

   J. H. J. (8th Ohio), Letter dated March 26, 1862, *The Sandusky Register,* April 3, 1862.

   Captain James E. Gregg (8th Ohio), Letter dated March 26, 1862, *The Sandusky Register*, April 3, 1862.

   Lieutenant Alfred T. Craig was killed two years later at the Battle of the Wilderness. According to his widow's pension application, Craig left a wife and five young children.

9. Sawyer, *A Military History of the 8th Ohio Inf'y*, pp. 42–43.

10. OR, XII, pt. 1, pp. 370–371.

11. A. C. Voris, "The Battle of the Boys," Sketches of War History 1861–1865: *Papers Read Before the Ohio Commandery of the Military Order of the Loyal Legion of the United States* (Cincinnati, Ohio: The Robert Clarke Company, 1896), pp. 96–97.

    Captain John B. Stafford (67th Ohio), Letter dated March 30, 1862, *Weekly Perrysburg Journal*, April 7, 1862.

12. OR, XII, pt. 1, p. 388.

    Samuel J. C. Moore (2nd Va.), Letter to wife, March 26, 1862, Moore Papers, Southern Historical Collection, University of North Carolina, Chapel Hill, N.C.

13. Kimball, Brigade Strength Report, March 31, 1862, Box 19, Folder 3, Nathaniel Banks Papers, LC.

S. F. Forbes (67th Ohio), Letter dated March 27, 1862, *Daily Toledo Blade*, April 3, 1862.

Spiegel, Letter to his family, March 28, 1862, *A Jewish Colonel*, p. 85.

J. E. B. (67th Ohio), Letter dated March 30, 1862, *The Summit Beacon* (Akron, Ohio), April 10, 1862.

The strength of the 67th Ohio is estimated. On March 31, they had nine companies of 424 men—an average of forty-seven men per company. Adding back the forty-seven casualties claimed at Kernstown, the 67th Ohio likely averaged approximately fifty men per company, or 350 men for seven engaged companies.

14. Voris, "The Battle of the Boys," p. 99.

John Faskin, " The Killed and Wounded of the 67th," *Daily Toledo Blade*, April 3, 1862.

S. F. Forbes (67th Ohio), Letter dated March 27, 1862, *Daily Toledo Blade*, April 3, 1862.

An alternative scenario leading to Captain Ford's death is provided by John Stafford (*Weekly Perrysburg Journal*, April 7, 1862) who claims: "When we engaged the enemy. . . word was passed along the line that we were firing on our own troops. Capt. Ford stepped out in front of his company and had just succeeded in stopping their fire when a volley from the enemy killed him. . ." Both Forbes's and Stafford's accounts are reasonable. No accounts confirming either have been found.

Xenophon Wheeler, "The Experiences of an Enlisted Man in the Hospital in the Early Part of the War," *Sketches of War History*, MOLLUS, Ohio, vol. 7, 1908, p. 277.

James M. King (13th Indiana), Journal, IHS.

15. A. R. B., Jr., (Rockbridge Artillery), Letter dated March 26, 1862, *Lynchburg Virginian*, April 5, 1862.

Thomas M. Nelson (2nd Virginia), "A Gentleman of Verona," *Old Chapel: Clarke County, Virginia*, The Blue Ridge Press, Berryville, Virginia, 1906, pg. 21.

"List of killed and Wounded of the 1st Brigade commanded by Genl. Garnett at the Battle of Kernstown March 23, 1862," Mss 1 P4299L, VSL.

This partial list indicated the source of wounds. After F. Whiting's name is "Bayonet-puncture in eyelid." The wound may have been accidentally self-inflicted during the excitement of loading and firing in battle.

16. OR, XII, pt. 1, pg. 388.

"List of killed and Wounded of the 1st Brigade commanded by Genl. Garnett at the Battle of Kernstown March 23, 1862," Mss 1 P4299L, VSL.

17. G. W. Fahrion (67th Ohio), "Courage of a Virginia Color Bearer," *Confederate Veteran*, vol. 17, no. 2, March 1909, p. 125.

David E. Roth, "Stonewall Jackson's Only Defeat: The Battle of Kernstown (or First Winchester) March 23, 1862," *Blue and Gray Magazine*, June–July 1986, p. 51.

Mr. Roth's research corrected the SHSP account which mistakenly places Fahrion in the 62nd Ohio (instead of the 67th Ohio), facing off against the 5th Virginia (instead of the 2nd Virginia). Any of the color-bearers who fell at the stone wall could have been the one in Fahrion's account.

18. OR, XII, pt. 1, p. 388.

"List of killed and Wounded of the 1st Brigade commanded by Genl. Garnett at the Battle of Kernstown March 23, 1862," Mss 1 P4299L, VSL.

Samuel J. C. Moore, Letter to his wife, March 26, 1861, University of North Carolina.

Pendleton, Letter to his mother, March 29, 1862, VMHB, p. 343.

19. Whitelaw Reid, *Ohio in the War: Her Statesmen, Generals and Soldiers,* p. 1001.

20. OR, XII, pt. 1, p. 374.

Matthew Schwab (5th Ohio), Letter to his parents, March 28, 1862, Matthew Schwab Letters, 1861–1865, Box 1, Folder 4, Cincinnati Historical Society, Cincinnati Ohio.

H. E. S. Letter to his brother, March 25, 1862, *Cincinnati Daily Commercial,* April 8, 1862.

21. OR, XII, pt. 1, pp. 374, 400.

22. Voris, "The Battle of the Boys," p. 97.

H. E. S., Letter to his brother, March 25, 1862, *Cincinnati Daily Commercial,* April 8, 1862.

E. J. (5th Ohio), Letter dated March 27, 1862, *Cincinnati Daily Commercial,* April 8, 1862.

23. OR, XII, pt. 1, p. 374.

Whitelaw Reid, *Ohio in the War: Her Statesmen, Generals and Soldiers,* p. 43.

H. E. S., Letter to his brother, March 25, 1862, *Cincinnati Daily Commercial,* April 8, 1862.

24. 84th Pennsylvania Infantry Regimental Orders and Furlough Book, RG 94, NA.

Alex Read (84th Pa.), Letter to friends, March 26, 1862, *Clearfield Republican,* April 16, 1862.

Lt. Col. Thomas MacDowell (84th Pa.), Letter to Governor Curtin, March 31, 1862, 84th Pennsylvania Regimental File, RG 19, Pennsylvania Historical and Museum Commission, Harrisburg, Pa.

Interestingly, the 84th Pennsylvania is the only Federal regiment whose engaged strength at Kernstown is recorded. Several sources, in addition to the MacDowell letter, cite the number "255" (See Merchant, *Eighty-Fourth Pennsylvania Volunteers,* p. 34; Craig, Reference #26, and Field and Staff of the 84th Pennsylvania, "Compiled Records Showing Service of Military Units in Volunteer Union Organizations" M594, NA).

25. A Volunteer (H. S. Wells, 84th Pa.), Letter dated March 31, 1862, *The Muncy Luminary,* April 15, 1862.

Fowler, "Criticizing Capehart," *The National Tribune,* May 16, 1889.

Both members of the 84th Pennsylvania describe the ruse, but do not name the opposing regiment that was responsible for fooling them. The March 26, 1862 evening edition of the *Boston Journal* claims the following: ". . . the Irish Battalion of 150, when brought forward and ordered to fire upon the Union troops, refused to fire. . ." The reporter received the story from a soldier in Shields's division who likely heard the Irish Battalion shout during the ruse "Don't fire upon your own men," and misinterpreted it a a refusal for them to fire upon the Federals.

26. Thomas H. Craig, "Shields's Division: A Delayed Report of the 84th Pennsylvania at Kernstown," *The National Tribune,* November 21, 1889.

27. James H. Simpson (14th Indiana), "Criticizing Capehart: Who took the Stone Wall at Kernstown," *The National Tribune,* May 9, 1889.

Jed Hotchkiss, Sketchbook, Cover Page, LC.

Simpson believed the wall was only 140–175 yards long. The Hotchkiss sketch indicates it was much longer than that.

28. OR, XII, pt. 1, p. 403.

Worsham, *One of Jackson's Foot Cavalry,* p. 68.

Neither Worsham and Patton use the word "stone wall" in their accounts (they describe it simply as a fence), thus assuring the concealment of this structure in all secondary interpretations of the Battle of Kernstown. The abundance of descriptions of the wall, provided by the 84th Pa., the 14th Indiana, and the Jed Hotchkiss sketches, leave no doubt that the wall existed at the position that Worsham and Patton decribe. Worsham's description of his company mounting the fence also hints that the structure was made of stone—a rail fence would not likely have supported a company of soldiers.

29. Thomas H. Craig, "Shields's Division: A Delayed Report of the 84th Pennsylvania at Kernstown," *The National Tribune,* November 21, 1889, pp. 4–5.

Rod Gainer (Arlington, Va.), Personal communication, 1994.

Rod Gainer is a direct descendant of Patrick Gallagher and owns the captain's sword. The "premonition note" is a family story without concrete support; however, all other family claims match well with information gleaned from Gallagher's service and pension records.

Thomas Gouldsberry, Letter to his father, May 6, 1862, Thomas Gouldsberry Papers, Save the Flags Collection, USAMHI.

Alfred Aurandt, Letter to his mother, March, 26, 1862, Aurandt Letters, Historical Collection, Penn State University.

30. *Adams Sentinel,* April 9, 1862.

Oneill resigned April 1862.

Joseph A. Pinkerton, Letter to his brother, March 26, 1862, *The Miner's Journal and Pottsville General Advertiser,* April 5, 1862.

C. F. Heverly, *Our Boys in Blue: A Complete History of Bradford County in the Civil War,* vol. 2 (Towanda, Pa.: Bradford Star Print, 1908), p. 451.

31. Samuel P. Bates, *Martial Deeds of Pennsylvania,* p. 546.

32. Thomas Craig, "Delayed Report," *The National Tribune,* November 21, 1889.

William Gallagher, Letter to his parents, April 22, 1862, William Gallagher Pension File, NA.

"List of Casualties at the Battle Near Winchester, Va." 84th Pennsylvania Regiment File, RG 19, Pennsylvania Historical and Museum Commission, Harrisburg, Pa.

Murray could have been killed by a member of the 21st Virginia; however, the fact that the bullet passed through his forehead (he was facing forward at the time), suggests that the shot was fired from someone directly in front of him. The 21st Virginia flanked Murray's left; the Irish Batallion stood in front of him.

33. Thomas C. Fowler (84th Pa.), "Criticizing Capehart: The Troops that Captured the Stone Wall at Kernstown," *The National Tribune,* May 16, 1889.

OR, XII, pt. 1, p. 403.

34. Harrow, Testimony, May 22, 1862, JCCW, p. 412.

35. Sifakis, *Who Was Who in the Civil War,* p. 288.

E. H. C. Cavins (14th Ind.), Letter to his father, April 6, 1862, EHC Cavins Collection, M42, Box 1, Folder 2, IHS.

Harrow's style and manner in the heat of battle may have been misinterpreted as intoxication. Fifteen months after Kernstown, Harrow took over a brigade at Gettysburg. A soldier described him on July 2, 1863: "Harrow said this battle must be won at all hazards, that the fate of the army depended upon it. Now said he, at the same time drawing out his pistol, the first God Damned man I see running or sneaking, I blow him to hell in an instant. This God Damned running is played out, just stand to it and Give them Hell. And he called upon all of us by all that was Good & Infernal to kill every son-of-a-bitch that runs without a cause. Said he, if you see me running I want you to kill me on the spot. . . This harangue pleased the boys much. One says bully for Harrow, another says he is tight, and a third remarked that he was just the man to lead us. All three of which I pronounced as correct. . ." (Roland E. Bowen (15th Mass.), "Nothing But Cowards Run," *Civil War Magazine*, #50, April 1995, p. 45.) The word "tight" in this account refers to drunk. Harrow may have produced a similar "harangue" at Kernstown that was subject to the same variety of interpretations from his men.

36. E. H. C. Cavins, Letter to his wife, March 28, 1862, EHC Cavins Collection, IHS.

   J. E. Gregg (8th Ohio), Letter dated March 26, 1862, *The Sandusky Register*, April 3, 1862.

37. Kimball, Brigade Strength Report, March 31, 1862, Box 19, Folder 3, Nathaniel Banks Papers, LC.

   James H.Simpson (14th Ind.), "Criticizing Capehart. Who Took the Stone Wall at Kernstown?", *The National Tribune*, May 9, 1889.

   E. H. C. Cavins, Letter to his wife, March 28, 1862, E. H. C. Cavins Collection, IHS.

   Augustus M. Van Dyke (14th Ind.), Letter to his family, March 28, 1862, Van Dyke Papers, Folder 1, IHS.

   William Houghton (14th Ind.), Letter to his father, March 27, 1862, Houghton Papers, M147, Box 1, Folder 4, IHS.

   On March 31, the 14th Indiana listed 400 men fit for duty. They had fifty-four casualties at Kernstown; therefore, their strength likely did not exceed 450 on the day of the battle.

38. "Prock," Undated letter, *Vincennes Western Sun*, April 12, 1862.

39. James H. Simpson (14th Ind.), "Criticizing Capehart. Who Took the Stone Wall at Kernstown?", *The National Tribune*, May 9, 1889.

40. James H. Simpson, "Battle of Kernstown: How Jackson was Beaten," *The National Tribune*, February 4, 1882.

41. Ibid.

   "Prock," Letter, March 29, 1862, *Vincennes Western Sun*, April 12, 1862.

   Paul Truckey, Compiled Pension Record, NA.

   William Houghton, "Capehart Criticized. The Part Taken by the 14th Ind. at Kernstown," *The National Tribune*, June 6, 1889.

   Both of Simpson's *National Tribune* accounts credit Truckey with initiating the charge. Since the author of the account is placing accolades on someone other than himself, the account has credibility. "Prock" took special note of Truckey as well. Others, like William Houghton, believed that many soldiers shouted "Forward!" and charged the wall at the same time. The prevailing sentiment that all agree upon is that the foot soldiers took matters into their own hands at this point.

CHAPTER EIGHT

1. Pendleton, Testimony, August 7, 1862, RBGCMP.

   Richard Brooke Garnett, Letter to Samuel Cooper, June 20, 1862, RBGCMP, p. 9.

2. John G. Marsh (29th Ohio), Letter to his father, April 10, 1862, in C. Calvin Smith, ed., "The Duties of Home and War: The Civil War Letters of John G. Marsh, 29th Ohio Volunteers (A Selection)," *Upper Ohio Valley Historical Review*, vol. 8 (2), 1979, p. 10.

3. OR, XII, pt. 1, pp. 382, 384.

   Garnett, Letter to Cooper, RBGCMP, p. 11.

   Elliott Johnston, Statement, July 25, 1862, RBGCMP.

   Garnett used one word to describe the men who left the ranks without legitimate reasons: "fugitives."

4. Elliott Johnston, Miscellaneous notes, RBGCMP, p. 3.

   Andrew Grigsby, Letter to Mr. William Garnett, July 12, 1862, RBGCMP.

5. P. Hirst (62nd OVI), Undated letter, *Zanesville Daily Courier*, April 4, 1862.

6. Thomas C. Fowler, "Criticizing Capehart. The Troops that Captured the Stonewall at Kernstown," *The National Tribune*, November 21, 1889.

   Had Kimball appointed a brigade commander, Colonel Carroll ranked everyone else in the brigade. Since he was unavailable (east of the Valley Pike), Colonel William Murray of the 84th Pennsylvania would have been the next ranking officer to lead Kimball's troops.

7. OR, XII, pt. 1, p. 407.

   Charles Alexander, "The First Battalion," *Richmond Times-Dispatch*, July 3, 1904.

   Charles W. Turner, ed., "Major Charles A. Davidson: Letters of a Virginia Soldier," *Civil War History*, vol. 22, 1976, p. 26.

   Augustus Van Dyke, Letter to his family, March 28, 1862, Van Dyke Papers, Folder 1, IHS.

8. E. H. C. Cavins, Letter to his wife, March 28, 1862, EHC Cavins Collection, IHS.

   OR, XII, pt. 1, p. 403.

   Patton's choice of words is compelling. The "general commanding" at the Battle of Kernstown was Stonewall Jackson; he obviously did not order Patton to withdraw. But Patton likely believed that Garnett was in charge of the battle on Sandy Ridge, indicating that Jackson was not at the site of action after the infantry fight began.

   The "Hoosier Yell" sounded across Sandy Ridge at the end of the fight. No description of the cheer has been provided by these soldiers in their writings.

9. Garnett, Letter to Cooper, RBGCMP, p. 11.

   Johnston, Statement, RBGCMP.

   The cavalry demonstration has not been confirmed in Northern accounts. There may have been cavalry flankers near his front; however, the Union cavalry did not attack until after Garnett ordered the retreat.

10. William Houghton, "Capehart Criticized. The Part Taken by the 14th Ind. at Kernstown," *The National Tribune*, June 6, 1889.

"Prock," Letter dated March 29, 1862, *Vincennes Western Sun*, April 12, 1862.

11. Jackson, Testimony, August 6, 1862, RBGCMP, p. 1.

12. Worsham, *One of Jackson's Foot Cavalry*, p. 68.

13. Jackson, Testimony, RBGCMP, pp. 1-2.

OR, XII, pt. 1, p. 382.

14. Pendleton, Letter to his mother, March, 29, 1862, VMHB, p. 342.

Fishburne, "Historical Sketch of the Rockbridge Artillery," p. 181.

Pendleton likely counted flags to arrive at this estimate. He probably assumed that each Federal regiment carried much more than the average of the 450–500 soldiers present for duty on March 23.

15. Winchester resident James Tubessing had been a relic hunter in the area since the 1960s. He indicates most of the bullets were found near the center and eastern end of the stone wall. Mr. Tubessing claims that he found very little near Fulkerson's position. This provides additional evidence that Fulkerson's force was not hard pressed after they repulsed the 1st West Virginia.

Allan, *Stonewall Jackson's Valley Campaign*, p. 231.

16. Frank Jones, Letter to his wife, September 6, 1861, HL.

Krick, *Lee's Colonels*, p. 163.

Obituary of Kenton Harper, *Staunton Spectator*, December 31, 1867.

17. OR, XII, pt. 1, pp. 391–392, 403–404.

18. OR, XII, pt. 1, pp. 375, 398.

James H. Simpson, "Criticizing Capehart. Who Took the Stone Wall at Kernstown?", *The National Tribune*, May 9, 1889.

19. OR, XII, pt. 1, pp. 389, 393, 395, 406–407.

20. "Volunteer," Letter dated March 30, 1862, *Painesville Telegraph*, April 10, 1862.

21. "Adjutant" (29th Ohio), Letter dated March 29, 1862, *Ashtabula Sentinel*, ca. April 9, 1862.

"Chaplin" (29th Ohio), Letter dated April 15, 1862, *Ashtabula Sentinel*, ca. April 30, 1862.

Myron Wright (29th Ohio), Letter to his father, March 25, 1862, *Summit Beacon*, April 1, 1862.

22. Wilson, *Itinerary of the Seventh Ohio Volunteer Infantry*, pp. 137–138.

23. William D. Lewis, Letter to Governor A. G. Curtin, March 30, 1862, pp. 3–4.

OR, XII, pt. 1, p. 359.

F. C. Gibbs, Letter dated March 26, 1862, *The Portsmouth Times*, April 12, 1862.

David Bard, Letter to his parents, March 29, 1862, HL.

Unnamed Soldier of 110th Pennsylvania, Letter to his cousin, March 29, 1862, *The* (Philadelphia) *Press*, April 11, 1862.

"Lovejoy," *A History of Company A, First Ohio Cavalry 1861–1865*, p. 64.

24. Charles Ballou (7th Ohio), Letter to his family, March 24, 1862, *Cleveland Morning Leader*, March 31, 1862.

Wilson, *Itinerary of the Seventh Ohio Volunteer Infantry*, p. 138.

"Prock," Letter, *Vincennes Western Sun*, April 12, 1862.

Charles Ballou identifies the trampled officer as "Lieutenant Kimball." The lieutenant was not recorded as an official battle casualty.

25. John Newton Lyle, "Stonewall Jackson's Guard," pp. 397–398.

Charles W. Turner, ed., *A Reminiscence of Lieutenant John Newton Lyle*, p. 159.

James H. Langhorne, Letter to his parents, April 3, 1862, *Lynchburg Virginian*, April 16, 1862.

White, *Sketches of the Life of Captain Hugh A. White*, p. 80.

26. A. R. B., Jr., Letter dated March 26, 1862, *Richmond Daily Dispatch*, April 3, 1862.

"The Confederate Prisoners In Jail," *Baltimore American*, March 31, 1862.

OR, XII, pt. 1, pp. 384, 389.

Prisoners of War Roster, Banks's Intelligence File, RG 393, entry 223, NA.

27. Hugh Barr obituary, *Winchester Times*, February 11, 1885.

Hugh Barr obituary, *Winchester News*, February 13, 1885.

The drummer "boy" story was picked up by G. F. R. Henderson, who wrote the following: "Seizing a drummer by the shoulder, he [Jackson] dragged him to a rise of ground in full view of the troops, and bade him in curt, quick tones, to 'Beat the Rally!' The drum rolled at his order and with his hand on the frightened boy's shoulder, amidst a storm of balls, he tried to check the flight of his defeated troops. His efforts were useless. . . ." Henderson also incorrectly placed the reserve position of the 5th Virginia at the foot of Sandy Ridge, rather than the Valley Turnpike. (Henderson, *Stonewall Jackson and the American Civil War*, pp. 184, 186). The "boy" drummer fallacy was picked up by most twentieth-century historians, including Douglas Southall Freeman (see *Lee's Lieutenants*, vol. 1, p. 314).

28. OR, XII, pt. 1, pp. 382, 392, 397.

Garnett, Letter to Cooper, RBGCMP, p. 12.

Jackson, Testimony, RBGCMP, p. 2.

Garnett had no battle experience prior to Kernstown. His placement of the 5th Virginia may have been based on West Point training more than twenty years earlier.

29. Voris, "The Battle of the Boys," p. 97.

William D. Lewis, Letter to Governor Curtin, p. 4.

H. E. S., Letter to his brother, March 25, 1862, *Cincinnati Daily Commercial*, April 8, 1862.

J. Jeff Parsons, Letter dated March 30, 1862, *Weekly Perrysburg Journal*, April 10, 1862.

Van Dyke, Letter to family, March 28, 1862, IHS.

30. Wilson, *Itinerary of the Seventh Ohio Volunteer Infantry*, p. 139.

James H. Simpson, "Criticizing Capehart," *The National Tribune*, May 9, 1889.

Corporal Day, whose account is recapped in Wilson's regimental history of the 7th Ohio, claimed that they captured the two cannons and Simpson took exception to the claim: "And this reminds me of hearing a few days later how a commissioned officer and a Sergeant of the 7th Ohio, strolling along in our rear, found the two cannon and some horses we had taken and left in our eager pursuit. These they took to the rear with a great hurrah, as captured by them in a charge. This may or may not be so, but it was one of the standing jokes in our camp at the time." The evidence strongly indicates that members of the 7th Ohio merely recaptured the guns that the 14th Indiana overran several minutes earlier.

31. E. H. C. Cavins, Letter to Nathan Kimball,1887, EHC Cavins Collection, M42, Box 2, Folder 4, IHS.

32. Fishburne, "Historical Sketch of the Rockbridge Artillery," p. 132.

Clement Fishburne, Memoirs, University of Virginia, Charlottesville, Va., p. 41.

OR, XII, pt. 1, pp. 372, 397.

G. K. Bedinger, Letter to his father, April 1, 1862, Bedinger-Dandridge Family Collection, DU.

"Prock," Letter dated March 29, 1862, *Vincennes Western Sun*, April 12, 1862.

William Houghton, "Capehart Criticized," *The National Tribune*, June 6, 1889.

Confederate States Almanac for 1862, p. 4.

33. William D. Lewis, Letter to Governor Curtin, p. 4.

OR, XII, pt. 1, p. 397.

Fishburne, "Historical Sketch of the Rockbridge Artillery", p. 132.

Rev. Philip Slaughter, *A Sketch of the Life of Randolph Fairfax* (Richmond, Va.: Tyler, Allegee and McDaniel, 1864), p. 21.

34. OR, XII, pt. 1, pp. 367, 392.

John B. Stafford (67th OVI), Letter dated March 30, 1862, *Weekly Perrysburg Journal*, April 17, 1862.

"Prock," Letter dated March 29, 1862, *Vincennes Western Sun*, April 12, 1862.

Van Dyke, Letter dated March 28, 1862, IHS.

James Oakey, Letter dated March 27, 1862, *Terre-Haute Daily Express*, April 5, 1862.

The 14th Indiana was the regiment most devastated by the volleys from the 5th Virginia, as indicated by the frequent loss of the color-bearers. Henderson, in his history of Stonewall Jackson, misnames the Federal regiment as the 5th Ohio and incorrectly places the 84th Pennsylvania in this assault: ". . . In front of the 5th Virginia the colours of the 5th Ohio changed hands no less than six times. . .The 84th Pennsylvania was twice repulsed. . ." These errors have been recycled when Henderson's work is cited as a Kernstown source by other historians. No flags from either side changed hands during the Battle of Kernstown.

35. William D. Lewis, Letter to Governor Curtin, pp. 4–5.

OR, XII, pt. 1, p. 397.

L. (Rockbridge Artillery), " The Battle of Barton's Mills," *Lexington Gazette*, April 3, 1862.

Fishburne, "Historical Sketch of the Rockbridge Artillery," p. 133.

Slaughter, *A Sketch of the Life of Randolph Fairfax*, p. 21.

Monroe F. Cockrell, ed., *Gunner with Stonewall: Reminiscence of William Thomas Poague, A Memoir written for his children in 1903* (Wilmington, N.C.: Broadfoot Publishing Company, 1989), p. 19.

36. OR, XII, pt. 1, p. 398.

McLaughlin's report, cited above, lists a total of eleven casualties. I am indebted to Jerry Reid for his work on Southern casualties at Kernstown. Reid tallies the fourteen total losses (including four mortal) in the Rockbridge Artillery and has uncovered the Gay brothers story from their service records.

37. OR, XII, pt. 1, pp. 392, 401, 404.

Spiegel (67th Ohio), Letter to family, March 28, 1862, *A Jewish Colonel*, p. 85.

Garnett, Report, RBGCMP, p. 4.

Jackson, Testimony, RBGCMP, p. 3.

38. OR, XII, pt. 1, pp. 372, 401, 404–405.

Spiegel (67th Ohio), Letter to family, March 28, 1862, *A Jewish Colonel*, p. 85.

39. Warner, *Generals in Blue*, p. 158.

Lee Frazier, "At Kernstown,Va.," *The National Tribune*, September 26, 1912.

40. Charles H. Ross (13th Indiana), "Old Memories," *War Papers Read Before the Commandery of the State of Wisconsin*, MOLLUS, vol. 1, Burdick, Armitage & Allen, 1891, p. 160.

41. Frank Ingersoll, Letter to his sister, March 26, 1862, Ingersoll Mss., Lilly Library, Indiana University, Bloomington, Ind., p. 3.

James M. King, Journal, IHS.

OR, XII, pt. 1, pp. 372, 384, 401.

"Prock," Undated letter, *Vincennes Western Sun*, April 12, 1862.

Van Dyke, Letter dated March 28, 1862, IHS.

Allen W. Wright, *The 42nd Virginia Infantry*, vol. 1, VHS, pp. 22–23.

"The Scales Brothers," *Confederate Veteran*, vol. 7 (9), Sept. 1899, p. 404.

Burks's herniation forced his resignation shortly after the battle. No indication is evident that the injury influenced his decision to withdraw the 42nd Virginia.

42. OR, XII, pt. 1, p. 372.

43. Wilson, *Itinerary of the Seventh Ohio Volunteer Infantry*, pp. 141–142.

Lee Frazier (13th Ind.), "At Winchester," *The National Tribune*, October 30, 1890.

Lee Frazier, "At Kernstown, Va.," *The National Tribune*, September 26, 1912.

"Lieut. George Junkin," *Lexington Gazette*, May 1, 1862.

W. G. Bean, "The Unusual War Experience of Lieutenant George G. Junkin, C. S. A.," *The Virginia Magazine of History and Biography*, vol. 76 (2), April, 1968, pp. 183–184.

There are others who also wish to take credit for capturing Junkin, including A. J. Weaver, Company D of the 110th Pennsylvania. (See S. C. B, Letter dated March 28, 1862, *The Shirleysburg Herald*, April 10, 1862.)

44. Garnett, Letter to Cooper, RBGCMP, p. 13.

OR, XII, pt. 1, p. 405.

The Confederate States Almanac, and repository of useful knowledge, for 1862, H. C. Clarke, comp., Vicksburg, Miss., p. 3.

Jed Hotchkiss, Journal, March 23, 1862, Hotchkiss Papers, LC.

The Magill house and the stone lane that runs to Barton's Woods still exist. The lane may have been specifically chosen to guide Jackson and his men through the darkness. Very little natural light was available to assist Jackson in his retreat.

45. "Lovejoy," Letter dated March 31, 1862, *Fayette County Weekly*, April 17, 1862.

OR, XII, pt. 1, pp. 355, 357.

Theodore Lang, *Loyal West Virginia from 1861 to 1865*, p. 159.

Much friction between the 1st West Virginia Cavalry and the 1st Ohio Cavalry is apparent from the post-battle letters sent home. One Buckeye told his sister "Somehow we are not mentioned in the papers, while the loyal Va. Cavalry, as arrant a set of cowards as ever lived, are." See "Joe," Letter to his sister, March 29, 1862, *Perry County Weekly*, April 9, 1862.

46. Henry G. Burr, Letter dated March 30, 1862, *Daily Toledo Blade*, April 5, 1862.

"Cosmus" (1st Ohio Cavalry), Letter dated March 31, 1862, *The* (Harrisburg, Pa.) *Patriot & Union*, April 12, 1862.

Randolph Barton, *Recollections*, privately printed, 1913, p. 33.

W. L. Curry, *Four Years in the Saddle*, p. 236.

47. OR, XII, pt. 1, pp. 386–387, 407.

George Baylor, *Bull Run to Bull Run or Four Years in the Army of Northern Virginia* (Richmond, Va.: B. F. Johnston, 1900), pp. 35–36.

Lee A. Wallace, *A Guide to Virginia Military Organizations 1861–1865*, second edition (Lynchburg, Va.: H. E. Howard, Inc., 1986), p. 48.

Because of the sparsity of firsthand Confederate cavalry accounts, it remains a mystery how the Union cavalry slipped through this portion of the field. Since Funsten's pickets were spread thin, it cannot be ruled out that Federal horsemen overran this small force prior to capturing their prisoners.

48. Charles W. Turner, ed., *A Reminiscence of Lieutenant John Newton Lyle*, pp. 160–161.

49. Casler, *Four Years in the Stonewall Brigade*, p. 67.

George C. Pile (37th Va.), "The War Story of a Confederate Soldier," *Bristol Herald Courier*, January 23–February 27, 1921.

50. James H. Langhorne, Letter to his parents, April 3, 1862, *Lynchburg Virginian*, April 16, 1862.

The infantry regiments that disrupted the square formation are unknown. The units closest to that part of the field were the 1st West Virginia and the 110th Pennsylvania.

51. Barton, *Recollections*, p. 33.

Charles W. Turner, ed., *John Newton Lyle*, p. 161.

52. James H. Langhorne, Letter to his parents, April 3, 1862, *Lynchburg Virginian*, April 16, 1862.

"Joe" (1st Ohio Cavalry), Letter to his sister, March 29, 1862, *Perry County Weekly*, April 9, 1862.

Lovejoy, Letter dated March 31, 1862, *Fayette County Weekly*, April 17, 1862.

Curry, *Four Years in the Saddle*, pp. 236–237.

These accounts agree with each other almost perfectly. The Federals misname Langhorne as "Preston," but Langhorne clarifies this by mentioning that he carried Preston's pistol. Perhaps the pistol was engraved. Langhorne does not mention the ring incident, but two separate Federal accounts make note of this poignant moment.

53. OR, XII, pt. 1, p. 357.

Cavins, Letter to Nathan Kimball, IHS.

"One of The Boys," Letter dated March 28, 1862, (Wheeling) *Daily Intelligencer*, April 7, 1862.

54. OR, XII, pt. 1, p. 348.

55. R. M. Copeland, Telegram to Gen. R. B. Marcy, March 23, 1862, Telegrams Collected by the Office of the Secretary of War, M473, Reel 98, NA, p. 231.

56. William F. Harrison, Letter to his wife, March 28, 1862, William F. Harrison Collection, DU.

57. Casler, *Four Years in the Stonewall Brigade*, p. 67.

58. Neese, *Three Years in the Confederate Horse Artillery*, p. 36.

59. Cockrell, ed., *Gunner with Stonewall: Reminiscences of William Thomas Poague*, p. 20.

A more familiar version of this anecdote is cited in Henderson, *Stonewall Jackson and the American Civil War*, pp. 188–189. I chose Poague's memoirs as being more accurate as he relates the story directly from Captain Carpenter, making this a second-hand account. Henderson does not cite the reference for his version, which may make it a story recycled several times before it reached his ears. Based on the previous mentioned errors in Henderson's work, his account—which suggests that Jackson was aware of his strategic victory on the night of March 23—lacks credibility.

60. Moore, *Rebellion Record*, p. 33.

Samuel J. C. Moore, Letter to his wife, March 26, 1862, University of North Carolina.

Frank Jones, Diary, March 23, 1862, HL.

61. William D. Lewis, Letter to Governor Curtin, p. 5.

Cavins, Letter to his wife, March 28, 1862, IHS.

Skidmore, *The Civil War Journal of Billy Davis*, p. 117.

Temperature readings, Georgetown, D.C., 9:00 P.M., March 23, 1862, National Weather Records.

62. "Prock," Undated letter, *Vincennes Western Sun*, April 12, 1862.

"Elliott" (Dr. C. E. Denig, 7th Ohio), Letter to his father, March 28, 1862, *State Capital Fact* (Columbus), April 12, 1862.

John G. Marsh (29th Ohio), Letter to his father, April 10, 1862, *Upper Ohio Valley Historical Review*, vol. 8 (2), 1979, p. 11.

Samuel V. List, Letter to his mother, March 29, 1862, Samuel V. List Collection, M444, Folder 19, Box 1, IHS.

CHAPTER NINE

1. Mrs. Cornelia McDonald, *A Diary With Reminiscences of the War and Refugee Life*, p. 53.

2. Mrs. Hugh Lee, Diary, March 25, 1862, HL.

Laura Lee, Diary, March 24, 1862, HL.

3. List of Prisoners of War Captured at Kernstown, and taken to Baltimore on March 24, 1862, Banks's Intelligence Reports, RG 393, Entry 223, NA.

Included among the captured was Lieutenant John Buford Lady. It is unknown if his brothers visited him prior to sending him to Baltimore.

4. Mrs. Hugh Lee, Diary, March 25, 1862, HL.

    Laura Lee, Diary, March 24, 1862, HL.

    Sperry, Diary, March 24, 1862, HL.

    John Peyton Clark, Journal, March 24, 1862, HL.

    Randolph Barton, *Recollections*, pp. 33–34.

    Market Street is today renamed as North Cameron Street. The biscuit transfer between the citizens and the soldiers occurred near the intersection of Cameron and Piccadilly Streets.

5. William T. McCoy (110th Pa.), Letter dated March 30, 1962, (Huntingdon) *Semi-Weekly Globe*, April 8, 1862.

    Levi Ritter, Letter dated March 29, 1862, *Hendricks County Ledger*, April 11, 1862.

    "The Winchester Battle-Field—The Wounded Rebels and the Secessionist Women," *Cincinnati Daily Commercial*, April 5, 1862.

6. Unknown soldier of the 110th Pa., Letter to his cousin, March 29, 1862, *The* (Philadelphia) *Press*, April 11, 1862.

    Alex Read, Letter dated March 26, 1862, *Clearfield Republican*, April 16, 1862.

    The Confederates were reinterred in Mt. Hebron Cemetery at the east end of Winchester.

7. No title, *The Philadelphia Inquirer*, April 21, 1862.

    Joseph Thoburn," (Wheeling) *Daily Intelligencer*, March 31, 1862.

    Old Town (84th Pa.), Letter to dated March 31, 1862, *Clearfield Republican*, April 23, 1862.

    "Colonel Murray's Remains," *Pittsburgh Post*, March 29, 1862.

8. Eby, p. 19.

9. Unknown soldier of 110th Pa., Letter to his cousin, March 29, 1862, *The* (Philadelphia) *Press*, April 11, 1862.

    Mrs. Cornelia McDonald, *A Diary With Reminiscences of the War and Refugee Life,* p. 54.

    OR, XII, pt. 1, p. 345.

    William S. Vohn, Letter dated April 2, 1862, *Weekly Perrysburg Journal,* April 10, 1862.

10. OR, XII, pt. 1, pp. 346–347.

    Wilson, *Itinerary of the Seventh Ohio Volunteer Infantry,* p. 133.

    Orville Thomson, *From Philippi to Appomattox: Narrative of the Service of the Seventh Indiana Infantry in the War for the Union*, published by the author, ca. 1907, p. 87.

    William F. Fox, *Regimental Losses in the American Civil War* (Dayton, Ohio: Morningside Bookshop, 1985), pp. 283, 311, 312, 313, 319, 330, 342, 364.

    "Killed and Wounded of the First Virginia Infantry," (Wheeling) *Daily Intelligencer,* April 23, 1862.

    Hamilton, *Manuscript History of the 110th Pa.*, p. 35.

11. Myron Wright, Letter to his father, March 25, 1862, *Summit Beacon,* April 1, 1862.

    Thomas Clark, Letter to his wife, March 29, 1862, Clark Letters.

12. Laura Lee, Diary, March 24, 1862, HL.

Mrs. Cornelia McDonald, *A Diary With Reminiscences of the War and Refugee Life*, pp. 54–55.

Strother, *Harper's*, p. 188.

13. "The Late Battle of Winchester," *Clearfield Republican*, April 9, 1862.

14. OR, XII, pt. 1, p. 335

James Shields, Letter to Nathaniel Banks, March 24, 1862, Box 19, Nathaniel Banks Papers, LC.

OR, XII, pt. 3, pp. 18–19.

15. Nathaniel Banks, Letter to Mary, March 24, 1862, Box 5, Folder 2, Nathaniel Banks Papers, LC.

Neese, *Three Years in the Confederate Horse Artillery*, pp. 37–39.

Wilder Dwight (2nd Mass.), Letter dated March 24, 1862, *Life and Letters*, p. 216.

16. Elisha Franklin Paxton, Letter to his wife, March 26, 1862, in *Memoir and Memorials*, p. 55.

Fornerdon, SHSP, pp. 133–134.

Neese, *Three Years in the Confederate Horse Artillery*, pp. 37–39.

Casler, *Four Years in the Stonewall Brigade*, p. 69.

Thomas J. Jackson, Letter to his wife, March 28, 1862, in *Life and Letters of General Thomas J. Jackson*, p. 247.

17. OR, XII, pt. 1, p. 379; pt. 3, p. 837.

18. OR, XII, pt. 1, p. 336.

Rawling, *History of the First Regiment Virginia Infantry*, pp. 68, 253.

Henry Capehart, "Shenandoah Valley: Operations in Virginia During the Year 1862," *The National Tribune*, March 21, 1889.

"W." "The Battle of Kernstown," *Richmond Daily Dispatch*, April 4, 1862.

Watkin Kearns (27th Va.), Diary, March 24, 1862, ViH MSS 5:1K2143:2, VHS.

19. James Shields, Letter to R. Morris Copeland, March 26, 1862, Box 19, Nathaniel Banks Papers, LC.

Special Orders No. 18, Shields Division, Box 19, Nathaniel Banks Papers, LC.

Festus P. Summers, "The Baltimore and Ohio—First in War," *Civil War History*, 7 (3), 1961, pp. 253–254.

20. James Shields, Letter to Senator Milton S. Latham, March 26, 1862, James Shields Papers, USAMHI.

21. OR, XII, pt. 1, pp. 375–377.

Warner, *Generals in Blue*, p. 515.

22. OR, XII, pt. 1, pp. 377–378.

William D. Lewis, Report of Battle of Kernstown, March 27, 1862, William D. Lewis Papers, HL.

E. W. Stephens, Letter to William D. Lewis, April 9, 1862, William D. Lewis Papers, HL.

William D. Lewis, Letter to Governor Curtin, March 30, 1862.

23. OR, XII, pt. 1, pp. 373–375.

George Whitcamp, Letter of resignation, March 28, 1862, Box 19, Nathaniel Banks Papers, LC.

24. OR, XII, pt. 1, pp. 349–351.

Eby, p. 23.

George H. Gordon, *Brook Farm to Cedar Mountain in the War of the Great Rebellion, 1861-62* (Boston, Mass.: James R. Osgood and Company, 1883), pp. 131–132.

25. Mrs. Hugh Lee, Diary, March 28, 1862, HL.

John Peyton Clark, Journal, March 29, 1862 & April 1, 1862, HL.

Sperry, Diary, March 29, 1862, HL.

Laura Lee, Diary, April 1, 1862, HL.

26. OR, XII, pt. 1, pp. 338–343.

Edwin Stanton, Letter to James Shields, March 30, 1862, Shields Papers, USAMHI.

In this revealing letter, Stanton begins: "I have received your two private letters and sympathise deeply with your bodily afflictions, and still more with your mental anxiety. Every effort in my power will be made to relieve you, and place you in a condition worthy of your skill and courage, and secure to the country the benefits of your superior military talents. . . ." Shields, likely by his own wishes, was not relieved from field command that spring. He returned to head his division in April.

27. "General Shields' Account of the Battle," *The Daily Toledo Blade*, April 1, 1862.

Kimball, Letter to J. J. Cravens, March 29, 1862, Cravens Mss., Lilly Library, Indiana University, Bloomington, Indiana.

George Rose, Letter to Nathan Kimball, May 3, 1862, Kimball Mss., Lilly Library, Indiana University, Bloomington, Indiana.

28. K. M. D., Letter dated March 27, 1862, *Cincinnati Daily Commercial*, April 9, 1862.

James Oakey (14th Indiana), Letter dated March 27, 1862, *Terre-Haute Daily Express*, April 5, 1862.

K. M. D., Letter dated March 28, 1862, *Parke County Republican* (Rockville, Indiana), April 16, 1862.

29. David Howell (14th Indiana), Letter to his cousin and parents, April 27, 1862, USAMHI.

"Prock," Letter dated March 29, 1862, *Vincennes Western Sun*, April 12, 1862.

W. C. F. (13th Indiana), Letter dated March 26, 1862, Indianapolis *Daily Journal*, April 2, 1862.

Thomson, *From Philippi to Appomattox*, p. 88.

George Washington Lambert, Diary, March 23, 1862, IHS.

30. Jed Hotchkiss, Journal, March 26 & 28, 1862, Hotchkiss Papers, LC.

31. Jacob Lemly, Diary, March 28, 1862, HL.

Frank Jones, Diary, March 28, 1862, HL.

32. John G. Paxton, ed., Letter to his wife, March 23, 1862, *Memoir and Memorials*, p. 54.

Pendleton, Letter to his mother, March 29, 1862, VMHB, p. 342.

A. R. B., Jr., Letter dated March 26, 1862, *Richmond Daily Dispatch*, April 5, 1862.

John Harman, Letter to his brother, March 26, 1862, Hotchkiss Papers, LC.

James H. Langhorne, Letter to his parents, April 3, 1862, *Lynchburg Virginian*, April 16, 1862.

33. Elisha Franklin Paxton, Letter to his wife, March 26, 1862, in *Memoir and Memorials*, p. 55.

    Frank Jones, Letter to his wife, March 30, 1862, HL.

    Thomas J. Jackson, Letter to his wife, March 28, 1862 in *Life and Letters of General Thomas J. Jackson*, p. 247.

34. OR, XII, pt. 1, pp. 392, 402, 404.

35. J. (23rd Va.), Letter dated April 3, 1862, *Richmond Daily Dispatch*, April 11, 1862.

    Cockrell, ed., *Gunner with Stonewall: Reminiscences of William Thomas Poague*, p. 18.

36. OR, XII, pt. 1, p. 384.

    "List of Confederates in Hospital," *Staunton Spectator*, April 1, 1862.

    Kernstown Casualty List, Jackson Papers, VHS.

    Banks's Intelligence Reports, RG 393, Entry 223, NA.

    Two hundred thirty-four Confederates were sent to Baltimore on March 24, 1862. In early April, an additional seventeen prisoners were sent there as well.

    The numbers of killed and mortally wounded were also obtained in roster studies conducted by Jerry Reid.

37. Fornerden, *A Brief History of the Military Career of Carpenter's Battery*, p. 134.

38. Allan, *Stonewall Jackson's Valley Campaign*, pp. 67–68.

    Hotchkiss, Journal, March 29, 1862, Hotchkiss Papers, LC.

39. OR, XII, pt. 1, pp. 338, 563.

    OR, XII, pt. 3, pp. 20–21.

    "Proceedings of the War Board," March 27, 1862, Reel #13, p. 287, Edwin Stanton Collection, LC.

40. Stephen W. Sears, *The Civil War Papers of George B. McClellan* (New York: Ticknor & Fields, 1989), pp. 222–223, 230, 233, 237.

    Allan, *Stonewall Jackson's Valley Campaign*, pp. 65, 236.

41. OR, XII, pt. 1, pp. 383–384.

    OR, XII, pt. 3, p. 840.

    Pendleton, Letter to his mother, March 29, 1862, VMHB, p. 343.

    Jed Hotchkiss, Letter to his wife, March 27, 1862, Hotchkiss Papers, LC.

    It is unknown if Jackson's informant was a spy or a Union deserter. Pendleton and Hotchkiss illustrate the easy availability of Northern newspapers.

42. Sears, *The Civil War Papers of George B. McClellan*, pp. 220–221.

43. OR, XII, pt. 3, p. 51.

    Averitt, *The Memoirs of General Turner Ashby*, p. 273.

    Dwight, Letter to his wife, March 15, 1862, in *Life and Letters of Wilder Dwight*, pp. 224–225.

    Worsham, *One of Jackson's Foot Cavalry*, p. 72.

    Jed Hotchkiss, Letter to his wife, April 2, 1862, Hotchkiss Papers, LC.

    Anonymous Soldier (8th Ohio), Letter dated April 5, 1862, *Bucyrus Weekly Journal*, April 18, 1862.

44. Thomas J. Jackson, Letter to A. R. Boteler, May 6, 1862, Boteler Papers, DU.

45. Pendleton, Letter to his mother, April 3, 1862, VMHB, p. 344.

    Jacob Lemly, Diary, April 2, 1862, HL.

    Jed Hotchkiss, Journal, April 2, 1862, Hotchkiss Papers, LC.

46. Pendleton, Letter to his mother, April 3, 1862, VMHB, p. 344.

    Garnett, Letter to Samuel Cooper, June 20, 1862, RBGCMP, p. 1.

    Frank Jones, Diary, April 2, 1862, HL.

    H. K. Douglas, Review of William Allan's book, *Hagerstown Mail*, November 5, 1880, Reel #50, Hotchkiss Papers, LC.

47. Hotchkiss, Journal, April 2, 1862, Hotchkiss Papers, LC.

    Allan, *Stonewall Jackson's Valley Campaign,* pp. 68–69, 238.

    Watkin Kearns, Diary, April 2, 1862, VHS.

48. OR, XII, pt. 3, pp. 843–844.

49. James Shields, Letter to Major R. Morris Copeland, April 5, 1862, Box 19, Nathaniel Banks Papers, LC.

    "Strange Suicide of a Colonel," *Cleveland Morning Leader*, April 16, 1862.

    G. G. Benedict, *Vermont in the Civil War,* vol. 2 (Burlington, Vermont: The Free Press Association, 1888), p. 544.

    Eby, p. 26.

    OR, XII, pt. 3, pp. 50, 52.

50. John Gale, Undated letter, (Wheeling) *Daily Intelligencer,* April 10, 1862.

51. Samuel V. List, Diary, June 8, 1862, IHS.

    "Dixie" (7th Indiana), Letter dated June 6, 1862, *Aurora Commercial*, June 1862.

CHAPTER TEN

1. Douglas, *I Rode with Stonewall,* p. 96.

2. Kimball, General's Report, March 20, 1864, M1098, R30, Vol. 3, NA, p. 883.

    OR, XII, pt. 1, p. 690.

3. Thomas Clarke (29th Ohio), Letter to his wife, May 27, 1862, Clark Letters.

    O. T. (7th Indiana), Letter dated June 11, 1862, *Indianapolis Journal*, June 19, 1862.

4. Henry Talcott (13th Indiana), Letter dated June 26, 1862, *Valparaiso Republic*, July 10, 1862.

5. "General Shields," (Wheeling) *Daily Intelligencer*, June 23, 1862.

    "General Shields," *Painesville Telegraph*, July 17, 1862.

    James Shields, Letter to Edwin Stanton, June 13, 1862, Reel #3, #51578, Edwin Stanton Papers, LC.

6. R. Morris Copeland, Letter to Nathaniel P. Banks, May 21, 1862, Box 20, Nathaniel Banks Papers, LC.

7. Ronald H. Bailey, *Forward To Richmond: McClellan's Peninsular Campaign* (Alexandria, Va.: Time-Life Books, Inc., 1983), p. 65.

    Allan G. Bogue, *The Earnest Men: Republicans of the Civil War Senate* (Ithaca, N.Y.: Cornell University Press, 1981), pp. 107, 135–136.

Keith A. Botterud, *The Joint Committee on the Conduct of the Civil War*, Master's Thesis for Georgetown University, 1949, pp. 1–16.

8. Third Session of the 39th Congress, *Report of the Joint Committee of the Senate on the Conduct of the War*, Vol. 3, pt. 2, no. 108, Government Printing Office, Washington, D.C., 1863, pp. 403–414.

The exchange with Dr. McAbee is on p. 411.

9. "The Battle of Port Republic," *Painesville Telegraph*, June 26, 1862.

"General Shields" *Painesville Telegraph*, July 17, 1862.

General James Shields, General's Report, September 25, 1872, M1098, R9, Vol. 6, NA, p. 286.

William H. Condon, *Life of Major-General James Shields: Hero of Three Wars and Senator from Three States* (Chicago, Ill.: Press of the Blakely Printing Company, 1900), p. 260.

Kimball, General's Report, p. 885.

Salmon Chase, Diary, August 2–3, 1862, Salmon Chase Papers, LC.

OR, XII, pt. 3, p. 435.

Shields's nomination vote is not indexed in the Senate records. The nomination was likely killed in committee; therefore, it never reached the Senate floor for a full vote.

10. Lowell Reidenbaugh, *27th Virginia Infantry* (Lynchburg, Va.: H. E. Howard, Inc., 1993), pp. 152, 156.

11. General Jackson's General Orders No. 218, April 29, 1862, Reel #49, Hotchkiss Papers, LC.

The transcript of Jackson's letter is punctuated in such a way to make it incomprehensible. The remarks about Garnett, therefore, have been re-punctuated to clarify his intent (See Freeman, *Lee's Lieutenants*, vol. 1, p. 318 for the corrected punctuation model).

12. Richard Brooke Garnett, Letter to R. M. Hunter, April 1862, G-385, RBGCMP.

Richard Brooke Garnett, Letter to Samuel Cooper, June 20, 1862, G-387, RBGCMP.

General Thomas J. Jackson, Letter to A. R. Boteler, May 6, 1862, Boteler Papers, DU.

13. Special Orders No. 146, June 25, 1862, G-386c, RBGCMP.

Garnett, Letter to Cooper, RBGCMP.

John E. Pierce, Jackson, Garnett and "The Unfortunate Breach," *Civil War Times Illustrated*, vol. 12 (6), 1973, p. 38.

Robert K. Krick, "The Army of Northern Virginia's Most Notorious Court Martial . . . Jackson vs. Garnett," *Blue & Gray Magazine*, June–July 1986, p. 30.

14. Freeman, *Lee's Lieutenants*, p. 325.

Cockrell, ed., *Gunner with Stonewall: Reminiscences of William Thomas Poague*, p. 20.

Thomas H. Williamson, Letter, G-383, RBGCMP.

15. Garnett, Letter to R. M. Hunter, G-385, RBGCMP.

16. Garnett, Letter to Cooper, RBGCMP.

17. Transcript, RBGCMP.

Garnett periodically wrote the word "Lie" on the margin of his copy of the transcript, the version which survives today. His opinion was scribbled several times near Jackson's responses.

Temperature readings, Georgetown, D.C., August 6, 1862, National Weather Records.

The mercury rose to ninety-nine degrees at 2:00 P.M.

18. Lenoir Chambers, *Stonewall Jackson,* vol. 2 (New York: William Morrow & Co., 1959), pp. 104, 498.

Chambers obtained Pendleton's letter from the Pendleton family papers at the University of North Carolina.

19. Pendleton, Testimony, August 7, 1862, RBGCMP.

Robert K. Krick, "Cedar Mountain," *The Civil War Battlefield Guide,* Frances H. Kennedy, ed., (Boston, Mass.: Houghton Mifflin Company, 1990), p. 70.

20. Turner Ashby, Letter to A. R. Boteler, April 25, 1862, Simon Gratz Manuscript Collection, Case 5, Box 11, Historical Society of Pennsylvania, Philadelphia, Pa.

21. F. W. Lander, Letter to Seth Williams, Jan. 20, 1862, #85938, McClellan Papers, LC. Lander's report details the small arms carried by his men who fight at Kernstown two months later. Most of his division was equipped with rifled muskets.

22. Pendleton, Letter to his mother, March 29, 1862, VMHB, p. 342.

EPILOGUE

1. John G. Marsh (29th Ohio), Letter to his father, April 10, 1862, *Upper Ohio Valley Historical Review,* 8 (2), 1979, p. 10.

2. Krick, *Lee's Colonels,* p. 275.

3. Ibid, p. 153.

Robert K. Krick, *Stonewall Jackson at Cedar Mountain* (Chapel Hill and London: The University of North Carolina Press, 1990), p. 26.

4. W. G. Bean, "The Unusual War Experience of Lieutenant George G. Junkin, C. S. A." *The Virginia Magazine of History and Biography,* 76 (2), 1968, pp. 185–190.

5. General James Shields, General's Report, September 25, 1872, M1098, R9, Vol. 6, NA, p. 286.

Sifakis, *Who Was Who in the Civil War,* pp. 363–364.

J. F. Huntington (1st Ohio Light Artillery), Letter, *The National Tribune,* December 5, 1889.

Samuel W. Cass (Ohio Artillery), Letter, *The National Tribune,* December 19, 1889.

6. Farwell, *Stonewall: A Biography of General Thomas J. Jackson,* p. 527.

7. Douglas, *I Rode with Stonewall,* p. 47.

8. Stephen Davis, "The Death and Burials of General Richard Brooke Garnett," *The Gettysburg Magazine,* 5, 1991, pp. 110–116.

Roland E. Bowen (15th Mass.), "Nothing But Cowards Run," Civil War Magazine, #50, April 1995, p. 45.

Davis's excellent article puts to rest the traditional notion that Garnett was wounded a few days before Gettysburg. The date of his injury is confirmed by a letter Garnett wrote the next day (June 21, 1863). The two eyewitnesses who saw Garnett shot through the head were R. H. Irvine and Captain John S. Jones. Both aides were at his side when he fell and give the same account of his death.

9. Sifakis, *Who Was Who in the Civil War,* pp. 199, 633–634.

   Joseph A. Whitehorne, "The 1864 Shenandoah Valley Campaign," *The Civil War Battlefield Guide,* pp. 223–224.

10. "Death of Adj't. Jas. A. Langhorne," *The Lynchburg Virginian,* June 2, 1864.

11. Warner, *Generals in Blue,* p. 515.

    Thomas A. Lewis and the editors of Time-Life Books, *The Shenandoah in Flames: The Valley Campaign of 1864* (Alexandria, Virginia: Time-Life Books, 1987), pp. 71, 73, 83.

12. Whitehorne, "The 1864 Shenandoah Valley Campaign," *The Civil War Battlefield Guide,* pp. 224–225, 239–242.

    Jed Hotchkiss, Diary, October 10–13, 1862 & July 25, 1864, in Archie P. McDonald, ed., *Make Me a Map of the Valley: The Civil War Journal of Stonewall Jackson's Topographer* (Dallas, Texas: Southern Methodist University Press, 1973), pp. 87–88, 217.

13. Scott C. Patchan, *Forgotten Fury: The Battle of Piedmont* (Fredericksburg, Va.: Sgt. Kirkland's Museum and Historical Society, Inc., 1996), pp. 140–146.

    "Funeral Obsequies of Col. Thoburn, Capt. Bier and Sergeant Jenkins,—The City in Mourning," (Wheeling) *Daily Intelligencer,* October 26, 1862.

    The Union officers at Kernstown who were commissioned (not brevetted) as generals by the end of the war are (Kernstown rank, name, and unit):

    Colonel Nathan Kimball, commanding First Brigade

    Colonel Jeremiah C. Sullivan, commanding Second Brigade

    Colonel Erastus B. Tyler, commanding Third Brigade

    Colonel John Mason, 4th Ohio Infantry (acting as division aide)

    Colonel Samuel Sprigg Carroll, 8th Ohio Infantry

    Colonel Thomas O. Osborn, 39th Illinois Infantry

    Lieutenant Colonel William Harrow, 14th Indiana Infantry

    Lieutenant Colonel Robert Foster, 13th Indiana Infantry

    Lieutenant Colonel Joseph T. Copeland, 1st Michigan Cavalry

    Major Isaac Duval, 1st West Virginia Infantry

    Lieutenant Robert Catterson, 14th Indiana Infantry

    Many deserving officers fighting for the Confederacy at Kernstown were killed or resigned early in the war. The following are those that received a general's commission:

    Colonel Turner Ashby, 7th Virginia Cavalry

    Colonel John Echols, 27th Virginia Infantry

    Major Elisha Franklin Paxton, 27th Virginia Infantry

    Lieutenant William Terry, 4th Virginia Infantry

14. Quarles, *Some Worthy Lives,* pp. 152–153.

15. Ibid, p. 143.

16. Warner, *Generals in Blue,* pp. 73, 488, 617.

    Sifakis, *Who Was Who in the Civil War,* pp. 279, 587.

OR, XLVI, pt. 2, p. 982.

17. S. Bassett French, "William H. Harman," S. Basset French Biographies, VSL, pp. 98–99.

18. Warner, *Generals in Blue*, p. 73.

Unidentified member of 2nd Virginia, "The Little Rooster on the Shenandoah," *Winchester Evening Star*, February 22, 1918.

19. Krick, *Lee's Colonels*, p. 263.

Paul Truckey, Compiled Pension Record, RG 94, NA.

Warner, *Generals in Blue*, p. 211.

Quarles, *Some Worthy Lives*, pp. 125–126.

Sifakis, *Who Was Who in the Civil War*, p. 314.

20. Condon, *Life of Major General James Shields*, pp. 301, 329–330.

Purcell, *James Shields: Soldier and Statesman*, pp. 85–87.

21. Warner, *Generals in Blue*, p. 268.

"Stonewall Jackson's Valley Campaign," *Hagerstown Mail*, November 5, 1880.

E. H. C. Cavins, Letter to Nathan Kimball, July 8, 1887, EHC Cavins Collection, M42, Box 2, Folder 4, IHS.

E. H. C. Cavins, Letter to Nathan Kimball, June 21, 1887, Kimball Mss., Lilly Library, Indiana University.

E. H. C. Cavins, Letter to Nathan Kimball, July 12, 1887, Kimball Mss., Lilly Library, Indiana University.

General John D. Imboden, "Stonewall Jackson in the Shenandoah," *Battles and Leaders of the Civil War*, II, pp. 283–284.

Kimball, "Fighting Jackson at Kernstown," *Battles and Leaders of the Civil War*, II, pp. 302–309.

22. "The Lost Sword of General Richard Brooke Garnett, Who Fell at Gettysburg," SHSP, vol. 33 (1905), pp. 26–31.

"Gen. Richard B. Garnett's Sword," *Confederate Veteran* 15 (1907), p. 230.

23. "Recognized Old Kernstown Rocks," *Winchester Evening Star*, September 3, 1912.

The veteran's name was W. H. Montgomery.

24. Voris, "The Battle of the Boys," p. 100.

APPENDIX B

1. OR, XII, pt. 1, pp. 383–410.

Freeman, *Lee's Lieutenants*, p. 315.

Allan, *Stonewall Jackson's Valley Campaign*, p. 232.

Henderson, *Stonewall Jackson and the American Civil War*, p. 199.

Roger G. Tanner, *Stonewall in the Valley* (Garden City, New York: Doubleday & Company, Inc., 1976), p. 123.

2. OR, XII, pt. 1, pp. 335, 336, 342.

3. Allan, *Stonewall Jackson's Valley Campaign*, pp. 230, 232.

4. OR, XII, pt. 3, pp. 4–5.

5. E. H. C. Cavins, Letter to Nathan Kimball, June 1885, EHC Cavins Collection, M42, Box 2, Folder 4, IHS.

6. "List of Casualties at the Battle Near Winchester, Va.," 84th Pennsylvania Regimental File, Pennsylvania State Archives, Harrisburg, Pa.

William D. Lewis, Letter to Governor Curtin, March 30, 1862, 110th Pennsylvania Regimental File, RG 19, Pennsylvania Historical and Museum Commission, Harrisburg, Pa.

OR, XII, pt. 1, pp. 368, 371.

7. Company K, 1st West Virginia, Morning Report, March 22, 1862, RG 94, NA.

8. J. C. Sullivan, Dispatch dated March 31, 1862, Box 19, Folder 3, Nathaniel Banks Papers, LC.

9. Lt. Col. Thomas MacDowell, Letter to Governor Curtin, March 31, 1862, 84th Pennsylvania Regimental File, RG 19, Pennsylvania Historical and Museum Commission, Harrisburg, Pa.

84th Pennsylvania, Field and Staff Report, March, 1862, "Compiled Records Showing Service of Military Units in Volunteer Union Organizations," M594, NA.

Thomas Craig, "Shields's Division: A Delayed Report of the 84th Pennsylvania at Kernstown," *The National Tribune*, November 21, 1889.

10. Hamilton, *Manuscript History of the 110th Pa.*, p. 35.

Samuel P. Bates, *History of Pennsylvania Volunteers, 1861–1865,* vol. 3, Harrisburg, 1869.

11. Frank Ingersoll, Letter to his sister, March 26, 1862, Ingersoll Mss., Lilly Library, Indiana University, Bloomington, Ind.

12. OR, XII, pt. 1, p. 370.

13. Company C, 7th Ohio, Record of Movements, March–April 1862, "Compiled Records Showing Service of Military Units in Volunteer Union Organizations," M594, NA.

Cleveland Morning Leader, April 4, 1862.

Cincinnati Daily Commercial, April 2, 1862.

14. Company K, 1st West Virginia, Morning Report, March 22, 1862, RG 94, NA.

15. Nathan Kimball, Dispatch dated March 31, 1862, Box 19, Folder 3, Nathaniel Banks Papers, LC.

16. J. C. Sullivan, Dispatch dated March 31, 1862, Box 19, Folder 3, Nathaniel Banks Papers, LC.

17. Erastus B. Tyler, Dispatch dated March 31, 1862, Box 19, Folder 3, Nathaniel Banks Papers, LC.

18. William D. Lewis, Letter to Governor Curtin, March 30, 1862, 110th Pennsylvania Regimental File, RG 19, Pennsylvania Historical and Museum Commission, Harrisburg, Pa.

BIBLIOGRAPHY

MANUSCRIPT SOURCES

Cincinnati Historical Society, Cincinnati, Ohio.

Matthew Schwab, Letter to his parents, March 28, 1862, Matthew Schwab Letters, 1861–1865, Box 1, Folder 4.

Chicago Historical Society, Chicago, Illinois.

Turner Ashby, Letter to Judah P. Benjamin, March 17, 1862, Turner Ashby Papers.

Duke University, William R. Perkins Library, Manuscript Department, Durham, North Carolina.

G. K. Bedinger, Letter to his father, April 1, 1862, Bedinger Dandridge Family Papers.

William F. Harrison, Letter to his wife, March 28, 1862, William F. Harrison Collection.

Thomas J. Jackson, Letter to A. R. Boteler, May 6, 1862, Boteler Papers.

Fredericksburg and Spotsylvania National Military Park, Fredericksburg, Virginia.

Charles Gibson, Letter to his parents, January 8, 1862, Vol. 182.

Oscar Rudd, Journal, March 23, 1862.

Handley Library, Archives Room, Winchester, Virginia.

David Bard, Letter to a friend, March 28, 1862, 361 WFCHS MMF.

Reverend B. F. Brooke, Journal, 226 WFCHS MMF.

War-Time Diary of Miss Julia Chase, 1861–1864, 973.78 C38.

John Peyton Clark, Journal, March 12, 1862, Louisa Crawford Collection, 424 WFCHS.

John H. Grabill, Diary, Charles Affleck Collection, 36 WFCHS, Box 2.

Frank Jones, Diary, Louisa Crawford Collection, 424 WFCHS.

Frank Jones, Letters to his wife, Ann Cary Randolph Jones Papers, 451 THL.

Laura Lee, Diary, Ben Ritter Collection, 12 WFCHS, Box 1.

Mrs. Hugh Lee, Diary, 1182 WFCHS.

Jacob Lemly, Diary, 1374 THL MMF Lemly, Jacob.

Colonel William D. Lewis Collection, 573 WFCHS.

Abraham S. Miller, Letter to his wife, January 6, 1862, James Miller Collection, 1 WFCHS, Box 1.

Kate S. Sperry, Diary, *Surrender? Never Surrender!*, 975.5991 Sp3.

Historical Society of Pennsylvania, Philadelphia, Pennsylvania.

Turner Ashby, Letter to A. R. Boteler, April 25, 1862, Simon Gratz Manuscript Collection, Case 5, Box 11.

Indiana Historical Society, Manuscript Department, Indianapolis, Indiana.

David Beem, Letter to his parents, March 15, 1862, David Beem Collection, M151, Folder 2, Box 1.

E. H. C. Cavins Collection, Collection M42, Box 2.

William Houghton, Letter to his father, March 27, 1862, Houghton Papers, M147, Box 1, Folder 4.

James M. King, Journal.

George Washington Lambert, Journal, M178, Box 2, Folder 3.

Samuel V. List Collection, M444, Folder 19, Box 1.

Van Dyke Family Papers.

Indiana Historical Society, W. H. Smith Memorial Library, Indianapolis, Indiana.

Isaac Banta, Letter to his brother, March, 1862.

John Cashner, Diary.

Indiana University, Lilly Library, Bloomington, Indiana.

Cravens Manuscript.

Frank Ingersoll, Letter to his sister, March 26, 1862, Ingersoll Manuscript.

Nathan Kimball Papers, Kimball Manuscript.

Library of Congress, Manuscript Division. Washington, D.C.

Nathaniel Banks Papers.

Salmon P. Chase Papers.

Jed Hotchkiss Papers.

Frederick Lander Papers.

Abraham Lincoln Papers.

George B. McClellan Papers.

Edwin Stanton Papers.

Military Order of the Loyal Legion of the United States, Civil War
    Library and Museum, Philadelphia, Pennsylvania.

    James C. M. Hamilton, "Manuscript History of the 110th
        Pennsylvania."

Museum of the Confederacy, Eleanor Brockenbrough Library,
    Richmond, Virginia.

    Richard Brooke Garnett Court-martial Papers.

    Major G. C. Coleman, Letter to his wife, March 25, 1862, Unfiled
        Manuscript.

    J. Tucker Randolph, Diary.

National Archives, Washington, D.C.

    Henry Anisansel Court-martial Transcript, Record Group
        153, Case File #II-693.

    Otto Burstenbinder Court-martial Case, Record Group 153,
        B1205, (VS) 1862, Box #23.

    Applications for Army Promotions, 15W3, Row 11,
        Compartment 5, Shelf A, Box 59, Record Group 107.

    Nathaniel Banks's Intelligence Reports, Record Group 393,
        Entry 223.

    Confederate States Army Casualties: Lists and Narrative
        Reports, Record Group 109.

    Compiled Service Records of Confederate Soldiers Who
        Served in Organizations from the State of Virginia, Record
        Group 109.

    Compiled Records Showing Service of Military Units in
        Volunteer Union Organizations, M594.

    Monthly Consolidation of the Weekly Class Reports including
        the Conduct Roll, U.S. Military Academy, Record
        Group 94.

    Population Schedules of the Sixth Census of the United
        States, Washington County, Pennsylvania, 1840, Record
        Group 29.

    Population Schedules of the Seventh Census of the United
        States, Ohio County, Virginia, 1850, Record Group 29.

Population Schedules of the Eighth Census of the United States, Virginia, 1860, Record Group 29.

Records of Volunteer Union Soldiers Who Served During the Civil War, Record Group 94.

Regimental Orders, Reports, and Furlough Books, Record Group 393.

David Taylor, Signal Corps, Official Report, April 17, 1862, Record Group 94.

Telegrams Collected by the Office of the Secretary of War, Record Group 94, M473.

U.S. Army General's Report of Civil War Service, Record Group 94, M1098.

U.S. Military Academy Application Papers, 1805–1866, Record Group 94, M688, Roll 91.

National Weather Records Center. Asheville, North Carolina.

"Weather Journal Recording Observations at . . . Georgetown, D.C., June 1858-May 1866."

"Weather Journal Recording Observations at . . . Cumberland, Md., January, 1859–1871."

"Weather Journal Recording Observations at . . . Sheets Mill, Hampshire County, Va., 1862."

Ohio Historical Society, Columbus, Ohio.

George Wood, Diary, Vol. 398.

Nathaniel L. Parmater, Diary, Mss. 246.

Pennsylvania Historical and Museum Commission, Division of Archives and Manuscripts, Harrisburg, Pennsylvania.

84th Pennsylvania Regiment Papers, Record Group 19.

110th Pennsylvania Regiment Papers, Record Group 19.

Private Collections

Marilyn Clark-Snyder, Annandale, Virginia. Lieutenant Colonel Thomas Clark, Letters to his wife.

David Richards, Gettysburg, Pennsylvania. Jacob Peterman, Letters to his father.

Stanford University Libraries, Department of Special Collections, Stanford, California.

Lander Family Papers.

United States Army Military History Institute, Carlisle Barracks, Pennsylvania.

Thomas Gouldsberry, Letter to his father, May 6, 1862, Gouldsberry Papers, Save the Flags Collection.

David Howell, Letter to his cousin and parents, April 27, 1862.

Lewis Owen, Letter to his cousin, March 22, 1862, David Howell Collection.

General James Shields Papers.

University of North Carolina, Southern Historical Collection, Chapel Hill, N.C.

Samuel J. C. Moore Letters.

University of Virginia, Charlottesville, Virginia.

Memoirs of Clement D. Fishburne.

Virginia Historical Society. Richmond, Virginia.

Thomas J. Jackson Papers.

"List of Killed and Wounded of the First Brigade Commanded by Gen'l. Garnett at the Battle of Kernstown, March 23, 1862."

Watkin Kearns, Diary.

William Kinzer, Diary.

Robert E. Lee Headquarter Papers.

Langhorne Family Papers.

Allen W. Wright, *"The 42nd Virginia Infantry."*

Virginia State Archives and Library, Richmond, Virginia.

John Apperson, Diary.

S. Bassett French Papers.

James W. Orr, "Recollections of the War Between the States," 1909.

Henry S. Shanklin (27th Va.), Letter to his father, March 31, 1862.

Washington and Lee University, Lexington, Virginia.

John N. Lyle, "Stonewall Jackson's Guard, the Washington College Company, or Imperialism in the American Union."

PUBLISHED PRIMARY SOURCES

Alexander, Charles. "The First Battalion." *Richmond Times-Dispatch*, July 3, 1904.

Allan, William. *Stonewall Jackson's Campaign in the Shenandoah Valley of Virginia from November 4, 1861 to June 17, 1862.* London: Hugh Rees, Ltd., 1912.

Avirett, Rev. James B. *The Memoirs of General Turner Ashby and His Compeers.* Baltimore, Md.: Selby & Dulany, 1867.

"A War Story." *Shenandoah Herald* (Woodstock, Va.), November 26, 1897.

Barton, Randolph. *Recollections.* Baltimore, Md.: Thomas & Evans Printing Company, 1913.

Baylor, George. *Bull Run to Bull Run or Four Years in the Army of Northern Virginia.* Richmond, Va.: B. F. Johnston, 1900.

Bean, W. G., ed. The Valley Campaign of 1862 as Revealed in Letters of Sandie Pendleton." *Virginia Magazine of History and Biography* 78 (1970): 326–364.

"Brigadier-General James Shields." *The Philadelphia Inquirer*, March 26, 1862.

Bowen, Roland E. "Nothing But Cowards Run." *Civil War Magazine* 50 (1995): 42–49.

Capehart, Henry. "Shenandoah Valley: Operations in Virginia During the Year 1862." *The National Tribune*, March 14–May 9, 1889.

Casler, John O. *Four Years in the Stonewall Brigade.* Guthrie, Okla.: State Capital Printing Company, 1893.

Cass, Samuel W. Letter to editor. *The National Tribune*, December 19, 1889.

Clark, Charles M. *The History of the Thirty-Ninth Regiment Illinois Volunteer Veteran Infantry (Yates Phalanx) in the War of the Rebellion, 1861–1865.* Chicago, Ill.: Veterans Association, 1889.

Clarke, H. C., comp. *The Confederate States Almanac and Repository of Useful Knowledge for 1862.* Vicksburg, Miss.: 1861.

Cockrell, Monroe F., ed. *Gunner With Stonewall: Reminiscences of William Thomas Poague.* Wilmington, N.C.: Broadfoot Publishing Company, 1989.

"Colonel Joseph Thoburn." (Wheeling) *Daily Intelligencer*, March 31, 1862.

"Colonel Murray's Remains." *Pittsburgh Post*, March 29, 1862.

Cooper, John S. "The Shenandoah Valley in Eighteen Hundred and Sixty-Two." *Military Order of the Loyal Legion of the United States, Illinois Commandery, Military Essays and Recollections.* Chicago: Cozzens & Beaton Company, V (1907): 36–60.

Cox, Jacob D. "McClellan in West Virginia." In *Battles and Leaders of the Civil War.* Edited by Robert U. Johnson and Clarence C. Buel. Secaucus, N.J.: Castle, 1: 126–148.

Craig, Thomas H. "Shields's Division: A Delayed Report of the 84th Pennsylvania at Kernstown." *The National Tribune*, November 21, 1889.

Cummins, D. Duane, and Daryl Hohweiller, eds. *An Enlisted Soldier's View of the Civil War: The Wartime Papers of Joseph Richardson Ward, Jr.* West Lafayette, Indiana: Belle Publication, 1989.

Curry, W. L., comp. *Four Years in the Saddle. History of the First Regiment Ohio Volunteer Cavalry. War of the Rebellion—1861–1865.* Jonesboro, Georgia: Freedom Hill Press, Inc., 1898.

"Death of Adj't. Jas. A. Langhorne." *The Lynchburg Virginian*, June 2, 1864.

"Death of Hugh Barr." *Winchester Times*, February 11, 1885.

"Death of Mr. Hugh Barr." *Winchester News*, February 13, 1885.

Douglas, H. K. "Stonewall Jackson's Valley Campaign." *Hagerstown Mail*, November 5, 1880.

Douglas, Henry Kyd. *I Rode With Stonewall.* Reprint Simons Island, Georgia: Mockingbird Books, Inc., 1987.

Dwight, Wilder. *Life and Letters of Wilder Dwight, Lieut.-Col. Second Mass. Inf. Vols.* Boston, Mass.: Ticknor and Field, 1868.

Eby, Cecil D., Jr., ed. *A Virginia Yankee in the Civil War: The Diaries of David Hunter Strother.* Chapel Hill, N.C.: The University of North Carolina Press, 1961.

Elwood, John W. *Elwood's Stories of the Old Ringgold Cavalry, 1847–1865, The 1st Three Year Cavalry of the Civil War.* Coal Center, Pa.: Published by the author, 1914.

Fahrion, G. W. "Courage of a Virginia Color Bearer." *Confederate Veteran* 17 (1909): 125.

Fishburne, Clement D. "Historical Sketch of the Rockbridge Artillery, C. S. Army, by a Member of the Famous Battery." *Southern Historical Society Papers* 23 (1895): 98–132.

Fornerden, C. A. *A Brief History of the Military Career of Carpenter's Battery: From its organization as a rifle company under the name of the Alleghany Roughs to the ending of the war between the states.* New Market, Va.: Henkel & Company Printers, 1911.

Fowler, Thomas C. "Criticizing Capehart. The Troops that Captured the Stonewall at Kernstown." *The National Tribune*, May 16, 1889.

Frazier, Lee. "At Kernstown, Va." *The National Tribune*, September 26, 1912.

Frazier, Lee. "At Winchester." *The National Tribune*, October 30, 1890.

"Funeral Obsequies of Col. Thoburn, Capt. Bier and Sergeant Jenkins—The City in Mourning." (Wheeling) *Daily Intelligencer*, October 26, 1862.

"General Richard B. Garnett's Sword." *The Confederate Veteran* 15 (1907): 230.

"General Shields' Account of the Battle." *Daily Toledo Blade*, April 1, 1862.

"General Shields." *Painesville Telegraph*, July 17, 1862.

"General Shields." (Wheeling) *Daily Intelligencer*, June 23, 1862.

Gordon, George H. *Brook Farm to Cedar Mountain in the War of the Great Rebellion, 1861–62.* Boston, Mass.: James R. Osgood and Company, 1883.

Green, Brian and Maria. "Unrecorded 'Stonewall' Jackson Cover and Letter Found." *The Confederate Philatelist* 1990: 2–6.

Haas, Ralph, ed. *Dear Esther: The Civil War Letters of Private Augier Dobbs, Centreville, Pennsylvania Company "A," The Ringgold Cavalry Company 22nd Pennsylvania Cavalry, June 29, 1861 to October 31, 1865.* Apollo, Pa.: Closson Press, 1991.

Harman, A. W. "The Valley after Kernstown. Jackson's Faith in his Little Army—Orders to Enforce Discipline." *Southern Historical Society Papers* XIX (1891): 318–320.

Houghton, William. "Capehart Criticized. The Part Taken by the 14th Ind. at Kernstown." *The National Tribune*, June 6, 1889.

Huntington, James F. "In the Valley: The Campaign in the Spring of 1862." *The National Tribune*, September 5, 1889.

———. Letter to the editor, *The National Tribune*, December 5, 1889.

———. "Operations in the Shenandoah Valley, From Winchester to Port Republic, March 10–June 9, 1862." In Theodore F. Dwight, ed. *Campaigns in Virginia 1861–1862. Papers of the Military Historical Society of Massachusetts.* Wilmington, N.C.: Broadfoot Publishing Company, 1: 303–337.

Imboden, John D. "Stonewall Jackson in the Shenandoah." In *Battles and Leaders of the Civil War*, edited by Robert U. Johnson and Clarence C. Buel. Secaucus, N.J.: Castle, 2: 282–298.

Jackson, Mary Anna. *Life and Letters of General Thomas J. Jackson (Stonewall Jackson).* New York: Harper Brothers, 1892.

Johnson, Bvt. Col. George K. *The Battle of Kernstown, March 23, 1862.* A Paper Read Before the Michigan Commandery of the Military Order of the Loyal Legion of the United States. Detroit, Michigan: Winn & Hammond Printers, 1890.

Johnston, General Joseph E. *Narrative of Military Operations During the Civil War.* Reprint New York: Da Capo Press, Inc., 1990.

Kepler, William. *History of the Three Month and Three Years Service from April 16th 1861, to June 22d, 1864, of the Fourth Regiment Ohio Volunteer Infantry in the War for the Union.* Cleveland, Ohio: Leader Printing Company, 1886.

"Killed and Wounded of the First Virginia Infantry." (Wheeling) *Daily Intelligencer*, April 23, 1862.

Kimball, Brevet Major–General Nathan. "Fighting Jackson at Kernstown." In *Battles and Leaders of the Civil War*, edited by Robert U. Johnson and Clarence C. Buel. Secaucus, N.J.: Castle, 2: 302–313.

Leatherman, Emily M. "James R. Smith Diary," in *Hancock: 1776–1976*. Hancock, Md.: Published by the author, 1976.

Lewis, Thomas A. and the editors of Time-Life Books. *The Shenandoah in Flames: The Valley Campaign of 1864*. Alexandria, Virginia: Time-Life Books, 1987.

"Lieut. George Junkin." *Lexington Gazette*, May 1, 1862.

"List of Confederates in Hospital." *Staunton Spectator*, April 1, 1862.

"Lovejoy." *A History of Company A, First Ohio Cavalry 1861–1865*. Washington Court House, Ohio: Published by the author, 1898.

Martin, Kenneth R. and Ralph Linwood Snow, ed. *"I am Now a Soldier!" The Civil War Diaries of Lorenzo Vanderoef*. Bath, Maine: Patten Free Press, 1990.

Massachusetts Adjutant–General's Report, January 1863, Public Document No. 7.

McClellan, George B. *McClellan's Own Story*. New York: Charles L. Webster & Company, 1887.

McDonald, Archie P., ed. *Make Me a Map of the Valley: The Civil War Journal of Stonewall Jackson's Topographer*. Dallas, Texas: Southern Methodist University Press, 1973.

McDonald, Mrs. Cornelia. *A Diary With Reminiscences of the War and Refugee Life in the Shenandoah Valley; 1860–1865*. Nashville, Tenn.: Cullom & Ghertner Co., 1934.

McGuire, Dr. Hunter. "General T. J. ('Stonewall') Jackson, Confederate States Army. His Career and Character." *Southern Historical Society Papers* 25 (1897): 91–112.

Merchant, Thomas A. *Eighty-Fourth Pennsylvania Volunteers, An Address*. Philadelphia, Pa.: Sherman and Company, 1889.

Moore, Edward A. *The Story of a Cannoneer Under Stonewall Jackson*. Lynchburg, Va.: J. P. Bell, Inc., 1910.

Moore, Frank, ed. *The Rebellion Record*. 11 vols. New York: D. Van Nostrand, 1861–1868.

Moore, Samuel J. C. (2nd Virginia). Letter dated May 7, 1888. *Spirit of Jefferson* (Charlestown, Va.), June 12, 1888.

Neese, George. *Three Years in the Confederate Horse Artillery*. Dayton, Ohio: Press of Morningside Bookshop, 1983.

Nelson, Thomas M. "A Gentleman of Verona," *Old Chapel: Clarke County, Virginia.* Berryville, Va.: The Blue Ridge Press, 1906: 19–24.

Nickerson, A. H. (8th Ohio). Letter dated April 13, 1888, *Shepherdstown* (W.Va.) *Register,* May 18, 1888.

Obituary of Kenton Harper, *Staunton Spectator,* December 31, 1867.

Paxton, John G., ed. *Elisha Franklin Paxton Brigadier-General C. S. A. Composed of his Letters From Camp and Field...and Arranged by His Son.* New York: The Neale Publishing Company, 1907.

Pile, George C. "The War Story of a Confederate Soldier Boy." *Bristol* (Tenn.-Va.) *Herald-Courier,* January 23, 1921.

Quaife, Milo M., ed. *From the Cannon's Mouth: The Civil War Letters of Alpheus S. Williams.* Detroit, Michigan: Wayne State University Press and the Detroit Historical Society, 1959.

Quint, Alonzo H. *The Potomac and the Rapidan, Army Notes From the Failure at Winchester to the Reinforcement of Rosecrans: 1861–3.* New York: Crosby and Nichols, 1864.

Rawling, C. J. *History of the First Regiment Virginia Infantry.* Philadelphia, Pa.: J. B. Lippincott Company, 1887.

Read, Alexander. Letter to Martin Watts, January 30, 1862. *The Progress* (Clearfield, Pa.), April 9, 1961.

"Recognized Old Kernstown Rocks." *Winchester Evening Star,* September 3, 1912.

Register of the Officers and Cadets of the U.S. Military Academy, June, 1841, J. P. Wright, New York, 1841, n.p.

Robertson, James I., ed. "An Indiana Soldier in Love and War: The Civil War Letters of John V. Hadley." *Indiana Magazine of History* 59 (1963): 203.

Ross, Charles H. "Old Memories." Military Order of the Loyal Legion of the United States, Wisconsin Commandery, *War Papers,* 1 (1891): 141–163.

Sawyer, Franklin. *A Military History of the 8th Ohio Vol. Inf'y: Its Battles, Marches and Army Movements.* Cleveland, Ohio: Fairbanks & Co. Printers, 1881.

Sears, Stephen W. *The Civil War Papers of George B. McClellan.* New York: Ticknor & Fields, 1989.

SeCheverell, J. Hamp. *Journal History of the Twenty-Ninth Ohio Veteran Volunteer, 1861–1865, Its Victories and Its Reverses.* Cleveland, Ohio: Published by the author, 1883.

"Sharp Fighting." *Adams Sentinel,* April 9, 1862.

Simpson, J. H. "Battle of Kernstown." *The National Tribune*, February 4, 1882.

———. "Criticizing Capehart. Who Took the Stonewall at Kernstown?" *The National Tribune*, May 9, 1889.

Skidmore, Richard S., ed. *The Civil War Journal of Billy Davis.* Greencastle, Ind.: The Nugget Publishers, 1989.

Slaughter, Rev. Philip, ed. *A Sketch of the Life of Randolph Fairfax.* Richmond, Va.: Tyler, Allegee, & McDaniel, 1864.

Smart, James G., ed. *A Radical View: The "Agate" Dispatches of Whitelaw Reid 1861–1865.* Vol. 1. Memphis State University Press, 1976.

Smith, Calvin C., ed. "The Duties of Home and War: The Civil War Letters of John G. Marsh, 29th Ohio Volunteers (A Selection)." *Upper Ohio Valley Historical Review* 8 (2), 1979: 7–20.

Soman, Jean Powers and Frank L. Byrne, eds. *A Jewish Colonel in the Civil War: Marcus M. Spiegel of the Ohio Volunteers.* Lincoln, Nebraska: University of Nebraska Press, 1995.

"Strange Suicide of a Colonel." *Cleveland Morning Leader*, April 16, 1862.

Strother, David Hunter. "Personal Recollections of the War by a Virginian." *Harper's New Monthly Magazine* (1867): 181–191.

Swiger, Elizabeth Davis, ed. *Civil War Letters and Diary of Joshua Winters: A Private in the Union Army Company G, First Western Virginia Volunteer Infantry.* Parsons, W.Va.: McClain Printing Company, 1991.

Taylor, James E. *With Sheridan Up the Shenandoah Valley in 1864: Leaves From a Special Artist's Sketchbook and Diary.* Cleveland, Ohio: The Western Reserve Historical Society, 1989.

"The Battle of Port Republic." *Painesville Telegraph*, June 26, 1862.

"The Battle of Winchester: A Bloody But Glorious Record." *Cleveland Morning Leader*, March 31, 1862.

"The Confederate Prisoners In Jail." *Baltimore American*, March 31, 1862.

"The Late Battle Near Winchester." (Wheeling) *Daily Intelligencer*, March 28, 1862.

"The Late Battle of Winchester." *Clearfield Republican*, April 9, 1862.

"The Little Rooster on the Shenandoah." *Winchester Evening Star*, February 22, 1918.

"The Lost Sword of General Richard Brooke Garnett, Who Fell at Gettysburg." *Southern Historical Society Papers* 33 (1905): 26–31.

The Massachusetts Register, 1862, Containing a Record of the Government and Institution of the State Together with a Very Complete Account of the Massachusetts Volunteer. Series #94: Adams Sampson and Co., 1862.

"The Scales Brothers." *Confederate Veteran* 7 (1899) 9: 404.

"The Serenade to General Shields by the Irish Brigade." *Semi-Weekly Dispatch* (Chambersburg, Pa.), January 14, 1862.

"The Winchester Battle-Field—The Wounded Rebels and the Secessionist Women." *Cincinnati Daily Commercial*, April 5, 1862.

Third Session of the 39th Congress, *Report of the Joint Committee of the Senate on the Conduct of the War*, vol. 3, pt. 2, No. 108, Government Printing Office, Washington, D.C., 1863, pp. 403–414.

Thomson, Orville. *From Philippi to Appomattox: Narrative of the Service of the Seventh Indiana Infantry in the War for the Union.* Published by the author, ca. 1907.

Turner, Charles W., ed. *A Reminiscence of Lieutenant John Newton Lyle of the Liberty Hall Volunteers.* Roanoke, Va.: The Virginia Lithography & Graphics Company, 1987.

———. *Ted Barclay, Liberty Hall Volunteers: Letters from the Stonewall Brigade, 1861–1864.* Natural Bridge Station, Va.: Rockbridge Publishing Company, 1992.

———. "Major Charles A. Davidson: Letters of a Virginia Soldier." *Civil War History* 22 (1976): 26.

United States War Department. *War of the Rebellion: A Compilation of the Official Records of the Union and Confederate Armies.* 70 vols. in 128 parts. Washington, D.C.: Government Printing Office, 1881–1902.

Voris, Brevet Major General Alvin C. "The Battle of the Boys." Military Order of the Loyal Legion of the United States, Ohio Commandery, *Sketches of War History 1861–1865,* 4 (1896): 87–100.

Wells, Harvey S. "The Eighty-fourth Volunteer Infantry in the Late War." *Philadelphia Weekly Times*, April 10, 1886.

———. "With Shields in 1862." *Philadelphia Weekly Times*, March 28, 1885.

Wheeler, Xenophon. "The Experiences of an Enlisted Man in the Hospital in the Early Part of the War." Military Order of the Loyal Legion of the United States, Ohio Commandery, *Sketches of War History 1861–1865,* 7 (1908): 275–284.

White, William S., ed. *Sketches of the Life of Captain Hugh A. White of the Stonewall Brigade.* Columbia, S.C.: South Carolina Steam Press, 1864.

Willis, N. P. "General F. W. Lander." *Williams County Leader* (Bryan, Ohio), April 3, 1862.

Wilson, Lawrence. *Itinerary of the Seventh Ohio Volunteer Infantry, 1861–1864, With Roster, Portraits and Biographies.* New York: The Neale Publishing Company, 1907.

Wood, George. *The Seventh Regiment: A Record.* New York: James Miller Publisher, 1865.

Worsham, John H. *One of Jackson's Foot Cavalry.* New York: The Neale Publishing Company, 1912.

Young, William S. "Shenandoah Valley. Criticizing Gen. Capehart's Article on That Campaign." *The National Tribune,* April 18, 1889.

LETTERS PUBLISHED IN 1862 NEWSPAPERS

(Unless stated otherwise, all papers are from same state as the regiment the soldier belonged to.)

"A Volunteer" (H. S. Wells, 84th Pa.). Letter dated January 8, 1862. *Muncy Luminary,* January 14, 1862.

————. Letter dated March 31, 1862. *The Muncy Luminary,* April 15, 1862.

A. R. B., Jr. (Rockbridge Artillery). Letter dated March 26, 1862. *Lynchburg Virginian,* April 5, 1862.

A. T. (42nd Virginia). Letter dated March 8, 1862. Lynchburg *Daily Republican,* March 17, 1862.

"Adjutant" (29th Ohio). Letter dated March 29, 1862. *Ashtabula Sentinel,* ca. April 15, 1862.

Anonymous soldier (1st W.Va.). Letter to his sister, January 2, 1862. (Wheeling) *Daily Intelligencer,* January 10, 1862.

Anonymous soldier (5th Ohio). Letter dated January 9, 1862. *Cincinnati Daily Commercial,* January 16, 1862.

Anonymous soldier (5th Ohio). Letter dated January 12, 1862. *Cincinnati Daily Commercial,* January 21, 1862.

Anonymous soldier (7th Ohio). Undated letter and sketch. *Painesville Telegraph,* April 10, 1862.

Anonymous soldier (8th Ohio). Letter dated April 5, 1862. *Bucyrus Weekly Journal,* April 18, 1862.

Anonymous soldier (110th Pa.). Letter to his cousin, March 29, 1862. *The* (Philadelphia) *Press,* April 11, 1862.

Asper, Captain J. F. (7th Ohio). Letter dated March 26, 1862. *Western Reserve Chronicle* (Cleveland), April 2, 1862.

Baker, Samuel C. (110th Pa). Letter dated January 6, 1862. *The Shirleysburg Herald*, January 12, 1862.

Ballou, Charles (7th Ohio). Letter to his family, March 24, 1862. *Cleveland Morning Leader*, March 31, 1862.

Burr, Henry G. (1st Ohio Cavalry). Letter dated March 30, 1862. *Daily Toledo Blade*, April 5, 1862.

Butterfield, Captain Francis W. (8th Ohio). Letter dated March 22, 1862. *Bucyrus Weekly Journal*, April 4, 1862.

"Chaplin" (29th Ohio). Letter dated April 15, 1862. *Ashtabula Sentinel*, ca. April 30, 1862.

"Coley" (13th Indiana). Letter dated March 29, 1862. *Franklin Democrat*, April 11, 1862.

"Cosmus" (1st Ohio Cavalry). Letter dated March 31, 1862. *The* (Harrisburg, Pa.) *Patriot and Union*, April 12, 1862.

Denig, Dr. C. Elliott (7th Ohio). Letter to his father, March 28, 1862. *State Capital Fact* (Columbus, Ohio), April 12, 1862.

"Dixie" (7th Indiana). Letter dated June 6, 1862. *Aurora Commercial*, June 1862.

E. J. (5th Ohio). Letter dated March 27, 1862. *Cincinnati Daily Commercial*, April 8, 1862.

"Eugene" (8th Ohio). Letter dated March 14, 1862. *Bucyrus Weekly Journal*, March 28, 1862.

Faskin, John (67th Ohio). "The Killed and Wounded of the 67th." *Daily Toledo Blade*, April 3, 1862.

"Frank" (5th Ohio). Letter dated March 29, 1862. *The Cincinnati Times*, April 8, 1862.

Frisbee, W. L. (46th Pa.) Letter dated March 23, 1862 *The Pittsburgh Evening Chronicle*, March 17, 1862.

Forbes, S. F. (67th Ohio). Letter dated March 27, 1862. *Daily Toledo Blade*, April 3, 1862.

———. (67th Ohio). Letter to his family, March 25, 1862. *Daily Toledo Blade*, April 1, 1862.

G. B. (1st W.Va.). Letter dated March 27, 1862. (Wheeling) *Daily Intelligencer*, April 2, 1862.

Gale, John (Unknown Confederate Unit). Undated letter. (Wheeling) *Daily Intelligencer*, April 10, 1862.

Gibbs, Frank C. (1st Ohio Artillery). Letter dated March 26, 1862. *The Portsmouth Times*, April 12, 1862.

Gregg, Captain James E. (8th Ohio). Letter dated March 26, 1862. *The Sandusky Register*, April 3, 1862.

G. S. F. (1st Michigan Cavalry). Letter dated March 30, 1862. *Detroit Tri-Weekly Tribune*, April 7, 1862.

H. E. S. (5th Ohio). Letter to his brother, March 25, 1862. *Cincinnati Daily Commercial*, April 8, 1862.

H. J. J. (1st W.Va.). Letter dated March 28, 1862. *The Wellsburg Herald*, April 4, 1862.

Hirst, P. (62nd Ohio). Undated Letter. *Zanesville Daily Courier*, April 4, 1862.

Hooper, Isaac (84th Pa). Letter dated January 6, 1862. *Altoona Tribune*, January 16, 1862.

Howard, E. B. (29th Ohio). Letter dated April 1, 1862. *Conneant Reporter*, April 9, 1862.

J. (23rd Va). Letter dated April 3, 1862. *Richmond Daily Dispatch*, April 11, 1862.

J. E. B., (29th Ohio). Letter dated March 30, 1862. *The Summit Beacon* (Akron, Ohio), April 10, 1862.

J. H. J. (8th Ohio). Letter dated March 26, 1862. *The Sandusky Register*, April 3, 1862.

"Joe" (1st Ohio Cavalry). Letter to his sister, March 29, 1862. *Perry County Weekly*, April 9, 1862.

"John" (39th Illinois). Letter dated January 6, 1862. *The Shirleysburg Herald,* January 23, 1862.

"Justice" (1st W.Va. Artillery). Undated letter to Augustus Pollack. (Wheeling) *Daily Intelligencer*, May 1, 1862.

K. M. D. (14th Indiana). Letter dated March 27, 1862. *Cincinnati Daily Commercial*, April 9, 1862.

———. Letter dated March 28, 1862. *Parke County Republican* (Rockville, Indiana), April 16, 1862.

"Keystone" (84th Pa.). Letter dated January 8, 1862. *The Press* (Philadelphia), January 13, 1862.

———. Letter dated January 20, 1862. *The Press* (Philadelphia), January 27, 1862.

Kirkpatrick, Captain T. M. (13th Indiana). Undated letter to his wife. *Howard Tribune*, April 8, 1862.

L. (Rockbridge Artillery). "The Battle of Barton's Mills." *Lexington Gazette*, April 3, 1862.

Langhorne, James H. Letter to his parents, April 3, 1862. *Lynchburg Virginian*, April 16, 1862.

"Lovejoy" (1st Ohio Cavalry). Letter dated March 31, 1862. *Fayette County Weekly*, April 17, 1862.

Lutz, John, Jr. (110th Pa.). Letter dated March 21, 1862. *The Shirleysburg Herald*, April 3, 1862.

M. D. (8th Ohio). Letter dated March 21, 1862. *The Sandusky Register*, April 1, 1862.

McCoy, William T. (110th Pa.). Letter dated March 30, 1962. (Huntingdon) *Semi-Weekly Globe*, April 8, 1862.

McReading, C. S. (39th Illinois). Letter dated January 14, 1862. *Ohio State Journal* (Columbus), January 17, 1862.

Miller, D. Ross (110th Pa). Letter dated January 20, 1862. *The Shirleysburg Herald*, January 20, 1862.

———. Letter dated March 21, 1862. *Semi-Weekly Globe* (Huntingdon, Pa.), March 27, 1862.

Molineaux, Joseph (7th Ohio). Undated interview. *Cleveland Morning Leader*, April 1, 1862.

Moore, Sergeant (1st W.Va.). Letter dated January 9, 1862. (Wheeling) *Daily Intelligencer*, January 21, 1862.

N. N. H. (1st W.Va. Cavalry). Letter dated January 8, 1862. (Wheeling) *Daily Intelligencer*, January 14, 1862.

"Notae" (7th Ohio). Letter dated March 29, 1862. *Lawrenceville (Pa.) Journal*, April 20, 1862.

Ogle, Captain Benjamin F. (8th Ohio). Letter dated March 26, 1862. *Tifflin Weekly Tribune*, April 11, 1862.

O. P. H. (4th Virginia Militia). Letter dated January 14, 1862. *Rockingham Register and Virginian*, January 24, 1862.

O. T. (7th Indiana). Letter dated June 11, 1862. Indianapolis *Daily Journal*, June 19, 1862.

Oakey, James (14th Indiana). Letter dated March 27, 1862. *Terre-Haute Daily Express*, April 5, 1862.

"Old Town" (84th Pa.). Letter dated March 21, 1862. *Clearfield Republican*, April 2, 1862.

———. Letter dated March 31, 1862. *Clearfield Republican*, April 23, 1862.

"One Of The Boys" (1st W.Va. Cavalry). Letter dated March 28, 1862. (Wheeling) *Daily Intelligencer,* April 7, 1862.

P. A. B. (1st W.Va.). Letter dated April 6, 1862. (Wheeling) *Daily Intelligencer*, April 15, 1862.

Parsons, J. Jeff (67th Ohio). Letter to friends, March 30, 1862. *Weekly Perrysburg Journal*, April 10, 1862.

Pinkerton, Joseph A. (84th Pa.). Letter to his brother, March 26, 1862. *The Miner's Journal and Pottsville General Advertiser*, April 5, 1862.

"Prock" (14th Indiana). Letter dated February 13, 1862. *Vincennes Western Sun*, February 26, 1862.

———. Letter dated January 8, 1862. *Vincennes Western Sun*, January 18, 1862.

———. Letter written prior to March 29, 1862. *Vincennes Western Sun*, April 12, 1862.

———. Letter dated March 29, 1862. *Vincennes Western Sun*, April 12, 1862.

Read, Alexander (84th Pa.). Letter dated March 26, 1862. *Clearfield Republican*, April 16, 1862.

Ritter, Dr. Levi (Indiana). Letter dated March 29, 1862. *Hendricks County Ledger*, April 11, 1862.

S. C. B. (110th Pa.). Letter dated February 5, 1862. *The Shirleysburg Herald*, February 13, 1862.

———. Letter dated March 28, 1862. *The Shirleysburg Herald*, April 10, 1862.

S. F. (84th Pa.). Letter dated January 23, 1862. *Clearfield Republican*, February 12, 1862.

S. M. (1st W.Va.). Letter dated March 29, 1862. (Wheeling) *Daily Intelligencer*, April 8, 1862.

"Sixty-Seventh Regiment." Letter dated March 16, 1862. *Williams County Leader* (Bryan, Ohio), April 3, 1862.

Stafford, John B. (67th Ohio). Letter dated March 30, 1862. *Weekly Perrysburg Journal*, April 17, 1862.

Steen, D. Q. (7th Ohio). Letter dated March 27, 1862. *Cleveland Daily Plain Dealer*, April 8, 1862.

T. F. A. (5th Ohio). Letter dated January 10, 1862. *Cincinnati Daily Commercial*, January 14, 1862.

Talcott, Henry W. (13th Indiana). Letter dated June 26, 1862. *Valparaiso Republic*, July 10, 1862.

Treher, Hiram (5th Ohio). Letter dated February 15, 1862. *Semi-Weekly Dispatch* (Chambersburg, Pa.), February 25, 1862.

———. Letter to his father, March 26, 1862. *Chambersburg (Pa.) Valley Spirit*, April 30, 1862.

———. Letter to his parents, January 15, 1862. *Semi-Weekly Dispatch* (Chambersburg, Pa.) January 28, 1862.

Vohn, William S. (Unknown Ohio Unit). Letter dated April 2, 1862. *Weekly Perrysburg Journal*, April 10, 1862.

"Volunteer" (13th Indiana). Letter dated March 18, 1862. *Madison Daily Courier*, March 29, 1862.

"Volunteer" (V. E. Smalley, 7th Ohio). Letter dated January 9, 1862. *Painesville Telegraph*, January 23, 1862.

———. Letter dated March 23, 1862. *Painesville Telegraph*, April 3, 1862.

———. Letter dated March 30, 1862. *Painesville Telegraph*, April 10, 1862.

"W." (27th Va.). Undated letter. *Richmond Daily Dispatch*, April 4, 1862.

W. C. F. (13th Indiana). Letter dated March 21, 1862. Indianapolis *Daily Journal*, March 28, 1862.

———. Letter dated March 26, 1862. Indianapolis *Daily Journal*, April 2, 1862.

W. C. H. (5th Ohio). Letter to his father, March 30, 1862. *Perry County Weekly*, April 16, 1862.

W. D. S. (7th Ohio). Letter dated August 31, 1861. *Painesville Telegraph*, September 12, 1861.

W. E. C. (110th Pa.). Letter dated March 17, 1862. *Semi-Weekly Globe* (Huntingdon, Pa.), March 25, 1862.

W. S. (1st W.Va. Cavalry). Letter dated February 28, 1862. (Wheeling) *Daily Intelligencer*, March 5, 1862.

"Wanderee" (Huntington's Battery). Letter dated March 30, 1862. *Daily Toledo Blade*, April 3, 1862.

Winship, T. S. (29th Ohio). Letter to J. H. Kilborn, March 29, 1862. *Conneant Reporter*, April 9, 1862.

Wright, Captain Myron (29th Ohio). Letter to his father, March 25, 1862. *Summit Beacon*, April 1, 1862.

"Younger" (1st W.Va. Cavalry). Letter dated February 26, 1862. (Wheeling) *Daily Intelligencer*, March 5, 1862.

KERNSTOWN BATTLEFIELD MAPS

Jed Hotchkiss, Sketchbook, Geography and Map Division, Library of Congress.

"Sketch of the Battle of Kernstown," Hotchkiss Papers, Carton #39 (Reel #39), Library of Congress.

Captain Eddy D. Mason, Four Sketches of the Battle of Winchester, United States, War Department. *War of the Rebellion: A Compilation of the Official Records of the Union and Confederate Armies.* Washington, D.C.: Government Printing Office, 1881–1902. Vol. 12, Pt. 1: 362–365.

United States Department of the Interior, Geological Survey Map, Winchester Quadrangle.

SECONDARY SOURCES

Armstrong, Richard L. *7th Virginia Cavalry*. Lynchburg, Va.: H. E. Howard, Inc., 1992.

Bailey, Ronald H. *Forward To Richmond: McClellan's Peninsular Campaign*. Alexandria, Va.: Time Life Books, Inc., 1983.

Bates, Samuel P. *History of Pennsylvania Volunteers, 1861–1865*. 5 vols. Harrisburg, Pa.: B. Singerly, State Printer, 1869.

———. *Martial Deeds of Pennsylvania*. Philadelphia Pa.: T. H. Davis & Co., 1876.

Baxter, Nancy Niblack. *Gallant Fourteenth: The Story of an Indiana Civil War Regiment*. Traverse City, Ind.: Pioneer Study Center Press, 1980.

Bean, W. G. *The Liberty Hall Volunteers: Stonewall's College Boys*. Berryville, Va.: The University Press of Virginia, 1964.

———. "The Unusual War Experience of Lieutenant George G. Junkin, C. S. A." *The Virginia Magazine of History and Biography* 70, (1968): 181–190.

Benedict, G. G. *Vermont in the Civil War*. 2 vols. Burlington, Vermont: The Free Press Association, 1888.

Bogue, Allan G. *The Earnest Men: Republicans of the Civil War Senate*. Ithaca, N.Y.: Cornell University Press, 1981.

Botterud, Keith A. *The Joint Committee on the Conduct of the Civil War*. Master's Thesis for Georgetown University, 1949.

Bowman, John S., ed. *The Civil War Almanac*. New York: World Almanac Publications, 1983.

Candenquist, Arthur. "Did Anyone Really Know What Time It Was?" *Blue & Gray Magazine* 8 (6) 1991: 32–35.

Cartmell, T. K. *Shenandoah Valley Pioneers and Their Descendants: A History of Frederick County, Virginia from its Formation in 1738 to 1908*. Berryville, Va.: Chesapeake Book Co., 1963.

Castle, Henry A. "General James Shields, Soldier, Orator, Statesman." *Collections of the Minnesota Historical Society* 15 (1915): 710–740.

Catton, Bruce. *The American Heritage Picture History of the Civil War*. (Reprint) New York: Crown Publishers, Inc., 1982.

Chambers, Lenoir. *Stonewall Jackson*. 2 vols. New York: William Morrow & Co., 1959.

Condon, William H. *Life of Major General James Shields.* Chicago, Ill.: Press of the Blakely Printing Co., 1900.

Couper, William. *History of the Shenandoah Valley.* 2 vols. New York: Lewis Historical Publishing Company, Inc., 1952.

Davis, Stephen. "The Death and Burials of General Richard Brooke Garnett." *The Gettysburg Magazine* 5 (1991): 108–116.

Delauter, Roger U. *Winchester in the Civil War.* Lynchburg, Va.: H. E. Howard, Inc., 1992.

Dodge, Grenville W. "General James A. Williamson." *Annals of Iowa* 6 (1903): 164.

Dyer, Frederick H. *A Compendium of the War of the Rebellion.* 3 vols. New York: Sagamore Press, Inc., 1959.

Ebert, Rebecca A. and Teresa Lazazzera. *Frederick County, Virginia: From the Frontier to the Future, A Pictorial History.* Norfolk, Va.: The Donning Company Publishers, 1988.

Farwell, Byron. *Stonewall: A Biography of General Thomas J. Jackson.* New York & London: W. W. Norton & Company, 1992.

Fox, William F. *Regimental Losses in the American Civil War.* Reprint Dayton, Ohio: Press of Morningside Bookshop, 1985.

Freeman, Douglas Southall. *Lee's Lieutenants: A Study in Command.* 3 vols. New York: Charles Scribner's Sons, 1942.

Garnett, James Mercer. *Genealogy of the Mercer-Garnett Family of Essex County, Virginia.* Richmond, Va.: Whittet & Shepperson, ca. 1910.

Gold, Thomas D. *History of Clarke County, Virginia and its Connection with the War Between the States.* Berryville, Va.: Published by the author, 1914.

Henderson, G. F. R. *Stonewall Jackson and the American Civil War.* Reprint New York: Da Capo Press, 1988.

Heverly, C. F. *Our Boys in Blue. A Complete History of Bradford County in the Civil War.* Vol. 2. Towanda, Pa.: Bradford Star Print, 1908.

Kennedy, Francis H., ed. *The Civil War Battlefield Guide: The Conservation Fund.* Boston, Mass.: Houghton Mifflin Company, 1990.

Krick, Robert K. "Armistead and Garnett: The Parallel Lives of Two Virginia Soldiers." In *The Third Day at Gettysburg & Beyond.* Gary W. Gallagher, ed. Chapel Hill, N.C.: The University of North Carolina Press, 1994.

————. *Lee's Colonels.* Dayton, Ohio: Press of Morningside Bookshop, 1979.

————. *Stonewall Jackson at Cedar Mountain.* Chapel Hill and London: The University of North Carolina Press, 1990.

————. "The Army of Northern Virginia's Most Notorious Court Martial . . . Jackson vs. Garnett." *Blue & Gray Magazine*, June-July (1986): 27–32.

Lang, Theodore F. *Loyal West Virginia from 1861 to 1865: With an Introductory Chapter on the Status of Virginia for Thirty Years Prior to the War.* Baltimore, Md.: The Deutsch Publishing Co., 1895.

Lewis, Thomas A. and the editors of Time-Life Books. *The Shenandoah in Flames: The Valley Campaign of 1864.* Alexandria, Virginia: Time-Life Books, 1987.

McCash, William B. *Thomas R. R. Cobb: The Making of a Southern Nationalist.* Macon, Ga.: Mercer University Press, 1983.

Miller, Nyle H., ed. "Surveying the Southern Boundary Line of Kansas." *Kansas Historical Quarterly* 1 (February 1932): 107–127.

Miller, William J. *The Training of an Army: Camp Curtin and the North's Civil War.* Shippensburg, Pa.: White Mane Publishing Company, Inc., 1990.

Myers, James E. *The Astonishing Saber Duel of Abraham Lincoln,* Springfield, Ill.: Lincoln-Herndon Building Publishers, 1968.

Newton, J. H., G. G. Nichols & A. G. Sprankle. *History of the Pan-Handle; Being Historical Collections of the Counties of Ohio, Brooke, Marshall and Hancock, West Virginia.* Wheeling, W.Va.: J. A. Caldwell, 1879.

Noll, Arthur H., ed. *Doctor Quintard, Chaplain C. S. A. and Second Bishop of Tennessee.* Sewanee, Tenn.: University Press of Sewanee Tennessee, 1905.

Patchan, Scott C. *Forgotten Fury: The Battle of Piedmont.* Fredericksburg, Virginia: Sgt. Kirkland Museum and Historical Society, Inc., 1996.

Pierce, John E. "Jackson, Garnett, and the 'Unfortunate Breach'. " *Civil War Times Illustrated* 23 (1973): 33–41.

Purcell, Joseph R. *James Shields: Soldier and Statesman.* Dublin. 1932, 73–87.

Quarles, Garland R. *Some Old Homes in Frederick County, Virginia.* Winchester, Va.: Winchester-Frederick County Historical Society, 1990.

————. *Some Worthy Lives: Mini-Biographies Winchester and Frederick County.* Winchester, Va.: Winchester-Frederick County Historical Society, 1988.

———. *The Story of One Hundred Old Homes in Winchester, Virginia.* Winchester, Va.: Winchester-Frederick County Historical Society, 1967.

Reid, Whitelaw. *Ohio in the War: Her Statesmen, Generals and Soldiers.* 2 vols. Columbus, Ohio: Eclectic Publishing Company, 1893.

Reidenbaugh, Lowell. *27th Virginia Infantry.* Lynchburg, Va.: H. E. Howard, Inc., 1993.

Ritter, Ben. "A Favorite Portrait of Stonewall." *Civil War Times Illustrated* 17 (1979): 36–39.

Robertson, James I., Jr. *Soldiers Blue and Gray.* Columbia, S.C.: University of South Carolina Press, 1988.

———. *Stonewall Jackson - The Man, The Soldier, The Legend.* New York: MacMillan Publishing, USA. 1997.

Robertson, John. *Michigan in the War.* Lansing, Michigan: W. S. George & Co., State Printers and Binders, 1882.

Roth, David E. "Stonewall Jackson's Only Defeat: The Battle of Kernstown (or First Winchester), March 23, 1862." *Blue & Gray Magazine,* June–July 1986: 4–22, 49–62.

Sauers, Richard A. *Advance the Colors! Pennsylvania Civil War Battle Flags.* 2 vols. Commonwealth of Pennsylvania: Capitol Preservation Committee, 1987–1991.

Sifakis, Stewart. *Who Was Who in the Civil War.* New York & Oxford: Facts on File Publications, 1988.

Summers, Festus P. "The Baltimore and Ohio—First in War." *Civil War History* 7 (1961): 239–253.

Tanner, Robert G. *Stonewall in the Valley.* Garden City, New York: Doubleday & Company, Inc., 1976.

Thomas, Clarence. *General Turner Ashby: the Centaur of the South, a Military Sketch.* Winchester, Va.: The Eddy Press Corporation, 1907.

Walker, Charles D. *Memorial, Virginia Military Institute. Biographical Sketches of the Graduates and Eleves of the Virginia Military Institute Who Fell During the War Between the States.* Philadelphia, Pa.: J. B. Lippincott & Co., 1875.

Wallace, Lee A. *A Guide to Virginia Military Organizations 1861–1865.* 2nd ed. Lynchburg, Va.: H. E. Howard, Inc., 1986.

Warner, Ezra J. *Generals in Blue: Lives of the Union Commanders.* Baton Rouge, La.: Louisiana State University Press, 1964.

———. *Generals in Gray, Lives of the Confederate Commanders.* Baton Rouge, Louisiana: Louisiana State University Press, 1959.

Wayland, John W. *History of Shenandoah County*. Strasburg, Va.: Shenandoah Publishing House, 1927.

———. *The Valley Turnpike from Winchester to Staunton and Other Roads*. Winchester, Va.: Winchester-Frederick County Historical Society, 1967.

Wessels, William L. *Born to be a Soldier: The Military Career of William Wing Loring of St. Augustine, Fla.* Fort Worth, Texas: Texas Christian University Press, 1971.

PERSONAL CORRESPONDENCES

William J. Miller, Churchville, Virginia. Camp Curtin.

Rod Gainer, Arlington, Virginia. Captain Patrick Gallagher.

Ben Ritter, Winchester, Virginia. Winchester Citizens.

James Tubbesing, Winchester, Virginia. Kernstown Battlefield Excavations.

Index